Global Perspectives on the Applications of Computer Vision in Cybersecurity

Franklin Tchakounté
University of Ngaoundere, Cameroon

Marcellin Atemkeng
Rhodes University, South Africa

A volume in the Advances in
Information Security, Privacy, and
Ethics (AISPE) Book Series

Published in the United States of America by
    IGI Global
    Engineering Science Reference (an imprint of IGI Global)
    701 E. Chocolate Avenue
    Hershey PA, USA 17033
    Tel: 717-533-8845
    Fax: 717-533-8661
    E-mail: cust@igi-global.com
    Web site: http://www.igi-global.com

Library of Congress Cataloging-in-Publication Data

Names: Tchakounté, Franklin, 1985- editor. | Atemkeng, Marcellin, 1986- editor.
Title: Global perspectives on the applications of computer vision in cybersecurity / edited by Franklin Tchakounte, and Marcellin Atemkeng.
Description: Hershey, PA : Information Science Reference, [2024] | Includes bibliographical references and index. | Summary: "The book highlights the real-world applications of CV in various domains, including computer system security, Web security, network security, IoT security, and digital forensics. It also emphasizes the importance of responsible CV for cybersecurity, ensuring that CV models adhere to ethical principles and are transparent and interpretable. By reading this book, cybersecurity professionals and researchers can gain a better understanding of how to use CV techniques to design solid cybersecurity solutions and address the challenges involved. With the guidance of the editors, Franklin Tchakounte and Marcellin Atemkeng, who are experts in both cybersecurity and computer vision, readers can leverage the power of CV to secure the future of our digital world"-- Provided by publisher.
Identifiers: LCCN 2023019954 (print) | LCCN 2023019955 (ebook) | ISBN 9781668481271 (hardcover) | ISBN 9781668481288 (paperback) | ISBN 9781668481295 (ebook)
Subjects: LCSH: Computer vision. | Computer security.
Classification: LCC TA1634 .G56 2023 (print) | LCC TA1634 (ebook) | DDC 006.3/7--dc23/eng/20230614
LC record available at https://lccn.loc.gov/2023019954
LC ebook record available at https://lccn.loc.gov/2023019955

This book is published in the IGI Global book series Advances in Information Security, Privacy, and Ethics (AISPE) (ISSN: 1948-9730; eISSN: 1948-9749)

British Cataloguing in Publication Data
A Cataloguing in Publication record for this book is available from the British Library.
All work contributed to this book is new, previously-unpublished material.
The views expressed in this book are those of the authors, but not necessarily of the publisher.
For electronic access to this publication, please contact: eresources@igi-global.com.

Advances in Information Security, Privacy, and Ethics (AISPE) Book Series

Manish Gupta
State University of New York, USA

ISSN:1948-9730
EISSN:1948-9749

MISSION

As digital technologies become more pervasive in everyday life and the Internet is utilized in ever increasing ways by both private and public entities, concern over digital threats becomes more prevalent.

The **Advances in Information Security, Privacy, & Ethics (AISPE) Book Series** provides cutting-edge research on the protection and misuse of information and technology across various industries and settings. Comprised of scholarly research on topics such as identity management, cryptography, system security, authentication, and data protection, this book series is ideal for reference by IT professionals, academicians, and upper-level students.

COVERAGE

- Electronic Mail Security
- CIA Triad of Information Security
- Privacy Issues of Social Networking
- Computer ethics
- Tracking Cookies
- Device Fingerprinting
- Access Control
- Security Classifications
- IT Risk
- Global Privacy Concerns

IGI Global is currently accepting manuscripts for publication within this series. To submit a proposal for a volume in this series, please contact our Acquisition Editors at Acquisitions@igi-global.com or visit: http://www.igi-global.com/publish/.

Titles in this Series

701 East Chocolate Avenue, Hershey, PA 17033, USA
Tel: 717-533-8845 x100 • Fax: 717-533-8661
E-Mail: cust@igi-global.com • www.igi-global.com

Table of Contents

    Fahim Anzum, University of Calgary, Canada
    Ashratuz Zavin Asha, University of Calgary, Canada
    Lily Dey, University of Calgary, Canada
    Artemy Gavrilov, University of Calgary, Canada
    Fariha Iffath, University of Calgary, Canada
    Abu Quwsar Ohi, University of Calgary, Canada
    Liam Pond, University of Calgary, Canada
    Md. Shopon, University of Calgary, Canada
    Marina L. Gavrilova, University of Calgary, Canada

    Naomi Dassi Tchomte, University of Ngaoundere, Cameroon
    Franklin Tchakounte, Faculty of Science, University of Ngaoundere,
        Cameroon
    Ismael Abbo, Faculty of Sciences, University of Ngaoundere, Cameroon

    Wyclife Ong'eta, Kenyatta University, Kenya

Detailed Table of Contents

    Fahim Anzum, University of Calgary, Canada
    Ashratuz Zavin Asha, University of Calgary, Canada
    Lily Dey, University of Calgary, Canada
    Artemy Gavrilov, University of Calgary, Canada
    Fariha Iffath, University of Calgary, Canada
    Abu Quwsar Ohi, University of Calgary, Canada
    Liam Pond, University of Calgary, Canada
    Md. Shopon, University of Calgary, Canada
    Marina L. Gavrilova, University of Calgary, Canada

Responsible, ethical, and trustworthy decision-making powered by the new generation of artificial intelligence (AI) and deep learning (DL) recently emerged as one of the key societal challenges. This chapter provides a comprehensive review of state-of-the-art methods that emerged very recently in the domain of trustworthiness, fairness, and authenticity of online social media. Furthermore, this chapter discusses open problems, provides examples of other application domains in the realm of computer vision and intelligent computing, recommends bias mitigation strategies, and provides insights on the future developments in this key research domain.

    Naomi Dassi Tchomte, University of Ngaoundere, Cameroon
    Franklin Tchakounte, Faculty of Science, University of Ngaoundere,
        Cameroon
    Ismael Abbo, Faculty of Sciences, University of Ngaoundere, Cameroon

The integration of case-based reasoning (CBR) and computer vision (CV) holds significant promise for enhancing cybersecurity, enabling the analysis and interpretation of visual data to detect security threats. This study provides an investigation of the synergy between case-based reasoning and computer vision techniques in the context of cybersecurity, aiming to address open challenges and identify opportunities for advancing security operations. Three main steps are realized. First, a taxonomy declining categories and sub-categories of the studied works is designed. Second, the collected literature is analysed in terms of (1) CBR for leveraging past security incidents and patterns in visual data analysis, facilitating threat detection, incident response, and threat intelligence analysis; (2) CV for cybersecurity modelling and to support cybersecurity decision making; (3) association between CBR and CV to design cybersecurity approaches. Third, open issues are discussed. This study exploiting CBR in computing vision for cybersecurity opens doors for further research.

Chapter 3

This chapter reviews how new technologies driven by artificial intelligence have a wide range of impact in advancing violent ideologies in Africa. In particular, the chapter analyses how computer vision is helping to advance radical and extreme ideologies and how to build resilience against the phenomenon. This work has found that terrorist organisations are tapping artificial intelligence through computer vision to develop synthetic videos, graphics, and images to advance their goals. It was revealed that transformative education has the potential to develop all round humans capable to thrive and navigate in ever changing and dynamic online ecosystem.

Chapter 4

The rate of use of cryptocurrencies through smart contracts and decentralized applications remains continually increasing. Ethereum is particularly gaining popularity in the blockchain community. In this work, the authors are interested in retraining vulnerability and timestamping. They propose a detection method based on the transformation of contracts into images and the processing of the latter using Simhash and n-gram techniques to obtain our contracts into images of size 32*32. They combine a technique to preserve the useful characteristics of images for exploitation. Training carried out with the convolutional neuronal network (CNN) model on a sample of 50 normal contracts, 50 contracts vulnerable to retraining, and 33 vulnerable to timestamping gave an accuracy of 88.98% on the detection of vulnerable contracts. The singular value decomposition (SVD) technique is capable of efficiently extracting from images, the key features that characterize contracts in Ethereum.

Chapter 5

Cecile Simo Tala, University of Ngaoundéré, Cameroon

Speech is the main source of communication between humans and is an efficient way to exchange information around the world. Emotion recognition through speech is an active research field that plays a crucial role in applications. SER is used in several areas of life, more precisely in the security field for the detection of fraudulent conversations. A pre-processing step was done on audios in order to reduce the noise and to eliminate the silence in the set of audios. The authors applied two approaches of the deep learning namely the LSTM and CNN for this domain in order to decide of the approach which saw better with the problem. They transformed treated audios into spectrograms for the model of the CNN. Then they used the technique of the SVD on these images to extract the matrices of characteristics for the entries of the LSTM. The proposed models were trained on these data and then tested to predict emotions. They used two databases, RAVDESS and EMO-DB, for the evaluation of the approaches. The experimental results proved the effectiveness of the model.

Chapter 6

Ismael Abbo, Faculty of Sciences, University of Ngaoundere, Cameroon
Naomi Dassi Tchomte, University Institute of Technology, Cameroon

In cybersecurity, the fusion of feature engineering and computer vision presents a promising frontier. This study delves into their symbiotic relationship, highlighting their combined potential in bolstering cybersecurity measures. By examining tailored feature engineering techniques for intrusion detection, malware analysis, access control, and threat intelligence, this work sheds light on the transformative impact of visual data analysis on cybersecurity strategies. Harnessing feature engineering pipelines alongside computer vision algorithms unlocks novel avenues for threat detection, incident response, and risk mitigation. However, challenges such as overfitting, adversarial attacks, and ethical concerns necessitate ongoing research and innovation. This chapter lays the groundwork for future advancements in feature engineering for computer vision in cybersecurity, paving the way for more robust and resilient security solutions.

Chapter 7

With the increase in malware attacks, the need for automated malware detection in cybersecurity has become more important. Traditional methods of malware detection, such as signature-based detection and heuristic analysis, are becoming less effective in detecting advanced and evasive malware. It has the potential to drastically improve the detection of malware, as well as reduce the manual efforts required in scanning and flagging malicious activity. This chapter also examines the advantages and limitations and the challenges associated with deploying object detection in cybersecurity, such as its reliance on labeled data, false positive rates, and its potential for evasion. Finally, the review presents the potential of object detection in cybersecurity, as well as the future research directions needed to make the technique more reliable and useful for cybersecurity professionals. It provides a comparison of the results obtained by these techniques with traditional methods, emphasizing the potential of object detection in detecting advanced and evasive malware.

Chapter 8

Digital forensics plays an important role in investigating cybercrimes, data breaches, and other digital misdeeds in an increasingly connected world. With the proliferation of blockchain technology, a new dimension has emerged in the world of digital forensics. This work presents a comprehensive review of the intersection between blockchain and digital forensics, exploring the various ways blockchain technology influences and challenges the traditional practices of digital forensic investigations. This work begins by elucidating the fundamental concepts of blockchain technology, emphasizing its decentralized and immutable nature, cryptographic underpinnings, and its uses in cryptocurrency transactions. Subsequently, it delves into the potential benefits of blockchain for digital forensics, such as providing transparent and tamper-proof logs of digital activities and transactions. However, this chapter also discusses the unique challenges posed by blockchain in digital forensic investigations.

Research in image processing of digital color photography is in full expansion, especially on CFA (color filter array) images. These raw CFA images are very important for image analysis because they have not undergone any processing (interpolation, demosaicking, etc.) that would alter their reliability. The chapter presents three robust hybrid algorithms combining chaotic encryption and blind watermarking techniques of CFA images based on the quaternionic wavelet transform (QWT) to propose solutions related to the problems of confidentiality, security, authenticity of these images transmitted over digital networks, the size of some CFA images, and the large amount of data to be transferred in a non-secure environment where resources in terms of throughput and bandwidth are quite limited. The three hybrid algorithms were implemented simultaneously and successively.

Preface

Welcome to *Global Perspectives on the Applications of Computer Vision in Cybersecurity*. In the rapidly evolving landscape of cybersecurity, the fusion of computer vision (CV) with innovative technologies has emerged as a potent force in safeguarding digital environments. This edited reference book, meticulously curated by Franklin Tchakounte and Marcellin Atemkeng, delves into the transformative role of CV in fortifying cybersecurity measures worldwide.

Computer vision, an AI application mirroring human vision, has revolutionized decision-making processes by deciphering visual inputs like images and videos. Deep learning, transfer learning, and explainable AI have propelled CV into the forefront of cybersecurity, enabling professionals and scientists to harness its prowess for tasks ranging from image-based malware classification to object detection surveillance.

Amidst this paradigm shift, this compilation serves as a beacon, illuminating the myriad applications of CV in cybersecurity through real-world case studies. It bridges the gap between theory and practice, equipping scientists, academics, and practitioners with invaluable insights to craft robust cybersecurity solutions.

In an era characterized by unprecedented digital interconnectivity, the intersection of CV and cybersecurity assumes paramount significance, particularly in Cyber-Physical Systems (CPS). This book fills a crucial void by offering a comprehensive exploration of this intersection, paving the way for advancements in secure digital ecosystems.

Tailored for those at the vanguard of emerging technologies, this book serves as a compass for navigating the intricate terrain of CV-enhanced cybersecurity. From collecting and processing cybersecurity vision data to integrating CV processes seamlessly, readers will find pragmatic guidance to address contemporary cybersecurity challenges.

Each chapter offers a unique vantage point, illuminating the innovative applications, challenges, and future directions within this burgeoning field. From ethical considerations in AI-powered decision-making to the fusion of case-based reasoning and computer vision for cybersecurity, our contributors delve into diverse facets of this dynamic landscape. As we navigate through chapters examining the influence of AI-driven technologies on violent ideologies, the vulnerabilities within smart contracts, and the complexities of emotion recognition through speech, we uncover the transformative potential of computer vision in safeguarding digital ecosystems. From feature engineering to object detection and digital forensics, each chapter offers invaluable insights and practical guidance for researchers, practitioners, and enthusiasts alike, as we chart a course towards a more secure and ethically-driven digital future.

Chapter 1: In the first chapter, we embark on a journey through the intricate landscape of responsible, ethical, and trustworthy decision-making in the era of new AI and deep learning technologies. A comprehensive review is provided about cutting-edge methods dedicated to ensuring the trustworthiness, fairness, and authenticity of online social media platforms. Through insightful discussions and illustrative examples from various application domains in computer vision and intelligent computing, we illuminate the challenges and opportunities in this vital research domain. Our exploration extends to bias mitigation strategies and offers visionary insights into future developments, promising a roadmap for fostering ethical AI practices in a rapidly evolving digital world.

Chapter 2: Chapter 2 dives into the fusion of case-based reasoning (CBR) and computer vision (CV) as we uncover their collaborative potential in fortifying cybersecurity measures. This chapter conducts a thorough investigation into the synergy between CBR and CV techniques, particularly in the context of threat detection and security operations. Through a structured taxonomy and meticulous analysis of relevant literature, we delineate the key categories and sub-categories driving advancements in this domain. From leveraging past security incidents to designing innovative cybersecurity approaches, this study elucidates the transformative impact of this symbiotic relationship, while also addressing open challenges and charting future research directions.

Chapter 3: The main focus shifts to the African continent in Chapter 3, where we confront the pervasive influence of new AI-driven technologies on the propagation of violent ideologies. Delving into the role of computer vision in advancing radical narratives, we examine the tactics employed by extremist groups to harness synthetic media for propagandistic purposes. This chapter underscores the imperative of building resilience against such nefarious endeavors through transformative education and proactive measures. By shedding light on the intersection of AI, computer vision, and ideological extremism, we aim to equip readers with the knowledge and tools to combat this emerging threat in the digital age.

Chapter 4: Ethereum and the realm of cryptocurrencies take center stage in Chapter 4 as we delve into the vulnerabilities lurking within smart contracts and decentralized applications. Through a novel detection method leveraging computer vision techniques, we illuminate the process of identifying vulnerabilities and timestamps within Ethereum contracts. By harnessing the power of convolutional neural networks (CNNs) and singular value decomposition (SVD), we demonstrate the efficacy of the proposed approach in detecting vulnerable contracts with high accuracy. This chapter serves as a roadmap for securing smart contracts in an increasingly digitized financial landscape.

Chapter 5: The realm of emotion recognition through speech (SER) is explored in Chapter 5, where we unravel the intricate dynamics of identifying emotions from spoken words. Through a multi-faceted approach encompassing deep learning, spectrogram analysis, and singular value decomposition, we elucidate effective models for discerning emotional cues in audio data. Drawing from extensive experimentation and evaluation, the effectiveness of our models is showcased in diverse real-world scenarios, particularly in the realm of security and fraud detection. This chapter promises to illuminate the path toward more nuanced and accurate emotion recognition systems, with far-reaching implications for various applications.

Chapter 6: A journey into the symbiotic relationship between feature engineering and computer vision is provided in Chapter 6, as we explore their combined potential in fortifying cybersecurity defenses. Through an in-depth examination of tailored feature engineering techniques, we unveil their transformative impact on threat detection, intrusion analysis, and access control. By harnessing the power of visual data analysis alongside computer vision algorithms, we illuminate novel avenues for bolstering cybersecurity strategies. This chapter lays the groundwork for future advancements in feature engineering, paving the way for more resilient security solutions in an ever-evolving threat landscape.

Chapter 7: In Chapter 7, we confront the escalating threat of malware attacks and the pressing need for automated detection mechanisms in cybersecurity. Through a comprehensive review of object detection techniques, we unveil their potential to revolutionize malware detection by offering improved accuracy and efficiency. From signature-based detection to heuristic analysis, we dissect traditional methods and highlight the advantages of object detection in detecting advanced and evasive malware. This chapter serves as a call to action for embracing innovative approaches in cybersecurity, with object detection poised to play a pivotal role in safeguarding digital ecosystems.

Chapter 8: The intersection of blockchain technology and digital forensics takes center stage is the essence of Chapter 8 as we navigate the complexities of investigating cybercrimes in an increasingly decentralized digital landscape. Through a comprehensive review, the potential benefits and challenges posed by blockchain for digital forensic investigations, are explored. From transparent transaction logs to cryptographic challenges, we illuminate the evolving role of blockchain in shaping the future of digital forensics. This chapter offers invaluable insights for navigating the intersection of blockchain technology and digital investigations, paving the way for more effective and transparent forensic practices.

Chapter 9: Our exploration culminates in Chapter 9, where we delve into the realm of digital color photography and the challenges of securing raw Color Filter Array (CFA) images in digital networks. Through the lens of quaternionic wavelet transform (QWT) and chaotic encryption, we unveil robust hybrid algorithms designed to safeguard the confidentiality, security, and authenticity of CFA images. By blending cutting-edge encryption techniques with blind watermarking, we offer solutions to the inherent vulnerabilities of transmitting raw CFA images over insecure digital channels. This chapter promises to be a beacon for securing digital imagery in an age of increasing connectivity and digital proliferation.

As stewards of responsible innovation, we acknowledge the ethical considerations inherent in the deployment of CV for cybersecurity. Hence, this book underscores the importance of ethical frameworks and responsible practices to ensure the safe and equitable use of CV in safeguarding digital landscapes.

We invite you to embark on a journey through the realms of computer vision and cybersecurity, as we unravel the myriad dimensions of this symbiotic relationship. With an array of recommended topics spanning from computer vision principles to image reconstruction and beyond, *Global Perspectives on the Applications of Computer Vision in Cybersecurity* promises to be an indispensable resource for all stakeholders invested in securing the digital frontier.

Franklin Tchakounté
University of Ngaoundere, Cameroon

Marcellin Atemkeng
Rhodes University, South Africa

Chapter 1
A Comprehensive Review of Trustworthy, Ethical, and Explainable Computer Vision Advancements in Online Social Media

Fahim Anzum
ⓘD https://orcid.org/0000-0002-1846-3957
University of Calgary, Canada

Ashratuz Zavin Asha
University of Calgary, Canada

Lily Dey
University of Calgary, Canada

Artemy Gavrilov
University of Calgary, Canada

Fariha Iffath
University of Calgary, Canada

Abu Quwsar Ohi
University of Calgary, Canada

Liam Pond
University of Calgary, Canada

Md. Shopon
University of Calgary, Canada

Marina L. Gavrilova
University of Calgary, Canada

ABSTRACT

Responsible, ethical, and trustworthy decision-making powered by the new generation of artificial intelligence (AI) and deep learning (DL) recently emerged as one of the key societal challenges. This chapter provides a comprehensive review of state-of-the-art methods that emerged very recently in the domain of trustworthiness, fairness, and authenticity of online social media. Furthermore, this chapter discusses open problems, provides examples of other application domains in the realm of computer vision and intelligent computing, recommends bias mitigation strategies, and provides insights on the future developments in this key research domain.

DOI: 10.4018/978-1-6684-8127-1.ch001

1. INTRODUCTION

Responsible, ethical, and trustworthy decision-making powered by the new generation of artificial intelligence (AI) and deep learning (DL) has recently emerged as a key societal challenge. Politicians, government officials, industry experts, and end users alike agree that in order for AI and DL to be used in commercial and public domains, safety mechanisms must be built to protect individuals. ("Directive on Automated Decision-Making," 2019). Recent theoretical, technological, and computational developments have enabled new-generation computing systems to process incredibly large amounts of visual information in a fraction of a second and to learn advanced data patterns in a human-like manner (Zhu et al., 2023). However, while advancements in information processing, data collection and information visualization have grown exponentially, research on the explainability and trustworthiness of visual systems has remained limited. In recent years, the mysterious nature of highly publicized commercial products, such as OpenAI's ChatGPT and Google's Gemini chatbots, has highlighted the need to understand the inner workings of such complicated systems. As a result, more than ever, people are turning to societal and regulatory bodies to solve difficult problems surrounding the ethics, trust, privacy, security, legal, and policy issues of these emerging AI technologies.

In online social media applications, the increasing influence of computer vision techniques underscores the critical importance of explainability and trust. Because these algorithms control the curation and dissemination of content that increasingly shapes public opinion, transparency is paramount. Understanding the inner workings of computer vision systems will not only protect individual privacy and improve user experiences, but also can help address potential training data biases and verify the authenticity of data.

Furthermore, explainable AI systems are inherently more trustworthy, meaning that users can better understand and have confidence in the decisions made by the AI, leading to increased acceptance and adoption of AI technologies. However, establishing trust in these AI-driven platforms requires a commitment to explainability, ensuring that users can understand and hold accountable the algorithms shaping their online interactions. This is why striking the balance between innovation and ethical transparency is key, creating a digital environment where computer vision can be used to the fullest extent without compromising trust in these systems. This chapter makes the following contributions:

1. Presenting a comprehensive overview of the existing research surrounding trustworthiness, bias, fairness, and explainability in online social media.

2. Exploring diverse application domains within computer vision and intelligent computing in online social media, shedding light on the intricate and multi-dimensional aspects of trust-related issues.

3. Introducing a unified framework for trustworthy computer vision applications, which underscores the significance of ethical data practices, robust data processing, bias mitigation, explainability, accountability, and user-centric design.

4. Proposing a conceptual framework to determine trust factors for computing weighted trust scores that are leveraged to ensure the explainability of the model. This approach applies to a trust-aware recommender system in social media.

5. Identifying critical research gaps in the emerging field of explainable AI (XAI) and trustworthy decision-making within computer vision techniques across diverse domains. We also outline open problems, paving the way for future investigations and advancements.

Firstly, the Literature Review section presents a comprehensive review of the existing research on the trustworthiness and explainability of computer vision algorithms in online social media. Next, we introduce a unified framework tailored for trustworthy

computer vision applications, followed by a new trust-aware computing technique for online social media. The expansive application of computer vision across diverse domains, along with a discussion of open problems and future research directions, is encapsulated in Applications and Open Problems. Finally, the insights and findings are synthesized to conclude this book chapter.

2. DEFINITIONS AND PRELIMINARIES

In this section, we define the most relevant terms, namely trustworthiness, explainability, ethics, and bias in the context of computer vision in online social media.

2.1 Trustworthiness

In the landscape of computer vision in online social media, several foundational principles stand out as guides for research and development.

Prominent among these is trustworthiness, which is defined as the ability of an intelligent computer system to perform a real-time task repeatedly, reliably, and dependably in complex real-world conditions (Lyu et al., 2021). Within the domain of computer vision on social media platforms, trustworthiness extends to the proficiency of algorithms and models to consistently and accurately interpret visual data, encompassing both images and videos, under diverse and intricate use cases. This principle emphasizes the importance of users, whether individual consumers or larger social media platforms, being able to trust the outputs and decisions generated by these computer vision systems (Duenser and Douglas, 2023). A key component of trustworthiness is transparency Li et al., 2023. The decisions made by the intelligent systems, the utilized data, and the processes governing them should be clear and interpretable to all stakeholders involved. Such clarity ensures that the intelligent system does not remain an enigmatic "black box" and becomes an entity whose actions and decisions are understandable and, more importantly, accountable.

2.2 Explainability

One of the fundamental principles of trustworthiness is explainability (Thiebes et al., 2021). In the context of computer vision, explainability refers to the transparency and comprehensibility of the decision-making process behind the analysis and interpretation of visual data by AI algorithms (Confalonieri et al., 2021). It

involves making the inner workings of these algorithms understandable to users, helping them to comprehend why certain decisions or classifications are made based on the visual input. In online social media, explainability is crucial for building trust and fostering user confidence in AI-driven features, ensuring users can grasp the rationale behind content recommendations, image tagging, or facial recognition (Jain et al., 2021). To ensure model explainability and transparency, self-explainable models that can visually explain their decisions via attribution maps and counterfactuals can be developed (Wilms et al., 2022). However, explainable AI models do not release details on the models' decision-making process, making them unreliable and misleading. Thus, developing inherently interpretable models that can provide their explanations is paramount (Rudin, 2019).

2.3 Ethics

Ethics in computer vision pertains to the moral principles and guidelines that govern the development, deployment, and use of visual recognition technologies in online social media platforms (Waelen, 2023). It ensures that these technologies are designed and employed to uphold fundamental human values, respect privacy rights, and avoid harm or discrimination toward individuals or communities. Ethical considerations in computer vision encompass data privacy, consent, fairness, accountability, and the equitable representation of diverse demographics within training datasets (Anzum et al., 2022).

2.4 Bias

Bias in computer vision refers to the systematic and unfair skewing of algorithmic outcomes or predictions based on certain characteristics or attributes present in the visual data (Yang et al., 2022). This bias can stem from various sources, including imbalanced training data, algorithmic limitations, or societal prejudices embedded in the data collection process (Anzum et al., 2022). In the context of online social media, bias in computer vision algorithms can lead to discriminatory outcomes, such as misidentification or misclassification of individuals based on factors like race, gender, or cultural background (Makhortykh et al., 2021). Addressing and mitigating bias is essential for ensuring fairness, equity, and inclusivity in the application of computer vision technologies within social media platforms (Peng, 2018; Zhao et al., 2021). There are three categories of biases that
could cause a feedback loop, namely, data to algorithm, algorithm to user, and user to data (Mehrabi et al., 2021). Firstly, "data to algorithm" bias occurs when the data used to train AI systems is not representative or contains inherent prejudices. This can lead to AI algorithms that perpetuate or even amplify these biases in their outcomes. Secondly, there is a potential for "algorithm to user" bias, where AI algorithms' biased outputs influence users' decisions or perceptions. This interaction can subtly shape user behavior and judgments. Lastly, "user to data" bias reflects the impact of human biases on user-generated data, which can introduce or reinforce biases when used to train AI systems.

In summary, to navigate the complexities of computer vision within online social media, the principles of trustworthiness, explainability, ethics, and bias play pivotal roles in shaping the landscape of AI-driven technologies. While trustworthiness emphasizes reliability and transparency in algorithmic decision-making, explainability ensures users can understand and trust these decisions. While ethical considerations promote fairness and inclusivity in developing and deploying computer vision technologies, biases can undermine these goals by potentially perpetuating inequalities. Therefore, recognizing and addressing these biases is crucial for fostering equitable and trustworthy online social experiences.

3. LITERATURE REVIEW

This section presents a comprehensive overview of the diverse application domains in computer vision and intelligent trust-aware computing within the realm of social media.

3.1 Trust-Aware Computing in Cybersecurity

Trust-aware computing in the cybersecurity domain refers to the integration of trust-related considerations into the design, implementation, and operation of computing systems and technologies used to safeguard digital assets, networks, and information from unauthorized access, cyberattacks, and data breaches (Pienta et al., 2020). Trust has been extensively studied across diverse domains, including cybersecurity, where it plays a pivotal role in ensuring the reliability and integrity of systems and data. Cybersecurity encompasses a broad spectrum of issues related to protecting computer systems, networks (Govindan and Mohapatra, 2011), and data from unauthorized access (Nakajima et al., 2007), cyberattacks, and data breaches (Jiang et al., 2022). For example, in the context of information security, AI-driven intrusion detection systems analyze network traffic patterns to identify potential threats and malicious activities, such as denial-of-service attacks or unauthorized access attempts. Similarly, biometric security systems utilize AI algorithms to authenticate users based on unique physiological or behavioral characteristics, such as fingerprints or gait patterns, to prevent unauthorized access to sensitive information or physical locations. However, while AI offers significant benefits in enhancing cybersecurity defenses, there are concerns regarding potential biases in AI models and the trustworthiness of automated decision-making processes (Sanclemente, 2022). For example, AI algorithms trained on biased or incomplete data may inadvertently perpetuate discriminatory practices or fail to detect emerging threats, undermining the overall effectiveness of cybersecurity measures. Addressing these challenges requires careful consideration of ethical principles, transparency in AI algorithms, and ongoing monitoring and evaluation of cybersecurity solutions to ensure their trustworthiness and effectiveness in real-world scenarios.

Paradesi et al. (Paradesi et al., 2009) proposed a trust-aware web service by incorporating user feedback to enhance confidence in a specific web service while Caverlee et al. (Caverlee, 2008) delved into the characteristics of large-scale online social media platforms, analyzing user-profiles and tracking activities. Although these studies provide valuable insight into platform dynamics, they fail to investigate the evolving nature of user behavior over time and the influence of platform changes on trust dynamics, indicating a need for longitudinal studies. Meanwhile, Adali et al. (Adali and Golbeck, 2012) proposed trust measures inferred from online social media interaction behavior. However, further research must be done to comprehensively explore the contextual factors that influence users' trust formation in dynamic online social environments.

Researchers have also highlighted the importance of considering affective trust since emotions play a critical role in decision-making (Granatyr et al., 2019; Granatyr et al., 2016). Granatyr et al. (2019) incorporated personality traits to compute users' trust, improving correlation and accuracy. However, relying solely on personality or emotion to compute trust scores has its drawbacks because it represents only a part of a user's profile and is difficult to extrapolate across different cultures and age groups. Future work should explore a holistic approach to trust computation by considering diverse user attributes and cultural nuances. Similarly, Aramanda et al. (2021) introduced Emotion-Specific Prediction, which uses emotion detection to refine user ratings. While innovative, this approach prompts further research to understand the impact of emotion-specific predictions on users' trust in recommender systems. Granatyr et al. (Granatyr et al., 2016) computed reputation scores based on emotions extracted from textual reviews. However, a limitation lies in the generalizability of these emotion-based reputation scores across different domains, calling for domain-specific investigations to enhance the robustness of trust-based systems.

In summary, relying solely on personality or emotion for trust scores has drawbacks, particularly, a lack of consideration of diverse user attributes and cultural nuances. Additionally, the absence of explicit trust factors and disregard for temporal aspects pose limitations, requiring further research. Integrating handcrafted and context-aware features alongside deep learning architectures can enhance transparency and trustworthiness.

3.2 Misinformation and Trust Dynamics

The proliferation of fake news in online social media not only reflects pervasive biases but also raises ethical concerns about the deliberate dissemination of misinformation. The lack of explainability in the algorithms that govern content distribution further erodes trust, highlighting the urgent need for transparent and accountable measures in the digital information landscape. Recently, Saxena et al. (Saxena et al., 2023) introduced FWRRS (Fairness-aware Weighted Reversible Reachable System) to combat fake news from a rival entity, utilizing weighted reversible reachable trees and maximin fairness. Similarly, Chien et al. (2022) proposed an explainable AI (XAI) framework named XFlag to identify fake news articles and explain the decision-making process. While both works contribute to fake news detection, they acknowledge a common limitation regarding the generalizability of their solutions across diverse user groups and cultural contexts.

Researchers have also leveraged the ratings and reputations of news sources to study users' trust and combat fake news on online social media. Kim et al. (2019) evaluated the effectiveness of three mechanisms for source ratings, namely expert rating, user rating, and user source rating, discovering that source rating significantly impacts source media users' trust in articles. However, further research must be done to better understand the complexity of the broader contextual factors influencing users' trust in news sources. Babaei et al. (2021) conducted a large-scale survey with

15,000 participants to analyze biases in users' perceptions of truth or misinformation in social media news. The study revealed that user perceptions are not always aligned with the actual level of truth in these news stories, emphasizing the need for a new prioritizing framework in fact-checking to address the most impactful perception biases first. Future research could build on this work by investigating the underlying factors contributing to these perception biases and exploring the psychological dynamics shaping users' perceptions of truth and misinformation.

Recognizing the vital role images play in shaping our trust in news, especially in the era of widespread misinformation, Karduni et al. (2023) uncovered how repeated exposure to emotional facial expressions and systematic emotional portrayal of politicians influences users' trust in news. Two studies were conducted to investigate the impact of emotional facial images on news perception. The findings revealed that negative (angry) facial emotions led to higher perceptions of bias in content, and systematic negative portrayal of politicians resulted in lower perceptions of source credibility.

However, a potential research gap lies in understanding the cross-cultural variations in the impact of emotional facial expressions on trust, necessitating further exploration into the cultural nuances influencing users' trust perceptions.

In summary, the existing research reveals significant insights into combating fake news and understanding trust formation on online social media platforms. However, more comprehensive investigations into trust formation across diverse demographics and cultural contexts are needed. A potential solution could involve conducting multi-disciplinary studies integrating socio-cultural, psychological, and technological perspectives to deepen our understanding of the nuanced factors shaping trust perceptions across diverse user groups and cultural contexts.

3.3 Trustworthy Computer Vision in Online Social Media

This subsection delves into the development of trustworthy computer vision in social media and highlights the importance of reliability, transparency, authenticity, and explainability in this field. Franco et al. (Franco et al., 2021) propose a privacy-preserving, fair, and explainable system using homomorphic encryption. While their approach shows promise, the scalability and real-world applicability needs further exploration, particularly across diverse datasets and scenarios. Wang et al. (M. Wang and Deng, 2020) address racial bias in face recognition with the introduction of adaptive margin. However, the generalizability and effectiveness of their proposed RL-RBN method requires validation across different demographic groups and environmental conditions. Alam et al. (Alam, 2020) explored the impact of artificial intelligence fairness on activity recognition for older adults in wireless wearable sensor networks (WSN). While existing research has focused on WSN integration and signal processing for activity recognition, this study addresses the unique challenges of AI fairness in this domain. The authors argue that fairness in detecting activities for older adults differs from other protected attributes like age, gender, or race due to the diversity in activities based on functional abilities and variations over time and space. The paper introduces a novel approach, employing signal processing and a bidirectional LSTM model for recognizing diverse multi-label activities using a single WSN sensor. It identifies biases related to age and functional ability as protected attributes and proposes bias mitigation techniques at different ML model development stages.

Karmakar et al. (Karmakar et al., 2021) proposed two novel deep learning-based models for assessing the trustworthiness of driverless cars and their on-board unit (OBU) components. Unlike existing non-learning models, these deep learning models aim to capture the distributed, dynamic, and complex nature of traffic systems. Results obtained from real and simulated traffic data demonstrate that the proposed models outperform other machine learning models in evaluating the trustworthiness of individual cars and their components. The outcomes suggest the practical application of these models in assessing the trust level of driverless cars in real-world scenarios. Roy et al. (Roy et al., 2019) focused on the challenge of activity recognition in videos, aiming to accurately infer the set of activities and their assignment to each frame. While existing deep learning systems can achieve high accuracy in this task, their use in interactive settings is hindered by the black-box nature of these models. The lack of transparency makes it difficult for users to trust and understand the system's decisions, particularly for end-users who rely on the system regularly. To address this issue, the proposed solution integrated the output of deep learning into an interpretable probabilistic graphical model. This combined approach enables high accuracy through deep learning while ensuring interpretability.

Overall, this section highlights the challenges and importance of trustworthy, ethical, and explainable AI systems, emphasizing the integration of explainable AI technologies in real-world applications. Evaluating trust in critical decision-making, such as risk and rescue and national defense, is crucial in cognitive and probabilistic approaches.

Additionally, incorporating human behavioral and communication patterns into AI-based decision-making, considering social, spatio-temporal, and emotional human traits, is a significant research avenue explored in this chapter. This comprehensive overview encompasses cutting-edge methods, open challenges, diverse application domains, and practical strategies for mitigating biases, providing valuable insights for researchers and practitioners in the dynamic realm of online social media.

Figure 1. Flowchart for the unified framework for trustworthy computer vision applications

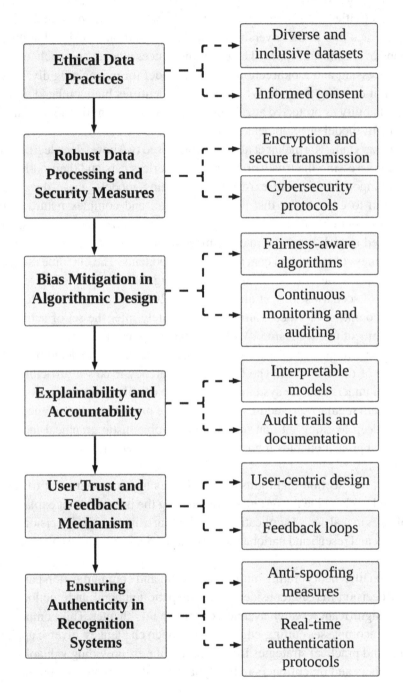

4. UNIFIED FRAMEWORK FOR TRUSTWORTHY COMPUTER VISION APPLICATIONS

Within social media platforms, establishing trust in utilizing biometric data through computer vision is imperative. This section introduces a comprehensive and unified framework for instilling trustworthiness in computer vision applications, addressing biometric privacy, cybersecurity, facial/gait online recognition systems, autonomous vehicle driver state/emotion detection, and computer vision for smart devices. The framework emphasizes ethical data practices, robust data processing, bias mitigation, explainability, accountability, and user-centric design, providing detailed insights into the implementation and advantages of each step across various sectors.

The proposed unified framework for trustworthy computer vision applications serves as a comprehensive guide to address the trustworthiness and ethical use of computer vision applications. This framework aims to bring ethics, transparency, and user trust into various research areas. Figure 1 depicts the flowchart of the proposed unified framework. To enhance understanding, we explain the framework within the context of a computer vision system designed for detecting unauthorized access using surveillance cameras in secure facilities. This system aims to prevent unauthorized access to make the facility more secure.

4.1 Ethical Data Practices

The framework begins with ethical data practices, which stand as a fundamental framework for responsible and conscientious handling of information. At its core, ethical data practices prioritize principles that respect individuals' privacy, ensure fairness, and
promote transparency in the collection, processing, and usage of data. This ethical approach recognizes the potential implications of biases and discrimination inherent in data and seeks to mitigate them. It emphasizes the importance of diversity and inclusivity in datasets, providing trust between data collectors, users, and the broader community.

Ethical data practices can be performed with the following procedures:

- **Diverse and Inclusive Datasets:** This step involves curating datasets that represent a wide spectrum of demographics, ensuring that the model is trained on a comprehensive set of data. In biometric privacy, diversity mitigates recognition biases. For smart devices, inclusive datasets ensure robustness in handling varied visual inputs.
- **Informed Consent:** Transparency is achieved by explicitly informing users about the purpose, extent, and handling of their data. In biometric privacy,

informed consent empowers users to understand and control the use of their biometric data. For smart devices, it ensures users are aware of and comfortable using computer vision features.

In the context of our problem statement, it's imperative to ensure that the collection of visual data encompasses a wide range of demographics and scenarios. By incorporating diverse datasets, surveillance systems can mitigate biases and enhance the accuracy and fairness of threat detection and monitoring activities. Furthermore, obtaining informed consent from individuals before monitoring them using surveillance cameras. Clear signage indicating the presence of surveillance cameras informs individuals of their use and purpose, enabling them to make informed decisions about entering monitored areas.

Additionally, limiting the retention period of surveillance footage and restricting access to authorized personnel helps mitigate privacy risks and ensures compliance with data protection regulations.

4.2 Robust Data Processing and Security Measures

Robust data processing and security measures form the next component of the framework. They constitute a crucial part of ethical data practices, focusing on safeguarding sensitive data during the entire lifecycle. This framework segment delves into implementing encryption and sector-specific cybersecurity protocols to fortify data against unauthorized access and potential vulnerabilities. By emphasizing secure transmission and storage, this component contributes significantly to the overall trustworthiness of computer vision applications. The following methods can be obtained for robust data processing and security measures:

- **Encryption and Secure Transmission:** This step emphasizes implementing encryption mechanisms to secure data during transmission and storage. In biometric privacy, encryption safeguards sensitive biometric data. For smart devices, it ensures the confidentiality of visual data during transmission.
- **Cybersecurity Protocols:** Sector-specific cybersecurity protocols are integrated to identify and address vulnerabilities. In facial/gait recognition, these protocols protect against unauthorized access to recognition models. Similarly, autonomous vehicles safeguard the integrity of driver state/emotion data against cyber threats.

Within the context of our problem statement, implementing encryption and secure transmission protocols for surveillance footage ensures confidentiality and integrity during storage and transmission. Access control mechanisms, such as user authentication and role-based access control, restrict access to surveillance footage to authorized personnel only. Furthermore, employing tamper detection technologies, such as digital signatures or watermarking, helps detect and prevent unauthorized alterations to surveillance footage, enhancing its trustworthiness and evidentiary value.

4.3 Bias Mitigation in Algorithmic Design

Following the establishment of robust data processing and security measures, the framework contains bias mitigation in its algorithmic design. To achieve fairness and equitable results, this aspect focuses on addressing subtle challenges related to potential biases in algorithms, especially in areas such as biometric privacy and facial/gait recognition. The objective is to develop and deploy algorithms that actively recognize and counteract biases, ensuring that diverse user groups are accurately represented without discrimination. Bias mitigation can be performed using the following methods:

- **Fairness-Aware Algorithms:** Fairness-aware algorithms ensure equitable outcomes in areas like biometric privacy and facial/gait recognition. Adversarial training helps identify and mitigate biases by training against adversarial networks. Reweighting instances adjusts the importance of different groups in the training dataset, promoting fair treatment. Demographic parity ensures equalized positive outcomes across diverse groups, contributing to unbiased recognition. Equalized odds minimize disparate impact, enhancing fairness in algorithmic decisions. Counterfactual fairness examines the influence of changing individual characteristics, aiding in addressing biases in attributes like facial features. Implementing these algorithms can significantly contribute to fostering fairness in evolving technological domains.
- **Continuous Monitoring and Auditing:** Continuous monitoring detects biases in real-time, while regular audits ensure ongoing fairness in applications like facial/gait recognition systems. Continuous monitoring in facial recognition systems allows real-time detection of biases, ensuring swift identification and mitigation of any unfair outcomes.

In the scope of our outlined problem, developing fairness-aware algorithms for threat detection helps mitigate biases and ensures equitable surveillance outcomes across diverse demographic groups. These algorithms incorporate fairness metrics and bias detection mechanisms to identify and address biases in surveillance data or algorithmic decision-making processes. Continuous monitoring and auditing of algorithmic performance enable surveillance operators to detect and rectify biases in real-time, improving the accuracy and fairness of threat detection outcomes.

4.4 Explainability and Accountability

Expanding on the need to address bias in algorithm design, the framework underscores the significance of explainability and accountability, aspects that are essential for ensuring transparency and trust in computer vision applications. Using interpretable machine learning models is a key component, enabling stakeholders to grasp the decision-making processes behind algorithmic outputs. For instance, in biometric privacy, interpretable models provide insights into how biometric data is processed, fostering user trust. In smart devices, interpretability ensures users understand how computer vision enhances device functionality. Concrete examples of interpreting a machine learning model include understanding how the model identifies and distinguishes facial features ensuring transparency in driver state and emotion assessments in autonomous vehicles. The emphasis on audit trials and documentation practices further assures accountability, offering a clear understanding of system decisions and facilitating post-incident analysis, particularly in facial/gait recognition systems. Building on ethical considerations, the framework now focuses on user trust and feedback mechanisms. Understanding that user confidence is crucial for adopting computer vision applications, this component emphasizes user-friendly design principles and ongoing feedback loops. By infusing interfaces with user-centric design, the goal is to create intuitive, responsive, and user-friendly applications. Simultaneously, feedback mechanisms facilitate an ongoing dialogue between users and developers, refining the system through user input. These practices not only focus on improving user experience but also contribute to the ongoing enhancement of computer vision applications across different sectors.

- **User-Centric Design:** Design principles prioritize user trust through intuitive interfaces. In biometric privacy, user-centric design ensures interfaces are user-friendly. For smart devices, it ensures a seamless integration of computer vision features, enhancing overall user experience.
- **Feedback Loops:** Implementing feedback mechanisms enables users to provide insights, fostering collaboration. In autonomous vehicles, user feedback enhances emotion detection accuracy. In cybersecurity, it aids in refining intrusion detection models.

In the context of our problem statement, utilizing interpretable machine learning models for threat detection enhances transparency and accountability in surveillance operations. These models provide insights into the decision-making process of surveillance systems, enabling stakeholders to understand how threat detection outcomes are generated and evaluated. Establishing comprehensive audit trails and documentation of surveillance activities facilitates traceability and accountability, enabling surveillance operators to demonstrate compliance with legal and ethical standards and address concerns raised by stakeholders effectively.

4.5 User Trust and Feedback Mechanisms

Ensuring authenticity in recognition systems is the final step in the framework, following user trust and feedback mechanisms. Here, the focus shifts to guaranteeing the genuine and unaltered nature of the identified content or information. This step becomes pivotal to maintaining the integrity and reliability of recognition systems, particularly in the face of potential manipulations or deceptive practices. To make the system trustworthy, we use strong measures to check if the recognized data is original, ensuring a safe and reliable environment for users. We achieve authenticity through the following methods:

- **Anti-Spoofing Measures:** Anti-spoofing measures, such as liveness detection, verify the authenticity of presented biometric data. For facial/gait recognition, this could involve checking for features like eye movements or facial expressions to prevent fraudulent attempts. In smart devices, touch-based liveliness tests enhance the authenticity of user interactions by ensuring a real, live user is involved, preventing spoofing attempts using photos or replicas.
- **Real-Time Authentication Protocols:** Implementing real-time authentication protocols ensures continuous and accurate verification. In autonomous vehicles, they authenticate driver's state/emotion in real time. In cybersecurity, they protect against unauthorized access.

In addressing our defined challenge, implementing community engagement initiatives and feedback mechanisms encourages collaboration and communication between surveillance operators and the community. Outreach programs and public forums provide opportunities for stakeholders to voice their concerns, provide feedback, and contribute to the development of surveillance policies and practices. Actively soliciting and addressing community feedback helps build trust and confidence in surveillance operations, fostering cooperation and support for security initiatives within the community.

In summary, the unified framework for trustworthy computer vision applications presented in this section offers a comprehensive guide to addressing the ethical use and trustworthiness of computer vision across diverse sectors. By incorporating ethical data practices, robust data processing, bias mitigation, explainability, accountability, user-centric design, and authenticity measures, the framework establishes a solid foundation for responsible and conscientious handling of information. Each step within the framework contributes to fostering user trust, transparency, and fairness in evolving technological domains such as biometric privacy, facial/gait recognition, autonomous vehicles, and smart devices. This framework would provide practical insights for researchers and serve as a guide for navigating the intricate landscape of ethical and trustworthy AI systems.

However, despite its comprehensive approach, the framework may encounter challenges in implementation and effectiveness. Diverse and inclusive datasets, while crucial for mitigating biases, may be challenging to curate comprehensively, leading to potential gaps in representation. Algorithmic bias mitigation techniques may not fully address complex societal biases embedded in data or algorithms, potentially perpetuating inequities.

Interpretable models may sacrifice predictive performance for transparency, impacting overall system accuracy. Additionally, while user feedback mechanisms are valuable, they may be subject to user bias or limited engagement, affecting the quality of system improvements. Finally, the framework's reliance on robust cybersecurity measures may face evolving threats and vulnerabilities, requiring continuous adaptation to emerging risk.

5. TRUST-AWARE COMPUTING IN ONLINE SOCIAL MEDIA

In the context of trust-aware computing in online social media, key considerations include responsible artificial intelligence, trustworthy decision-making, privacy concerns, and the analysis of physiological and behavioral traits. These aspects collectively shape the landscape of reliable and ethical AI systems within the dynamic realm of online social platforms. In the following, we emphasize the importance of responsible AI, trustworthy decision-making, privacy, understanding human traits, and bias mitigation strategies to foster a more transparent, secure, and trustworthy online environment.

- **Responsible AI:** Generally, the deep neural network is considered a black box that does not provide precise information about its internal processes. The emergence of more complex architectures, such as attention mechanisms, transformer models, and federated learning, further proliferate that notion. To achieve explainability of AI-based systems, data representation, feature engineering, prediction, and classification outcomes of AI models must be transparent and understood by humans (Linardatos et al., 2020). As such, developing new approaches to responsible AI becomes crucial from a scientific and societal point of view.

- **Trustworthy Decision-Making:** Trustworthy decision-making is defined as the ability of an intelligent computer system to perform a real-time task repeatedly, reliably, and dependably in complex real-world conditions (Lyu et al., 2021). However, not all decision-making systems include metrics to report how accurate or correct their decision. To assist in this task, multi-modal fusion approaches can be combined with trustworthiness estimation based on multi-variable dynamic game theories, to estimate and report confidence in the decisions made by the system (Y. Wang et al., 2018).

- **Privacy Considerations:** Data privacy and bias mitigation have emerged as some of the key challenges of modern society (Collmann and Matei, 2016). Debates on who can access data, how it should be stored, when it can be retired, and whether it can be shared with a third-party are ongoing in academia and industry. While an EU data protection regulation addresses some of the aspects of data ownership and sharing, a coordinated effort of policy-makers, academicians, and the public is long overdue to address the issues of data privacy, bias mitigation, and ethical use (Anzum et al., 2022).

- **Analysis of Physiological and Behavioral Traits:** Physiological and behavioral human traits play a key role in online media analytics. This is evident from their increased importance in biometrics, human-robot interactions, online communication, medical care, customer relationships, creative design, and many other domains. These traits enable AI-based systems to incorporate human behavior factors (M. Gavrilova et al., 2017), human sentiment (KN and Gavrilova, 2021), and aesthetic preferences (Bari et al., 2020) into decision-making. Novel methodologies are being actively researched for obtaining insights on behavioral traits from remotely observable actions and online communications (Paul et al., 2014). Finally, incorporating different levels of uncertainties, emotions, and nonverbal expressions into the decision-making system will assist humans in gaining a better insight into how those decisions were obtained.

- **Bias Mitigation Strategies:** In order to reduce algorithmic bias, which is when certain groups are favoured because of flawed principles, we must consider privacy, security, ethics, data bias, and fairness in system development and decision-making (Gupta and Krishnan, 2020). In addition, proper protocols for data collection must involve ethical procedures, informed consent, and legal compliance. The active inclusion of diverse samples in datasets helps prevent skewed outcomes and discriminatory results (Anzum et al., 2022). Identifying and explicitly considering protected variables, such as age and race, during data processing ensures fairness. Furthermore, the use of proxy variables, like place of birth, indirectly captures these effects, addressing biases while maintaining privacy. Comprehensive datasheets for datasets enhance transparency by documenting collection procedures and potential biases (Anzum et al., 2022). Training decision-making system administrators and users is critical for ethical considerations and compliance, contributing to responsible outcomes. Developing algorithms with built-in mechanisms, like fairness-aware algorithms, continuous monitoring, and auditing processes, actively addresses and rectifies biases during system operation. There are recently developed commercially available toolkits (such as Microsoft's Fairlearn) that can be used to mitigate algorithmic bias and arrive at fair and ethical decision-making (Bird et al., 2020).

Here, we propose a conceptual framework, shown in Figure 2, for determining trust factors and computing weighted trust scores that are leveraged to ensure the explainability of a trust-aware recommender system in social media. The proposed workflow can be adapted to systems that leverage computer vision models, natural language processing techniques, etc., for data exploration and decision-making.

- **Determining Trust Factors:** Understanding the factors shaping user trust in content and intelligent systems is vital for overall trustworthiness. Developing trust-aware recommender systems requires identifying elements influencing trust in system decisions. Behavioral and psychological traits, key in this context, are often analyzed during system design. Existing research (Granatyr et al., 2019) has introduced trust and reputation models that demonstrate how trust could be formulated using personality traits and other handcrafted features extracted from the dataset. Current models, often numeric or cognitive, may have limitations in capturing emotions' impact on trust within evaluations (Granatyr et al., 2015). Trust, as a psychological state influenced by emotional and cognitive processes, presents an opportunity to integrate trust models into the affective paradigm (Wade and Robinson, 2012; Granatyr et al., 2017). Granatyr et al. (Granatyr et al., 2016) incorporated emotions from textual reviews to compute reputation scores, considering emotions in computing reputation scores. Our investigation explores effective utilization of emotional, personality, and temporal traits, in conjunction with trust scores, to enhance recommender system trustworthiness.

Figure 2. Different phases of developing a trust-aware recommender system to ensure trustworthy recommendation

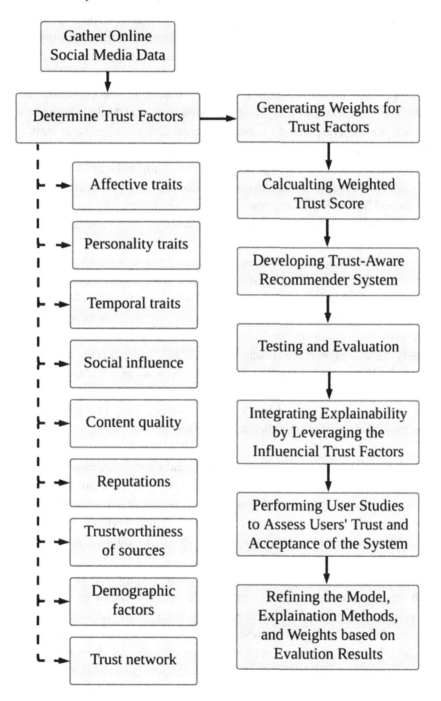

Several publicly available datasets, namely the Amazon reviews dataset (Ni et al., 2019), Trip Advisor dataset (Roshchina et al., 2015), Ciao review dataset (Cai et al., 2017), and Epinions dataset (Cai et al., 2017), among others, can be explored to train and evaluate the trust-aware recommender system. These datasets contain information about the user ID, item ID, rating, text review, timestamp, reviewer reputation, review helpfulness votes, and others. Notably, the Epinions dataset (Hamedani et al., 2021) contains an additional field for user trust relationships within the trust network. The trust relationships are represented as directed edges between users, where each node corresponds to a user, and each directed edge represents a trust or distrust relationship between the two users. From the dataset, different types of features, namely emotional traits, personality traits, temporal traits, and trust scores, can be extracted. Anzum et al. (Anzum and Gavrilova, 2023) introduced a novel feature named SSEL that incorporates stylistic, sentiment, and linguistic features to capture users' emotional traits expressed in microblogs which can be leveraged to calculate emotion-based features for this recommender system.

Personality traits can be extracted using the most commonly used Big Five personality model that defines personality traits as openness, conscientiousness, extraversion, agreeableness, and neuroticism (Christian et al., 2021). We hypothesize that incorporating emotional and personality traits in a recommender system would enhance its trustworthiness by creating a more personalized, transparent, explainable, and satisfying user experience (Dhelim et al., 2022). To extract the temporal traits (J. Wu et al., 2020), we can use the time of the reviews as a feature and compute additional temporal features such as the time between reviews, the frequency of reviews, and the time of day when the reviews were posted. These would provide insights into the users' temporal behavior and preferences.

- **Deriving Trust Score:** The trust factors and their significance can be used to derive the weighted trust score. Moreover, incorporating the trust score with additional pertinent features, like the linguistic quality (including writing style, vocabulary, and readability) of text reviews, product-related attributes, and more, can help to creating more reliable and trustworthy recommendations (Victor et al., 2011).
- **Model Development:** The combined feature vector can then be used as an input to the machine learning models (support vector machine, random forest, decision tree, XGBoost, etc.) to predict either the user's rating for a particular item or the likelihood of the user liking or purchasing a specific item. This derived feature vector could be effective for deep learning-based architecture as well. While deep learning models are powerful for extracting features automatically from the dataset, handcrafted features are essential to guarantee the model's personalization, transparency, and explainability.

Consequently, we hypothesize that incorporating users' emotional traits, personality traits, and temporal traits with trust scores would improve the trustworthiness of the recommender system.

- **Performance Evaluation:** To evaluate the performance of the trust-aware recommender system, we can use the mean absolute error (MAE) (Botchkarev, 2018), which measures the absolute difference between the predicted and actual ratings for each user-item pair, and how well the model can predict the actual ratings. In addition to MAE, we can also use other commonly used metrics for recommender systems, such as root mean squared error and normalized root mean squared error (Aramanda et al., 2021) for achieving more comprehensive evaluations. Additionally, the system's trustworthiness can be evaluated by adopting human evaluation through qualitative feedback. This can capture subjective aspects that offer practical insights for building a more trustworthy system, which is often difficult to capture using standard evaluation metrics (Liao et al., 2022).

- **Integrating Explainability:** To enhance explainability, we can employ post-hoc methods (LIME and SHAP) for transparent insights into recommendations. Moreover, built-in attention mechanisms directly integrate explainability into the model, highlighting crucial trust factors that help users understand the decision-making process (Knapič et al., 2021).

In the development of the trust-aware recommender system, the incorporation of weighted trust scores assumes a critical role in enhancing explainability. By assigning weights to different trust factors such as user trust relationships, emotional traits, personality traits, and temporal behavior, the system aims to provide a clearer rationale behind its recommendations. This comprehensive approach would allow users to understand why certain recommendations are being made (Vultureanu-Albişi and Bădică, 2021). In addition, weighted trust scores add a transparent view into how the system evaluates various aspects of user interactions and preferences. For instance, by considering user trust relationships, the system can account for the reliability of information provided by different users, helping users discern the credibility of recommendations. Similarly, integrating emotional and personality traits into the trust scores would enable the system to personalize recommendations based on individual preferences and characteristics, while including temporal behavior in the computation of trust scores would allow the system to adapt to evolving user preferences over time (Lex et al., 2021). The system would provide contextually relevant suggestions by analyzing user behavior patterns, further enhancing user trust. Moreover, the transparency of weighted trust scores would empower users to decide whether to trust the system's recommendations. By understanding the factors contributing to each recommendation, users can assess the reliability and relevance of the suggestions, leading to a more engaging and satisfying user experience.

- **Conducting User Studies:** Conducting user studies is vital to evaluate the effectiveness and acceptance of the proposed trust-aware recommender system (Vultureanu-Albişi and Bădică, 2021). The focus is on assessing users' trust in recommendations and overall system acceptance. Through surveys, interviews, and interactions, we aim to gather insights into trust factors and the effectiveness of explainability. This user-centric approach ensures the system meets user expectations, providing accurate, trustworthy recommendations aligned with transparency preferences.
- **Refinement:** Post-implementation, an iterative refinement process is crucial for improving the system. This involves analyzing system performance metrics and user feedback to adjust the model architecture, fine-tuning explanation methods, and optimizing trust factor weights. This ensures the system evolves to meet user expectations and effectively provides trustworthy recommendations.

In summary, this section outlined the key factors shaping ethical AI systems in online social media. Considering the addressed aspects, a conceptual framework is presented to develop a trust-aware recommender system that incorporates users' personality, emotional, and temporal traits. The framework also highlights how deriving a weighted trust score using different factors could be leveraged to enhance users' trust in the recommender system's decision-making. One potential limitation of the proposed framework is the complexity of determining the appropriate weights for different trust factors. Assigning accurate weights would require a deep understanding of user behavior and preferences, which could be challenging to capture comprehensively. Additionally, the subjective nature of emotional and personality traits adds another layer of complexity, potentially leading to biases in the weighting process. However, rigorous validation and refinement processes would ensure the reliability and effectiveness of the weighted trust scores in enhancing explainability.

6. APPLICATIONS AND OPEN PROBLEMS

This section presents a brief overview of the emerging field of XAI and trustworthy decision-making within computer vision techniques in diverse domains, followed by identifying critical research gaps and outlining open problems.

6.1 Computer Visual Social Media Content

- **Domain Overview:** In the highly interconnected era of information technology, social media platforms have become a vital source of online news in the form of various multimedia contents such as images, videos, text (Flaxman et al., 2016; Comito et al., 2023). Users are exposed to such information beyond social media platforms, extending to specialized communities such as discussion forums (e.g., Reddit), blogs (e.g., Medium), and microblogs (e.g., Twitter) (Kessler, 2018). Online translation technology enhances blog interactions, allowing users to engage with content in diverse languages and media formats (Ku and Chen, 2007).

  Due to the rapid spread of fake news, establishing trust in online information is difficult. Moreover, biases in the translation of online articles present another challenge, where the translated content may introduce alterations in semantic meaning, potentially leading to a distortion of the intended context. Since online news and translation increasingly shape public opinion, they raise ethical concerns regarding privacy, responsible reporting, and the potential manipulation of information. Using deepfake technology and advanced image editing tools, visual content can be manipulated easily (Langguth et al., 2021). This includes fake images or videos designed to deceive and mislead viewers. Addressing these multifaceted challenges is important for maintaining a trustworthy, unbiased, authentic, and ethically sound online information ecosystem.

- **Current Research:** Addressing challenges in sharing digital information is an essential research domain. Doumit et al. (Doumit and Minai, 2011) addressed the issue of media bias in news outlets, where biases can vary. It introduces a unified system that extracts information from political news texts and analyzes it within a cognitive network. Treating news outlets as agents with unique personalities, the system uses Latent Dirichlet Allocation (LDA) and Natural Language Processing (NLP) to identify their traits about different topics. While their unified system effectively extracts and analyzes information from political news texts, it primarily focuses on textual content, overlooking the influence of multimedia elements like images and videos, a common gap in current research. Balmau et al. (Balmau et al., 2018) further introduced a mechanism to combat the spread of fake news on social media platforms without relying on content-based criteria, which can be bypassed by adversaries. The proposed solution involves a plugin that utilizes a team of fact-checkers to review a small subset of popular news items, gauging users' inclination to share fake news. Employing a Bayesian approach, the system estimates the trustworthiness of future news items and treats those surpassing a certain "untrustworthiness" threshold accordingly. However, the reliance on a small subset of popular news items for fact-checking limits the scalability and effectiveness of the proposed system. Lago et al. (Lago et al., 2019) addressed the problem of misinformation and manipulation in online news articles that predominantly feature images or videos. Given the influence of images on readers' opinions and behaviors, the paper proposes an automatic technique to assess the authenticity of images in online news. This dual-method approach aims to enhance accuracy by cross-verifying information from both visual and textual sources. While their dual-method approach combines image forensic algorithms with textual analysis, it primarily focuses on image verification within the context of textual content. This approach overlooks the potential for standalone image-based misinformation, such as memes and manipulated visuals, thereby highlighting a gap in research concerning comprehensive multimedia verification techniques.

- **Open Problems and Future Work:** In this domain, an essential challenge is to distinguish between authentic and manipulated visual content. Advanced algorithms capable of identifying deepfake visual content are needed to detect subtle alterations in videos and images. As a result, future research should explore robust solutions that leverage cutting-edge techniques, potentially integrating blockchain or cryptographic methods to ensure the integrity and authenticity of visual media. Another open problem lies in developing robust methods to identify and mitigate the impact of fake news, safeguarding users from misinformation, and maintaining the credibility of online information sources. Future research can explore integrating advanced AI technologies into online platforms to enhance the accessibility and integrity of news articles and translation services.

In summary, the current research addresses the challenges of establishing trust and mitigating bias in online news and translation platforms. Despite promising outcomes, issues persist regarding the reliance on textual analysis, scalability, and oversight of standalone image-based misinformation. It is crucial to develop robust algorithms capable of identifying manipulated visual content, integrating multi-modal analysis for comprehensive verification, and addressing ethical frameworks to promote responsible practices and safeguard against misinformation.

6.2 Aesthetic Systems

- **Domain Overview:** Aesthetic biometrics is a sub-domain of social behavioral biometrics that integrates technology, human perception, and personal preference for identification (M. Gavrilova et al., 2017). Users' activities across social media platforms, such as reacting to posts, sharing content, engaging in discussions, etc., provide valuable insights about their unique aesthetic preferences. These behavioral traits have potential applications in various fields such as situation awareness, cybersecurity, digital monitoring, psychological assessment, marketing, etc. (M. L. Gavrilova et al., 2022; Paul et al., 2014).

The widespread availability of aesthetic content on social media platforms introduces a potential risk of misuse of such biometric systems, which can undermine users' trust in these systems. Recently developed aesthetic systems utilize advanced AI methods. However, the black-box nature of such computational methods requires explainability of the system's decision-making process. There exists a potential risk of ensuring the integrity and originality of the presented aesthetic data. The widespread availability of such content also introduces various ethical concerns, highlighting the issues of responsible usage of user-generated content.

- **Current Research:** Research in aesthetic biometrics is still emerging, with relatively few studies. In 2012, pioneering research in this domain was conducted by introducing a visual aesthetic system (Lovato et al., 2012). The system leveraged hand-crafted image features along with LASSO regression algorithm. Subsequently, in 2021, another aesthetic modality, audio aesthetics, was introduced by incorporating intra- and inter-song features (Sieu and Gavrilova, 2021). Both systems relied on manual feature engineering, prone to limitations such as subjectivity and scalability constraints. However, these limitations were further overcome by leveraging automatic feature extraction using advanced deep learning techniques and achieving significantly higher precision in aesthetic evaluation. In 2020, the first deep learning-based visual aesthetic system was developed by leveraging high-level features extracted from VGG16 (Bari et al., 2020). Similarly, the first deep learning-based audio aesthetic system was developed by including high-level features extracted from ResNet50 and meta-heuristic feature optimization algorithms to generate the most optimal feature set for identification (Iffath and Gavrilova, 2022). The aesthetic biometric systems further extended beyond uni-modal systems by integrating multiple aesthetic modalities for more robust and reliable aesthetic biometric systems. Sieu et al. (Sieu and Gavrilova, 2021) and Iffath et al. (Iffath and Gavrilova, 2023) explored late fusion and intermediate fusion techniques, respectively, to integrate multiple aesthetic modalities. Existing aesthetic biometric systems have yielded promising identification results; however, there are still potential issues regarding biases, authenticity, explainability, and ethics. The dataset used in the developed systems lacks temporal preference changes, demographic information, or correlation among aesthetic modalities, resulting in biased preference patterns and decision-making. Furthermore, current systems fail to explain how preference data contributes to outcomes.

- **Open Problems and Future Work**: Until now, very limited research has been done in the aesthetic visual domain. Adaptability to dynamic changes in aesthetic preferences over time and analyzing negative preferences continue to be problems. Additionally, the long-term societal impact of aesthetic profiling on social dynamics and user behavior can be explored. Aesthetic biometric systems are vulnerable to various attacks that need to be addressed by making them resilient against potential threats. To protect the integrity and privacy of user-generated aesthetic data, necessary guidelines should be formed for the responsible usage of aesthetic content.

In summary, existing research in aesthetic biometrics showcases advancements in visual and audio systems, transitioning to deep learning-based approaches. Despite promising results in identification tasks, concerns persist regarding biases and authenticity due to limited dataset diversity and explainability issues. Future efforts must prioritize mitigating biases and ensuring the trustworthiness of aesthetic systems to foster responsible usage and safeguard user privacy in applications such as cyber security and recommender systems.

6.3 Cybersecurity and Biometrics

- **Domain Overview:** Cybersecurity is a comprehensive approach that guards against cyberattacks on data, networks, and computer programs. Various methods are used to guarantee the privacy, accuracy, and accessibility of data. To manage breaches in any cybersecurity system, researchers are currently working on biometric security, network security, application security, data protection, identity management, and incident response, among others (M. L. Gavrilova et al., 2021). Critical issues in biometric and cybersecurity research encompass trust, bias, explainability, and authenticity (Jain et al., 2021). The current trend in biometric research underscores the ethical use and reliability of systems dedicated to securing digital environments and safeguarding sensitive information. The limitations associated with traditional password or token-based authentication methods have fueled the exploration of more accurate and trustworthy user authentication and identification management systems (Jain et al., 2021). Security concerns in modern biometric systems extend to potential manipulations by adversaries, including insiders like system administrators or direct attacks on system infrastructure (Jain and Nandakumar, 2012). Recent research has delved into the fairness of facial recognition algorithms (H. Wu et al., 2023) and highlighted biases in their outputs due to factors like lighting, posture, expression, and picture quality. Some biometric systems may exhibit gender or demographic bias, demonstrating variations in performance across different user groups.

- **Current Research:** Addressing bias in biometric systems is also challenging. A recent article discusses responsible AI from a scientific and societal perspective, addressing trustworthy decision-making, privacy considerations, visual knowledge discovery, and bias mitigation strategies (M. L. Gavrilova, 2023). In addition to a thorough review of bias and ethical issues in AI-based information security applications, it offers specific suggestions for minimizing bias and fairness in AI-generated judgments. Another study highlights the use of deep learning and artificial intelligence in cybersecurity by emphasizing physiological, behavioral, and social behavioral biometrics to the psychological characteristics of individuals (M. L. Gavrilova et al., 2022). Multi-pose-specific deep convolutional neural network (CNN) models studied by (AbdAlmageed et al., 2016) process facial images to produce a variety of pose-specific features and convert the input image into various facial poses using 3D rendering. However, the recognition system's sensitivity to changes in posture is decreased because an ensemble of pose-specific CNN features is employed. Furthermore, another study uses a two-way approach to investigate bias in face detection (Alshareef et al., 2021). In the first phase, the impact of gender distribution in Spoof in the Wild (SiW) data on model performance is explored, and CNN models (ResNet50 and VGG16) are used to evaluate the fairness of detecting impostor attacks based on gender. A debiasing variational autoencoder (DB-VAE) is used in conjunction with VGG16 in the second phase to assess its efficacy in mitigating bias in attack detection.

- **Open Problems and Future Work:** Establishing a user-centric, ethical environment and improving security measures are essential to the ever-evolving process of fostering trust in biometric systems. Although some research has investigated trustworthy biometric systems, more work is still needed to establish users' trust. It is always a challenge to develop a strong approach to counter different techniques like unbiased face recognition, voice recordings, facial masks, or fake fingerprints. Creating face recognition models resilient to adversarial attacks is a key challenge in many biometric systems. Future studies can focus on techniques such as adversarial training and model regularization to enhance the robustness of face recognition models against adversarial attacks.

In summary, ongoing research in Cybersecurity and Biometrics addresses critical issues such as trust, bias, explainability, and authenticity. Recent studies focus on bias in face recognition algorithms, proposing strategies for minimizing bias and ensuring fairness in AI-generated judgments. The integration of deep learning in cybersecurity, particularly in utilizing physiological and behavioral biometrics, is a notable trend. Future challenges include building user-centric, ethical environments, countering adversarial attacks on face recognition models, and exploring techniques like adversarial training for enhanced robustness.

6.4 Tele-medicine and Psychology

- **Domain Overview:** Online medicine encompasses delivering healthcare services through digital platforms, enabling virtual consultations, remote diagnoses, and the issuance of electronic prescriptions. The COVID-19 pandemic brought online medicine services into the public eye, and as a result, individuals have become used to digital medicine services. Patients can access medical expertise from the convenience of their own homes and receive prescribed medications through home delivery. The flexibility of virtual consultations allows for a diverse range of healthcare needs, including follow-up appointments, preventive care discussions, and lifestyle management. Moreover, integrating emerging technologies, such as artificial intelligence and wearable devices, hold the potential to further optimize diagnostic accuracy and treatment recommendations in the evolving landscape of online medicine. As the field continues to evolve, addressing regulatory considerations, ensuring data security, and fostering patient trust remain essential components for the sustained growth and effectiveness of online medicine. Online medicine impacts psychology, bias, and security in healthcare. Virtual consultations enhance well-being, breaking barriers to timely healthcare while addressing biases in online platforms helps ensure equitable treatment. Although online medicine chatbots (Gilson et al., 2023) can save valuable clinician time, they raise concerns about misdiagnosis and the limited expertise compared to human professionals. As a result, human oversight is needed to verify AI-generated data (Arif et al., 2023). Additional security concerns involve safeguarding patient privacy and ensuring data protection for trust in digital healthcare platforms. Users' trust is vital for enduring product-consumer relationships (Elphinston et al., 2023). Patients' tech comfort and literacy can also influence effective interactions in online healthcare.

- **Current Research:** A recent study Uncovska et al., 2023 investigated the acceptance of mobile health (mHealth) in Germany, focusing on factors influencing patients' intention to use and the impact of prescription and reimbursement status. When looking into therapeutic areas, most mHealth users had experience with apps for either mental and behavioral or endocrine and nutritional issues. Another study (van der Stigchel et al., 2023) has investigated whether humans recognize potential biases provided by an agent and whether they can neutralize this when it occurs. A final study (Gravel et al., 2023) found that more than two-thirds of the references provided by ChatGPT to a diverse set of medical questions were fabricated, although most seemed deceptively real.

- **Open Problems and Future Work:** One of the most challenging factors for virtual treatment is the accuracy of medical advice. Research can be done by integrating artificial intelligence and advanced technologies to improve diagnostic accuracy and personalizing healthcare in virtual settings. Moreover, enhancing security and privacy measures is paramount to protecting patient data, while establishing interoperability standards can facilitate efficient data exchange between platforms. Discovering a balance between virtual and in-person care, especially for chronic conditions, also remains a challenge that requires innovative solutions to ensure the best outcomes for patients.

In summary, the domain of Online medicine revolutionizes healthcare with virtual consultations, prescription delivery, and AI-driven diagnostics. Core considerations include regulatory compliance, data security, and patient trust. In psychology, bias, and security, it impacts well-being and efficiency, urging efforts to address biases, ensure AI reliability, and protect patient privacy. Current research explores mHealth acceptance, bias recognition, and AI-generated medical information reliability. Future work aims to enhance diagnostic accuracy, security measures, and strike a balance between virtual and in-person care for seamless patient outcomes.

6.5 Autonomous Vehicle Technology

- **Domain Overview:** Autonomous vehicles (AVs) are expected to become an integral part of our future transportation landscape. Many automakers, such as Waymo and Cruise, have introduced commercial robotaxis, accumulating millions of miles of driving experience. With the advancement of AI and computer vision, there are considerable improvements in different components of autonomous driving technology (Zablocki et al., 2022). As we progress towards fully autonomous vehicles, trust in these safety-critical applications becomes paramount for widespread acceptance (Saleh et al., 2017). In this context, explainable AI approaches can improve operational safety and transparency by enabling stakeholders to understand the complex decision-making process of automated driving operations (Jirotka, 2021).

- **Current Research:** Researchers and practitioners in computer vision have been actively exploring methods to provide explainability for real-time decision-making and actions in AVs. For instance, Kim et al. (J. Kim et al., 2018) integrated textual descriptions and saliency maps to generate design justifications from an AV with end-to-end driving. They utilized post-hoc explanations from an attention-based video-to-text model, typically developed after the model has been trained, thereby lacking proper accuracy and faithful design of a transparent system. To address these limitations, Jing et al. (Jing et al., 2022) incorporated both explicit human annotations and implicit visual semantics, striving for comprehensive interpretability of automated systems. In the domain of human-computer interaction, researchers have incorporated human-machine interfaces (HMIs) to explain AV actions to passengers and pedestrians. For example, Asha et al. (Asha et al., 2020) designed explainable visualizations on external car bodies, offering context and user-specific information to different road users. While this work primarily considered external users of AVs, another study (Asha and Sharlin, 2023) delved into user-adaptive XAI, explicitly targeting vulnerable passengers like older adults, who preferred to receive less frequent explanations from AVs to reduce distractions and mental workload. While detailed information can enhance transparency, backend system reports that are too frequent can also overwhelm users, eventually decreasing trust. Du et al. (Du et al., 2023) investigated users' trust and opinions on explanations provided via AV HMIs from a cross-cultural perspective and found that participants from India and China exhibited a greater trust in AVs when seeking permission and receiving explanations before actions, reflecting their cultural norms of user authority. Conversely, this preference differed among participants from the United States and other countries. Thus, it is imperative to consider various contextual factors, such as user diversity and cross-cultural aspects to effectively develop and generalize human interpretability of AVs.

- **Open Problems and Future Work:** AVs have been tested and mainly researched in developed European countries, the US, and Canada over the last decade (Müller, 2019). Thus, it also raises questions about the trust, bias, and generalizability of gathered data and algorithm design of AVs, limiting their adaptability in other countries. To address this issue, we recommend enhancing the diversity of datasets for AVs with cross-cultural aspects by conducting tests in varied driving infrastructures with different traffic laws. Additionally, it is essential to consider diverse user perspectives and needs while incorporating XAI systems in AVs to reduce bias and increase trust, transparency, and authenticity.

In summary, existing research has explored approaches for designing interpretability in AVs, recognizing it as a multifaceted problem. However, challenges persist in effectively meeting human users' expectations by enhancing the quality of explainability in automated systems, whether by balancing the limitations of post-hoc applications or utilizing direct interpretations generated from the model. Overall, future work should investigate comprehensive explanations for AVs that are inclusive and understandable to a diverse range of users, regardless of their age, gender, abilities, or characteristics.

6.6 Unmanned Aerial Vehicles (UAVs)

- **Domain Overview:** Autonomous drones or unmanned aerial vehicles (UAVs) are gaining maturity for deployment in cities, supporting tasks related to surveillance, monitoring environments, and delivery of emergency items such as medicine and food (Hassanalian and Abdelkefi, 2017). To ensure improved performance in these emerging technologies, powerful AI models are being utilized, as any errors in the decision-making process of autonomous drones can cause damage to citizens or urban infrastructure (Dolph et al., 2018). To foster trust and acceptability for UAVs, it is important to understand their operations and working process so that human operators or technicians can identify any system malfunctions. Thus, the questions of explainability, bias, and authenticity arise for better interpretability of drone behaviors and functions.

- **Current Research:** Various studies have explored the potential usage of XAI methods in monitoring drone behavior to mitigate malfunctions or combat data poisoning attacks. Dolph et al. (Dolph et al., 2018) investigated explainability through feature visualization of various layers of convolutional neural networks (CNNs), aiming to enhance the trustworthiness of UAV's in executing safety-critical tasks. While the authors utilized imagery for human interpretability of internal networks, end-users may struggle to fully grasp the complex output of the XAI method. Subsequently, another study (He et al., 2021) introduced a deep reinforcement learning (DRL) controller for UAV path planning, incorporating visual and textual explanations. While this approach improved the explainability for path planning of autonomous drones, the model required further fine-tuning and feature attribution. For identifying potential failure or malfunction of UAVs, Hogan et al. (Hogan et al., 2022) proposed KernelSHAP, a visual explainer for bounding boxes produced by the detection algorithms of on-board UAVs. The explainer uses a saliency map to highlight the essential parts of an image, simplifying the identification of the reasons behind specific failures or data biases. In the realm of human-AI interaction, a study (Agrawal and Cleland-Huang, 2021) investigated user interface (UI) designs aimed at delivering timely and detailed explanations for swarms of UAVs. The research introduced the concept of a human-on-the-loop (HotL) system, emphasizing the importance of maintaining situational awareness for human operators to monitor the behavior of drones and intervene when necessary. The findings highlighted effective design strategies, such as information clustering and graphical animations, to facilitate meaningful interpretability of the UAVs' actions. However, further exploration is needed to assess the presented design principles and the effectiveness of the explanations for UAVs in real-world settings, particularly considering diverse events and autonomous features.

- **Open Problems and Future Work:** As UAV is still an emerging technology, research gaps exist in exploring user engagement with these autonomous drones and how their diverse perspectives and observations will contribute to XAI design in this context. It is crucial to investigate how information explanations should be formatted to support immediate and clear comprehension, reducing the potential distractions or overload of information. For human operators of autonomous drones as the HoTL system, proper explanation to increase situational awareness is essential to reduce automation bias, which can create overtrust in the autonomy of these drones and misinterpretation of their operations.

In summary, previous studies have predominantly focused on improving the interpretability of UAVs' internal networks to better understand autonomous behaviors and diagnose specific failures. Visual explanations for internal CNN and DRL models were commonly employed to enhance end-users comprehensibility. Additionally, some research explored design interfaces to augment situational awareness for human operators of UAVs' paths and actions. Overall, the challenges remain in fostering greater acceptance of this emerging technology by engaging with diverse end-users and experts and conducting studies considering various factors and variables in real-world settings. Therefore, future studies should inspect the scalability aspects of their models and designs to enhance the interpretability of UAVs in urban infrastructure to make their decision-making processes more transparent to end-users, ultimately leading to increased trust.

6.7 Online Social Media

- **Domain Overview:** Computer vision has revolutionized online activities by enabling applications such as face recognition on social platforms (Indrawan et al., 2013), generating captions for images (Hossain et al., 2019), augmented reality (Scavarelli et al., 2021), and so on. These technologies enhance user experiences, streamline the search and identification process, and provide efficiency in online interactions. With the increasing usage of automated systems in online activities, the question that arises is how responsibly these systems are implemented.

- **Current Research:** Despite the advancements of deep learning-based computer vision systems, concern persists in trust, bias, explainability, and authenticity of these systems. Face recognition systems show performance degradation due to due to biases of face pose, orientation, and illumination (Kortylewski et al., 2019). Moreover, facial recognition systems also have race bias (Cavazos et al., 2020), which gives a deviation in recognition performance for different races. In contrast, image captioning systems face societal bias (Zhao et al., 2021), which is a result of the imbalance of different populations in the training dataset. Among various societal biases, gender and racial biases are the most common in image captioning systems. Overall, as computer vision architectures are biased, the trustworthiness of these architectures is also questionable.

- **Open Problems and Future Work:** To explain how vision models mitigate bias, researchers are investigating various measures to explain what deep learning architectures are learning. Neural probing (Palmieri et al., 2020) is one of the common ways to measure what a deep learning architecture is learning by reverse engineering the embedding space of the penultimate layer. Biasness in facial pose, orientation, and illumination can be balanced by training recognition models with synthetic datasets (Kortylewski et al., 2019). However, efforts to mitigate racial and gender bias in face recognition and captioning systems have yet to be explored.

Computer vision has become a cornerstone of online social media for its performance and acceptability. However, the issue of bias is still a troublesome issue that needs to be addressed. Instead of only focusing on detecting biases, well-organized frameworks and datasets are required to measure the biases of the social media-based vision models.

6.8 Smart Sensors

- **Domain Overview:** Smart devices are typically connected to a network and can operate interactively and autonomously. In recent years, there has been a significant increase in the integration of computer vision into smart devices. Advanced vision architecture has enabled robots and automated systems to gain visual perception capabilities. Smart glasses equipped with vision perception can assist individuals with vision impairment by utilizing large language models (Waisberg et al., 2023). Additionally, computationally efficient object detection systems have been developed to detect and classify traffic incidents while determining the severity level of accidents (Basheer Ahmed et al., 2023).

- **Current Research:** While the incorporation of computer vision in smart devices is increasing rapidly, it is also giving rise to several important questions that need to be addressed. These questions revolve around trust, bias, explainability, and authenticity. With the growing use of computer vision in various applications, it becomes crucial to ensure that the decisions made by vision-based smart devices are not only accurate but also comprehensible to human users. This is where the concept of explainable AI comes into the picture (Doshi-Velez and Kim, 2017). By incorporating explainable AI techniques, we can provide transparent and understandable reasons behind the decisions made by these vision-based robots, thus emphasizing the importance of fairness in their functioning.

Moreover, it is worth noting that gender and race-based biases are unfortunately quite common in many commercial computer vision-based systems (Buolamwini and Gebru, 2018). This raises concerns about the potential discrimination and unfairness that may arise from using these systems. Therefore, it becomes imperative to address these biases and work towards developing more inclusive and unbiased computer vision technologies. By doing so, we can ensure that these systems are not only accurate and reliable but also ethical and fair in their operation.

- **Open Problems and Future Work:** Current research investigates class activation maps highlighting the substantial properties that lead vision-based systems to choose a particular object label (Sun et al., 2020). Class activations have made vision-based deep learning systems explainable. It has also increased the authenticity of vision-based systems as they can help in fault diagnostics (Sun et al., 2020). Deep learning architectures often exhibit bias based on their training dataset. Therefore, a crucial challenge for smart devices is to mitigate this bias in their training data effectively.

Although computer vision models are currently explainable, the methods still require extensive evaluation to be trustworthy. As bias has become a greater issue in sensor-based vision architectures, removing bias from data has become a crucial task. The present studies lack the investigation of bias-removal strategies and uniformity of vision data that are used to train smart vision systems.

In summary, this section provides insights into key areas where computer vision intersects with various domains, highlighting the challenges and opportunities within each context, where common themes of trust, bias, explainability, and authenticity emerge as central concerns. Researchers explored the ethical implications of biased algorithms, and the importance of transparent decision-making processes by ensuring inclusivity and fairness in technological advancements. Proposed solutions include leveraging explainable AI techniques, diversifying datasets, and incorporating cross-cultural perspectives to address biases and enhance trustworthiness. By addressing these challenges, the field aims to build more accountable, reliable, and user-centric computer vision systems that positively impact society, fostering trust and transparency in technological advancements.

7. CONCLUSION

This chapter provided a comprehensive overview of pivotal advancements in trustworthy, ethical, and explainable computer vision within online social media systems. It defined the notion of trust and proposed a unified framework to promote trust in future computer vision applications. This chapter also highlighted the significance of integrating explainability to ensure the trustworthiness of an intelligent system in addition to emphasizing other performance evaluation metrics. It listed key application domains of importance to industries, academia, and the public, including cybersecurity, online social media, recommender systems, misinformation detection, healthcare, smart cities, and autonomous vehicles. Furthermore, the chapter explored potential novel applications arising from this research and outlined open challenges that pave the way for future developments in this dynamic and evolving domain.

ACKNOWLEDGMENT

The authors acknowledge the Natural Sciences and Engineering Research Council (NSERC) Discovery Grant funding, as well as the NSERC Strategic Partnership Grant (SPG) and the University of Calgary Transdisciplinary Connector Funding for the partial funding of this project.

REFERENCES

AbdAlmageed, W., Wu, Y., Rawls, S., Harel, S., Hassner, T., Masi, I., Choi, J., Lekust, J., Kim, J., & Natarajan, P. (2016). Face recognition using deep multi-pose representations. 2016 IEEE winter conference on applications of computer vision (WACV), 1–9.

Adali, S., & Golbeck, J. (2012). Predicting personality with social behavior. *2012 IEEE/ACM International Conference on Advances in Social Networks Analysis and Mining*, 302–309. 10.1109/ASONAM.2012.58

Agrawal, A., & Cleland-Huang, J. (2021). Explaining autonomous decisions in swarms of human-on-the-loop small unmanned aerial systems. *Proceedings of the AAAI Conference on Human Computation and Crowdsourcing, 9*, 15–26. 10.1609/hcomp.v9i1.18936

Alam, M. A. U. (2020). AI-fairness towards activity recognition of older adults. *MobiQuitous 2020-17th EAI International Conference on Mobile and Ubiquitous Systems: Computing, Networking and Services*, 108–117.

Alshareef, N., Yuan, X., Roy, K., & Atay, M. (2021). A study of gender bias in face presentation attack and its mitigation. *Future Internet, 13*(9), 234. doi:10.3390/fi13090234

Analyzing and reducing the damage of dataset bias to face recognition with synthetic data. (2019). *IEEE/CVF Conference on Computer Vision and Pattern Recognition Workshops (CVPRW)*, 2261–2268. doi:10.1109/CVPRW.2019.00279

Anzum, F., Asha, A. Z., & Gavrilova, M. L. (2022). Biases, fairness, and implications of using AI in social media data mining. *2022 International Conference on Cyberworlds (CW)*, 251–254. 10.1109/CW55638.2022.00056

Anzum, F., & Gavrilova, M. L. (2023). Emotion detection from micro-blogs using novel input representation. *IEEE Access : Practical Innovations, Open Solutions, 11*, 19512–19522. doi:10.1109/ACCESS.2023.3248506

Aramanda, A., Abdul, S. M., & Vedala, R. (2021). Refining user ratings using user emotions for recommender systems. *The 23rd International Conference on Information Integration and Web Intelligence. Linz, Austria*, 3–10.

Asha, A. Z., & Sharlin, E. (2023). Designing inclusive interaction with autonomous vehicles for older passengers. *Proceedings of the 2023 ACM Designing Interactive Systems Conference*, 2138–2154. 10.1145/3563657.3596045

Babaei, M., Kulshrestha, J., Chakraborty, A., Redmiles, E. M., Cha, M., & Gummadi, K. P. (2021). Analyzing biases in perception of truth in news stories and their implications for fact checking. *IEEE Transactions on Computational Social Systems*, 9(3), 839–850. doi:10.1109/TCSS.2021.3096038

Balmau, O., Guerraoui, R., Kermarrec, A.-M., Maurer, A., Pavlovic, M., & Zwaenepoel, W. (2018). Limiting the spread of fake news on social media platforms by evaluating users' trustworthiness. *arXiv preprint arXiv:1808.09922*.

Bari, A. H., Sieu, B., & Gavrilova, M. L. (2020). Aestheticnet: Deep convolutional neural network for person identification from visual aesthetic. *The Visual Computer*, 36(10-12), 2395–2405. doi:10.1007/s00371-020-01893-7

Basheer Ahmed, M. I., Zaghdoud, R., Ahmed, M. S., Sendi, R., Alsharif, S., Alabdulkarim, J., Albin Saad, B. A., Alsabt, R., Rahman, A., & Krishnasamy, G. (2023). A real-time computer vision based approach to detection and classification of traffic incidents. *Big Data and Cognitive Computing, 7*(1), 22.

Bird, S., Dudík, M., Edgar, R., Horn, B., Lutz, R., Milan, V., Sameki, M., Wallach, H., & Walker, K. (2020). Fairlearn: A toolkit for assessing and improving fairness in ai. *Microsoft, Tech. Rep. MSR-TR-2020-32*.

Botchkarev, A. (2018). Performance metrics (error measures) in machine learning regression, forecasting and prognostics: Properties and typology. *arXiv preprint arXiv:1809.03006*.

Buolamwini, J., & Gebru, T. (2018). Gender shades: Intersectional accuracy disparities in commercial gender classification. *Conference on fairness, accountability and transparency. New York, USA*, 77–91.

Cai, C., He, R., & McAuley, J. (2017). SPMC: Socially-aware personalized markov chains for sparse sequential recommendation. *arXiv preprint arXiv:1708.04497*. doi:10.24963/ijcai.2017/204

Cavazos, J. G., Phillips, P. J., Castillo, C. D., & O'Toole, A. J. (2020). Accuracy comparison across face recognition algorithms: Where are we on measuring race bias? *IEEE Transactions on Biometrics, Behavior, and Identity Science*, 3(1), 101–111. doi:10.1109/TBIOM.2020.3027269 PMID:33585821

Caverlee, J. (2008). A large-scale study of myspace: Observations and implications for online social networks. *Proceedings of the International AAAI Conference on Web and Social Media, 2* (1), 36–44.

Chien, S.-Y., Yang, C.-J., & Yu, F. (2022). Xflag: Explainable fake news detection model on social media. *International Journal of Human-Computer Interaction, 38*(18-20), 1808–1827. doi:10.1080/10447318.2022.2062113

Christian, H., Suhartono, D., Chowanda, A., & Zamli, K. Z. (2021). Text based personality prediction from multiple social media data sources using pre-trained language model and model averaging. *Journal of Big Data, 8*(1), 1–20. doi:10.1186/s40537-021-00459-1 PMID:33425651

Collmann, J., & Matei, S. A. (2016). *Ethical reasoning in big data: An exploratory analysis.* Springer. doi:10.1007/978-3-319-28422-4

Comito, C., Caroprese, L., & Zumpano, E. (2023). Multimodal fake news detection on social media: A survey of deep learning techniques. *Social Network Analysis and Mining, 13*(1), 101. doi:10.1007/s13278-023-01104-w

Confalonieri, R., Coba, L., Wagner, B., & Besold, T. R. (2021). A historical perspective of explainable artificial intelligence. *Wiley Interdisciplinary Reviews. Data Mining and Knowledge Discovery, 11*(1), e1391. doi:10.1002/widm.1391

Dhelim, S., Aung, N., Bouras, M. A., Ning, H., & Cambria, E. (2022). A survey on personality-aware recommendation systems. *Artificial Intelligence Review*, 1–46.

Directive on automated decision-making. (2019). Government of Canada.

Dolph, C. V., Tran, L., & Allen, B. D. (2018). *Towards explainability of uav-based convolutional neural networks for object classification. 2018 Aviation Technology.* Integration, and Operations Conference.

Doshi-Velez, F., & Kim, B. (2017). Towards a rigorous science of interpretable machine learning. *arXiv preprint arXiv:1702.08608.*

Doumit, S., & Minai, A. (2011). Online news media bias analysis using an lda-nlp approach. *International Conference on Complex Systems.*

Du, N., Robert, L., & Yang, X. J. (2023). Cross-cultural investigation of the effects of explanations on drivers' trust, preference, and anxiety in highly automated vehicles. *Transportation Research Record: Journal of the Transportation Research Board, 2677*(1), 554–561. doi:10.1177/03611981221100528

Duenser, A., & Douglas, D. M. (2023). Whom to trust, how and why: Untangling artificial intelligence ethics principles, trustworthiness, and trust. *IEEE Intelligent Systems, 38*(6), 19–26. doi:10.1109/MIS.2023.3322586

Elphinston, R. A., Vaezipour, A., Fowler, J. A., Russell, T. G., & Sterling, M. (2023). Psychological therapy using virtual reality for treatment of driving phobia: A systematic review. *Disability and Rehabilitation, 45*(10), 1582–1594. doi:10.10 80/09638288.2022.2069293 PMID:35532316

Flaxman, S., Goel, S., & Rao, J. M. (2016). Filter bubbles, echo chambers, and online news consumption. *Public Opinion Quarterly, 80*(S1), 298–320. doi:10.1093/ poq/nfw006

Franco, D., Oneto, L., Navarin, N., & Anguita, D. (2021). Toward learning trustworthily from data combining privacy, fairness, and explainability: An application to face recognition. *Entropy (Basel, Switzerland), 23*(8), 1047. doi:10.3390/e23081047 PMID:34441187

Gavrilova, M., Ahmed, F., Azam, S., Paul, P. P., Rahman, W., Sultana, M., & Zohra, F. T. (2017). Emerging trends in security system design using the concept of social behavioural biometrics. *Information Fusion for Cyber-Security Analytics*, 229–251.

Gavrilova, M. L. (2023). Responsible artificial intelligence and bias mitigation in deep learning systems. *2023 27th International Conference Information Visualisation (IV)*, 329–333.

Gavrilova, M. L., Ahmed, F., Bari, A. H., Liu, R., Liu, T., Maret, Y., Sieu, B. K., & Sudhakar, T. (2021). Multi-modal motion-capture-based biometric systems for emergency response and patient rehabilitation. In *Research anthology on rehabilitation practices and therapy* (pp. 653–678). IGI global.

Gavrilova, M. L., Anzum, F., Hossain Bari, A., Bhatia, Y., Iffath, F., Ohi, Q., Shopon, M., & Wahid, Z. (2022). A multifaceted role of biometrics in online security, privacy, and trustworthy decision making. In *Breakthroughs in digital biometrics and forensics* (pp. 303–324). Springer. doi:10.1007/978-3-031-10706-1_14

Gilson, A., Safranek, C. W., Huang, T., Socrates, V., Chi, L., Taylor, R. A., & Chartash, D. (2023). How does chatgpt perform on the united states medical licensing examination? the implications of large language models for medical education and knowledge assessment. *JMIR Medical Education, 9*(1), e45312. doi:10.2196/45312 PMID:36753318

Govindan, K., & Mohapatra, P. (2011). Trust computations and trust dynamics in mobile adhoc networks: A survey. *IEEE Communications Surveys and Tutorials, 14*(2), 279–298. doi:10.1109/SURV.2011.042711.00083

Granatyr, J., Barddal, J. P., Weihmayer Almeida, A., Enembreck, F., & dos Santos Granatyr, A. P. (2016). Towards emotion-based reputation guessing learning agents. *2016 International Joint Conference on Neural Networks (IJCNN)*, 3801–3808. 10.1109/IJCNN.2016.7727690

Granatyr, J., Botelho, V., Lessing, O. R., Scalabrin, E. E., Barthès, J.-P., & Enembreck, F. (2015). Trust and reputation models for multiagent systems. *ACM Computing Surveys*, *48*(2), 1–42. doi:10.1145/2816826

Granatyr, J., Gomes, H. M., Dias, J. M., Paiva, A. M., Nunes, M. A. S. N., Scalabrin, E. E., & Spak, F. (2019). Inferring trust using personality aspects extracted from texts. *2019 IEEE International Conference on Systems, Man and Cybernetics (SMC)*, 3840–3846. 10.1109/SMC.2019.8914641

Granatyr, J., Osman, N., Dias, J., Nunes, M. A. S. N., Masthoff, J., Enembreck, F., Lessing, O. R., Sierra, C., Paiva, A. M., & Scalabrin, E. E. (2017). The need for affective trust applied to trust and reputation models. *ACM Computing Surveys*, *50*(4), 1–36. doi:10.1145/3078833

Gravel, J., D'Amours-Gravel, M., & Osmanlliu, E. (2023). Learning to fake it: Limited responses and fabricated references provided by chatgpt for medical questions. *Mayo Clinic Proceedings. Digital Health*, *1*(3), 226–234. doi:10.1016/j.mcpdig.2023.05.004

Gupta, D., & Krishnan, T. (2020). Algorithmic bias: Why bother. *California Management Review*, *63*(3).

Hamedani, R. M., Ali, I., Hong, J., & Kim, S.-W. (2021). TrustRec: An effective approach to exploit implicit trust and distrust relationships along with explicitones for accurate recommendations. *Computer Science and Information Systems*, *18*(1), 93–114. doi:10.2298/CSIS200608039H

Hassanalian, M., & Abdelkefi, A. (2017). Classifications, applications, and design challenges of drones: A review. *Progress in Aerospace Sciences*, *91*, 99–131. doi:10.1016/j.paerosci.2017.04.003

He, L., Aouf, N., & Song, B. (2021). Explainable deep reinforcement learning for uav autonomous path planning. *Aerospace Science and Technology*, *118*, 107052. doi:10.1016/j.ast.2021.107052

Hogan, M., Aouf, N., Spencer, P., & Almond, J. (2022). Explainable object detection for uncrewed aerial vehicles using kernelshap. *2022 IEEE International Conference on Autonomous Robot Systems and Competitions (ICARSC)*, 136–141. 10.1109/ICARSC55462.2022.9784772

Hossain, M. Z., Sohel, F., Shiratuddin, M. F., & Laga, H. (2019). A comprehensive survey of deep learning for image captioning. *ACM Computing Surveys*, *51*(6), 1–36. doi:10.1145/3295748

Iffath, F., & Gavrilova, M. (2023). Raif: A deep learning-based architecture for multi-modal aesthetic biometric system. *Computer Animation and Virtual Worlds*, *34*(3-4), 2163. doi:10.1002/cav.2163

Iffath, F., & Gavrilova, M. L. (2022). A novel three stage framework for person identification from audio aesthetic. *IEEE Access : Practical Innovations, Open Solutions*, *10*, 90229–90243. doi:10.1109/ACCESS.2022.3200166

Indrawan, P., Budiyatno, S., Ridho, N. M., & Sari, R. F. (2013). Face recognition for social media with mobile cloud computing. *International Journal on Cloud Computing: Services and Architecture*, *3*(1), 23–35. doi:10.5121/ijccsa.2013.3102

Jain, A. K., Deb, D., & Engelsma, J. J. (2021). Biometrics: Trust, but verify. *IEEE Transactions on Biometrics, Behavior, and Identity Science*, *4*(3), 303–323. doi:10.1109/TBIOM.2021.3115465

Jain, A. K., & Nandakumar, K. (2012). Biometric authentication: System security and user privacy. *Computer*, *45*(11), 87–92. doi:10.1109/MC.2012.364

Jiang, Y., Wu, S., Yang, H., Luo, H., Chen, Z., Yin, S., & Kaynak, O. (2022). Secure data transmission and trustworthiness judgement approaches against cyber-physical attacks in an integrated data-driven framework. *IEEE Transactions on Systems, Man, and Cybernetics. Systems*, *52*(12), 7799–7809. doi:10.1109/TSMC.2022.3164024

Jing, T., Xia, H., Tian, R., Ding, H., Luo, X., Domeyer, J., Sherony, R., & Ding, Z. (2022). Inaction: Interpretable action decision making for autonomous driving. *European Conference on Computer Vision*, 370–387. 10.1007/978-3-031-19839-7_22

Jirotka, M. (2021). Explanations in autonomous driving: A survey. *IEEE Transactions on Intelligent Transportation Systems*, 23.

Karduni, A., Wesslen, R., Markant, D., & Dou, W. (2023). Images, emotions, and credibility: Effect of emotional facial expressions on perceptions of news content bias and source credibility in social media. *Proceedings of the International AAAI Conference on Web and Social Media, 17*, 470–481. 10.1609/icwsm.v17i1.22161

Karmakar, G., Chowdhury, A., Das, R., Kamruzzaman, J., & Islam, S. (2021). Assessing trust level of a driverless car using deep learning. *IEEE Transactions on Intelligent Transportation Systems*, *22*(7), 4457–4466. doi:10.1109/TITS.2021.3059261

Kessler, G. (2018). Technology and the future of language teaching. *Foreign Language Annals*, *51*(1), 205–218. doi:10.1111/flan.12318

Kim, A., Moravec, P. L., & Dennis, A. R. (2019). Combating fake news on social media with source ratings: The effects of user and expert reputation ratings. *Journal of Management Information Systems*, *36*(3), 931–968. doi:10.1080/07421222.201 9.1628921

Kim, J., Rohrbach, A., Darrell, T., Canny, J., & Akata, Z. (2018). Textual explanations for self-driving vehicles. *Proceedings of the European conference on computer vision (ECCV)*, 563–578.

KN, P. K., & Gavrilova, M. L. (2021). Latent personality traits assessment from social network activity using contextual language embedding. *IEEE Transactions on Computational Social Systems*, *9*(2), 638–649.

Knapič, S., Malhi, A., Saluja, R., & Främling, K. (2021). Explainable artificial intelligence for human decision support system in the medical domain. *Machine Learning and Knowledge Extraction*, *3*(3), 740–770. doi:10.3390/make3030037

Ku, L.-W., & Chen, H.-H. (2007). Mining opinions from the web: Beyond relevance retrieval. *Journal of the American Society for Information Science and Technology*, *58*(12), 1838–1850. doi:10.1002/asi.20630

Lago, F., Phan, Q.-T., & Boato, G. (2019). Visual and textual analysis for image trustworthiness assessment within online news. *Security and Communication Networks*, *2019*, 2019. doi:10.1155/2019/9236910

Langguth, J., Pogorelov, K., Brenner, S., Filkuková, P., & Schroeder, D. T. (2021). Don't trust your eyes: Image manipulation in the age of deepfakes. *Frontiers in Communication*, *6*, 632317. doi:10.3389/fcomm.2021.632317

Lex, E., Kowald, D., Seitlinger, P., Tran, T. N. T., Felfernig, A., & Schedl, M. (2021). Psychology-informed recommender systems. *Foundations and Trends® in Information Retrieval*, *15*(2), 134–242.

Li, B., Qi, P., Liu, B., Di, S., Liu, J., Pei, J., Yi, J., & Zhou, B. (2023). Trustworthy ai: From principles to practices. *ACM Computing Surveys*, *55*(9), 1–46. doi:10.1145/3555803

Liao, M., Sundar, S. S., & Walther, B., J. (2022). User trust in recommendation systems: A comparison of content-based, collaborative and demographic filtering. *Proceedings of the 2022 CHI Conference on Human Factors in Computing Systems*, 1–14. 10.1145/3491102.3501936

Linardatos, P., Papastefanopoulos, V., & Kotsiantis, S. (2020). Explainable ai: A review of machine learning interpretability methods. *Entropy (Basel, Switzerland)*, *23*(1), 18. doi:10.3390/e23010018 PMID:33375658

Lovato, P., Perina, A., Sebe, N., Zandonà, O., Montagnini, A., Bicego, M., & Cristani, M. (2012). Tell me what you like and i'll tell you what you are: Discriminating visual preferences on flickr data. *Proceedings of the 11th Asian conference on Computer Vision*, 45–56.

Lyu, D., Yang, F., Kwon, H., Dong, W., Yilmaz, L., & Liu, B. (2021). Tdm: Trustworthy decision-making via interpretability enhancement. *IEEE Transactions on Emerging Topics in Computational Intelligence*, *6*(3), 450–461. doi:10.1109/TETCI.2021.3084290

Makhortykh, M., Urman, A., & Ulloa, R. (2021). Detecting race and gender bias in visual representation of ai on web search engines. *International Workshop on Algorithmic Bias in Search and Recommendation*, 36–50. 10.1007/978-3-030-78818-6_5

Mehrabi, N., Morstatter, F., Saxena, N., Lerman, K., & Galstyan, A. (2021). A survey on bias and fairness in machine learning. *ACM Computing Surveys*, *54*(6), 1–35. doi:10.1145/3457607

Müller, J. M. (2019). Comparing technology acceptance for autonomous vehicles, battery electric vehicles, and car sharing—A study across europe, china, and north america. *Sustainability (Basel)*, *11*(16), 4333. doi:10.3390/su11164333

Ni, J., Li, J., & McAuley, J. (2019). Justifying recommendations using distantly-labeled reviews and fine-grained aspects. *Proceedings of the 2019 conference on empirical methods in natural language processing and the 9th international joint conference on natural language processing (EMNLP-IJCNLP)*, 188–197. 10.18653/v1/D19-1018

Palmieri, F. A., Baldi, M., Buonanno, A., Di Gennaro, G., & Ospedale, F. (2020). Probing a deep neural network. *Neural Approaches to Dynamics of Signal Exchanges*, 201–211.

Paradesi, S., Doshi, P., & Swaika, S. (2009). Integrating behavioral trust in web service compositions. *2009 IEEE International Conference on Web Services*, 453–460. 10.1109/ICWS.2009.106

Paul, P. P., Gavrilova, M., & Klimenko, S. (2014). Situation awareness of cancelable biometric system. *The Visual Computer*, *30*(9), 1059–1067. doi:10.1007/s00371-013-0907-0

Peng, Y. (2018). Same candidates, different faces: Uncovering media bias in visual portrayals of presidential candidates with computer vision. *Journal of Communication, 68*(5), 920–941. doi:10.1093/joc/jqy041

Pienta, D., Tams, S., & Thatcher, J. (2020). Can trust be trusted in cybersecurity? Roshchina, A., Cardiff, J., & Rosso, P. (2015). TWIN: Personality-based intelligent recommender system. *Journal of Intelligent & Fuzzy Systems, 28*(5), 2059–2071.

Roy, C., Shanbhag, M., Nourani, M., Rahman, T., Kabir, S., Gogate, V., Ruozzi, N., & Ragan, E. D. (2019). Explainable activity recognition in videos. *IUI Workshops, 2*(4).

Rudin, C. (2019). Stop explaining black box machine learning models for high stakes decisions and use interpretable models instead. *Nat Mach Intell, 1*, 206–215. . doi:10.1038/s42256-019-0048-x

Saleh, K., Hossny, M., & Nahavandi, S. (2017). Towards trusted autonomous vehicles from vulnerable road users perspective. *2017 Annual IEEE International Systems Conference (SysCon)*, 1–7. 10.1109/SYSCON.2017.7934782

Sanclemente, G. L. (2022). Reliability: Understanding cognitive human bias in artificial intelligence for national security and intelligence analysis. *Security Journal, 35*(4), 1328–1348. doi:10.1057/s41284-021-00321-2

Saxena, A., Gutiérrez Bierbooms, C., & Pechenizkiy, M. (2023). Fairness-aware fake news mitigation using counter information propagation. *Applied Intelligence, 53*(22), 27483–27504. doi:10.1007/s10489-023-04928-3

Scavarelli, A., Arya, A., & Teather, R. J. (2021). Virtual reality and augmented reality in social learning spaces: A literature review. *Virtual Reality (Waltham Cross), 25*(1), 257–277. doi:10.1007/s10055-020-00444-8

Sieu, B., & Gavrilova, M. (2021). Multi-modal aesthetic system for person identification. *2021 International Conference on Cyberworlds (CW)*. doi:10.1109/ACCESS.2021.3096776

Sun, K. H., Huh, H., Tama, B. A., Lee, S. Y., Jung, J. H., & Lee, S. (2020). Vision-based fault diagnostics using explainable deep learning with class activation maps. *IEEE Access: Practical Innovations, Open Solutions, 8*, 129169–129179. doi:10.1109/ACCESS.2020.3009852

Thiebes, S., Lins, S., & Sunyaev, A. (2021). Trustworthy artificial intelligence. *Electronic Markets, 31*(2), 447–464. doi:10.1007/s12525-020-00441-4

Uncovska, M., Freitag, B., Meister, S., & Fehring, L. (2023). Patient acceptance of prescribed and fully reimbursed mhealth apps in germany: An utaut2-based online survey study. *Journal of Medical Systems*, *47*(1), 14. doi:10.1007/s10916-023-01910-x PMID:36705853

van der Stigchel, B., van den Bosch, K., van Diggelen, J., & Haselager, P. (2023). Intelligent decision support in medical triage: Are people robust to biased advice? *Journal of Public Health (Oxford, England)*, *45*(3), fdad005. doi:10.1093/pubmed/fdad005 PMID:36947701

Victor, P., De Cock, M., & Cornelis, C. (2011). Trust and recommendations. *Recommender systems handbook*, 645–675.

Vultureanu-Albişi, A., & Bădică, C. (2021). Recommender systems: An explainable ai perspective. *2021 International Conference on INnovations in Intelligent SysTems and Applications (INISTA)*, 1–6. 10.1109/INISTA52262.2021.9548125

Wade, L., & Robinson, R. (2012). *The psychology of trust and its relation to sustainability*. Global Sustainability Institute (Briefing Note 2).

Waelen, R. A. (2023). The ethics of computer vision: An overview in terms of power. *AI and Ethics*, 1–10.

Waisberg, E., Ong, J., Masalkhi, M., Zaman, N., Sarker, P., Lee, A. G., & Tavakkoli, A. (2023). Meta smart glasses—Large language models and the future for assistive glasses for individuals with vision impairments. *Eye (London, England)*, 1–3. PMID:38049627

Wang, M., & Deng, W. (2020). Mitigating bias in face recognition using skewness-aware reinforcement learning. *Proceedings of the IEEE/CVF conference on computer vision and pattern recognition. Seattle, USA*, 9322–9331. 10.1109/CVPR42600.2020.00934

Wang, Y., Howard, N., Kacprzyk, J., Frieder, O., Sheu, P., Fiorini, R. A., Gavrilova, M. L., Patel, S., Peng, J., & Widrow, B. (2018). Cognitive informatics: Towards cognitive machine learning and autonomous knowledge manipulation. *International Journal of Cognitive Informatics and Natural Intelligence*, *12*(1), 1–13. doi:10.4018/IJCINI.2018010101

Wilms, M., Bannister, J. J., Mouches, P., MacDonald, M. E., Rajashekar, D., Langner, S., & Forkert, N. D. (2022). Invertible modeling of bidirectional relationships in neuroimaging with normalizing flows: Application to brain aging. *IEEE Transactions on Medical Imaging*, *41*(9), 2331–2347. doi:10.1109/TMI.2022.3161947 PMID:35324436

Wu, H., Albiero, V., Krishnapriya, K., King, M. C., & Bowyer, K. W. (2023). Face recognition accuracy across demographics: Shining a light into the problem. *Proceedings of the IEEE/CVF Conference on Computer Vision and Pattern Recognition*, 1041–1050. 10.1109/CVPRW59228.2023.00111

Wu, J., Cai, R., & Wang, H. (2020). Déjà vu: A contextualized temporal attention mechanism for sequential recommendation. *Proceedings of The Web Conference 2020*, 2199–2209. 10.1145/3366423.3380285

Yang, Y., Gupta, A., Feng, J., Singhal, P., Yadav, V., Wu, Y., Natarajan, P., Hedau, V., & Joo, J. (2022). Enhancing fairness in face detection in computer vision systems by demographic bias mitigation. *Proceedings of the 2022 AAAI/ACM Conference on AI, Ethics, and Society. Oxford, United Kingdom*, 813–822. 10.1145/3514094.3534153

Zablocki, É., Ben-Younes, H., Pérez, P., & Cord, M. (2022). Explainability of deep vision-based autonomous driving systems: Review and challenges. *International Journal of Computer Vision*, *130*(10), 2425–2452. doi:10.1007/s11263-022-01657-x

Zhao, D., Wang, A., & Russakovsky, O. (2021). Understanding and evaluating racial biases in image captioning. *Proceedings of the IEEE/CVF International Conference on Computer Vision*, 14830–14840. 10.1109/ICCV48922.2021.01456

Zhu, S., Yu, T., Xu, T., Chen, H., Dustdar, S., Gigan, S., Gunduz, D., Hossain, E., Jin, Y., & Lin, F. (2023). Intelligent computing: The latest advances, challenges, and future. *Intelligent Computing, 2*, 6.

Chapter 2
Case–Based Reasoning and Computer Vision for Cybersecurity:
A Short Review

Naomi Dassi Tchomte
University of Ngaoundere, Cameroon

Franklin Tchakounte
 https://orcid.org/0000-0003-0723-2640
Faculty of Science, University of Ngaoundere, Cameroon

Ismael Abbo
Faculty of Sciences, University of Ngaoundere, Cameroon

ABSTRACT

The integration of case-based reasoning (CBR) and computer vision (CV) holds significant promise for enhancing cybersecurity, enabling the analysis and interpretation of visual data to detect security threats. This study provides an investigation of the synergy between case-based reasoning and computer vision techniques in the context of cybersecurity, aiming to address open challenges and identify opportunities for advancing security operations. Three main steps are realized. First, a taxonomy declining categories and sub-categories of the studied works is designed. Second, the collected literature is analysed in terms of (1) CBR for leveraging past security incidents and patterns in visual data analysis, facilitating threat detection, incident response, and threat intelligence analysis; (2) CV for cybersecurity modelling and to support cybersecurity decision making; (3) association between CBR and CV to design cybersecurity approaches. Third, open issues are discussed. This study exploiting CBR in computing vision for cybersecurity opens doors for further research.

DOI: 10.4018/978-1-6684-8127-1.ch002

1. INTRODUCTION

Cybersecurity is an ever-evolving field faced with the daunting challenge of defending against a myriad of sophisticated and constantly evolving cyber threats (Beghhith 2017). As organizations increasingly rely on digital technologies and data-driven processes, the need for robust and effective cybersecurity measures has never been more critical. Traditional approaches to cybersecurity often rely on signature-based detection systems and rule-based algorithms, which may struggle to keep pace with the rapidly evolving threat landscape (de Sousa, 2018). In recent years, there has been growing interest in exploring innovative approaches that leverage artificial intelligence (AI) and machine learning (ML) techniques to enhance cybersecurity capabilities. Among these approaches, the integration of case-based reasoning (CBR) and computer vision has emerged as a promising paradigm for analysing and interpreting visual data to detect and respond to security threats effectively.

Computer vision (CV), a subfield of AI, focuses on enabling computers to interpret and understand visual information from the world around them (Bachir, 2024). By leveraging advanced algorithms and techniques, computer vision systems can extract meaningful insights from diverse visual sources, including images, videos, network traffic visualizations, and log data. These insights are valuable for identifying anomalous behaviour, detecting suspicious activities, and investigating security incidents in real-time (D. Lopez-Sanchez, 2018) (Adedoyin et al., 2016). More specifically, visualizing binary files or network packets as images and applying convolutional neural networks (CNNs) can help detect malware signatures or anomalies (Yang et al. 2024); Anomaly detection algorithms based on computer vision can identify unusual behavior or suspicious activities in video feeds, alerting security personnel to potential threats (Zhao et al. 2021); Facial recognition and iris scanning, relying on computer vision algorithms provide robust authentication mechanisms difficult to spoof or replicate (Minaee et al. 2023); Analysing video streams in real-time, security personnel can quickly respond to incidents and mitigate potential risks (Wang et al. 2013); In forensics, computer vision techniques are employed in digital forensics to analyze visual evidence collected from crime scenes or digital devices based on image and video analysis tools (Kapoor et al. 2023).

On the other hand, case-based reasoning is a problem-solving methodology that relies on past experiences or cases to guide decision-making in new and similar situations (Nabila, 2013). By storing and retrieving relevant cases from a knowledge base, CBR systems can leverage historical data and patterns to inform security analyses, incident response, and threat intelligence operations. When combined with computer vision techniques, CBR systems can harness the power of visual data to enrich their knowledge base and improve decision-making capabilities (Wang et al. 2023). The association between CBR and CV can also increase reliability and performances in decision support systems (DSS) (Chen, 2023). In their works (Kaur et al. 2023; Sarker et al. 2023), authors reveal the potentials of combining CV and CBR in the context of cybersecurity. Indeed, this is gaining attention and authors are leveraging CV and CBR to combat infiltration of malware (Tripathi, 2022; Adedoyin et al., 2016; Akhtar, 2021; Abioye 2021; Rohatgi, 2023). It is therefore important to investigate research in this area and to provide details that researchers can rely on to contribute further.

This study is reflective essay that explores the synergy between CBR and CV in preserving cybersecurity. We seek to investigate the synergies between these two methodologies and evaluate their potential to address key challenges in cybersecurity operations. By shedding light on the potential benefits, challenges, and opportunities associated with combining case-based reasoning and computer vision in cybersecurity, this study seeks to contribute to the development of innovative and effective cybersecurity solutions for addressing the complex threats faced by organizations today.

This paper has two main contributions:

1.   Examine the current state-of-the-art in case-based reasoning and computer vision for cybersecurity and propose a taxonomy.
2.   Identify key issues and challenges in leveraging visual data for cybersecurity purposes.

The rest of the document is organized as follows. In section 2, similar works are discussed and the gaps are identified. In section 3, the research methodology is provided. In section 4, the key notions of CBR and CV are described. In section 5, the taxonomy is presented and literature is analysed. In section 6, open issues are discussed. In section 7, a conclusion and future directions are given.

2. RELATED WORKS

In this section, a batch of reviews and surveys on the use of artificial intelligence (AI), machine learning (ML), deep learning (DL), and computer vision (CV) for cybersecurity are discussed.

2.1 AI for Cybersecurity

With its potential to automate analysis of billions of network traffic data and cyberattacks data, AI is a faithful companion of human in cybersecurity. In (Iyer & Umadevi 2023), authors reviewed the role of AI and its impact on the development of cybersecurity applications. Kaur et al. (2023) surveyed 236 main studies of AI use cases for cybersecurity provisioning. They classified the identified AI use cases based on a National Institute of Standards and Technology (NIST) cybersecurity framework and provided with a comprehensive overview of the potential of AI to improve cybersecurity in different contexts. They also identified future directions in emerging cybersecurity application areas. Dangi et al. (2023) provided an essay that examined the place of AI in cybersecurity while analyzing the pertinent studies and their advantages.

OZKAN-OKAY et al. (2023) evaluated the efficiency of AI and machine learning techniques on the cyber security solutions and concluded that ChatGPT-like tools can be a valuable for cybersecurity despite the fact that they are subject to integrity, confidentiality, and availability of data. Akhtar et. (2021) overviewed AI-based applications of cybersecurity that can improve the security of cyberspace. In reference (de Azambuja et al. 2023), a systematic literature is provided to identify publications of artificial intelligence-based cyber-attacks and to analyze them for deriving cyber security measures.

2.2 ML and DL for Cybersecurity

More specifically, some works are dedicated to study machine learning variants in cybersecurity. Apruzzese et al. (2023) made the first tentative to provide a detailed understanding of the role of ML in cybersecurity by highlighting its advantages elucidating intrinsic problems affecting ML deployments in cybersecurity. Concerning IoT security, (Alwahedi et al. 2023) surveyed current trends, methodologies, and challenges in applying machine learning for cyber threat detection. Variants of ML has also been explored in the detection of malware. In Sewak et al. (2022), deep reinforcement learning techniques have been studied in regards to the threat defense. Another research concerns overviewing federated ML for IoT malware detection.

Dixit and Silakari (2020) analyzed and reviewed 80 papers about the usage of deep learning algorithms for cybersecurity applications. They found that DL improves the quality of automation and performance of DL tools. Miranda-Garcia et al. (2023) performed an in-depth review of the use of deep learning techniques in the field of security in specific areas such as spam, malware detection, adult content detection and deepfake. In their chapter, Dave and Gawade (2023) explored advancements made by deep learning applications in cyber security concerning applications such as intrusion detection and prevention systems, network traffic and user behavior analysis as well as spam, social engineering and malware detection. A similar study (Gopinath and Sibi 2022) is realized concerning detection schemes for mobile malware (both Android and iOS), Windows malware, IoT malware, Advanced Persistent Threats (APTs), and Ransomware. In Dunmore et al. (2023), the authors examined the use of Generative Adversarial Networks (GAN) in Intrusion Detection Systems (IDS) by detailing its place and objectives in detecting intrusions.

2.3 CV for Cybersecurity

ML variants are limited to methods relying on statistical features extracted from sources such as binaries, emails, and packet flows. Considerable research has been done using computer vision for network security to identify attacks. A comprehensive survey of such researches is provided under three topics: phishing detection, malware detection, and traffic anomaly detection. They explored the research gaps and future research directions in using computer vision methods for effective detection approaches.

2.4 Mentions of CBR in Cybersecurity

Sarker et al. (2023) studied multi-aspects of AI-based modeling and adversarial learning that address diverse cybersecurity issues. They emphasized future aspects of cybersecurity intelligence to encounter. In this work, the authors revealed the necessity to use hybrid techniques involving CBR and CV for instance, to create innovative models in cybersecurity. Mat et al. (2024) proposed a systematic review of 45 studies on methods of detecting Advanced persistent threats (APTs) by surveying research in the area, extracting gaps in the relevant studies, and proposing future directions. The authors presented the case-based paradigms as promising methods for detecting APT.

2.5 Gaps

To the best of our knowledge, there is no investigations specific to CBR and CV for cybersecurity. All the previous reviews and surveys are generic to combat malware relying independently on AI, ML, DL and CV. None of them is able to reveal for example the strengths CBR in cybersecurity or the place of CBR in CV during the detection of malicious behaviors. Moreover, rare are those that even mentioned authors who exploited CBR in their studies. This study therefore contributes in exploring specifically CBR and CV schemes in cybersecurity.

3. RESEARCH METHODOLOGY

This study outlines several key steps, beginning with planning and establishing a review protocol, followed by formulating research questions and designing the search strategy. Additionally, the current investigation entails defining exclusion and inclusion criteria and selecting relevant data. These steps provide a structured approach to conducting the review and ensure that the methodology is clearly outlined and adhered to throughout the process.

3.1 Research Questions

The following research questions guide this study.

RQ1: Which taxonomies federating these approaches can be built and how are they characterized?

RQ2: What approaches based on CBR (resp. CV) and combining CBR with CV, have been developed to combat cybersecurity?

RQ3: What are the open issues, that research oriented to case-based reasoning and computer vision for cybersecurity should focus on?

3.2 Search Strategy

The research conducted an extensive search across various digital libraries including IEEE, ACM Digital Library, Springer, ScienceDirect, and WileyOnline Library, utilizing specific keywords outlined in Table 1 for crawling purposes. Additionally, citation engines such as Google Scholar and Web of Knowledge were employed to ensure comprehensive coverage of relevant literature. Forward research on authors who cited identified papers was also conducted to gather recent works. This thorough approach aimed to minimize the likelihood of overlooking any relevant studies and to provide a comprehensive overview of the existing literature on the topic.

Table 1. Search keywords

Group	Keywords
1	Case-based reasoning AND|FOR detection of malware
2	Case-based reasoning AND computer vision AND detection of malware
3`	Case-based reasoning AND computer vision AND cybersecurity
4	Case-based reasoning AND cybersecurity
5	Computer vision AND cybersecurity
6	1 OR 2 OR 3 OR 4 OR 5
7	1 AND 2 AND 3 AND 4 AND 5

3.3 Inclusion Criteria

This essay exclusively focuses on studies published from 2010 onwards and restricted to those written in English. Extensive literature searches were conducted to gather relevant literature, including literature reviews and surveys pertaining to case-based reasoning and computer vision for cybersecurity. These sources are intended for utilization in the "related reviews" section of the research. Papers were selected based on the presence of specific keywords such as "case-based reasoning for cybersecurity," "computer vision for cybersecurity," and "detection of malware" to ensure alignment with the research objectives.

3.4 Exclusion Criteria

The exclusion criteria for papers encompass those published in predatory journals, papers lacking specificity to case-based reasoning and computer vision for cybersecurity in their title and abstract, and papers lacking peer review. These criteria ensure the selection of rigorous and relevant literature for the research, excluding sources from questionable publishing outlets and focusing exclusively on papers directly related to the research topic. Abstracts and conclusion sections of all relevant articles were thoroughly examined to ensure their alignment with the study's topic. This scrutiny aimed to verify that the selected articles provide pertinent insights and findings related to case-based reasoning and computer vision for cybersecurity, confirming their relevance to the research objectives and ensuring the inclusion of high-quality and pertinent literature in the essay.

3.5 Data Selection Process

Only studies meeting the inclusion criteria related to case-based reasoning and computer vision for cybersecurity were considered for further review, with Mendeley utilized for paper organization and duplicate removal. Any works not meeting the exclusion criteria were deemed irrelevant and excluded. While collecting relevant papers ensured inclusion based on criteria, the quality of each paper was ensured through full-text reading. Papers related to case-based reasoning and computer vision were collected separately and then filtered based on the cybersecurity focuses.

4. GENERAL BACKGROUND

In this section, key concepts about CBR and CV are described.

4.1 Case-Based Reasoning

Case-based Reasoning (CBR) is a type of reasoning that copies human behaviour, naturally drawing on experience to solve real-life problems according to (Adedoyin et al., 2016). An CBR uses the specific and practical knowledge of previously experienced problems to solve a current problem case. Increasingly used as a progressive and evolutionary approach, CBR retains new experience each time a problem or new problem is solved, making this experience available for future problems. CBR finds its place because similar problems often have similar solutions and because we are often faced with problems that we have already encountered. CBR is exploited in several sectors.

4.1.1 Fundamentals of CBR

The concept of CBR is based on the search for problems like the new problem and historically saved in a memory. According to (Lieber, 2008), the different stages of an CBR are:

- Elaboration, which is the concrete description of the target problem;
- Retrieval or recollection (search and selection in the case database or memory of the source case most like the target problem);
- Reuse or adaptation (adapting the solution of the recovered source problem to the target problem);
- Validation or revision, which consists of checking whether the solution to the target problem really does coincide with that of the source problem, by an expert human;
- Recording or memorisation (storage of the target problem and its solution in the case database).

The memory contains a finite set of pre-registered cases and their solutions and uses a similarity measurement mechanism to extract similar cases.

Knowledge

The knowledge containers used in CBR are grouped into four categories (Luc, 2014).

- Indexing vocabulary or attributes;
- The case base such as structured experiments exploited in research, reuse and maintenance;
- The similarity measure is used to assess the similarities between two or more basic cases;
- Adaptation knowledge, which refers to domain heuristics, often represented in the form of rules that enable new solutions to be modified and their applicability to be assessed.

Attribute

Attributes are knowledge or features that characterise the description of the problem and the solution. Attributes form part of the constitution of the case base, hence their importance in the selection phase of similar cases.

Case

A case is composed of several attributes. The structure of a case and the content of its attributes condition the quality of case-based reasoning (Luc, 2014). A case can also be defined as an entity that brings together various pieces of information about a past situation (Nabila, 2013). A case is an entity from which reasoning can be used to situate a new situation in relation to the circumstance defined in the case.

Let C be the case and BC the case base consisting of different cases, then $BC = \{C_1, C_2, ...C_n\}$. Denoting $Cs = (Pbs, Sol[P\ bs])$ the source case, where

- *Pbs*: the source problem
- *Sol[P bs]*: the solution to the source problem.

Also, noting Cc the target case, $Cc = (P\ bc, Sol[P\ bc])$, with:

- *Pbc:* the target problem
- *Sol[P bc]*: the solution to the target problem.

Case Database

The case base is a storage memory or database of cases containing old and new cases (Nabila, 2013). As new solved cases arise, these cases are added to the memory or case base of the others and indexed to update this memory. Storage in the case base involves learning the CBR system. It can be in the form of a table, or in the form of a graph. Table 2 illustrates an example of a case base in table form, where each row relates to a case associated with its solution and each column relates to a characteristic of the case.

Table 2. Case base in tabular form

Case	Attributes					Solutions
	Attribute₁	*Attribute₂*	...	...	*Attributeₘ*	
$case_1$	$value_{11}$	$value_{12}$	...	...	$value_{1n}$	$solution_1$
$case_2$	$value_{21}$	$value_{22}$	...	...	$value_{2n}$	$solution_2$
...	...	...	...	...	...	...
$case_n$	$value_{n1}$	$value_{n2}$	...	...	$value_{nn}$	$solution_n$

Problem and Solution

The problem and the solution are parts of a case. The description of a problem contains the context in which the case occurred (Nabila, 2013). The solution is the solution to the problem or the reaction to the given problem (for example, a doctor's decision or a court's deliberation). The solution is also the outcome of the description of a case. According to (Kolodner 1994), the description generally contains the goals to be achieved in solving the problem, the constraints on these goals, the characteristics of the situation and the various relationships between these parts. In (Kolodner, 1994), it is specified that the solution to a problem may be a classification, a plan, an interpretation or an explanation, all of which depend on the nature of the problem to be solved. The following notations are considered:

- D, the descriptive data set for the problem ;
- R, the query to indicate the objective of the reasoning, which is always known, then $Pb = (D, R)$. In other words, the problem is made up of a description of the problem and a known query for how to reason about solving the problem.

4.1.2 Architecture

Figure 1 presents a generic model of an CBR system. It presents the CBR as a set of processes and knowledge that allows the exploitation of past experiences. In this diagram, cases are created and acquired using the indexing vocabulary, the case base, the similarity metric and the adaptation process. In this model, the main processes are the search, adaptation, maintenance and preservation of experience.

The Fuch decomposed form of case-based reasoning (Nabila, 2013) is shown in Figure 2.

By associating the generic CBR model with the Fuch decomposition, we can see that there are four types of decomposition. These are the essential steps in implementing a CBR. These are the recovery of similar cases, the reuse or adaptation, the revision of the new solution and finally the conservation or recording of the new case in the case base. These four phases form the backbone of case-based reasoning. They can also be broken down into several sub-phases for an efficient design of a CPMR, such as the retrieval or search for similar cases, which is broken down into three actions: elaboration, search and selection. Figure 3 shows the cycle of a CBR.

Figure 1. Generic model of a CBR system (Luc, 2014)

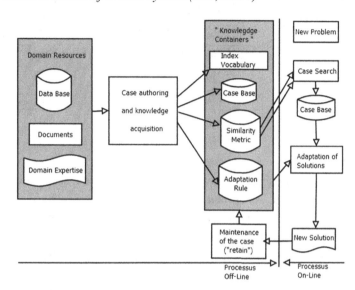

Figure 2. CBR decomposition (Nabila, 2013)

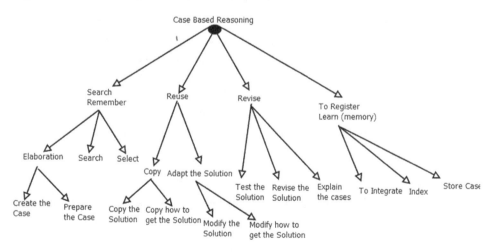

Figure 3. CBR cycle

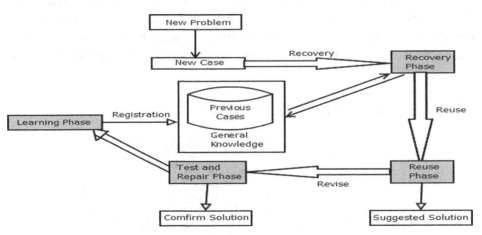

Recovery

The retrieval phase represents the process of searching for cases that are most like the problem to be solved. As shown in Figure 1.3, the retrieval phase consists of knowledge extraction and the retrieval of the most relevant cases by similarity to solve the target problem. This phase is the most important one in CBR. It consists of finding similar cases in the case base and comparing them with the new case. Classical distance methods such as the k- nearest neighbour algorithm is used for this search. The nearest neighbours approach classifies or measures the correspondences between each case in the case base and the new problem to be solved. In its distance calculation, K-NN uses methods such as Euclidean distance or cosine to calculate the different similarities between two or more attributes. (Kwon, 2019) show that the reliability of the predictions of an CBR is due to the good methods used in the search of similarity. In this article, the authors explain that the use of similarity distances such as the Euclidean distance depends on the type of input attribute. Euclidean distance is widely used in the search for similar cases. The consideration of weights to the different attributes for the calculation of similarities is of paramount importance (Tchomte, 2019). Considering different weights, this distance is calculated as shown in equation (1).

$$S^2\left(x_0, x_i\right) = 1 - WEuc\left(x_0, x_i\right) = 1 - \sqrt{\sum_{i=1}^{n}\left(WD\left(x_0\left(k\right), x_i\left(k\right)\right)\right)^2} \qquad (1)$$

Where S, is the similarity, x_0 and x_i are attributes.

$$WD\big(x_0(k),x_i(k)\big)=\begin{cases} w_i \times \big(x_0(k)-x_i(k)\big), & if \ \big(x_i(k)\big) \ is \ numeric \\ w_i, & if \ \big(x_i(k)\big) \ is \ numeric \ and \ \big(x_i(k)\big) \neq \big(x_0(k)\big) \\ 0, & if \ \big(x_i(k)\big) \ is \ numeric \ and \ \big(x_i(k)\big)=\big(x_0(k)\big) \end{cases}$$

(2)

Cosine is one of the popular distance-based metrics (N. Tchomté, 2019). It is determined by the formula given in equation (1.3) and its value is always between 0 and 1. The more the result of calculating the cosine between two vectors tends towards 1, the more similar the two vectors are.

$$\cos(A,B)=\frac{\sum_{i=1}^{N}A_iB_i}{\sqrt{\sum_{i=1}^{N}A_i^2}\times\sqrt{\sum_{i=1}^{N}B_i^2}}$$

(3)

A and B being two vectors to compare.

There are several other distance schemes, such as the Manhattan distance and the Hemming distance, but these will not be used in this work. The search and retrieval of cases can also be carried out using an induction approach, which consists of generating a tree distributing the cases according to the different attributes. However, this approach proves difficult when the number of attributes in a case is large to manipulate. (Y.-J. Park, 2006) show that statistics can also be used to recover the best similar cases, by recovering the optimal number of neighbours according to their similarity probity.

The search is generally carried out in two stages.

- Obtaining a set of plausible candidates (similar cases) through an initial search;
- An in-depth search that selects the best candidate (the best similar case) from the plausible candidates obtained from the initial search.

The selection of the best similar case is sometimes determined by the evolution of the degree of similarity, by generating explanations that tend to justify dissimilarities between the case found and the problem to be treated. This is often done using general knowledge of the domain, or by additional information provided by users.

At the end of the recovery process, similar cases are recalled through a process of successive refinement of the recovered cases. Similarities can be obtained locally or globally between the target case (target problem) and the source case (source problem). Local similarity is calculated between the value of an attribute in the target case and the value of the same attribute in the source case. It is equal to 1 if the values of the two attributes are equal and is equal to zero otherwise. Equation (1.4) expresses this assertion.

$$\text{Sim}\left(S_i, C_i\right) = \begin{cases} 1 & if \ S_i = C_i \\ 0 & if \ S_i \neq C_i \end{cases} \tag{1.4}$$

With:

C_i: value of an attribute i in the target problem.
S_i: value of the same attribute i in the source problem.

Global similarity is calculated between a set of attributes in the target problem and the same set of attributes in the source problem. It is the average of local similarity, and its value is always within the interval [0,1] (H. Meguehout, 2013). It is given by the formula in equation (1.5).

$$\text{Sim}\left(CS, CC\right) = \frac{1}{n} \sum_{i=1}^{n} Sim_i \left(S_i, C_i\right) \tag{1.5}$$

With:

CC: Target case;
CS: Case Source ;
n: number of attributes for which local similarity has been calculated ;
Sim_i (S_i, C_i): local similarity value for attribute i. Here, a similarity threshold is set at 0.5 and we have:
If Sim $(CS, CC) < 0.5$ then the source case is considered negligible (not similar);
If Sim $(CS, CC) > 0.5$ then the source case is considered important (partially similar);
If Sim $(CS, CC) = 1$ then the source case is perfectly similar;
If there are no similar cases, we repeat the recall or retrieval step without filtering the case base.

Reuse

Reuse is the second phase of case-based reasoning or CBR. Following the selection and recovery of similar cases during the search, the similar cases found are reused to determine the current solution. The differences between the past case, the present case and the part of the recovered case that can be transferred to the new case are aspects on which the reuse of solutions from past cases focuses. Many systems make do with a simple copy of the solution of the recovered case (Nabila, 2013). This copy consists of a simple classification of the differences, considering these differences as irrelevant in relation to the similarities, and the solution of the case found is transferred to the new case. This is a trivial method of reuse. Other systems use adaptation, which does not radically change the solution, but modifies certain parts by reorganising it. This step proposes a solution to the new problem (al. R. L., 2005). This is easy when the similar case in the recovery step is sufficiently like the new case because the solution of the new case will be the same as the similar case found.

The following approaches can be used in this phase (López, 2013).

- Majority Rule (MR): the solution is the class C_i with the highest number of votes (*maxcount*), i.e., the class that has solved the highest number of cases in the list of recovered cases RC (Recovered Cases). The formula used to apply MR is given in equation (1.6).

$$S_q = \arg_i maxcount(c_i, RC) \tag{1.6}$$

- The Probabilistic Scheme (PM): this procedure allocates probabilities to each possible outcome or class ci. Here, the class with the highest probability is selected and its formula is given in equation (1.7).

$$P(S_q = C_i) = \frac{\sum_{j \in RC} \mathrm{Sim}\left(P_q, P_j\right)^{\lambda^j}}{\sum_{j \in RC} \mathrm{Sim}\left(P_q, P_j\right)} \tag{1.7}$$

Where:

$$\lambda^j = \begin{cases} 1 & if \ S_i = C_i \\ 0 & otherwise \end{cases} \tag{1.8}$$

- Class-based scheme (CM): this procedure determines, for each class c_i, the average distance of the case sought from the cases belonging to c_i and takes the class with the minimum average (*minmean*). Its model is given in equation (1.9).

$$S_q = \arg_i minmeanc_i \times \mathrm{Sim}(P_q, P_j), \forall j \tag{1.9}$$

The recovery process becomes more difficult when there are significant differences between the recovered cases. It is therefore necessary to be able to adapt the solutions of the recovered cases to obtain new solutions. According to (Kolodner, An introduction to case-based reasoning, 1992), adaptation can be done in two ways: substitution and transformation.

Revise

The case-based reasoning system offers the possibility of learning from mistakes when the solution obtained in the reuse phase is not right. The revision process begins when the reuse phase is complete. After adaptation, the resulting solution is proposed. Two tasks are observed in this stage: on the one hand, evaluating the solution generated by the user to detect failures, and on the other, adding corrections if necessary. The revision phase is often considered to be a continuation of the adaptation phase since adaptation involves modifying a solution that does not fit with the expected solution (Nabila, 2013).

When the solution is evaluated, if it is successful, the system learns from this success, and if it is not successful, the system learns from it. On the contrary, the use of domain-specific information is important for the repair of the solution. It should also be noted that simulations sometimes neglect important aspects of reality, as it is not always possible to formulate all the aspects that might occur in the real world (R. Faia, 2017).

Retain

Retain is the last phase of the CBR (Lopez 2022). It consists of recording the correct solution in the case database. This phase enables the CBR system to record the successes and failures of the proposed solutions. It also involves selecting the relevant case information to be retained, considering how to store it and how to index it to facilitate the resolution of similar problems in the future. It is also often important to record the problem specification for future use. This step stores the resulting experience as a new case in memory after the solution has been successfully adapted to the target problem.

4.2 Computer Vision

Computer vision is a field of artificial intelligence (AI) and computer science that focuses on enabling computers to interpret and understand visual information from the world around them (Bachir, 2024). It seeks to replicate and augment human vision capabilities using computational methods and algorithms.

4.2.1 Motivations

The history of computer vision spans several decades, originating in the 1960s and 1970s as researchers embarked on endeavours to imbue computers with the ability to comprehend visual data. Initially, efforts concentrated on fundamental tasks like image classification and pattern recognition. However, the field gained significant traction with the advent of digital imaging technologies and advancements in image processing techniques (Kaur N. a., 2024). Techniques like edge detection, feature extraction, and image segmentation emerged as pivotal components of early computer vision algorithms. In recent years, the landscape of computer vision has been transformed by the widespread adoption of machine learning and deep learning methodologies, particularly convolutional neural networks (CNNs) (Bhatt, 2021). These innovations have ushered in a new era of enhanced accuracy and performance in tasks ranging from object detection to image recognition and generation. The applications of computer vision are vast and diverse, permeating various industries and domains such as healthcare, automotive, retail, agriculture, robotics, security, and entertainment (Sarvajcz, 2024). It underpins technologies like facial recognition, autonomous vehicles, medical image analysis, augmented reality (AR), and surveillance systems, driving innovation and transformation across sectors.

4.2.2 Key Concepts and Techniques

Computer vision encompasses several key concepts and techniques essential for understanding and analysing visual data. Image processing involves a range of techniques for manipulating and analysing digital images, including filtering, transformation, and enhancement, to extract meaningful information. Feature extraction plays a crucial role in identifying and extracting relevant features from images, such as edges, corners, textures, and shapes, facilitating the representation and characterization of visual data (Yan, 2024). Object detection and recognition are pivotal tasks in computer vision, involving the localization and identification of objects within images or videos, often employing machine learning algorithms and deep neural networks for accurate detection. Semantic segmentation further enhances understanding by partitioning images into meaningful segments or regions and assigning semantic labels to each segment, enabling a nuanced comprehension of visual content. Pose estimation is another significant aspect, focusing on estimating the spatial orientation and position of objects or subjects within images or videos, with applications ranging from gesture recognition to human activity analysis. Deep learning architectures, notably convolutional neural networks (CNNs) and recurrent neural networks (RNNs), have revolutionized computer vision tasks by autonomously learning hierarchical representations of visual data, advancing the field's capabilities and applications (Genc, 2024).

4.2.3 Relation between CBR and CV

The relationship between Case-Based Reasoning (CBR) and Computer Vision, although distinct fields within artificial intelligence (AI) and machine learning, exhibits several points of intersection. Firstly, both methodologies share a problem-solving approach: CBR leverages past experiences or cases to address new problems, mirroring the utilization of past instances or examples in computer vision to train models for recognizing patterns or objects in new images (Yan, 2024). Secondly, there is a common emphasis on feature extraction and representation. In both CBR and computer vision, the focus lies on extracting relevant features from data (Belghith, 2017). While computer vision deals with visual features like edges, textures, or key points from images, CBR may employ features representing different aspects of a problem or case for comparison and retrieval. Moreover, similarity measurement plays a pivotal role in both realms. CBR often relies on measuring the similarity between the current problem and past cases to retrieve the most relevant ones (N. Kwon, 2019). Similarly, in computer vision, similarity metrics are employed to compare extracted features from different images, determining their degree of similarity (Yan, 2024). Adaptation and learning are inherent to both CBR and computer vision methodologies. CBR adapts solutions from past cases to fit the current problem context, while in computer vision, models are trained on extensive datasets to learn patterns and enhance performance over time. Finally, their applications overlap in various domains. For instance, in medical imaging, CBR may retrieve similar cases from a database based on features extracted from medical images, while computer vision techniques aid in object and situation recognition (Mohammed Benamina, 2018). In contexts like autonomous vehicles, computer vision technologies recognize objects and situations, while CBR contributes to decision-making processes based on past experiences (Yan, 2024). Overall, while CBR and computer vision are distinct fields, they share common principles and can be complementary in solving complex problems, especially in domains where both visual data and past experiences are important for decision-making.

4.2.4 Challenges and Future Directions

Addressing the challenges and future directions of computer vision entails navigating several key areas. Firstly, the acquisition and labelling of large, diverse datasets pose significant hurdles for robust system training, necessitating meticulous attention to data quality and quantity. Secondly, the interpretability and explainability of deep learning models remain crucial concerns, particularly in critical domains like healthcare and autonomous driving, where trust and understanding are paramount. Furthermore, ensuring the robustness and generalization of computer vision algorithms across varying environmental conditions, lighting scenarios, viewpoints, and object variations presents ongoing challenges. Ethical and societal implications loom large, with considerations surrounding privacy, bias, fairness, and misuse requiring thoughtful scrutiny and management. Advancing the field involves exploring multimodal fusion techniques, integrating information from diverse sources such as images, text, and audio to enhance perception in complex environments. Finally, enabling continual learning mechanisms for computer vision systems to adapt and evolve over time in dynamic settings without encountering catastrophic forgetting represents a crucial frontier for future development and innovation.

Despite these challenges, computer vision continues to advance rapidly, driven by ongoing research and technological innovation. It holds tremendous promise for transforming industries, enhancing human-machine interaction, and shaping the future of AI-enabled systems.

5. TAXONOMY AND LITERATURE ANALYSIS

Several works that concern CBR in cybersecurity, CV in cybersecurity and association between CBR and CV for cybersecurity, are discussed. The taxonomy in Figure 4 is designed to logically group the different studies. Three categories of works are identified. The first one is named "CBR used for cybersecurity domains" concerns research that exploits CBR to solve cybersecurity issues. This category is then partitioned into six (1) sub-categories related to the detection of Android malware, detection of phishing, detection of botnet, detection of virus and (2) sub-categories related to profiling the attacker and the attack, forensics, and to support network IDS. The second category concerns research works for that deal with exploiting computer vision for cybersecurity issues including four sub-categories such as CV for detecting Android malware, for detecting Windows malware, for detecting bad network traffic and for supporting forensics. The third category concerns studies that combine CBR and CV, as supporting cybersecurity activities.

5.1 CBR for Cybersecurity

CBR is a powerful tool that is used to support cybersecurity. Various directions found in literature are discussed here.

Figure 4. Taxonomy

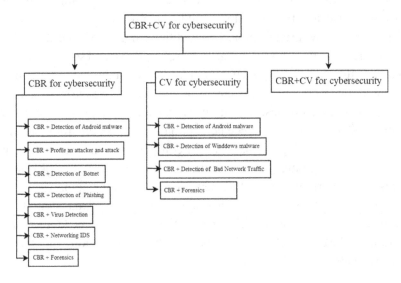

5.1.1 CBR and Detection of Android Malware

The use of CBR is increasing to detect Android malware based on past resolutions. In this work, Qaisar and Li (2022) exploit CBR and take APK as cases made up of attributes such as permissions, services provider, intents, features, and app status. Based on similarity matching with K-mean with a certain threshold, the approach classifies the new case by designated it as Malware or Normal. Results obtained show that their proposed work achieves better accuracy, higher precision and reduced false-negative rate compared to related approaches.

CBR is used in (Al-Abri et al. 2023) for Android malware detection in which a current security issue is solved based on historically matched solved security issues.

5.1.2 CBR and Profiling an Attacker and an Attack

A direction that is found in literature consists to guess an attack based on previous intentions of the attacker. In this work (Kapetanakis et al. 2014), authors argue that the cyber traces left by a human attacker during an intrusion attempt can be exploited to profile that human. They developed an approach based on CBR that indirectly measures an attacker's characteristics for given attack scenarios. The objective is to identify an attacker's profile relying on observable characteristics from intrusion attempts.

In (Han et al. 2016), CBR is used to profile web hacking based on a complete analysis of historical hacker's activities. They implemented WHAP that includes

CBR to analyze the hacker's activities and to provide the investigators with evidence to attribute attacks and unveil criminals. They evaluated WHAP's using a large scale of web defacement cases including North Korean hacker's attacks against South Korea. They discovered a relationship between those attacks and another set of attacks against Sony Pictures Entertainment.

In (Nakid 2021), CBR is used here to profile the cybercriminal based on past activities and therefore to predict the type of attack that has been executed on the target. The authors design an approach for predicting the attack type in cybercrime based of attack patterns stored in the case base.

Authors in (Al-Mousa 2021) monitor the attack intentions with CBR to identify the strategy and tools required in the attack, and therefore to catch the perpetrator of the attack with higher confidence.

In (Guerra 2023), the authors deal with mitigating the incidents and avoiding the unavailability of services, based on past solved experiences. Authors proposed an ontology-based representation of past incident cases, built by exploiting domain expert knowledge. CBR is used to rely on similarity-based knowledge in supporting the resolution of incident problems.

5.1.3 CBR and Detection of Botnet

Detecting botnet in networks is a concern since Distributed Deny of Service (DDoS) are so popular. Authors in (Panimalar et al. 2019) combined case-based reasoning (CBR) and fuzzy pattern recognition to detect botnet. CBR is exploited to prepare and maintain the knowledge base observed from the series of previous network traces. The objective is to avoid predicting the same domain names or IP addresses which are well known. A case is made up of domain name, IP address, condition, payload, and hop count.

5.1.4 CBR and Detection of SQL Injection

SQL injection is easily profiled based on CBR characterization. This direction is found in literature.

This article (Pinzón Trejos 2015) introduces the SQLCBR classifier, which employs a hybrid detection strategy comprising signature detection and anomaly detection techniques to identify SQL injection attacks. The system leverages a Case-Based Reasoning (CBR) mechanism combined with a Perceptron Multilayer neural network, enabling rapid learning and adaptation to evolving attack patterns. By integrating CBR with neural networks, the classifier effectively distinguishes between simple and complex attacks, enhancing its ability to detect SQL injection attacks in user requests.

CBR in (Recio-Garcia et al. 2023) is used for the understanding of why a SQL sentence is considered as an attack by the ML model through the comparison between such sentences and similar explanation cases. The cases include 82 binary and numerical features from the SQL sentence obtained through investigation of the existing literature. Most features are the use of SQL keywords like "select", "from", and "where". The keywords like drop, delete, alter, or update susceptible to clearly indicate an injection attack are also considered in the database.

In (Schoenborn et al. 2021), a case-based reasoning approach is introduced to detect similar attacks like cross-site scripting (XSS) and SQL injection (SQLi) by leveraging previous attack cases. Through the SEASALT framework instantiation, expandability towards additional attack vectors such as authentication testing is facilitated by incorporating topic agents. By distinguishing between request-level and overall traffic analysis, the system can detect timed attacks like authentication testing and identify clients generating suspiciously high traffic volume. The focus of the paper is on identifying XSS and SQLi attacks, utilizing case bases to detect similar instances, and identifying relevant 16 attributes, predominantly text-based, depending on the specific use-case. The following 10 features constitute the different attributes of a case: IP Address, Length, Protocol, Timing, Description, Request/Info, User-Agent, Status, Cookie, Referer, Time, Method and Number

5.1.5 CBR and Detection of Virus

Some authors tried to model CBR for detecting specific virus. Authors in (Venmaa Devi & Karpagam 2028) exploited CBR to monitor some cyberattacks such as in other to propose detection and prevention strategies. They showed how the four phases are performed.

5.1.6 CBR for Network IDS

CBR is relevant to represent network traces and therefore to detect bad activities happening in the flow based on past events.

An approach based on CBR and description logic (DL) is designed in (Jiang et al. 2014) for Network security emergency response (NSER).

In (Zakaria & Kiah 2012), the authors demonstrated that CBR can be suitable to build smart honeypot due to its ability to learn and adapt in each cycle and the flexible way of building case base.

In this study (Nunes et al. 2029), CBR is integrated to reuse past correction procedures in the resolution of cybersecurity incident problems, in the resolution of new incidents.

A hybrid approach for network intrusion detection including an agent, a Case-Based Reasoning (CBR) and a learning system is proposed in (Leite & Girardi 2017). The role of CBR is to enable learning of new reactive rules by observing recurrent good solutions from the past.

This work (Erbacher et al. 2013) deals with identifying schemes by which these naïve and well-known attack alerts can effectively be handled by a Case-Based Reasoning (CBR). More specifically, CBR is used to match the current alert to the historical alerts in the knowledge base and use an associated template to fill in the report form.

In (Colome et al. 2029), IODEF is used to represent the incidents as cases in the case base and CBR is used to rely on past relevant cybersecurity incident solutions to solve the current ones.

In (Beliz et al. 2012), the authors use CBR combined with multi-agent capabilities to classify and filter incoming flows related to SOAP messages.

A CBR based intelligent is designed in (Zakaria 2015) to recommend the solutions based on existing incidents previously stored.

In (EL AJJOURI et al. 2016), CBR is combined to agents to learn abnormal profiles that correspond to attacks. It is also used to rely on existing attack patterns and attacks observed in the past to identify similarities with a current suspicious sequence of event which does not correspond to a normal sequence, or a known attack. Based on the degree of similarity, classification as new or known attack is made. In case it is new, the profile is updated by the administrator in knowledge base.

CBR is used in (Kruge 2022) to profile cases of cybercrime attacks based on existing stored cases. The stored cases are scanned from publicly available sources such as police web portals using a web crawler and stored in the case database in an attribute-to-attribute matching process.

A multi-agent case-based reasoning system is proposed in (Schoenborn & Althoff 2022) to detect categories of malicious traffic in a network based of previously stored traffic profiles. There are nine agents for nine categories of attacks and one agent for benign flows

5.1.7 CBR and Forensics

The use of CBR in forensics is an option which is also found in literature. In this paper (Al-Mousa 2021), a model to analyze the intentions of cyber-attacks using a case-based reasoning is proposed.

In (Boehmer 2010), CBR is used to support compliance analysis with W7 questionnaires to show a direct relationship between possible internal intruder behavior (insider threats) and unauthorized actions initiated by users called explorers.

In (Horsman & Vickers 2011), the authors demonstrate that a case-based reasoning system can be effectively used to record and store digital forensics examinations, and that it can be used to fully automate decision aid concerning digital forensic examinations. This is due to their ability to process complex problems without human interaction.

5.1.8 Summary of Works

Table 3 depicts a synthesis of works in the category "CBR for cybersecurity" based on four criteria. The first criteria is about the number of phases that are used in the work. The second criteria refers to the similarity scheme used in the work. The third criteria concerns the type or the number of attributes included in a case. The last criteria includes some other details.

Table 3. Summary of CBR for cybersecurity works (N.D: Not Defined)

Sub-Category	Paper	Phases	Similarity	Cases	Other Precisions
CBR and Detection of Android Malware	Qaisar and Li (2022)	4 phases	N.D	APK	Euclidean distance for similarity. Principle Component Analysis (PCA) and Co-relation attribute evaluation (CAE) for feature selection
	(Al-Abri and Salih, 2023)	4 phases	N.D	APK	
CBR and Profiling an attacker and an attack	(Kapetanakis et al. 2014),	Retrieve	N.D	9 attributes	
	(Han et al. 2016),	N.D	N.D	18 attributes	Importance of attribute considered
	(Nakid 2021),	4R	KNN algorithm	26+ features	
	(Al-Mousa 2021)	Retrieve	weighted similarity		Importance of attribute considered
CBR and Detection of Botnet	(Panimalar et al. 2019)	4R		5 attributes	Fuzzy algorithm
Detection of SQL injection	(Pinzón Trejos 2015)	4R	cosine similarity-based	13 attributes	
	(Recio-Garcia et al. 2023)	Not defined	Machine Learning.	82 attributes	
	(Schoenborn et al. 2021),	Retrieve		10 features	Importance of attribute considered; Implementation in Java.

Table 3 continued

Sub-Category	Paper	Phases	Similarity	Cases	Other Precisions
CBR and Detection of Virus	(Venmaa Devi & Karpagam 2028)	4R	N.D	N.D	
CBR for Network IDS	(Jiang et al. 2014)	Retrieve	correction similarity & overall similarity	three tuples	Association with description logic; Importance of attribute considered;
	(Zakaria & Kiah 2012),	N.D	N.D	N.D	It's an exploratory work
	(Nunes et al. 2029),	4R	N.D	Each computer network intrusion	Coupling with the IODEF standard
	(Leite & Girardi 2017).	Retrieve	N.D	events made of flow fields	Involvement of the analyst: expert to confirm the results
	(Erbacher et al. 2013)	Retrieve	K-NN	incidents	Importance of attribute considered;
	(Colome et al. 2029),	2R	Classification and Regression Tree (CART)	19 features	Couple with multi-agent; Reuse: Neural Network
	(Beliz et al. 2012),	4R	N.D	11 features	
	(Zakaria 2015)	2R	N.D	N.D	
	(EL AJJOURI et al. 2016),	N.D	07 schemes	5 features	
	(Kruge 2022)	N.D	Hamming similarity	47 features	Importance of attribute considered
CBR and Forensics	(Al-Mousa 2021),	4R	N.D	N.D	Importance of attribute considered
	(Boehmer 2010),	4R	Hamming similarity	7 features	Couple to graph theory (DAG)
	(Horsman & Vickers 2011),				

5.2 CV for Cybersecurity

The aim here is to discuss different sub-categories of works dealing with CV for cybersecurity.

5.2.1 CV and Detection of Android Malware

Some studies that focus on using CV for the detection of Android malware, are investigated in this section.

In (Grosse et al. 2017), they enhance existing adversarial example crafting algorithms to create a highly potent attack that employs adversarial examples to undermine malware detection models. They demonstrate that neural networks-based android malware detection, despite achieving performance levels comparable to the state-of-the-art, is vulnerable to deception through adversarial examples.

Authors in (Zhu et al. 2023) proposed a detection approach that extracts vital parts of the Dalvik executable (Dex) and convert into an RGB (Red/Green/Blue) image. This method is convolutional neural network (CNN)-based using max pooling and average pooling simultaneously (MADRF), that captures the dependencies between different parts of the image with capitalizing on multi-scale context information.

An efficient vision-based Android Malware Detection is designed in (Almomani et al. 2022) and composed 16 well-developed and fine-tuned CNN algorithms. This model precludes the need for a pre-designated features extraction process while generating accurate predictions. Their approach requires a transformation of DEX files to colored and grayscale malware images before forwarding to the Xception CNN.

A Vision Transformer (ViT)-based computer vision model that uses self-supervised learning is proposed in (Seneviratne et al. 2022) for Android malware detection. They use the visualization method to transform DEX executable into RGB images.

5.2.2 CV and Detection of Windows Malware

Authors also focus on using CV for the detection of Windows malware. Authors represented the malware signature (byte) as a 2D image and exploit deep learning techniques to characterize the signature of malware (Ahmed et al. 2023).

In (Jian et al. 2021), an approach in which data augmentation method is used with computer vision for malware detection. Firstly, executable file samples are converted into bytes files and ASM files through disassembly technology. Secondly, the samples are converted into three-channel RGB images using visualization technology and data augmentation to extract high-dimensional intrinsic features from data samples.

In (Ben abdel ouahab et al. 2023), authors exploited Vision Transformers (ViT) for malware detection and showed that their ViT-based approach outperforms the traditional Convolutional Neural Networks (CNNs) in terms of accuracy and robustness.

In (Abijah Roseline et al. 2020), the detection of malware is made using visualization technique and lightweight Convolutional Neural Networks deep learning model.

In (Hashemi & Hamzeh 2019), the authors designed a scheme to identify unknown malware based on micro-patterns within the executable files. They use machine learning-based method on visual features extracted from executable files to detect malware. First, files are transformed into 2D digital images; second, visual features of the image corresponding to each file are extracted using Local Binary Pattern (LBP) and third, the features are used to train machine learning tools.

Authors in (Ravi et al. 2023) designed ViT4Mal as a lightweight vision transformer (ViT) based malware detection on an edge device. ViT4Mal transforms executable byte-codes into images to characterize malware features and to profile malware with high accuracy. They demonstrated that ViT4Mal is 41x speedup compared to the original ViT model.

This study in (Hemalatha et al. 2021) employs a visualization-oriented approach, representing malware binaries as two-dimensional images and categorizing them using a deep learning model. The system employs a reweighted class-balanced loss function in the last classification layer of the DenseNet model, resulting in notable performance enhancements in malware classification by addressing imbalanced data challenges.

This research in (Ravi & Alazab 2023) incorporates a multi-headed attention mechanism into a CNN to pinpoint and recognize small infected areas within the complete image. A thorough examination and analysis of this method were conducted using a dataset of malware images. The performance of the proposed CNN approach, which utilizes multi-headed attention, was assessed against several CNN approaches without attention mechanisms across different training and testing data splits of a benchmark dataset for malware images. Across all data splits, the attention-based CNN method consistently surpassed non-attention-based CNN methods, while also maintaining computational efficiency.

The main contribution in (Vinayakumar et al. 2019), that combines visualization and deep learning architectures, lies in introducing a new image processing technique with optimized parameters for machine learning algorithms (MLAs) and deep learning architectures, resulting in an efficient model for detecting zero-day malware. Through a comprehensive comparative analysis, our study shows that our proposed deep learning architectures outperform traditional machine learning algorithms.

5.2.3 CV and Detection of Bad Network Traffic

Some studies that focus on using CV for the detection of malicious network traffic, are investigated in this section. In (El-Ghamry et al. 2023), authors developed a machine learning image-based IoT malware using visual representation (i.e., images) of the network traffic. In this paper, a novel optimized machine learning image-based IoT malware detection method is proposed using visual representation (i.e., images) of the network traffic. Ant colony optimizer (ACO) and PSO algorithms are used to optimize the number of features.

5.2.4 CV and Forensics

Forensics with CV is the focus of some researches that are discussed here. Authors propose in (Shah et al. 2022) a computer vision-based scheme for detecting malware that resides in the main computer memory. This work takes portable executables and extract memory dump files from the volatile memory and transform them into images.

The authors in (Bozkir et al. 2021) proposed a two-options method. In the first option, the of visual patterns memory dump of suspicious processes is captured and represented as a RGB image and classification is realized using computer vision and machine learning methods in a multi-class open-set recognition regime. UMAP is used later to improve the detection of unknown malware files through binary classification.

5.2.5 Summary

Table 4 depicts a synthesis of works in the category "CV for cybersecurity" based on four criteria. The first criteria is the technique of preprocessing that is used in the work. The second criteria refers to the datasets used in the work. The third criteria concerns the size and type of images that are fed into computer vision algorithms. The last criteria refers to the CV models used in the work.

Table 4. Summary of CV for cybersecurity works (N.D: Not defined)

Sub-Category	Paper	Pre-Processing Technique	Datasets	Images and Size	CV Models
CV and Detection of Android Malware	(Grosse et al. 2017)	-	DREBIN dataset	-	-
	(Zhu et al. 2023)	Capitalizing on multi-scale context information	Dataset made of apps from Google Play Store and Virusshare	RGB	(CNN)-based
	(Almomani et al. 2022)	Transformation of DEX files to images	Leopard Android dataset	Color and RGB	Xception CNN
	(Seneviratne et al. 2022)	Visualization method	MalNet dataset	Size 224x224	Vision Transformer (ViT)

Table 4 continued

Sub-Category	Paper	Pre-Processing Technique	Datasets	Images and Size	CV Models
CV and Detection of Windows Malware	(Ahmed et al. 2023).	Deep learning	Microsoft BIG15 dataset with nine specific classes	2D 1024 x 1	Transfer learning and inception v3
	(Jian et al. 2021),	Disassembly	-	RGB	Deep neural network SERLA based on SEResNet50, Bi-LSTM, and attention
	(Ben abdel ouahab et al. 2023),	-	Malimg database	-	Vision Transformers, CNN
	(Abijah Roseline et al. 2020),	Visualization technique	Malimg dataset and Kaggle's Microsoft Malware Classification Challenge (BIG 2015) dataset.	Size: 32 × 32	Visualization and CNN
	(Hashemi & Hamzeh 2019),	Automatic feature extraction	Malimg, MaleVis, virus-MNIST, and Dumpware10	**Size: 32 x 32 x 1**	ECOC coding matrices
	(Ravi et al. 2023)	Zigzag method and Markov chain, K-Nearest Neighbor	03 datasets	Gray scale	Visual Features are extracted using LBP
	(Hemalatha et al. 2021)	Transformation of executable byte-codes into images	-	-	vision transformer
	(Ravi & Alazab 2023)	visualization-oriented approach	Malimg dataset, BIG 2015 dataset, MaleVis dataset, Malicia dataset	Size: 64x 64 Grayscale images	DenseNet model, Deep learning
	(Vinayakumar et al. 2019),	CNN preprocessing	Malimg dataset	Grayscale and color	CNN, multi-headed attention
	(Ahmed et al. 2023).	CNN preprocessing	Ember, Malimg	Size: 32 x 32	deep neural network (DNN)
CV and Detection of Bad Network Traffic	(El-Ghamry et al. 2023),	Visual representation	Dataset from literature	2D RGB images	Ant colony optimizer (ACO) and PSO algorithms

Table 4 continued

Sub-Category	Paper	Pre-Processing Technique	Datasets	Images and Size	CV Models
CV and Forensics	(Shah et al. 2022)	Preprocessing based on vizualization	Microsoft Malware Classification Challenge, Malicia, Malimg, and Malevis	112 x 112 and 56 x 56	Computer vision-based, histogram equalization and wavelet transform
	(Bozkir et al. 2021)	N.D	4294 samples in total, including 10 malware families	RGB	Computer vision and machine learning methods

5.3 CBR+CV for Cybersecurity

This section discusses the last category of the taxonomy. First, works that couple CV and CBR are discussed and second, the works integration CV and CBR to support cybersecurity are discussed.

5.3.1 CV and CBR

The integration of CV and CBR has been explored for various applications, with several related works presenting promising results yet identifying limitations. In (Wang Y., 2023), the authors demonstrated an early exploration of using CBR for object recognition but faced scalability and efficiency challenges when handling large datasets and complex scenes. Building on this work, (Shin, 2024) proposed a framework combining computer vision and CBR for image interpretation, though gaps remained in terms of scalability, efficiency, and adaptability.

In the field of content-based image retrieval (CBIR), (Roy Chowdhury, 2020) and (Li, 2021) presented a CBR approach to automatic annotation based on visual content. However, this work faced challenges in adapting CBR systems to evolving datasets and dynamic user preferences while maintaining scalability for large-scale image repositories. The integration of CBR with deep learning was explored in (Jaafar, 2023), (Wang S. a., 2024) and (Chen, 2023) where the authors proposed a hybrid system leveraging the strengths of both methodologies. Yet, gaps persisted in effectively utilizing the complementary capabilities while addressing interpretability and explainability challenges. In medical image analysis, (Barnett, 2021) and (Lamy, 2019) investigated CBR for assisting medical professionals but struggled with evaluating the robustness of CBR systems when handling noisy or incomplete visual data and integrating domain-specific knowledge into the CBR process.

To overcome these limitations, future research should focus on developing scalable, efficient, and robust CBR systems capable of handling large-scale visual datasets while maintaining the ability to adapt to evolving user needs. Additionally, exploring methodologies for integrating CBR with emerging technologies like deep learning while addressing interpretability and explainability challenges would be beneficial in advancing this area of research.

5.3.2 CV and CBR in Cybersecurity

A comprehensive study on the integration of computer vision and case-based reasoning (CBR) for cybersecurity applications is presented here, highlighting several related works along with their identified limitations. In (Sarker 2023) and (Kaur 2023), the authors explore the potential of using visual data and historical cases to identify and mitigate cybersecurity threats. However, gaps exist in scalability and efficiency, especially when handling large-scale datasets and real-time threat detection requirements. In (Sarker 2022) and (Lopez-Sanchez 2028), the authors investigate the application of CBR with computer vision for malware analysis, demonstrating its effectiveness in identifying and categorizing malware variants based on visual features. Nonetheless, these studies face limitations in terms of robustness against advanced malware evasion techniques and scalability for analysing large datasets.

Furthermore, authors in (Tripathi 2022) and (Adedoyin 2029), present a framework for leveraging visual evidence from security cameras or network traffic analysis to guide incident response actions. Despite its potential benefits, this approach faces challenges in integrating real-time visual data with historical case repositories and automating decision-making processes for incident response. In (Akhtar, 2021) and (Abioye, 2021), the authors explore the use of computer vision and CBR techniques for network intrusion detection by matching visual patterns in network traffic data with historical cases to detect anomalous behaviour. However, this methodology lacks scalability when analysing large-scale network traffic and adapting to evolving attack strategies. Lastly, (Rohatgi, 2023), investigates the application of CBR with computer vision for threat intelligence analysis by integrating visual features extracted from security logs or threat reports to identify emerging threats. Still, these studies face limitations in effectively combining visual evidence with other data sources and automating the threat analysis process. In (Lansley et al. 2019), the authors proposed an effective method that detects social engineering attacks by associating CBR and Deep learning.

Overall, the integration of computer vision and case-based reasoning in cybersecurity offers promising opportunities for various applications such as intrusion detection, malware analysis, and threat intelligence. However, several gaps need to be addressed, including scalability, efficiency, robustness against advanced techniques, automation of decision-making processes, and effective integration with other data sources.

6. OPEN ISSUES

While the integration of computer vision and case-based reasoning (CBR) in cybersecurity presents promising avenues, several open issues and challenges should be considered. Based on the previous discussions in related works, the following open issues are highlighted.

Integrating computer vision with CBR in cybersecurity often encounters scalability challenges, especially when dealing with large-scale datasets and real-time processing requirements. Existing approaches may struggle to efficiently process and analyse vast amounts of visual data, hindering their applicability in enterprise-scale cybersecurity operations. This issue is related to scalability.

Visual data in cybersecurity can be highly complex and heterogeneous, including images, videos, network traffic visualizations, and log data. Effectively extracting relevant features and patterns from diverse visual sources poses significant challenges, requiring advanced computer vision techniques tailored to cybersecurity applications. This issue is related to complexity of visual data.

While computer vision algorithms can effectively process visual data, the interpretability and explainability of their decisions remain limited. Understanding how and why a particular decision or inference was made is crucial for trust and accountability in cybersecurity applications. Integrating CBR techniques that provide explanations based on past cases could enhance the interpretability of computer vision-based cybersecurity systems. This issue is related to interpretability and explainability.

Cyber threats evolve rapidly, necessitating cybersecurity systems to adapt and learn from new data and experiences. However, existing computer vision and CBR approaches may struggle to adapt to emerging threats and novel attack techniques. Developing adaptive and self-learning systems that continuously update their knowledge base and detection mechanisms is essential to stay ahead of cyber adversaries. This issue is related to adaptability to evolving threats.

Seamless integration of computer vision and CBR techniques with existing cybersecurity tools and frameworks is crucial for practical deployment and adoption. However, interoperability challenges may arise when integrating these advanced techniques with legacy systems, requiring standardization efforts and interoperability protocols in cybersecurity domains. This issue is related to integration with existing cybersecurity tools.

Leveraging visual data in cybersecurity raises privacy and ethical concerns, particularly regarding the collection, storage, and analysis of sensitive information. Protecting the privacy of individuals while still extracting actionable insights from visual data poses a significant challenge. Developing privacy-preserving techniques and adhering to ethical guidelines are paramount in computer vision-based cybersecurity applications. This issue is related to privacy and ethical concerns.

Deploying computer vision and CBR systems in resource-constrained environments, such as edge devices or IoT devices, presents additional challenges. These systems must balance the computational and memory requirements of sophisticated algorithms with the limited resources available in such environments, without compromising performance or security. This issue is related to resource constraints.

Addressing these open issues opens doors to new research directions in the community.

7. CONCLUSION

The aim of this study was to provide a brief state-of-the-art concerning exploiting CBR with CV in cybersecurity approaches. A taxonomy is designed and researches have been analysed. Integration CBR and CV is revealed a promising avenue for bolstering cybersecurity capabilities. This study also poses pressing challenges that should be overcome by the community. Throughout our exploration, we have identified key issues such as scalability, interpretability, adaptability to evolving threats, integration with existing cybersecurity tools, and privacy concerns. While these challenges remain significant, they also present opportunities for innovation and advancement in the field of cybersecurity. The future step will be to consider one issue and to explore possible technical solutions. Future research directions should focus on developing scalable, interpretable, and adaptive computer vision-based cybersecurity solutions that address the evolving threat landscape while upholding privacy and ethical standards.

REFERENCES

Abijah Roseline, S., Hari, G., Geetha, S., & Krishnamurthy, R. (2020). Vision-based malware detection and classification using lightweight deep learning paradigm. In *Computer Vision and Image Processing: 4th International Conference, CVIP 2019, Jaipur, India, September 27–29, 2019, Revised Selected Papers, Part II 4* (pp. 62-73). Springer Singapore. 10.1007/978-981-15-4018-9_6

Abioye, S. O., Oyedele, L. O., Akanbi, L., Ajayi, A., Davila Delgado, J. M., Bilal, M., Akinade, O. O., & Ahmed, A. (2021). Artificial intelligence in the construction industry: A review of present status, opportunities and future challenges. *Journal of Building Engineering*, *44*, 103299. doi:10.1016/j.jobe.2021.103299

Adedoyin, A., Kapetanakis, S., Petridis, M., & Panaousis, E. (2016). Evaluating Case-Based Reasoning Knowledge Discovery in Fraud Detection. In ICCBR Workshops (pp. 182-191). Academic Press.

Ahmed, M., Afreen, N., Ahmed, M., Sameer, M., & Ahamed, J. (2023). An inception V3 approach for malware classification using machine learning and transfer learning. *International Journal of Intelligent Networks*, *4*, 11–18. doi:10.1016/j.ijin.2022.11.005

Akhtar, M. a. (2021). An overview of the applications of Artificial Intelligence in Cybersecurity. *EAI Endorsed Transactions on Creative Technologies, 8*(29).

Al-Abri, A. A., & Salih, N. K. (2023, September). Mobile Application Malware Self-Diagnosis. In *2023 10th International Conference on Electrical Engineering, Computer Science and Informatics (EECSI)* (pp. 338-342). IEEE. 10.1109/EECSI59885.2023.10295583

Al-Mousa, M. R. (2021). Analyzing cyber-attack intention for digital forensics using case-based reasoning. *arXiv preprint arXiv:2101.01395*.

Almomani, I., Alkhayer, A., & El-Shafai, W. (2022). An automated vision-based deep learning model for efficient detection of android malware attacks. *IEEE Access : Practical Innovations, Open Solutions*, *10*, 2700–2720. doi:10.1109/ACCESS.2022.3140341

Anandita Iyer, A., & Umadevi, K. S. (2023). Role of AI and its impact on the development of cyber security applications. In *Artificial Intelligence and Cyber Security in Industry 4.0* (pp. 23–46). Springer Nature Singapore. doi:10.1007/978-981-99-2115-7_2

Bachir, N. a. (2024). Benchmarking YOLOv5 models for improved human detection in search and rescue missions. *Journal of Electronic Science and Technology*, 100243.

Barnett, A. J. (2021). Interpretable mammographic image classification using case-based reasoning and deep learning. arXiv preprint arXiv:2107.05605.

Belghith, H. Y. (2017). A Multi-Agent Case-Based Reasoning Architecture for Phishing Detection. *Procedia Computer Science, 110*, 492–497. doi:10.1016/j.procs.2017.06.131

Belghith, H. Y. (2017). Using Case-Based Reasoning for Phishing Detection. *Procedia Computer Science, 109*, 281288. doi:10.1016/j.procs.2017.05.352

Beliz, N., Rangel, J. C., & Hong, C. S. (2012). Detecting DoS attack in Web services by using an adaptive multiagent solution. *ADCAIJ: Advances in Distributed Computing and Artificial Intelligence Journal, 1*(2), 57–63. doi:10.14201/ADCAIJ2012125763

Ben Abdel Ouahab, I., Elaachak, L., & Bouhorma, M. (2023). Enhancing Malware Classification with Vision Transformers: A Comparative Study with Traditional CNN Models. In *Proceedings of the 6th International Conference on Networking, Intelligent Systems & Security* (pp. 1-5). Academic Press.

Bhatt, D., Patel, C., Talsania, H., Patel, J., Vaghela, R., Pandya, S., Modi, K., & Ghayvat, H. (2021). CNN variants for computer vision: History, architecture, application, challenges and future scope. *Electronics (Basel), 10*(20), 2470. doi:10.3390/electronics10202470

Boehmer, W. (2010). Analyzing human behavior using case-based reasoning with the help of forensic questions. In *2010 24th IEEE International Conference on Advanced Information Networking and Applications* (pp. 1189-1194). IEEE. 10.1109/AINA.2010.73

Bozkir, A. S., Tahillioglu, E., Aydos, M., & Kara, I. (2021). Catch them alive: A malware detection approach through memory forensics, manifold learning and computer vision. *Computers & Security, 103*, 102166. doi:10.1016/j.cose.2020.102166

Chen, M.-Y. a. (2023). Guest editorial: Machine learning-based decision support systems in IoT systems. *Computer Science and Information Systems, 20*(2).

Colome, M., Nunes, R. C., & de Lima Silva, L. A. (2019). Case-Based Cybersecurity Incident Resolution. In SEKE (pp. 253-330). doi:10.18293/SEKE2019-204

Dangi, A. K., Pant, K., Alanya-Beltran, J., Chakraborty, N., Akram, S. V., & Balakrishna, K. (2023). A Review of use of Artificial Intelligence on Cyber Security and the Fifth-Generation Cyber-attacks and its analysis. In *2023 International Conference on Artificial Intelligence and Smart Communication (AISC)* (pp. 553-557). IEEE. 10.1109/AISC56616.2023.10085175

De Azambuja, A. J. G., Plesker, C., Schützer, K., Anderl, R., Schleich, B., & Almeida, V. R. (2023). Artificial intelligence-based cyber security in the context of industry 4.0—A survey. *Electronics (Basel)*, *12*(8), 1920. doi:10.3390/electronics12081920

El Ajjouri, M., Benhadou, S., & Medromi, H. (2016). LnaCBR: Case Based Reasoning Architecture for Intrusion Detection to Learning New Attacks. *Revue Méditerranéenne des Télécommunications*, *6*(1).

El-Ghamry, A., Gaber, T., Mohammed, K. K., & Hassanien, A. E. (2023). Optimized and efficient image-based IoT malware detection method. *Electronics (Basel)*, *12*(3), 708. doi:10.3390/electronics12030708

Erbacher, R. F., & Hutchinson, S. E. (2013). *Extending Case-Based Reasoning (CBR) Approaches to Semi-automated Network Alert Reporting*. Academic Press.

Faia, R., Pinto, T., Abrishambaf, O., Fernandes, F., Vale, Z., & Corchado, J. M. (2017). Case based reasoning with expert system and swarm intelligence to determine energy reduction in buildings energy management. *Energy and Building*, *155*, 269281. doi:10.1016/j.enbuild.2017.09.020

Grosse, K., Papernot, N., Manoharan, P., Backes, M., & McDaniel, P. (2017). Adversarial examples for malware detection. *Computer Security–ESORICS 2017: 22nd European Symposium on Research in Computer Security, Oslo, Norway, September 11-15, 2017 Proceedings*, *22*(Part II), 62–79.

Guerra, P. A. C., Barcelos, F. A., Nunes, R. C., De Freitas, E. P., & Silva, L. A. D. L. (2023). An Artificial Intelligence Framework for the Representation and Reuse of Cybersecurity Incident Resolution Knowledge. In *Proceedings of the 12th Latin-American Symposium on Dependable and Secure Computing* (pp. 136-145). 10.1145/3615366.3615369

Han, M. L., Han, H. C., Kang, A. R., Kwak, B. I., Mohaisen, A., & Kim, H. K. (2016, October). WHAP: Web-hacking profiling using case-based reasoning. In *2016 IEEE Conference on Communications and Network Security (CNS)* (pp. 344-345). IEEE. 10.1109/CNS.2016.7860503

Hashemi, H., & Hamzeh, A. (2019). Visual malware detection using local malicious pattern. *Journal of Computer Virology and Hacking Techniques, 15*(1), 1–14. doi:10.1007/s11416-018-0314-1

Hemalatha, J., Roseline, S. A., Geetha, S., Kadry, S., & Damaševičius, R. (2021). An efficient densenet-based deep learning model for malware detection. *Entropy (Basel, Switzerland), 23*(3), 344. doi:10.3390/e23030344 PMID:33804035

Horsman, G., Laing, C., & Vickers, P. (2011). *A case-based reasoning system for automated forensic examinations.* Academic Press.

Jaafar, R. a. (2023). CBHIR-based approach for histological image analysis on large scale datasets. *2023 International Conference on Cyberworlds (CW)* (pp. 502-503). IEEE. 10.1109/CW58918.2023.00088

Jian, Y., Kuang, H., Ren, C., Ma, Z., & Wang, H. (2021). A novel framework for image-based malware detection with a deep neural network. *Computers & Security, 109*, 102400. doi:10.1016/j.cose.2021.102400

Jiang, F., Gu, T., Chang, L., & Xu, Z. (2014). Case retrieval for network security emergency response based on description logic. *Intelligent Information Processing VII: 8th IFIP TC 12 International Conference, IIP 2014, Hangzhou, China, October 17-20, 2014 Proceedings, 8*, 284–293.

Kapetanakis, S., Filippoupolitis, A., Loukas, G., & Al Murayziq, T. S. (2014). *Profiling cyber attackers using case-based reasoning.* Academic Press.

Kapoor, N., Sulke, P., Pardeshi, P., Kakad, R., & Badiye, A. (2023). Introduction to Forensic Science. In *Textbook of Forensic Science* (pp. 41–66). Springer Nature Singapore. doi:10.1007/978-981-99-1377-0_2

Kaur, N., Rani, S., & Kaur, S. (2024). Real-time video surveillance based human fall detection system using hybrid haar cascade classifier. *Multimedia Tools and Applications*, 1–19. doi:10.1007/s11042-024-18305-w

Kaur, R., Gabrijelčič, D., & Klobučar, T. (2023). Artificial intelligence for cybersecurity: Literature review and future research directions. *Information Fusion, 97*, 101804. doi:10.1016/j.inffus.2023.101804

Kolodner, J. L. (1992). An introduction to case-based reasoning. *Artificial Intelligence Review, 6*(1), 3–34. doi:10.1007/BF00155578

Kolodner, J. L. (1994). Understanding creativity: A case-based approach. Lecture Notes in Computer Science (including subseries Lecture Notes in Artificial Intelligence and Lecture Notes in Bioinformatics), 837, 3-20. doi:10.1007/3-540-58330-0_73

Krüger, M. (2022). An Approach to Profiler Detection of Cyber Attacks using Case-based Reasoning. In LWDA (pp. 234-245). Academic Press.

Kwon, N., Cho, J., Lee, H.-S., Yoon, I., & Park, M. (2019). Compensation Cost Estimation Model for Construction Noise Claims Using Case-Based Reasoning. *Journal of Construction Engineering and Management*, *145*(8), 04019047. Advance online publication. doi:10.1061/(ASCE)CO.1943-7862.0001675

Lamy, J.-B., Sekar, B., Guezennec, G., Bouaud, J., & Séroussi, B. (2019). Explainable artificial intelligence for breast cancer: A visual case-based reasoning approach. *Artificial Intelligence in Medicine*, *94*, 42–53. doi:10.1016/j.artmed.2019.01.001 PMID:30871682

Lansley, M., Polatidis, N., Kapetanakis, S., Amin, K., Samakovitis, G., & Petridis, M. (2019). Seen the villains: detecting social engineering attacks using case-based reasoning and deep learning. *Proceedings of the ICCBR Workshops*, 39–48.

Leite, A., & Girardi, R. (2017). A hybrid and learning agent architecture for network intrusion detection. *Journal of Systems and Software*, *130*, 59–80. doi:10.1016/j.jss.2017.01.028

Li, X., Yang, J., & Ma, J. (2021). Recent developments of content-based image retrieval (CBIR). *Neurocomputing*, *452*, 675–689. doi:10.1016/j.neucom.2020.07.139

Lieber, J. (2008). *Contributions à la conception de systèmes de raisonnement à partir de cas*. Academic Press.

López, B. (2022). *Case-based reasoning: a concise introduction*. Springer Nature.

Lopez-Sanchez, D., Herrero, J. R., Arrieta, A. G., & Corchado, J. M. (2018). Hybridizing metric learning and case-based reasoning for adaptable clickbait detection. *Applied Intelligence*, *48*(9), 29672982. doi:10.1007/s10489-017-1109-7

Luc, L. G. (2014). *Raisonnement à base de cas textuels-état de l'art et perspectives*. Academic Press.

Meguehout, T. B.-T. (2013). *Un Raisonnement à Partir de Cas pour la Traduction Automatique Arabe-Francais Basée sur la Sémantique*. Academic Press.

Minaee, S., Abdolrashidi, A., Su, H., Bennamoun, M., & Zhang, D. (2023). Biometrics recognition using deep learning: A survey. *Artificial Intelligence Review*, *56*(8), 8647–8695. doi:10.1007/s10462-022-10237-x

Mohammed Benamina, B. A. (2018). Diabetes Diagnosis by Case-Based Reasoning and Fuzzy Logic. *Int. J. Interact. Multimed. Artif. Intell.*, *4*(7), 7280. doi:10.9781/jimai.2017.03.003

Nabila, N. a. (2013). *Une approche d'optimisation par essaim de particules pour la recherche en mémoire de cas* [PhD thesis]. University of Montreal, Canada.

Nakid, S. S. (2021). *Evaluation and detection of cybercriminal attack type using machine learning* (Doctoral dissertation, Dublin, National College of Ireland).

Nunes, R. C., Colomé, M., Barcelos, F. A., Garbin, M., Paulus, G. B., & Silva, L. A. D. L. (2019). A case-based reasoning approach for the cybersecurity incident recording and resolution. *International Journal of Software Engineering and Knowledge Engineering, 29*(11-12), 1607-1627.

Ozkan-Ozay, M., Akin, E., Aslan, Ö., Kosunalp, S., Iliev, T., Stoyanov, I., & Beloev, I. (2024). A Comprehensive Survey: Evaluating the Efficiency of Artificial Intelligence and Machine Learning Techniques on Cyber Security Solutions. *IEEE Access : Practical Innovations, Open Solutions*, *12*, 12229–12256. doi:10.1109/ACCESS.2024.3355547

Panimalar, P., & Rameshkumar, K. (2019). A novel traffic analysis model for botnet discovery in dynamic network. *Arabian Journal for Science and Engineering*, *44*(4), 3033–3042. doi:10.1007/s13369-018-3319-7

Park, Y.-J., Kim, B.-C., & Chun, S.-H. (2006). New knowledge extraction technique using probability for case-based reasoning: Application to medical diagnosis. *Expert Systems: International Journal of Knowledge Engineering and Neural Networks*, *23*(1), 2–20. doi:10.1111/j.1468-0394.2006.00321.x

Pinzón Trejos, C., De Paz, J., Bajo, J., & Corchado, J. (2015). *An Adaptive Mechanism to Protect Databases against SQL Injection*. Academic Press.

Qaisar, Z. H., & Li, R. (2022). Multimodal information fusion for android malware detection using lazy learning. *Multimedia Tools and Applications*, *81*(9), 1–15. doi:10.1007/s11042-021-10749-8

Ravi, A., Chaturvedi, V., & Shafique, M. (2023). ViT4Mal: Lightweight Vision Transformer for Malware Detection on Edge Devices. *ACM Transactions on Embedded Computing Systems*, *22*(5s), 1–26. doi:10.1145/3609112

Ravi, V., & Alazab, M. (2023). Attention-based convolutional neural network deep learning approach for robust malware classification. *Computational Intelligence*, *39*(1), 145–168. doi:10.1111/coin.12551

Recio-Garcia, J. A., Orozco-del Castillo, M. G., & Soladrero, J. A. (2023). Case-based Explanation of Classification Models for the Detection of SQL Injection Attacks. *Proceedings of the: XCBR, 23*.

Rohatgi, S. a. (2023). Introduction to Artificial Intelligence and Cybersecurity for Industry. *Artificial Intelligence and Cyber Security in Industry 4.0*, 1-22.

Roy Chowdhury, A., Banerjee, S., & Chatterjee, T. (2020). A cybernetic systems approach to abnormality detection in retina images using case based reasoning. *SN Applied Sciences*, *2*(8), 1–15. doi:10.1007/s42452-020-3187-0

Sarker, I. H. (2022). Ai-based modeling: Techniques, applications and research issues towards automation, intelligent and smart systems. *SN Computer Science*, *3*(2), 158. doi:10.1007/s42979-022-01043-x PMID:35194580

Sarker, I. H. (2023). Multi-aspects AI-based modeling and adversarial learning for cybersecurity intelligence and robustness: A comprehensive overview. *Security and Privacy*, *6*(5), 295. doi:10.1002/spy2.295

Sarvajcz, K., Ari, L., & Menyhart, J. (2024). AI on the Road: NVIDIA Jetson Nano-Powered Computer Vision-Based System for Real-Time Pedestrian and Priority Sign Detection. *Applied Sciences (Basel, Switzerland)*, *14*(4), 1440. doi:10.3390/app14041440

Schoenborn, J. M., & Althoff, K. D. (2021). Detecting SQL-Injection and Cross-Site Scripting Attacks Using Case-Based Reasoning and SEASALT. In LWDA (pp. 66-77). Academic Press.

Schoenborn, J. M., & Althoff, K. D. (2022). Multi-Agent Case-Based Reasoning: a Network Intrusion Detection System. In LWDA (pp. 258-269). Academic Press.

Seneviratne, S., Shariffdeen, R., Rasnayaka, S., & Kasthuriarachchi, N. (2022). Self-supervised vision transformers for malware detection. *IEEE Access : Practical Innovations, Open Solutions*, *10*, 103121–103135. doi:10.1109/ACCESS.2022.3206445

Shah, S. S. H., Ahmad, A. R., Jamil, N., & Khan, A. U. R. (2022). Memory forensics-based malware detection using computer vision and machine learning. *Electronics (Basel)*, *11*(16), 2579. doi:10.3390/electronics11162579

Shin, Y., Choi, Y., Won, J., Hong, T., & Koo, C. (2024). A new benchmark model for the automated detection and classification of a wide range of heavy construction equipment. *Journal of Management Engineering*, *40*(2), 04023069. doi:10.1061/JMENEA.MEENG-5630

Sousa, A. J. (2018). *Application of knowledge acquisition methods in a casebased reasoning tool*. Master thesis, FEUP.

Tchomté, S. A. (2019). A Case Based Reasoning Coupling Multi-Criteria Decision Making with Learning and Optimization Intelligences: Application to Energy Consumption. *EAI Endorsed Trans. Smart Cities, 4*(9), 162-292. doi:10.4108/eai.26-6-2018.162292

Tripathi, V. a. (2022). Enhanced CNN Is Used For Mal Image Anomaly Detection And Classification. *Scandinavian Journal of Information Systems*, *34*(2), 37–44.

Venmaa Devi, P., & Karpagam, G. R (2018). R4 Model for Malware Detection And Prevention Using Case Based Reasoning. *IJCRT, 6*(2).

Vinayakumar, R., Alazab, M., Soman, K. P., Poornachandran, P., & Venkatraman, S. (2019). Robust intelligent malware detection using deep learning. *IEEE Access : Practical Innovations, Open Solutions*, *7*, 46717–46738. doi:10.1109/ACCESS.2019.2906934

Wang, S., Zou, P., Gong, X., Song, M., Peng, J., & Jiao, J. R. (2024). Visual analytics and intelligent reasoning for smart manufacturing defect detection and judgement: A meta-learning approach with knowledge graph embedding case-based reasoning. *Journal of Industrial Information Integration*, *37*, 100536. doi:10.1016/j.jii.2023.100536

Wang, X. (2013). Intelligent multi-camera video surveillance: A review. *Pattern Recognition Letters*, *34*(1), 3–19. doi:10.1016/j.patrec.2012.07.005

Wang, Y. (2023). *Vision-assisted behavior-based construction safety: Integrating computer vision and natural language processing*. Academic Press.

Yan, J. a. (2024). Exploring better image captioning with grid features. *Complex & Intelligent Systems*, 1-16.

Yang, D., Ding, Y., Zhang, H., & Li, Y. (2024). PVitNet: An Effective Approach for Android Malware Detection Using Pyramid Feature Processing and Vision Transformer. In *ICASSP 2024-2024 IEEE International Conference on Acoustics, Speech and Signal Processing (ICASSP)* (pp. 2440-2444). IEEE.

Zakaria, W. Z. A. (2015). Application of case based reasoning in it security incident response. In *Int. Conf. Recent Trends in Engineering and Technology* (pp. 106-109). Academic Press.

Zakaria, W. Z. A., & Kiah, M. L. M. (2012). A review on artificial intelligence techniques for developing intelligent honeypot. In *2012 8th International Conference on Computing Technology and Information Management (NCM and ICNIT)* (Vol. 2, pp. 696-701). IEEE.

Zhu, H., Wei, H., Wang, L., Xu, Z., & Sheng, V. S. (2023). An effective end-to-end android malware detection method. *Expert Systems with Applications, 218*, 119593. doi:10.1016/j.eswa.2023.119593

Chapter 3
Computer Vision and Building Resilience Against Online Violent Extremism in Africa:
Computer Vision for Fake News Detection

Wyclife Ong'eta
Kenyatta University, Kenya

ABSTRACT

This chapter reviews how new technologies driven by artificial intelligence have a wide range of impact in advancing violent ideologies in Africa. In particular, the chapter analyses how computer vision is helping to advance radical and extreme ideologies and how to build resilience against the phenomenon. This work has found that terrorist organisations are tapping artificial intelligence through computer vision to develop synthetic videos, graphics, and images to advance their goals. It was revealed that transformative education has the potential to develop all round humans capable to thrive and navigate in ever changing and dynamic online ecosystem.

INTRODUCTION

Globally, the number of terrorist attacks has increased by 17% to 5,226. In Africa, cases have exponentially increased particularly in Sub-Saharan Africa (Burkina Faso, the Democratic Republic of the Congo, Mali, and Niger). For example, deaths in the Sahel region account for 35% of global terrorism deaths in 2021, compared

DOI: 10.4018/978-1-6684-8127-1.ch003

with just 1% in 2007 (Institute for Economics and Peace, 2022). In Africa, like the rest of the world, technological innovation has always shaped the dynamics of conflicts. Advances in computing as well as the development of artificial intelligence (AI) have wide-ranging impacts in advancing violent extremism (VE) (Heidelberg Institute for International Conflict Research (HIIK), 2022; RAN, 2021). An exemplar, synthetically computer audios and videos so called deep fakes continue to capture the imagination of the computer-graphics and computer-vision communities, at the same time, the democratization of access to technology that can create a sophisticated manipulated video of anybody saying anything continues to be of concern because of its power to disrupt democratic elections, commit small to large-scale fraud, fuel disinformation campaigns, and promote radical and extreme ideologies (Agarwal, Farid, El-Gaaly and Lim, 2020; Crawford, Keen and Suarez de-Tangil, 2020). Not only are people accessing synthetic videos of executions and those amplifying violent ideologies, but they can now more easily be targeted by terrorists and extremists in online chat rooms, gaming platforms and other open and dark spaces online (RAN, 2021; Albahar, 2017).

Through artificial intelligence, the social world is becoming available to algorithms, which read not emotions or faces but structured data, tabulations that can be contained in a data file. This is, increasingly, the work of the digital camera. Far from generating images, what digital cameras produce is not only standardized data files containing data that enable a data reader to display an image, but also metadata that apart from specifying how to read the file and possibly containing a thumbnail preview of its contents enables open tagging as well as geotags, timestamps, equipment tags, and a myriad of other operations of describing and or classifying the files (Rocco et al., 2021). A previous Islamic State (ISIS) case study by Gambetta and Hertog revealed that engineers and technological gurus are overrepresented among violent Islamist extremists who are tapping computer vision driven by artificial intelligence to advance violent extremism (Muro, 2017). This is not different to other extremism groups in Africa who are affiliated to ISIS. So if new technologies can be used for a wrong course, it is likely to cause more harm than good to humanity especially computer algorithms which may not comply with required ethics as programmed or when driven by AI unlike the way humans who could distinguish between the right and wrong. Since new technologies is not going away, there is need to build human capability to counter its harmful effects. As such, the proposed chapter provides an analysis of computer vision and how to build resilience against online VE in Africa.

THE STUDY OBJECTIVES

This chapter will seek to achieve the following objectives:

1.   To analyse how computer vision helps in advancing radical and extreme ideologies; and,
2.   To examine tools to build resilience against online violent extremism in Africa.

COMPUTER VISION AND EXTREME IDEOLOGIES

There is a myriad of factors driving individuals to and out of violent extremism groups globally, these ranges from socio-economic conditions, psychological elements, conflict contexts, political contexts, marginalisation, illiteracy, racial or ethnic profiling, ideological orientation to conflicting ideological standpoint and values system (Diego Muro, 2017). For example, Gambetta and Hartog observe that relative deprivation and extremist ideologies have driven both educated and uneducated youth to join violent extremism groups in Africa and the rest of the world even though there is no causal link between education, poverty, inequality and radicalization (Diego Muro, 2017). While individuals join terrorist groups, certain forces again are pushing them out of the group. For example, Daniel Koehler (2017) opines that events such as violence within terrorist group ranks, latent homosexuality paired with militant homophobe actions, drug abuse, life-changing situations especially when in prison, loss of identity prompt some individuals to reconsider getting out of al-Qaeda, Islamic State (ISIL), Boko Haram, Al shabaab extremist groups.

The growth of new technologies, together with evolution of social media platforms have created a new ecosystem which terrorist organisations are tapping to advance extreme ideologies. This state of affairs has been worsened with vulnerabilities associated with computer system such as hyper-speed in data retrieval, anonymity among users, lack of delineated cyber borders and so forth (Nnam and Ajah, 2019). Through computer vision, terrorists can manipulate digital data to generate images to advance misinformation, abhorrence videos, extreme Islamic anecdotes, conspiracy narratives, spread extremist content and promote recruitment drive in online chat rooms, social platforms, webs or dark spaces (Rudner, 2013; RAN, 2021; Ogunlana, 2019) as exemplified my activities of Boko Haram, Al-shabaab and Salafi-jihadist terrorist organisations in subsequent sections. This kind of violence is the foundation upon which the force of computation rests when it comes to computer vision tasks through the conversion of those images into other data formats by computer vision systems, be that unique descriptors, captions, matches with faces in a known database, face recognition data, colour description, or some other parameter that the system is developed to produce (Rocco et al., 2021).

Terrorist organisations are exploiting computer vision to attract new members and expand their network of followers. The organisations are using graphic images of suffering around the Muslim World as they call upon their members and followers to take action in alleviating suffering of people. Through computer vision, the militant jihadist recruiters are able to show potential recruits graphically the inequality and evil actions inflicted upon Muslims convincing recruits that they have a role to play in building a fair prosperous world (Anne and Molly, 2020). To recruit minors, the recruiters are using narratives accompanied with cartoons, computer games, and popular music videos carrying messages that glorify acts of terror (UNODC, 2012). The same computer recruitment platforms provide avenues for dissemination of synthetic video clips, decrees, and documents on religious ethics, magazines, and manuals with topics such as how to plan and execute terrorist attacks; how to construct explosives; how to join terrorist organisations; hazardous materials and so forth (UNODC, 2012; Besenyö and Sinkó, 2021). For example, Alshabaab through al-Kata'ib Media Foundation has launched online recruitment campaigns including the one on: 'And Rouse the Believers'. This entails a series of synthetic videos encouraging more followers to join the terrorist group. These recruitment campaign videos have also featured in the other social media platforms such as telegram, Reddit, Facebook, and Twitter blended with images of martyrs and suffering of Muslims and the need for the youth to join the group to fight their enemies (Badurdeen, 2018). The group additionally reaches its followers and to-be recruiters in chat-rooms and dark web to conduct private conversations that may not be possible in the other social platforms (János Besenyö, Gábor Sinkó, 2021). While Boko Haram uses computer cyberspace to recruit and re-train members, share information and intelligence (Nnam and Ajah, 2019). Salafi-jihadist networks in Sahel is using offensive cyber capabilities, encrypted communications, the Dark Web, and artificial intelligence to distribute propaganda, recruit new members, conduct disinformation campaigns, and plan and orchestrate attacks (Byrne et al., 2018).

Computer vision is the primary tool terrorist organisations are using to disseminate propaganda. This generally takes the form of multimedia communications providing, ideological explanations or practical instruction, justifications or promotion of terrorist activities. These may include virtual messages, magazines, treatises, presentations, video and audio files and video games developed by terrorist organizations (UNODC, 2012: 3). Al-shabaab has released various propaganda videos for example, the African Crusaders: Fighting the West's War.' The video gives the message that all African suffering are of the West's interest (Besenyö and Sinkó, 2021). So they are campaigning against the West civilisation and ideals. For Boko Haram, it primarily uses social media platforms such as YouTube, Facebook, and Twitter as propaganda tools (Ogunlana, 2019; Besenyö and Sinkó, 2021).

The use of internet and computer vision systems has provided terrorist organisations a platform to propagate violence. The notable platform is chan sites that are facilitating in group status rotating around the consumption of violent extremism ideologies through the modern pop-cultural aesthetic deployed by users via memes, attracting a younger generation of digital natives who are initially drawn in by the visual culture, and then become slowly more tolerant of radical and extreme ideologies. Through this gradual indoctrination, a seemingly infinite number of racist, bigoted and misogynist worldviews are made more palatable (Crawford, Keen and Suarez de-Tangil, 2020). This platform is mostly used by Islamic State of Iraq and Syria (ISIS) normally trying to create fear in civilized societies by circulating video films of executions (Albahar, 2017). The other dominant terror groups in Africa are using internet, websites, videos, discussion forums and file hosting services to disseminate violence. For example during 2013 Westgate attack in Kenya, Al-shabaab generated Twitter content justifying the attack, creating fictional threats, providing news on hostages and mocking the police and military response (Mair, 2016). While, Boko Haram uses YouTube to transmit its activities as a way of intimidating people with messages of fear to force the Nigerian government to admit to its demands (Ogunlana, 2019).

Unchecked Online extremism has also caused unrest and violence with devastating impact to humanity. For example, online planning of the US Capitol invasion on January 6, 2021; the terrorist attack against French history teacher, Samuel Paty on October 16, 2020 who was falsely believed to have shown the image of Prophet Muhammad in offensive way. His assassination was planned and executed using Twitter platform; and the Christchurch mosque shootings on March 15, 2019 which was live streamed on Facebook before users could report the incident to Twitch to have the video removed from the platform (Joe Burton, 2020; Chandell Gosse and Jaigris Hodson, 2021). Another example where online hate speech and activism have contributed to sustainability of offline violence is the fight between Armenia and Azerbaijan over disputed Nagorno-Karabakh territory. Pro-Azerbaijani and Pro-Armenian diaspora online activists tapped social platform to share information about the conflict to international community since the conflict was given low coverage by international media due to its minimal international strategic importance. The activists also used the platform to pay tribute to causalities and soldiers, submit online petitions, and to coordinate online and offline resource mobilization to support the war (Dmitry Chernobrov, 2022). As such, Chandell Gosse and Jaigris Hodson (2021) discourages viewing online and offline contexts as distinct as this could potentially create a barrier in fighting online disinformation and misinformation campaigns as wellas conspiracy theories ending up to miss important opportunity to mitigate threats as they appear across online platforms.

BUILDING RESILIENCE AGAINST ONLINE VIOLENT EXTREMISM

One way of building resilience against violent extremism is through education. Transformative education is pertinent in forming the whole person as it help learners to reflect on themselves, examine their beliefs, values and knowledge, and challenge preconceived ideas about the other. This kind of education enables humans to think outside the box as it promotes open-mindedness regarding divergent worldviews, trust in the processes of reasoned inquiry, being self-critical, fair-mindedness in appraising reasoning besides inculcating values essential when it comes to countering online ideologies leading to violent extremism through strengthening commitment to non-violence and peace (UNESCO-IICBA, 2019; UNESCO, 2018). And as learning transcends the mind and connects with hearts and body by transforming knowledge, attitudes, skills, and the learner (Adeto, 2019) essential to thrive in the online ecosystem. Through education, we are able to critically asses what we see and hear through different media. This can help us to avoid the risk of believing false information and ensuring that our personal data is not misused as we reduce the risk of being the victim of cybercrime and violent ideologies (Teicher, 2019). More importantly, education develops in a person the art of asking questions: What are the sources of information? What is the source's background, what are their skills and area of expertise? What is their intention? (Teicher, 2019). Another example, when one offer a generalization or perception about another's behaviour, we need to ask him/her what the evidence for that statement is or how they know it is true. "Did Y say those actual words? Could there be another explanation for what Y said or did?" (OSCE and ODIHR, 2018). Furthermore, through education, one is able to understand anti-Semitism that is central in preventing extremism through acquired competencies fundamental to identify and reject anti-Semitic representations, extremist claims and conspiracy theories (OSCE and ODIHR, 2018).

While navigating within the social platforms, one is not supposed to like or share or comment about a message before carrying proper verification about its truthfulness. Failure to do so, in case the message was propagating violent ideologies, conspiracy theories, misinformation, hate speech and you have liked it for example, other online users might associate you with the content the message is carrying with possible negative repercussions. That is why UNESCO (2018) advises before sharing or liking or forwarding a message in a social media, we ought to do fact checking. This is composed of three phases:

1. Finding fact-checkable claims by scouring through legislative records, media outlets and social media. This process includes determining which major public claims (a) can be fact-checked and (b) ought to be fact-checked;

2. Finding the facts by looking for the best available evidence regarding the claim at hand; and,
3. Correcting the record by evaluating the claim in light of the evidence, usually on a scale of truthfulness.

Put in another way, we ought to be careful always on what we share as Papathanasaki and Maglaras (2020) enlightens, in case we detect spam accounts in our mails we should block them. In case we find unknown online users want to side chat us, we should avoid such advances. The authors further advise against the tendency of using hash-tags, this makes our profiles vulnerable to cyber criminals. And whenever we face misinformation or hate speech, we should do fact checking adhering to three phases we had highlighted above. And when reading an article, do not depend on the title of the article alone; get to read the content of the article before having to make any comment or remark about it. This is crucial if at all we have to win the war against misinformation and dis-information or propagandas disseminating violent ideologies. And in case if we have to do a counter-narrative, this should happen with a strong factual foundation and this may be accompanied with images and videos (United Nations Office on Drugs and Crime (UNODC), 2012).

Through computer vision, one might expose private information especially when using search engines such as Google to get very important information from diverse websites. This happens through cookies. For a website to work optimally well there are optional cookies which you can accept, reject or go to the option to manage preferences. By accepting cookies, one gives the computer consent to process your personal data or transfer your data to the third party sometimes to territories with minimal protection standards. In other words, this immersive sound installation exposes the proliferation of ubiquitous online surveillance via the real time sonification of internet tracking. Cookies are used for data profiling by advertising, corporations and governments, by placing a small file on the user's computer (Guffond, 2020 b). So if your personal data gets to wrong hands for example cyber criminals, terrorised organisations and so on it might be used to cause unintended harm. That is why one must be extremely cautious when making decision to accept cookies as this will go along the way in building resilience against violent extremism despite the fact that data protection and privacy commissioners have made a forceful intervention by adopting a declaration on ethics and data protection in artificial intelligence which spells out six principles for the future development and use of artificial intelligence that include fairness, accountability, transparency, privacy by design, empowerment and non-discrimination (Buttarelli, 2018).

To safeguard online users further technology companies are adding end-to-end encryption service when sending massages in platforms such as whatsapp and Gmail. Knutsson (2023) shares that in Gmail one can send encrypted emails both within and outside domain. This keeps messages extra safe as only the sender and the receiver are able to read the message. In addition, one could create a unique password for the file which the receiver should have in order to access the content of the file or decrypt personal data. This is especially important in this era of technology with many cyber elements including terrorists who could infiltrate online users Gmail accounts. One could also protect confidential and sensitive information from unlawful admission by getting allowed to set an expiration date for the messages or revoke access at any time. Recipients of these emails will not be allowed to forward, copy, download or print any content contained within the email (Knutsson, 2023).

Today, computer vision is being tapped as a tool for prevention of hate speech and violence. Artificial intelligence methods leverages large unstructured language datasets and convert them to structured data are helping relate specific language to outcomes; for example, the relationship between influential actors' language and violence is significant. As such, a language that can cause a violent behaviour from the recipient could be prevented through holding those responsible accountable (Chris Mahony, Jim Brumby and Huong Thi Lan Tran, 2021). Another tool is Spotlight which uses machine-learning capabilities to identify words, numbers, clusters, odd and/or unusual font, and other markers in advertisements that promote violent ideologies (Graham, 2022; Maras, 2017). Oggero et al. (2018) suggests that agile data algorithms, machine learning software, and threat alert mechanisms must be developed to automatically create alerts and drive quick response in countering and preventing violent extremism. However, these tools are likely to invade privacy of online users, therefore, causing violation of online ethical standards.

Despite the significant contributions computer vision and artificial intelligence is making towards detection and prevention of online violent extremism and hate speech, the new technology is posing some challenges. For instance, both state and nonstate actors can feed their own narratives and mis- and disinformation to their constituents within and across borders. Often, these narratives and falsehoods deliberately aim to stoke ethnic, religious, or political conflict (Eleonore Pauwels, 2020). Or it can infringe fundamental human rights from privacy and data confidentiality to freedom of choice and freedom of conscience (Audrey Azoulay, 2018). As such, many actors including international organizations, United Nations Member States, science academies, businesses, research centres, and civil society associations are calling for an ethical framework for AI development. While there is a growing understanding of the issues, related initiatives need more robust coordination as the issues are global in nature and reflection on them must take place at the global level so as to avoid a 'pick-and-choose' approach to ethics (Audrey Azoulay, 2018).

International community, however, is at forefront in establishing the framework that could help in mitigating online hate speech and violent extremism even though the process has been confronted with some challenges for example major powers

(China, USA, and Russia) refusing to get involved in the process despite support by major tech companies such as Facebook, Google and Microsoft (Joe Burton, 2020). For USA, the framework might have a negative impact on the first amendment to US constitution which guarantees freedom of speech, civil liberties, privacy, and civil rights (Joe Burton, 2020). However, the government of United States has continued to support efforts seeking to mitigate and prevent online violent extremism. For example, the Department of Homeland Security is supporting Counter-Messaging Efforts by Tech Companies, Non-Governmental Organizations, and Civic Partners: Private organizations and technology companies through providing grant funding to effective campaigns, sharing threat information, evaluating the efficacy of counternarrative efforts, engaging the technology sector to identify and amplify credible voices online and the convening of Digital Forums for Terrorism Prevention (Global Internet Forum to Counter Terrorism) that connect technology sector experts with civic leaders to catalyze prevention activities online (USA Department of Homeland Security, 2019). Furthermore, Daniel Koehler Ed (2017) has suggested counter-radicalization activities including involvement in research, participation in counter-narrative projects as strong and credible voices, workshops in schools explaining the risks of radicalization to the students, media projects, restorative justice, and Victim-Perpetrator Dialogue.

TECH AGAINST TERRORISM: A CASE STUDY OF COMPUTER VISION AND PREVENTION OF ONLINE VIOLENT EXTREMISM

Tech against Terrorism is one of the organisations applying computer vision and artificial intelligence driven platform to prevent terrorists and violent extremists from exploiting the internet. The organisation utilizes Terrorist Content Analytics Platform (TCAP) which automates the alerting of terrorist content (Tech against Terrorism, 2023). TCAP is the world's largest database of verified terrorist content, collected in real time from verified terrorist channels on messaging platforms and apps. The platform is a secure and transparent online tool to detect and verify terrorist content and notify technology companies of the presence of such content on their platforms (Tech Against Terrorism, 2020-2021). For example this year, Tech Against Terrorism disrupted several Terrorist Operated Websites (TOWs), responded to the hacking of a prominent social media account by a neo-Nazi, and discovered the latest creative attempts by Islamic State (IS) networks to exploit new and emerging platforms. IS -affiliated networks began using an emerging messaging app run by a company registered in Malta in mid-May. By early June, Tech Against Terrorism was monitoring 20+ IS-affiliated channels on the platform, most of which were posting identical content and posing as "official" IS propaganda channels (Tech Against Terrorism, 2023).

CONCLUSION

Computer vision driven by artificial intelligence is becoming a game changer for terrorist organisation in advancing their goals in Africa and the rest of the world in the one hand. On the other, governments and bodies engaging in war against terror are utilizing computer technology in gathering intelligence as they neutralise intended devastating impact by terrorist organisation. Artificial intelligence has helped to improve the welfare and well-being of people, to increase innovation and productivity, to contribute to positive sustainable global economic activity, and to help respond to key global challenges of peace (OECD, 2022). As seen from above discussion, this work is not real intended to change policy directions with regard to use of online platforms, but it seeks to enlighten online users so as to build their resilience against violent extremism through advocacy for transformative education, and digital literacy which entails use of data mining tools for intelligence gathering, fact checking, promoting the art of asking good questions while engaging with controversial online narratives and free thinking. All these, is likely to cushion online users from religious or politically motivated extreme ideologies that can cause violence.

REFERENCES

Adeto, Y. (2019). Transformative Pedagogy for Building Peace. In *Reconciliation, Peace and Global Citizenship Education: Pedagogy and Practice*. Author.

Agarwal, S., Farid, H., El-Gaaly, T., & Lim, S. (2020). Detecting Deep-Fake Videos from Appearance and Behavior. *WIFS, 2020*(December), 6–11. doi:10.1109/WIFS49906.2020.9360904

Albahar, M. (2017). Cyber Attacks and Terrorism: A Twenty-First Century Conundrum. *Sci Eng Ethics*. DOI doi:10.1007/s11948-016-9864

Azoulay, A. (2018). Towards an Ethics of Artificial Intelligence. New Technologies: Where To?

Badurdeen, F. (2018). Online Radicalisation and Recruitment: Al-Shabaab Luring Strategies with New Technology. In M. Ruteere & P. Mutahi (Eds.), *Confronting Violent Extremism in Kenya: Debates, Ideas and Challenges*. Centre for Human Rights and Policy Studies.

Besenyö, J., & Sinkó, G. (2021). The Social Media Use of African Terrorist Organizations: A Comparative Study of Al-Qaeda in the Islamic Maghreb, Al-Shabaab and Boko Haram. *Insights into Regional Development, 3*(3), 66–78. doi:10.9770/IRD.2021.3.3(4)

Burton, J. (2020). *Christchurch's Legacy of Fighting Violent Extremism Online Must go Further Deep into the Dark Web*. Retrieved August 23, 2023 from https://theconversation.com/christchurchs-legacy-of-fighting-violent-extremism-online-must-go-further-deep-into-the-dark-web-133159

Buttarelli, G. (2018). *What Do we Learn from Machine Learning?* European Data Protection Supervisor. Retrieved January 3, 2023 from https://edps.europa.eu/press-publications/press-news/blog/what-do-we-learn-machine-learning_en

Byrne et al. (2018) *The Evolution of the Salafi-Jihadist Threat: Current and Future Challenges from the Islamic State, Al-Qaeda, and Other Groups*. A Report of Center for Strategic and International Studies Transnational Threat Project.

Chernobrov, D. (2022). Diasporas as Cyberwarriors: Infopolitics, Participatory Warfare and the 2020 Karabakh War. *International Affairs, 98*(2), 631–651. doi:10.1093/ia/iiac015

Crawford, B., Keen, F., & Suarez de-Tangil, G. (2020). *Memetic Irony and the Promotion of Violence within Chan Cultures*. CREST Centre for Research and Evidence on Security Threats.

Gosse, C., & Hodson, J. (2021). *Not two Different Worlds: QAnon and the Offline Dangers of Online Speech*. Retrieved August 23, 2023 from https://theconversation.com/not-two-different-worlds-qanon-and-the-offline-dangers-of-online-speech-159668

Guffond, J. (2020). *The Web Never Forgets*. Retrieved January 10, 2023 from http://jasmineguffond.com/?path=art/The+Web+Never+Forgets

Heidelberg Institute for International Conflict Research (HIIK). (2022). *Conflict Barometer*. Author.

Jamie Kay Graham. (2022). *The Dark Web and Human Trafficking*. PhD Dissertation Liberty University.

Koehler, D. (2017). *Understanding Deradicalization Methods, tools and programs for countering violent extremism*. Routledge.

Kurt Knutsson. (2023). *Turn this Gmail Security Feature on ASAP*. Retrieved January 2, 2023 from https://www.foxnews.com/tech/turn-gmail-security-feature-asap

Mahony, C., Brumby, J., & Thi Lan Tran, H. (2021). *AI can help trace language to violence*. Retrieved August 24, 2023 from https://blogs.worldbank.org/governance/ai-can-help-trace-language-violence

Mair, D. (2016). Westgate: a Case Study-How al-Shabaab Used Twitter During an Ongoing Attack. In A. Aly, S. Macdonald, L. Jarvis, & T. Chen (Eds.), *Violent Extremism Online: New Perspectives on Terrorism and the Internet*. Routledge Publishers.

Maras, M. (2017). Social Media Platforms: Targeting the "Found Space" of Terrorists. *Journal of International Law*.

Muro, D. (2017). Engineers of Jihad: The Curious Connection between Violent Extremism and Education. *Terrorism and Political Violence*, *29*(6), 1154–1156. do i:10.1080/09546553.2017.1377559

Nnam, M., & Ajah, B. (2019). The War Must be Sustained: An Integrated Theoretical Perspective of the Cyberspace-Boko Haram Terrorism Nexus in Nigeria. *International Journal of Cyber Criminology*, *13*(2).

OECD. (2022). *Recommendation of the Council on Artificial Intelligence*, OECD/LEGAL/0449. http://www.jasmineguffond.com/?path=art/Listening+Back

Oggero. (2018). Content-based Multimedia Analytics: US and NATO Research. *Proc. SPIE*. doi:10.1117/12.2307756

Ogunlana, S. (2019). Halting Boko Haram / Islamic State's West Africa Province Propaganda in Cyberspace with Cybersecurity Technologies. *Journal of Strategic Security*, *12*(1), 72–106. doi:10.5038/1944-0472.12.1.1707

OSCE & ODIHR. (2018). *Challenging Conspiracy Theories*. Authors.

Papathanasaki, M., & Maglaras, L. (2020). *The Current Posture of Cyber Warfare and Cyber Terrorism*. Global Foundation for Cyber Studies and Research.

Pauwels, E. (2020). *Artificial Intelligence and Data Capture Technologies in Violence and Conflict Prevention: Opportunities and Challenges for the International Community*. Global Center on Cooperative Security.

RAN. (2021). *Digital Challenges: Terrorists' Use of the Internet and the Challenges Coming out of Covid*. Author.

Rocco. (2021). Toward a Critique of Algorithmic Violence. *International Political Sociology*, *15*(1), 121–150. Advance online publication. doi:10.1093/ips/olab003

Rudner, M. (2013). Cyber-Threats to Critical National Infrastructure: An Intelligence Challenge. *International Journal of Intelligence and CounterIntelligence*, *26*(3), 453–481. doi:10.1080/08850607.2013.780552

Tech Against Terrorism. (2023). *The Disruption Report*. Retrieved August 24, 2023 from https://www.techagainstterrorism.org/2023/07/31/the-disruption-report/

Tech Against Terrorism. (2020-2021). *Transparency Report: Terrorist Content Analytics Platform*. Author.

Teicher, F. (2019). The role of Media and Information Literacy. In *Reconciliation, Peace and Global Citizenship Education: Pedagogy and Practice*. Author.

UNESCO. (2018). *Journalism, 'Fake News' and Disinformation*. UNESCO.

UNESCO-IICBA. (2019). *Youth Empowerment for Peace and Resilience Building and Prevention of Violent Extremism in Sahel and Surrounding Countries: A Guide for Teachers*. UNESCO-IICBA.

United Nations Office on Drugs and Crime (UNODC). (2012). *The Use of the Internet for Terrorist Purposes*. Author.

USA Department of Homeland Security. (2019). *Strategic Framework for Countering Terrorism and Targeted Violence*. Author.

Chapter 4
Detection of Vulnerabilities in Cryptocurrency Smart Contracts Based on Image Processing

Gabbi Evrard Tchoukouegno De Mofo
University of Ngaoundéré, Cameroon

Ali Joan Beri Wacka
University of Buea, Cameroon

Franklin Tchakounte
 https://orcid.org/0000-0003-0723-2640
University of Ngaoundéré Cameroon

Jean Marie Kuate Fotso
Ministry of Scientific Research and Innovation, Cameroon & University of Ngaoundéré, Cameroon

ABSTRACT

The rate of use of cryptocurrencies through smart contracts and decentralized applications remains continually increasing. Ethereum is particularly gaining popularity in the blockchain community. In this work, the authors are interested in retraining vulnerability and timestamping. They propose a detection method based on the transformation of contracts into images and the processing of the latter using Simhash and n-gram techniques to obtain our contracts into images of size 32*32. They combine a technique to preserve the useful characteristics of images for

DOI: 10.4018/978-1-6684-8127-1.ch004

exploitation. Training carried out with the convolutional neuronal network (CNN) model on a sample of 50 normal contracts, 50 contracts vulnerable to retraining, and 33 vulnerable to timestamping gave an accuracy of 88.98% on the detection of vulnerable contracts. The singular value decomposition (SVD) technique is capable of efficiently extracting from images, the key features that characterize contracts in Ethereum.

1. INTRODUCTION

A cryptocurrency is a digital, decentralized and virtual currency (no need for banknotes, coins, credit cards, checkbooks) which uses cryptographic algorithms and a protocol called blockchain to ensure the reliability and traceability of transactions.

The idea of this currency dates back to the 1980s. But in concrete terms, we will have, in 1983, David Chaum who will introduce the possibility of withdrawing money electronically from a bank and then spending it at merchants accepting this method of payment (Yazid, 2023). In 1998, Wei Dai was the first to propose the creation of virtual currencies through consensus. He did not issue details about the implementation of the consensus method (Sudhani, Divakar, & Girish, 2022). In 2008, Satoshi Nakamoto unveiled Bitcoin (Paul, 2023), considered the first successful project that was implemented on the blockchain. To ensure its operation, the creator unveils the "proof-of-work" consensus method. This allows peers in the network to communicate with each other and agree on the validity of transactions. However, there are so many cryptocurrencies (Figure 1) these days that it can be difficult to tell them apart. We can have in others: coins, the store of value, the means of exchange, the "exchange" of tokens, Decentralized Finance (DEFI), smart contract platforms (ADAM, 2023). Since its creation, the rate of users of cryptocurrencies has continued to grow over the years. At the end of 2019, there were nearly 2,400 cryptocurrencies on the coin-marketcap site (Vitalik). In 2015, the Ethereum cryptocurrency brought a major innovation to the field of blockchains. This platform enabled the development and deployment of applications on blockchains.

2. SMART CONTRACTS AND MINING

2.1 Smart Contract

Smart contracts are scripts stored on the blockchain. They have a unique address (Joonseok, Sumin, & Keunhyuk, 2023).

Figure 1. Popular cryptocurrencies in 2020 (Conti et al., 2018)

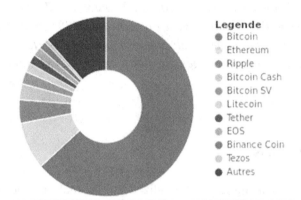

A Smart Contract, as Vitalik Buterin describes it, is "a program that directly controls digital assets". Vitalik Buterin is the senior developer who imagined ETHEREUM, sometimes referred to as bitcoin 2.0 (Roberto, 2019).

A smart contract can define rules, like a normal contract, and enforce them automatically through code. These contracts have a wide range of possibilities (Monika & Gernot, 2019; Sujeetha and Preetha, 2021):

- Operate as multi-signature accounts implementing additional conditions, such as the fact that funds can only be spent when a defined percentage of signatories agree;
- Manage agreements between users, like traditional contractual agreements;
- Can be used by other contracts, so that they "offset" certain functionalities to existing contracts;
- Store information about an app, such as app member logs.

The blockchain makes it possible to secure and verify the data allowing the execution of a smart contract; it is not possible to modify the conditions of the contract once deployed. A smart contract has several advantages (Antonios, Christos, & Georgios, 2023):

- Security: All data exchanged by the smart contract is protected by cryptography. It will be very difficult for a hacker to crack them;
- Autonomy: A smart contract deployed on the blockchain does not require any intervention from a third person to carry out the various operations programmed for it;

- Saving money: A smart contract makes it possible to eliminate the "man in the middle" (a notary in the case of a sale of real estate, for example). In this case, it allows you to save notary fees;
- Speed: As smart contracts replace the intermediary in the case of a transaction, the time spent on paperwork is no longer necessary; so we save time.

Different programming languages have been developed for the implementation of smart contracts, such as: Solidity, Serpent, Pact, Viper, Liquidity, Chaincode, or even Mutan (Lee, Purnima, Jonathan, & Peter) (Majd, · Gısli, & Mohammad).

2.2 Mining

Mining is an operation which consists of validating transactions on the blockchain (Figure 2). To carry out this task we need a miner. They validate and produce new blocks on the blockchain and each of them has a full copy of the data ledger and validates the contents. They recalculate the digital fingerprints of each block to ensure data integrity. When new transactions are accepted, they add them to the ledger. Since all this work requires a lot of computing power and consumes energy. They receive monetary compensation (Carlos, Carlis, & Julio, 2022).

Figure 2. Block in a blockchain system

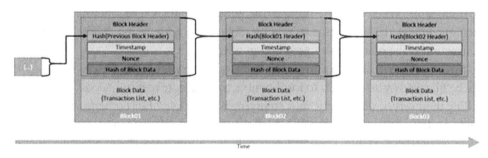

Since miners are paid on the basis of work done, it is important to produce proof. The concept of consensus defines the rules which will define the functioning of the blockchain. It lays the foundations of the system in terms of security and establishes trust so that the system is unanimous.

There are several consensus algorithms including: proof of stake (PoS), proof of activity (PoA), proof of knowledge (PoK), practical Byzantine fault tolerance (PBFT). Each algorithm has its own advantages and weaknesses depending on the use case (Jega, 2014).

2.2.1 Vulnerability of Smart Contracts

Hackers take advantage of vulnerabilities defined in consensus algorithms, network architecture and applications. Consensus algorithms define how storage technology will behave. They undergo various attacks to take control. A 51% attack is an attack that involves controlling the majority of nodes or more than 50% of the total computing power of the network. This makes it possible to reject valid blocks which will have to be added to the main chain, and added malicious content. This attack depends on the consensus algorithm used and the type of blockchain. The main threat of the 51% attack comes from public blockchains that use proof of work (Muhammed, 2020).

The downside with digital currencies is that data can be copied. As with physical currencies, these copies will massively increase the number of coins available, which will lower their value. This is the reason why Bitcoin verifies every transaction (Mubashar & Raimundas, 2021) (Sachin & Kaushal, 2022).

Double spending refers to an attacker spending currency twice by bypassing the verification mechanism. This is because it takes time to confirm transactions. There are two double payment techniques that attackers use in the world of cryptocurrencies:

Racing attack: the hacker launches two transactions at the same time. Only one of the transactions can be validated. This allows the attacker to recover twice as much well for the same amount. If both receivers do not wait for confirmation first.

Finney's attack: In a Finney attack, funds are used in a transaction, but the attacker withholds a pre-prepared block with the same transaction in one of their own accounts. When the store releases the goods, the attacker broadcasts his block, then invalidates the initial transaction by making the network believe that the real transaction is the one that was prepared in advance.

Smart contracts allow for invoking and using external code. This external call can be hijacked by an attacker to force contracts to execute reentrant code, including calling themselves recursively, thus emptying the contract of its contents. This is the vulnerability of reentrancy. We also have the timestamp dependence, which occurs when a contract uses block variables as call conditions to perform certain critical operations (such as token transfers). Some variables are rooted in the block header, including BLOCKHASH, TIMESTAMP, NUMBER... Consequently, they originate from miners. The TIMESTAMP block can be adjusted with a 900-second offset. If cryptocurrencies are transferred based on block variables, miners can exploit the vulnerability by altering them. These are not the only vulnerabilities; we also have transaction order dependence (TOD), integer overflow and underflow, and poorly handled exceptions (Samreen et al, 2021).

Blockchain technology is used by various applications. Each of these applications has its own strengths and weaknesses regarding cryptocurrency loss, as well as different areas of use. We have, among others: Cryptojacking, Timejacking, Replay attack (Firdaus, AlDharhani, Ismail, & Razak, 2023). However, two methodologies can be used to analyze its attacks. Static detection techniques analyze the smart contract in a static environment by examining its source code or bytecode. This first methodology generally exploits techniques such as: Symbolic execution, Construction of a CFG (control flow graph), Rule-based analysis, Decompilation analysis, Pattern recognition. Dynamic analysis compensates for analysis during operation through techniques such as execution traces, generation of fuzzing inputs.

3. EXIT SOLUTIONS

Researchers have proposed various approaches to make the world of cryptocurrencies more secure (Saad et al., 2019).

By analyzing the problems associated with mathematical constructs of blockchains, we proposed a Byzantine fault-tolerant blockchain protocol that addresses the problems of forks in blockchains (Eyal and Sirer, 2014).

Decker and Wattenhofer (2013) observed the propagation of information in the Bitcoin network and introduced a model that explains the formation of forks in blockchains. From their results, they concluded that delays in block propagation are the main cause of blockchain forks.

Kiffer et al. (2017) analyzed the Ethereum design space and studied a large-scale fork that partitioned Ethereum into two separate networks (Ethereum and Ethereum Classic). They then analyzed the impact of the fork on users, mining pools and both networks, exploring the possible gains and security vulnerabilities of the result.

Heilman (2016) and Solat and Potop-Butucaru (2017) proposed countermeasures for selfish mining and block retention. Heilman used tamper-proof timestamps to increase the mining power threshold to achieve selfish mining.

Bastiaan (2015) proposed a defense against the 51% attack through a stochastic analysis of the two-phase proof of work (2P-PoW), initially proposed by Eyal and Sirer (2014). 2P-PoW prevents a mining pool's hash rate from growing beyond a limit. It does this by forcing pool owners to reduce their hashing power or give up their private keys.

The area of DDoS attacks on blockchains and mempools remains an open problem and, as such, countermeasures are proposed, including: increasing throughput, increasing block size and limiting transaction size. Since DDoS attacks manifest themselves differently in a peer-to-peer architecture, as opposed to a centralized system, their prevention also requires unconventional approaches (Vyas, 2014).

Solat and Potop-Butucaru (2017) Use a modified signature scheme that exposes the double-spender's private key in fast transactions. Their proposed method protects an optimistic bitcoin user who might be ready to deliver the product before confirmation of the received transaction.

Atzei et al. (2017) Analyzed possible attacks on Ethereum smart contracts with a focus on DAO attacks. They classify attacks based on vulnerabilities associated with the Solidity programming language, the Ethereum Virtual Machine (EVM), and the Ethereum blockchain.

Chen et al. (2020) Introduced an adaptive gas cost mechanism for Ethereum to defend against underpaid denial-of-service attacks.

Luu et al. (2016), studied the different possibilities by which an adversary can compromise smart contracts on Ethereum. They also developed a symbolic execution tool, OYENTE, which reactively finds and fixes bugs in Ethereum smart contracts.

ContractWard detects smart contract vulnerability at the opcode level by extracting bigram features from the simplified opcode and training individual binary machine learning-based classifiers for each vulnerability class (Zhuang et al., 2021). The paper targets six vulnerabilities and experiments with RandomForests, K-Nearest Neighbors, SVM, AdaBoost, and XGBoost classifiers. This article uses "One versus Rest" algorithms and designs distinct learning models to detect each vulnerability class. This means that supporting a new vulnerability class requires training a new learning model to scratch, which is expensive.

Based on LSTM, the paper Tann et al. (2018) proposes a sequence learning approach to detect the weakness of the opcode of smart contracts. In particular, this paper uses one-shot encoding and an embedding matrix to represent the contract opcode. The resulting code vectors are used as input to train an LSTM model to determine whether the given smart contract is secure or vulnerable. The LSTM model only provides a binary decision on contract security without distinguishing between vulnerability types.

Based on GNN, the article Zhuang et al. (2021) proposes an approach based on networks (GNN). In particular, this work constructs a contract graph from the contract source code where the nodes and edges represent the critical function or variable calls and the temporal execution trace. This graph is normalized to highlight important nodes and fed to a temporal message propagation network for vulnerability detection. The article (Zhuang et al., 2021) requires constructing a graph from the contract source code. However, source code is generally difficult to obtain from the public blockchain.

Based on CNN, the paper (Huang, 2018) transforms the contract bytecode into fixed-size RGB color images and trains a convolutional neural network for vulnerability detection. The CNN architecture ignores the existing sequential information in the contract. The images that they pass to the CNN should be further processed to obtain a better quality result with an image preprocessing technique called SVD, which consists of decomposing a matrix into a product of 3 matrices U, S and V

(S is called the matrix of singular values whose contribution we have shown in the proposed method. The detection method based on CNN is neither discussed nor evaluated in this article. To remedy the limitations mentioned above and in noticing that vulnerable contracts, if they share the same vulnerability, will behave in the same way. All these detection tools and methods use different techniques to extract features and build an intelligent vulnerability detection system.

4. OUR APPROACH

Our approach to vulnerability detection in smart contracts using CNN is inspired by existing work. The goal is to combine several image processing techniques by extracting key features to detect reentrancy and timestamp dependency vulnerabilities. Through an experiment on a retraining and timestamp dependence sample, the detection performance will be evaluated.

The work relies on the n-gram and the simhash algorithm to visually represent contracts. We use the singular value decomposition (SVD) technique to extract useful values in the images before feeding them to our learning algorithm.

4.1 Architecture of the Approach

Figure 3. Architecture

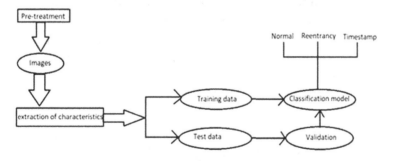

This architecture (Figure 3) can be summarized by the following steps:

- Data collection: This phase consists of collecting smart contracts which will constitute our data (samples) for training and testing our model.
- Data preprocessing: This involves the transformation of our various smart contracts into images.

- Extraction of image characteristics: This step allows us to have the different characteristics extracted from our images which will be ready to be provided by our learning algorithm.
- Division of data for testing and learning purposes: The division of our knowledge base or dataset is made into two main parts, one for learning and the other for testing.
- Learning model: The objective is to study the relevance and reliability of the proposed model according to performance and after comparison with similar work.

4.2 Data Collection

Data collection is defined as the procedure of collecting, measuring and analyzing accurate data for research using standard validated techniques. A researcher can evaluate his hypothesis based on the data collected. In most cases, data collection is the main and most important step of research, regardless of the age of the research. The approach to data collection is different across fields of study, depending on the information required.

The most important goal of data collection is to ensure that the data is rich in reliable information and is collected for statistical analysis so that data-driven decisions can be made for research.

Any process based on building a model from artificial intelligence uses the ETL (Extract Transform Load) method; In this method, it involves identifying data sources, transforming the data from these sources and loading it into an analysis engine.

Data collection is part of the first step in this process. This step involves identifying sources through which we can obtain smart contracts that can be used in our analysis. More precisely, it involves collecting a set of malicious smart contracts and analyzing them.

4.2.1 Image Transformation Approach

Regarding the construction of the image (Figure 4), this was carried out in several stages using a script written in Python, in which we used a good number of libraries (Nltk, Hashlib, Xmltodict, Binascii, Skimage) with:

Hashlib: This module implements an interface common to many secure algorithms for hashing and digesting SHA1, SHA224, SHA256 messages.

Nltk: Natural language toolkit is a pre-designed Python software library for automatic language processing.

Binascii: This module contains a number of methods for converting binary representations to various ASCII-encoded binary representations.

Figure 4. Image preprocessing

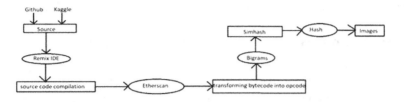

Skimage: SciKit image, or sKimage, is an open python package designed for image preprocessing.

For the extraction of features from images, we used the technique of Singular Value Decomposition (SVD), which is a mathematical method used in various applications in various fields of science and technology. After all its transformation, the data is trained with the CNN model.

5. EXPERIMENTS, RESULTS, AND DISCUSSIONS

For the working environment, the experimentation support is divided into two main components.

Hardware: Intel ® Corel ™i3-3110M CPU@2.40GHz microprocessor; 4GB RAM; 500GB hard drive.

Software: Kali linux 2020 operating system; Jupyter notebook text editor; VS Code; Python Programming Language.

5.1 Experimenting With the Classic CNN

The experimentation of our approach is based on the same steps as those planned by the model proposal. In this process we export the smart contracts on the tools in order to obtain a concrete detection model.

For our multiclass architecture we used several labels, 0 for normal contracts, 1 for contracts vulnerable to retraining and 2 for contracts vulnerable to timestamp dependence.

We first generated the operation codes for each contract, produced them using the python script, then we matched each opcode to a hash using the Simhash function. Since the length of opcode sequences for each vulnerable contract varies, it is difficult to compare the similarity of sequences of different length. SimHash, is used for sequence similarity comparison. SimHash is a local sensitive hashing algorithm proposed by Charikar (2002) and is mainly used for recognition of similar texts and identification of web page duplication (Manku et al., 2007).

5.2 Sample Collection

We collected 133 contracts (50 for normal smart contracts, 50 for contracts vulnerable (Figure 6) to retraining and 33/for those vulnerable to timestamp dependence). The normal contracts (Figure 6) were collected via Kaggle, which is a site which provides reliable datasets. Our vulnerable contracts were collected via a vulnerability detection tool, GNNSCVulDetector, available on GitHub, from which the source of the contracts comes from Etherscan.

Figure 5. Sample of normal contracts

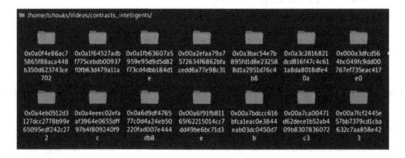

Figure 6. Sample of vulnerable contracts

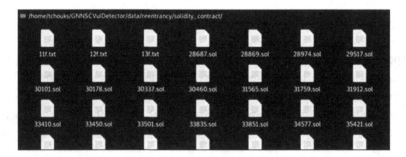

5.3 Sample Pretreatment

This part presents step by step the process to obtain images of our contracts before launching training with a multi-class learning model.

Step 1: After obtaining our sample (smart contracts), we go to Remix, which is a programming interface (Figure 7) for Ethereum smart contracts, and uses Solidity as a programming language. In Remix, we put each contract in the interface and compile the contract code in order to obtain the intermediate code between the machine instructions and the source code (bytecode).

Figure 7. Interface remix

Then we go to Etherscan (Figure 8) which is a public browser of the Ethereum blockchain to transform the bytecode obtained into operations code.

Step 2: this step consists of structuring the opcodes in a text file (Figure 9) to generate the 2- gram with a python script before applying the Simhash algorithm on the entire text. Figure 10 illustrates the hash obtained with Simhash. Since the length of opcode sequences for each vulnerable contract varies, it is difficult to compare the similarity of sequences of different lengths. SimHash,is used for sequence similarity comparison. SimHash is a local sensitive hashing algorithm proposed by Charikar (Jiang and Sun, 2011) and is mainly used for similar text recognition and web page duplication identification (Manku et al., 2007).

Figure 8. Etherscan browser interface

Figure 9. Structured operation codes

```
ne > tchouks > Vidéos > contracts_opcode
  1    PUSH1 0x60
  2    PUSH1 0x40
  3    MSTORE
  4    PUSH1 0x04
  5    CALLDATASIZE
  6    LT
  7    PUSH2 0x0171
  8    JUMPI
  9    PUSH4 0xffffffff
 10    PUSH1 0xe0
 11    PUSH1 0x02
 12    EXP
 13    PUSH1 0x00
 14    CALLDATALOAD
 15    DIV
 16    AND
 17    PUSH4 0x2c4e722e
```

Figure 10. Hash 512

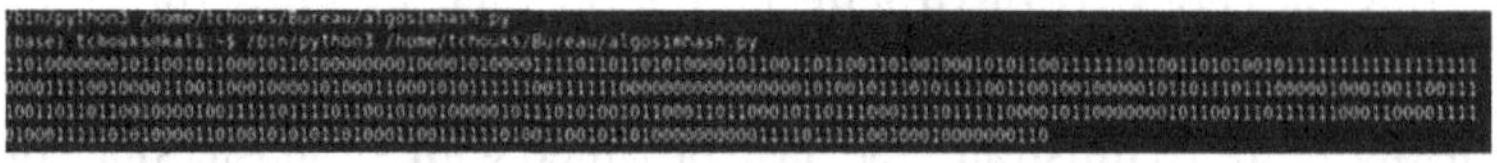

Step 3: We transform the hash obtained into an image using a python script. Figure 11 shows an example smart contract image.

Figure 11. Opcode

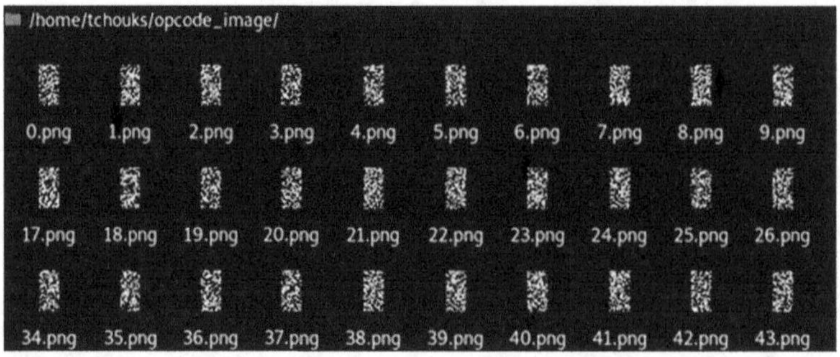

After transforming our smart contracts into an image, we will use them to do deep learning (Figure 12) using a multi-class CNN to make predictions on the retraining, timestamp dependence and contract classes normal.

Figure 12. Training data

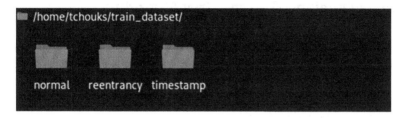

5.4 Prediction With CNN

Before seeing the different results, we defined different parameters depending on our dataset, the type of classification we want to perform and the divisions we want to make (Figure 13).

- Optimizer: Algorithm used to update the weights of our CNN. "Adam" (Gradient Descent) is one of the popular optimizers used to update weights.

Figure 13. CNN parameters

```
datagen = ImageDataGenerator(
                    rescale=1./255,
                    validation_split = 0.3)
train_generator = datagen.flow_from_directory(
    path_dir,
    target_size=(32,32),
    shuffle=True,
    subset='training'
)
validation_generator = datagen.flow_from_directory(
    path_dir,
    target_size=(32,32),
    subset='validation'
)

Found 94 images belonging to 3 classes.
Found 39 images belonging to 3 classes.
model.compile(
    optimizer=tf.keras.optimizers.Adam(lr=0.0001),
    loss=tf.keras.losses.CategoricalCrossentropy(from_logits=True)
    metrics=['accuracy']
```

- Loss: Cost function used to calculate the error between the predicted value and the actual value. In our case, we will use "categorical_crossentropy" since we are dealing with multiclass classification. In the case of binary classification, we need to use "binary_crossentropy" as the loss function.
- Metrics: Evaluation metric to check the performance of our model.

5.5 Results Obtained With the CNN Algorithm

After partitioning the test and training data, using a classification model based on the multi class CNN algorithm gives the following results (Table 2):

Table 1. Metrics obtained with CNN

	Precision	Accuracy	Recall	F1-Score
80-20	78.02%	72.35%	80.20%	79.09
75-25	78.45%	72.28%	81.05%	80.20
70-30	78.80%	72.60%	84.74%	81.64

Figure 14. Representative accuracy curve using CNN

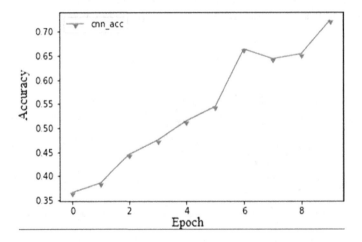

Figure 15 represents the loss during training and validation of our data. This is the sum of errors made for each training and validation set. The more the curve tends towards zero, the more efficient the model is. Unlike the accuracy curve (Figure 14) where the more the curve increases, the more precise the model is and performs correct classifications.

Figure 15. Representative curve of the loss using the CNN

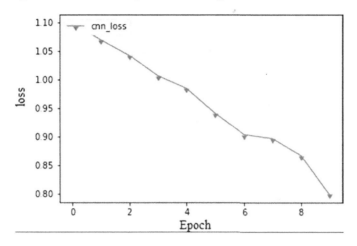

5.6 Experimentation With the SVD Method

This part consists of studying the performance of the model after extracting features with the SVD method (Figure 16). This script takes the input images and runs SVD on those images and produces the output singular matrix represented by the singular values specific to each image (Figure 17).

Figure 16. Applying the SVD script We use the SVD to extract the U and V matrices

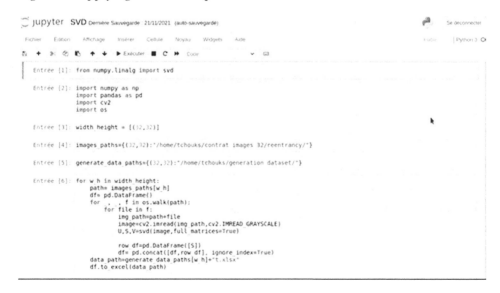

Figure 17. Matrices extracted by the SVD

```
Entrée [28]: U
    Out[28]: array([[-0.19385898,  0.25077113,  0.25653527, ...,  -0.2690864 ,
                      0.21001979, -0.06642302],
                     [-0.19736693, -0.12201352, -0.1372422 , ...,  -0.31691705,
                      0.19958164,  0.20434639],
                     [-0.21313057, -0.13809514, -0.1129197 , ...,  -0.03989136,
                      0.01558833,  0.23559561],
                     ....
                     [-0.1805329 ,  0.0628689 , -0.30238989, ...,  -0.02979757,
                      0.07578348,  0.20123727],
                     [-0.15308863,  0.02066764, -0.32790494, ...,   0.06740648,
                     -0.11883379, -0.02948016],
                     [-0.18676367, -0.11096195,  0.11128528, ...,  -0.1182789 ,
                      0.11832865, -0.26240452]]))

Entrée [29]: S
    Out[29]: array([[4.23327982e+03, 1.33813343e+03, 1.22060239e+03, 1.09053545e+03,
                     1.05546519e+03, 9.90039115e+02, 8.29272657e+02, 8.09557195e+02,
                     7.88057031e+02, 6.93462506e+02, 6.90625878e+02, 6.30965783e+02,
                     5.15246186e+02, 5.05693706e+02, 4.12595320e+02, 3.52074019e+02,
                     1.04243400e+01, 8.93578763e+00, 7.83901483e+00, 7.37906282e+00,
                     6.91415682e+00, 5.74422067e+00, 5.23863418e+00, 4.67914950e+00,
```

After extracting the matrix V, we transform the matrix S into a vector. Our new dataset is represented by Figure 18:

Figure 18. Data grouped according to their class

To carry out our learning we labeled our extracted data with the SVD: Normal: 0; Retraining: 1; Timestamp: 2.

After the two experiments, we note that depending on the different divisions noted noted the samples, the application of the SVD method provides better results in terms of accuracy, precision, recall and F1-Score. Which clearly shows us an improvement in performance metrics (Table 2).

Table 2. Metrics obtained with the SVD method

Splitting	Precision	Accuracy	Recall	F1-Score
80-20	90.02%	88.02%	90.5%	90.25
75-25	90.55%	88.50%	90.04%	90.29
70-30	90.70%	88.98%	91.26%	90.97

6. DISCUSSION

In the existing works, several focuses on the detection of vulnerabilities in smart contracts. But it focused on those dealing with static analysis based on pattern recognition and image processing, with particular attention to Huang's work, which presented a methodology for analyzing potential attacks on smart contracts. They translated the solidity bytecode into RGB color code, transformed it into images of fixed sizes and transmitted it to the convolutional neural network for machine learning. We therefore carry out a comparison according to several criteria between our approach and that of Huang (Table 3).

Table 3. Comparison with the existing

Criteria		Our Approach
Type of Samples	Smart Contracts	Smart Contracts
Structure	Bytecode	Opcode
Image processing	Convert bytecode into color code	Convert opcode into image based on 2-gram and Simhash
Image type	M*M	32*32
Accuracy	83.65	88.98

As a result, our approach has a contributory and significant result for the security of smart contracts.

CONCLUSION

The main objective of this work was to be able to detect vulnerabilities present in cryptocurrency smart contracts based on image processing. It emerges from our work that the image virtualization of smart contracts by considering the instruction sequence (N-gram) and the use of the Simhash algorithm to obtain similar hashes is of very great interest. This process makes it possible to classify a normal contract which is vulnerable to retraining or timestamping. The SVD method has proven to be very effective in improving the performance of the learning model. For future work it would be interesting to use other n-gram sequences and to classify several other types of vulnerability.

REFERENCES

Adam, H. (2023, August 25). *10 Important Cryptocurrencies Other Than Bitcoin.* Retrieved February 09, 2024, from https://www.investopedia.com/tech/most-important-cryptocurrencies-other-than-bitcoin/

Antonios, G., Christos, K. G., & Georgios, D. (2023, Decembre 23). A Comparative Analysis of Ethereum Solidity and Sui Move Smart Contract Languages: Advantages and Trade-Offs. *2023 6th World Symposium on Communication Engineering (WSCE).* 10.1109/WSCE59557.2023.10365887

Atzei, N., Bartoletti, M., & Cimoli, T. (2017). A survey of attacks on ethereum smart contracts (sok). *Principles of Security and Trust: 6th International Conference, POST 2017, Held as Part of the European Joint Conferences on Theory and Practice of Software, ETAPS 2017, Uppsala, Sweden, April 22-29, 2017 Proceedings, 6,* 164–186.

Bastiaan, M. (2015, January). *Preventing the 51%-attack: a stochastic analysis of two phase proof of work in bitcoin.* Available at http://referaat. cs. utwente. nl/ conference/22/paper/7473/preventingthe-51-attack-a-stochasticanalysis-oftwo-phase-proof-of-work-in-bitcoin. pdf

Carlos, G., Carlis, R., & Julio, L. (2022, September 29). eSi-BTC: an energy efficient Bitcoin mining core. *2022 35th SBC/SBMicro/IEEE/ACM Symposium on Integrated Circuits and Systems Design (SBCCI).* 10.1109/SBCCI55532.2022.9893218

Chen, H., Pendleton, M., Njilla, L., & Xu, S. (2020). A survey on ethereum systems security: Vulnerabilities, attacks, and defenses. *ACM Computing Surveys, 53*(3), 1–43. doi:10.1145/3391195

Conti, M., Kumar, E. S., Lal, C., & Ruj, S. (2018). A survey on security and privacy issues of bitcoin. *IEEE Communications Surveys and Tutorials, 20*(4), 3416–3452. doi:10.1109/COMST.2018.2842460

Decker, C., & Wattenhofer, R. (2013, September). Information propagation in the bitcoin network. In IEEE P2P 2013 Proceedings (pp. 1-10). IEEE. doi:10.1109/ P2P.2013.6688704

Eyal, I., & Sirer, E. G. (2014). *How to disincentivize large bitcoin mining pools.* http://hackingdistributed. com/2014/06/18/how-to-disincentivize-large-bitcoin-mining-pools

Firdaus, A., AlDharhani, G. S., Ismail, Z., & Razak, M. F. (2023, January 23). The Summer Heat of Cryptojacking Season: Detecting Cryptojacking using Heatmap and Fuzzy. *2022 International Conference on Cyber Resilience (ICCR).* 10.1109/ICCR56254.2022.9995891

Heilman, E. K. (2016, October). Eclipse attacks on bitcoin's peer-to-peer network. *Proceedings of the 2016 ACM SIGSAC conference on computer and communications security.*

Huang, T. H. D. (2018). Hunting the ethereum smart contract: Color-inspired inspection of potential attacks. *arXiv preprint arXiv:1807.01868.*

Jega, A. D. (2014, September 18). Bitcoin mining acceleration and performance quantification. *2014 IEEE 27th Canadian Conference on Electrical and Computer Engineering (CCECE).*

Jens, D. (2022, June). *Satoshi Nakamoto and the Origins of Bitcoin — Narratio in Nomine, Datis et Numeris.* doi:/arXiv.2206.10257 doi:10.48550

Jiang, Q., & Sun, M. (2011, June). Semi-supervised simhash for efficient document similarity search. In *Proceedings of the 49th annual meeting of the association for computational linguistics: Human language technologies* (pp. 93-101). Academic Press.

Joonseok, P., Sumin, J., & Keunhyuk, Y. (2023, July). Smart Contract Broker: Improving Smart Contract Reusability in a Blockchain Environment. *Sensors (Basel), 13*(13), 6149. Advance online publication. doi:10.3390/s23136149

Kiffer, L., Levin, D., & Mislove, A. (2017, November). Stick a fork in it: Analyzing the ethereum network partition. In *Proceedings of the 16th ACM Workshop on Hot Topics in Networks* (pp. 94-100). 10.1145/3152434.3152449

Lee, S. H., Purnima, M. M., Jonathan, P., & Peter, L. (n.d.). *An Integrated Smart Contract Vulnerability Detection Tool Using Multi-layer Perceptron on Real-time Solidity Smart Contracts.* IEEE. doi:10.1109/ACCESS.2024.3364351

Luu, L., Chu, D. H., Olickel, H., Saxena, P., & Hobor, A. (2016, October). Making smart contracts smarter. In *Proceedings of the 2016 ACM SIGSAC conference on computer and communications security* (pp. 254-269). 10.1145/2976749.2978309

Majd, S. (2023, October). Dissecting Smart Contract Languages. *Survey (London, England), 6.* arXiv2310.02799v2 [cs.CR]

Manku, G. S., Jain, A., & Das Sarma, A. (2007, May). Detecting near-duplicates for web crawling. In *Proceedings of the 16th international conference on World Wide Web* (pp. 141-150). 10.1145/1242572.1242592

Monika, A., & Gernot, S. (2019, July 16). Collateral Use of Deployment Code for Smart Contracts in Ethereum. *2019 10th IFIP International Conference on New Technologies, Mobility and Security (NTMS).* 10.1109/NTMS.2019.8763828

Mubashar, I., & Raimundas, M. (2021, May 19). *Exploring Sybil and Double-Spending Risks in Blockchain Systems.* doi:10.1109/ACCESS.2021.3081998

Paul, K. (2023, November 3). *Satoshi Nakamoto created Bitcoin in 2009. He mysteriously vanished in 2011, with billions to his name.* Retrieved February 09, 2024, from https://www.cbc.ca/documentaries/the-passionate-eye/satoshi-nakamoto-created-bitcoin-in-2009-he-mysteriously-vanished-in-2011-with-billions-to-his-name-1.7014958

Peter, G. K. (2023, December 21). Blockchain Ethics. Philosophies, 9(2). https://doi.org/ doi:10.3390

Roberto, I. (2019). *Building Ethereum Dapps: Decentralized applications on the Ethereum blockchain.* Academic Press.

Saad, M., Njilla, L., Kamhoua, C., Kim, J., Nyang, D., & Mohaisen, A. (2019, May). Mempool optimization for defending against DDoS attacks in PoW-based blockchain systems. In *2019 IEEE international conference on blockchain and cryptocurrency (ICBC)* (pp. 285-292). IEEE.

Sachin, S., & Kaushal, S. (2022, July 18). Exploring Security Threats on Blockchain Technology along with possible Remedies. *2022 IEEE 7th International conference for Convergence in Technology (I2CT).* 10.1109/I2CT54291.2022.9825123

Solat, S., & Potop-Butucaru, M. (2017). Brief announcement: Zeroblock: Timestamp-free prevention of block-withholding attack in bitcoin. *Stabilization, Safety, and Security of Distributed Systems: 19th International Symposium, SSS 2017, Boston, MA, USA, November 5–8, 2017 Proceedings, 19,* 356–360.

Sudhani, V., Divakar, Y., & Girish, C. (2022, January). Introduction of Formal Methods in Blockchain Consensus Mechanism and Its Associated Protocols. *IEEE Access : Practical Innovations, Open Solutions, 10,* 66611–66624. doi:10.1109/ACCESS.2022.3184799

Sujeetha, R., & Preetha, C. S. D. (2021, October). A literature survey on smart contract testing and analysis for smart contract based blockchain application development. In *2021 2nd International Conference on Smart Electronics and Communication (ICOSEC)* (pp. 378-385). IEEE.

Tann, W. J. W., Han, X. J., Gupta, S. S., & Ong, Y. S. (2018). Towards safer smart contracts: A sequence learning approach to detecting security threats. *arXiv preprint arXiv:1811.06632*.

Vyas, C. A. (2014). M. Security concerns and issues for bitcoin. *International Journal of Computer Applications*. Retrieved from https://goo.gl/cNACCq

Yazid, A. C. (2023). Blockchain Technology in Financial Transactions under Sharia Banking Practice. *Jurnal Ekonomi dan Bisnis, 7*, 65-75. Retrieved from doi:10.14421/EkBis.2023.7.2.2049

Zhuang, Y., Liu, Z., Qian, P., Liu, Q., Wang, X., & He, Q. (2021, January). Smart contract vulnerability detection using graph neural networks. In *Proceedings of the Twenty-Ninth International Conference on International Joint Conferences on Artificial Intelligence* (pp. 3283-3290). Academic Press.

Chapter 5
Extraction of Emotion From Spectrograms:
Approaches Based on CNN and LSTM

Cecile Simo Tala
University of Ngaoundéré, Cameroon

ABSTRACT

Speech is the main source of communication between humans and is an efficient way to exchange information around the world. Emotion recognition through speech is an active research field that plays a crucial role in applications. SER is used in several areas of life, more precisely in the security field for the detection of fraudulent conversations. A pre-processing step was done on audios in order to reduce the noise and to eliminate the silence in the set of audios. The authors applied two approaches of the deep learning namely the LSTM and CNN for this domain in order to decide of the approach which saw better with the problem. They transformed treated audios into spectrograms for the model of the CNN. Then they used the technique of the SVD on these images to extract the matrices of characteristics for the entries of the LSTM. The proposed models were trained on these data and then tested to predict emotions. They used two databases, RAVDESS and EMO-DB, for the evaluation of the approaches. The experimental results proved the effectiveness of the model.

INTRODUCTION

Societies are based on communication that responds to a set of rules allowing everyone to understand and be understood. These communications can be in voice, text, and gesture form. These different forms are intended to translate the thought,

DOI: 10.4018/978-1-6684-8127-1.ch005

to represent it using a set of words chosen from a lexicon, gestures responding to a culture, and articulated sounds to form syllables, words, and sentences. This work is situated in the context of the recognition of emotions during telephone conversations between two people. In these types of interactions, the telephone is the only channel of communication. The conversation to be studied becomes important since our only channel of expression is the voice. It contains a multitude of information about the speaker such as his emotions, his age, his identity, his gender as well as the physiological disorders felt during oral expression. The extraction of this information has given rise to several areas of speech research, in particular the recognition of emotions from the voice. Speech is the most widespread means of exchanging information between human beings all over the world (Kwon, 2021), and attention should be paid to it. However, the most significant factor in human speech is emotion (Nardelli et al., 2015), which can be analyzed for judgments about humans and other expressions. Speech is the most widespread means of exchanging information between human beings all over the world (Kwon, 2021), and attention should be paid to it. However, the most significant factor in human speech is emotion Nardelli et al. (2015), which can be analyzed for judgments about humans and other expressions. Speech is the most widespread means of exchanging information between human beings all over the world (Kwon S., (2021), and attention should be paid to it. However, the most significant factor in human speech is emotion (Nardelli et al., 2015), which can be analyzed for judgments about humans and other expressions.

Emotions or emotional states are fundamental for humans insofar as they permeate humanity consciously and unconsciously in the most varied areas of life. They influence our perceptions, our behaviors, our mental states, and our daily activities such as communication, learning, and decision-making. The importance of emotions in the learning process has been known for a long time (L. Kerkeni et al, 2020), Nowadays the recognition of emotions in a speech signal is one of the most emerging areas of research and plays an important role in applications. in real time where researchers have developed methods to detect emotions from a voice signal (Kwon, 2021; (Mustaqeem and Kwon, 2019; Anvarjon et al., 2020) It paves the way for human-computer interaction (HMI) and plays an important role in many effective services such as call centers and tracking customer emotions to provide better services (Gupta, et al. (2007). In the medical field, speech-based diagnostic systems are developed to assess the extent of depression and distress (Rana et al. (2019), and some emotion recognition systems are designed for healthcare centers to monitor depression. state of the speaker for bipolar patients (Badshah et al., 2019; Wang, et al., 2015) There are so many other applications, such as multimedia search systems, (Roberts et al., 2012) forensic science (Vögel et al., 2018) smart car systems that have as their aim to improve their performance by using an effective emotion recognition system. More and more man is dependent on machines. There are several approaches to detecting an emotion from an audio, video, or text file. However, is it possible to adapt the models of emotion recognition in the audio of the telephone conversations to detect a set of emotions?

The general objective of this work is to propose an intelligent approach to emotion recognition during a conversation. This general objective is broken down into several specific objectives, namely:

Understand generalists on voice and emotion then build a dataset of conversations using audio from the literature

Segment conversations according to the interventions of the speakers and bring out all the emotions during the conversation through deep learning based on LSTM and CNN.

Experiment with audio to get the right performance

Compare the two deep learning approaches and decide which produces a better quality of learning.

The chapter is structured as follows: The first part is devoted to the review of the techniques and models for the characterization of emotions, and the models proposed for the extraction of emotions during telephone conversations in the second part. The last part presents the experiments and the results, and finally a conclusion and perspectives.

I. RELATE RESEARCH

Emotion recognition in speech is a research area of growing interest. emotions and their characteristics, detecting emotion from a signal, and existing approaches for recognizing emotions.

1. Emotions

"Emotion" is a word derived from "motion" which concerns movement, a term appearing in the 13th century in French as in the Saxon languages and carrying the idea of a movement which is accomplished; the Latin root remover meaning "to set in motion". Emotion existed at the beginning of the 16th century through the word "emotion" which will induce the meaning used (Delacourt et al., 2000). An emotion is a complex, internal psychophysiological experience of an individual's state of mind related to a locatable object when responding to biochemical and environmental influences. (Claudon et al., 2009) defines emotion as a subjective and conscious experience characterized by a biological reaction and mental state. For him, reason plays a central role in daily life, especially when faced with decisions or judgments. Emotions are recognized as key factors in decision-making, especially those on the spur of the moment. It has an internal manifestation and generates an external reaction.

Robert Plutchilk was one of the pioneers in 1980 to propose his complex three-dimensional model and his two-dimensional wheel model to describe the relationships between these emotions. (Luo et al., 2015) proposes its 4 fundamental so-called primary emotions (fear, anger, joy, sadness), which combine with cognitive mechanisms involving memory and reflection to give 4 other fundamental so-called secondary emotions (confidence (linked to joy), disgust (linked to sadness), anticipation (linked to anger) and surprise (linked to fear), whose respective functions would be preservation, protection of acquired knowledge, reproduction, reintegration, and incorporation, Paul Ekman, consider only 4 to 6 primary emotions instead of 8 like Plutchik because insofar as the combined emotions involve mechanisms of reflection and memory (for example confidence is linked to a set of joyful memories) or even abstract thought, it is no longer about emotions but feelings by definition. Plutchik organized his primary emotions into pairs of opposites: joy and sadness, fear and anger, disgust and confidence, surprise and anticipation. However, research agrees on the existence of a minimum set of primary emotions, the number of which varies widely depending on the researcher.

According to P. Ekman the group of 6 emotions ("big six") because insofar as the combined emotions involve mechanisms of reflection and memory (for example confidence is linked to a set of joyful memories) or even of abstract thought, it is no longer a question of emotions but of feelings by primary definition that he uses would be universal and therefore present both in humans and in animals (Robert Plutchik, (2021). Plutchilk (2021) who postulates eight primary emotions (joy, acceptance, fear, surprise, sadness, disgust, anger, and anticipation) has inscribed in a wheel these elementary emotions which, in combining, produce other emotions: love would be the resultant of the elementary emotions of joy and acceptance; submission would result from acceptance and fear.

Basic emotions are categorized by:

- Joy: is a pleasant emotion or a feeling of pleasure, of intense happiness, characterized by its plenitude and its limited duration, and experienced by someone whose aspiration or desire is satisfied or in the process of being satisfied. It can be expressed by a smile, a relaxed posture, and a tone of voice i.e., an optimistic and pleasant way of speaking
- Sadness: State of someone who experiences grief, melancholy; or affliction. It is emotional pain associated with, or characterized by feelings of disadvantage, loss, despair, or grief. It can be manifested by crying, loss of appetite, or loss of vitality. In the most severe cases, sadness can lead to more or less profound lethargy, as well as social isolation.

- fear: more or less lasting affective state, which can begin with an emotional shock, made of apprehension (which can go as far as anxiety) and trouble (which can manifest itself physically by pallor, trembling, paralysis, disordered activity in particular), which accompanies the awareness or representation of a real or imaginary threat or danger. Fear is classified into two types: external fear and internal fear. External fear is an external fear that the individual wishes to avoid; Internal fear is inner fear linked to an often negative emotion. It manifests itself when the situation slips away when you think you no longer have any control. Fear is connected to several emotional and cognitive states including worry, anxiety, terror, horror, panic, and fear. Fear can be expressed through facial expressions such as eye-widening and chin withdrawal, body language such as attempting to hide or move away from the threat, and physiological responses such as breathing and heartbeat.
- Anger: is a strong emotion of the soul resulting in a violent physical and psychic reaction. It is an emotion characterized by a feeling of restlessness, hostility, frustration, and antagonism towards others or situations. Humans express their anger through facial expressions, such as frowning or staring. Body language: such as taking a strong stance or turning away Tone of voice: such as grumpy talking or yelling Physiological responses: such as sweating or turning red Aggressive behaviors: such as hitting, kicking, or throwing objects.
- Disgust: is a basic emotion felt by a person confronted with what he does not taste and/or which he instinctively or culturally rejects with a certain violence, instinctively to protect himself. This emotion can manifest itself through body language: turning away from the object of disgust, physical reactions: vomiting, facial expressions: wrinkling the nose and curling the upper lip, etc.
- Confidence: is the translation into a concept of the feeling one experiences when one feels that one can trust someone, something, or oneself to overcome the difficulties, and the challenges of life. It means feeling capable of responding to daily challenges, having confidence in one's thoughts, in one's ability to solve problems, to adapting to the changes that may occur in one's life.
- Surprise: is an emotion characterized by a physiological startle reaction following an event or something unexpected. Surprise is often characterized by facial expressions: raised eyebrows, widening eyes, opening of the mouth, physical reactions: like jumping back, verbal reactions: like shouting, yelling, or gasping.
- Anticipation: This involves eliminating as much as possible the uncertainty inherent in any decision-making. Anyone who anticipates well must be able

to predict a future course as completely and accurately as possible. It is an estimate of the future values of an economic variable by an economic agent, and it bases its decisions; anticipation is considered one of the fundamental principles in time management.

2. Voice and Emotion

The human voice can be characterized by several attributes such as pitch, timbre, volume, and tone. Speech carries linguistic content, i.e. sentences and words, and paralinguistic content such as mood; an effect of speaker states such as intoxication and drowsiness; speaker traits such as age, gender, and personality (Ekman, 1999). It has often been observed that humans express their emotions by varying different vocal attributes during speech generation. Therefore, inferring human emotions through voice and speech analysis has practical plausibility and could potentially be beneficial for improving human conversational and persuasive skills (Plutchik, (1988). Human voices are very personal, difficult to falsify, and contain startling information about our mental health and behaviors (Schuller et al., 2013). The key to voice analysis research is not what someone says. Technically, speech and music are acoustic signals, represented in the physical world by micro-variations in pressure, primarily atmospheric pressure, from the order of approx. 50-8000 Hz. Speech-based emotion detection offers a means to estimate human emotional states with considerable accuracy. Research on the detection of emotions from speech has made great strides in recent years. These authors found a correlation between emotion and facial signals. In (Dasgupta et al., (2017) the authors merged acoustic information with visual cues for emotion recognition. It can therefore be noted here that the detection of emotion from speech in a conversation between two interlocutors consists of extracting the emotion associated with each utterance in the speech of conversation. Research on emotions has increased over the past two decades in many fields including psychology, medicine, history, sociology of emotions, and computer science. Emotions are biologically based psychological states caused by neurophysiological changes, variously associated with thoughts, feelings, behavioral responses, and degree of pleasure or displeasure.

3. Emotion Detection Techniques

Emotion recognition is an active area of research that aims to identify ways to quantify and measure emotional expressions in a wide variety of applications. Speech recognition of emotions is a field that studies expressions by analyzing the acoustic characteristics of speech signals. Nowadays, researchers have developed a multitude of techniques for the recognition of vocal emotions. Deep learning approaches are used as a basic framework to represent emotional cues in speech and to explore learning possibilities efficiently.

Deep learning uses unstructured, big data with an autonomous learning method that performs complex tasks such as cyber security, voice assistance, etc. The CNN choice because it's an algorithm used for object analysis and detection.

CNN's choice because it's an algorithm used for object analysis and detection.

As for LSTM, this algorithm is used to learn and memorize dependencies over a long period of time; it is also used for voice processing and recognition.

The choice of these approaches is based on the fact that they have considerably improved results in several works in the literature in this field.

a) Deep Learning-Oriented Technique: CNN

A convolutional neural network or convolutional neural network (CNN) is a type of artificial neural network used in image recognition and processing and specifically designed to process pixel data (theverge.com (2021). CNNs are powerful artificial intelligence (AI) image-processing systems that use deep learning to perform both generative and descriptive tasks. Convolutional neural networks have a methodology similar to that of traditional supervised learning methods: they receive images as input, detect the characteristics of each of them, and then train a classifier on them. However, these characteristics are learned automatically! CNNs do all the tedious work of feature extraction and description themselves. This reduces the classification error rate, hence the importance of CNNs compared to other approaches. There are four types of layers for a convolutional neural network:

- The convolution layer: This is the key component of convolutional neural networks, and always constitutes at least their first layer. Its purpose is to identify the presence of a set of features in the images received as input. For this, we carry out convolution filtering, that is to say that we make the images slightly blurred to reduce the noise, or on the contrary to accentuate the details. It therefore receives several images as input and calculates the convolution of each of them with each filter.
- The pooling layer: This is the layer often placed between two convolution layers: It receives several feature maps as input and applies to each of them the pooling operation which consists of reducing the size of the images while preserving their important characteristics. It reduces the number of parameters and calculations in the network. This improves the efficiency of the network by avoiding over-fitting. Thus, the pooling layer makes the network less sensitive to the position of features. It can be done in 2 ways:
  * Average pooling: which calculates the average value of the information *

Max pooling: which retains only the maximum value of the information and uses it to create an under-sampled feature map.

- the ReLU correction layer: ReLU (Rectified Linear Units) designates the real non-linear function defined by ReLU(x)=max (0, x). The ReLU correction layer therefore replaces all the negative values received as inputs with zeros. It acts as an activation function.

- The fully-connected layer: The fully-connected layer always constitutes the last layer of a neural network, convolutional or not. It applies a linear combination and then possibly an activation function (this function will allow the passage of information or not if the stimulation threshold is reached) to the values received as input. The last fully connected layer is used to classify the input image of the network: it returns a vector of size N where N is the class number. This layer determines the link between the position of the features in the image and a class. Here is an architecture from CNN with the different parts mentioned above.

Figure 1. General view of the CNN

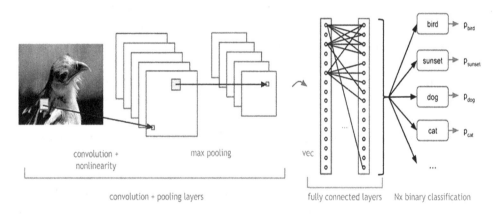

b) Techniques-Oriented Deep Learning: LSTM

Long-Short-Term Memory Networks commonly referred to as "LSTMs" are a special type of RNN, capable of learning long-term dependencies. They were introduced by (El Filali et al., (2022); The data consists of a "continuous" signal, it will therefore be necessary to process them sequentially. It is then possible to use recurrent neural networks (RNN) such as LSTMs (Long Short-Term Memory) networks which have shown far better results in the processing of sequential data (actualiteinformatique.fr,

(2021). LSTMs are explicitly designed to avoid the long-term dependency problem. Remembering information for long periods is pretty much their default behavior. It is a cell made up of three "gates": these are calculation areas that regulate the flow of information (by carrying out specific actions).

- Forget gate: This gate decides which information should be kept or discarded: The information of the previous hidden state is concatenated to the input data and then the sigmoid function is applied to it to normalize the values between 0 and 1. If the output of the sigmoid is close to 0, this means that we must forget the information and if we are close to 1 then we must memorize it for the future.

- Input gate: The role of the input gate is to extract information from the current data. We will apply in parallel a sigmoid to the two concatenated data and a tanh. The Sigmoid function will return a vector for which a coordinate close to 0 means that the coordinate in an equivalent position in the concatenated vector is not important. Conversely, a coordinate close to 1 will be considered "important", i.e. useful for the prediction that the LSTM seeks to make. Tanh at his level will simply normalize the values between -1 and 1 to avoid problems of overloading the computer in calculations. The product of the two will therefore make it possible to keep only the important information, the others being almost replaced by 0.

- Output gate: To talk about this last gate the researchers approach the subject on the state of the cell because it calculates the value that will be used in the output gate. The state of the cell is calculated fairly simply from the forgetting gate and the entry gate: first, we multiply the coordinate to coordinate the exit from forgetting with the old state of the cell. This makes it possible to forget certain information from the previous state which is not used for the new prediction to be made. Then, the whole is added with the output of the entrance gate, which makes it possible to record in the state of the cell what the LSTM has deemed relevant. The output gate must decide what the next hidden state will be, which contains information about previous entries in the network and is used for predictions.

To do this, the new state of the cell calculated just before is normalized between -1 and 1 thanks to Tanh. The concatenated vector of the current input with the previous hidden state passes, for its part, into a sigmoid function whose goal is to decide which information to keep. This all might sound like magic in the sense that it looks like the network has to guess what to hold in a vector on the fly, but let's remember that a weight matrix is applied as input. It is this matrix that will, concretely, store the fact that such information is important or not from the thousands of examples that the network will have seen. Structure of LSTM:

Figure 2. General view of the LSTM

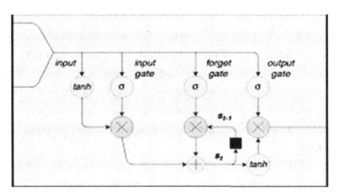

4. State of the Art

Researchers have adopted artificial intelligence (AI) and deep learning (DL) approaches to improve the way of Human-Computer Interaction (HCI), which includes emotion recognition in speech signals. Nowadays, new techniques are being developed for Emotion Recognition Systems (ERS) efficiently using AI and DL (Hochreiter et al., (1997). Acoustic, linguistic, and contextual information are the three main categories of features used in RES research (datavalueconsulting.com (2021). In addition to these features, hand-crafted features such as height, zero-crossing rate (ZCR), and MFCC are widely used in many research works (datavalueconsulting. com (2021), Abbaschian, et al. (2021), Noroozi et al. (2017).

Many researchers have achieved great success in this era in creating an efficient and robust SER system using some applications of DL, such as deep belief networks (Mao, et al. (2014) (DBN), CNNs (Handa, et al. (2021), and long-term memory. term (LSTM) (Zhu et al., (2017), Liu et al. (2019). Most DL-based CNN models operate on 2D data, so researchers use deep spectrum approaches for SER to extract high-level discriminating features from speech spectrograms using the CNN model. All CNN models work extremely well in the spatial domain to extract salient features from the data (Sajjad et al., 2020).

Recently, fully convolutional networks (FCNs) have been introduced as a variant of CNNs, which process inputs of varying sizes depending on their properties, and they have achieved state-of-the-art accuracy in time series problems (RNNs) and the LSTM exhibits good performance for modeling the temporal dependence between sequences. The RNN-LSTM network is suitable for learning long-term contextual dependencies, and it is widely used in the field of SER.

The authors proposed a new SER system based on a CNN stride to extract salient discriminating features and train them end-to-end (Karim et al., (2019).

A new technique for emotion recognition based on the DCNN. This method extracts features using the Alex Net model and a trained conventional classifier, which is a support vector machine (SVM), to predict emotions (Karim et al., (2019).

A bimodal approach for emotion recognition from audio and text. Emotions are recognized as key factors in decision-making processes, especially for out-of-the-box decisions. (Ekman, (1999) Defines an interactive influence model of emotions and cognition, identifying the factors that determine when emotions trump reason; this model makes it possible to elaborate the relationship between emotion and reason in decision-making.

(Wang et al., (2019) Presents a 3D CNN for audio-visual cross-correspondence recognition. Their audio-visual recognition system couples two non-identical 3D CNN architectures. This allows a pair of voice and video inputs to be mapped into a new representation space to assess the correspondence between them. The spectrograms are used as inputs, along with the first and second-order derivatives of the MFCC characteristics. The audio and video characteristics are merged.

(Zhang et al., (2017) The authors model the speakers and the sequential information in the dialogues through three different GRUs, namely the Global GRU, the Speaker GRU, and the Emotion GRU. Also, in the multimodal setting, the concatenation of acoustic, visual, and textual features is used when the speaker is speaking, but only the visual features otherwise. However, DialogueRNN does not improve much in multimodal contexts (Verkholyak et al. (2021).

Paria et al (Torfi et al., (2017), propose a bimodal approach for emotion recognition from audio and text. Emotions are recognized as key factors in decision-making processes, especially for out-of-the-box decisions.

Claudon and Weber (Ekman, 1999), propose an interactive influence model of emotions and cognition, identifying the factors that determine when emotions prevail over reason; this model makes it possible to elaborate the relationship between emotion and reason in decision-making. Démirel et al (Hajarolasvadi et al., (2019).), proposed an audio-visual ERS system for video clips. They extracted 88 features, including MFCC, pitch, intensity, mean, variance, and more. of the entire voice signal. No framing is performed. They then applied SVM and Random Forest to this feature space.

The various works covered in the literature propose methods and techniques for the recognition of emotions based on the fusion of acoustic, linguistic, or textual characteristics. Others rely on attention to detect emotion whether in speeches, video clips, or texts. These approaches are used in various areas of life. In this research, the authors propose a new approach for emotion recognition systems that take into account segmentation by the speaker and that returns all the emotions during the conversation. To achieve this, they constitute a conversation sample, and then carry out a segmentation by the speaker to bring out the sub-emotions of the conversation.

Indeed, the particularity of this approach is that it adds a segmentation module per speaker and detects all of the sub-emotions during the conversation. The model returns a sequence of emotions extracted during the conversation. This technique will be applied using fraudulent conversations in the field of cybersecurity for the detection of scams. One of the most applied forms of social engineering is vishing.

The overall project is to see how controlling these emotions can reduce this form of attack. Detecting emotions during a telephone conversation is one of the preliminary tasks.

II. PROPOSED METHODOLOGY

To evaluate the model according to the proposed approaches, a set of preprocessing steps must be taken into account. The proposed model is that of emotion recognition by exploiting CNN and LSTM deep learning approaches. The realization of the model follows several phases. The first phase concerns the signal considered as input. Depending on this dataset, the second is to perform pre-processing on this data. The third phase is based on the segmentation and the grouping by speakers the fourth phase consists in extracting from these audios the spectrograms and the features for the inputs of the models, The fifth phase a CNN model and an LSTM model are designed to detect the set of emotions during a conversation.

1. Constitution of the Sample

In this work, the researchers used two datasets TESS and RAVDESS. The first TESS dataset consisting of 2800 audios for 7 emotions (calm, anger, fearful, disgust, happy, surprised, and sad) at the rate of 400 per emotion is used to train and validate the two approaches. The second RAVDESS dataset is used for model testing. the researchers used the latter to simulate conversations by considering 4 actors in the database (2 women and 2 men), so we obtained 2 audio files containing the conversations between a man and a woman. A script is written to associate the audios of the 4 authors two by two and the conversations obtained are 17 to 20 seconds per conversation, 60 conversations in 2 files. And a third folder containing 15 audio files of 30 seconds of the duration of the conversation. With a total of 135 conversations.

Figure 3. Approach methodology

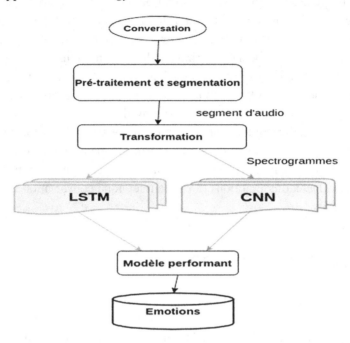

2. Pre-Processing and Segmentation

This is to eliminate silence in conversations and to remove all parts where no sound is emitted. The Audacity software was used to visualize certain conversations to see the variations in decibels of the signal and also to observe at what value to set for the threshold value of silence. The researchers found that in a conversation when the amplitude varies between -55dB and 55dB, this part represents the silence that must be eliminated. A conversation contains 5 interventions.

These conversations are visualized because the values of the silent parts in signals can vary depending on the signals and the value will be modified in our script. The time constraint is taken into account in this script; in conversations, there are moments of silence between segments of speech and moments of silence between turns of speech. The difference between speech turns and speech segments can be identified via the silence time. Considering that the silence time between speaking turns is higher than that between speaking segments. Speech segments are included in speaking turns; when we speak of speech segments, these are the words or expressions that a speaker can pronounce during his intervention. If during this intervention the time of silence is also high, it is considered that the speech segment conveys important information. It may also happen that during the conversation the signal is noisy due to degradation or background noise. The signal may suffer from the narrow bandwidth or the poor quality of the microphones of certain telephone terminals. To use the information effectively, these noises must be reduced. Among the multitudes of denoising algorithms, researchers apply the one based on the thresholding method because of its simplicity and efficiency. The signal may suffer from the narrow bandwidth or the poor quality of the microphones of certain telephone terminals. To use the information effectively, these noises must be reduced. Among the multitudes of denoising algorithms, researchers apply the one based on the thresholding method because of its simplicity and efficiency. The signal may suffer from the narrow bandwidth or the poor quality of the microphones of certain telephone terminals. To use the information effectively, these noises must be reduced. Among the multitudes of denoising algorithms, researchers apply the one based on the thresholding method because of its simplicity and efficiency.

During a conversation, the speakers speak in turn. Expressions can be based on a specific topic. It is a question of separating the different speaking turns of each speaker and to do this the silent parts are used. As seen previously, during a conversation there are moments of silence between speaking turns, this will be used as a segmentation parameter. Some conditions are defined in the script; if in the signal a part is considered silent, this part is eliminated and at the same time the conversation is segmented. In other words, the same script is used to eliminate silence and segment the audio. These audios are stored in a database.

3. Representation in the Form of a Spectrogram

One of the techniques for representing audio is the spectrogram. It is the visual representation of signal intensity over time at different frequencies. The spectrogram is generated by applying the STFT. STFT is a Fourier transform that determines the sinusoidal frequency and phase of local parts of a signal as it changes over time. By applying the Fourier transform to each image the Fourier spectrum of that image is revealed. The visualization of the spectra changes according to the given time. In these spectrograms the horizontal axis represents the time and the vertical axis represents the frequency of the signal. In a spectrogram, at a given time and a given frequency, the dark colors illustrate the low amplitude frequency, while light colors indicate the frequency of greater amplitude. Spectrograms are well-suited for a variety of speech analyses and are used as input for CNNs. Given the seven folders representing the set of emotions, a set of spectrograms for each folder of emotions emerged. However, the script allowing the representation of audio in the form of a spectrogram does not allow this transformation for the audios with a size higher than 550 kB therefore transforming it in the form of a spectrogram only applies to the audio of short size. These images are 432 pixels wide and 288 pixels high. With these values, the model will be too heavy so it is necessary to resize these images to make them light and speed up their fast loading. Figure 4 presents the spectrograms for the different emotions. These figures show the frequencies on the ordinate, the time taken by the signal on the abscissa with the color variation for the amplitude.

Figure 4. Spectrograms of emotions

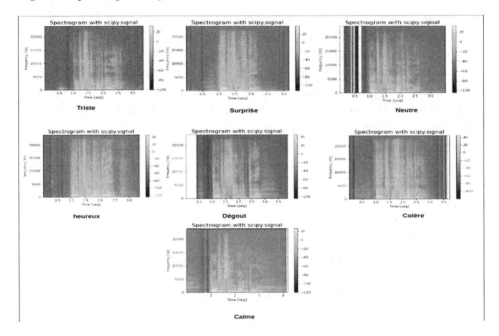

4. CNN Model Architecture

The proposed CNN architecture is shown in Figure 3.6. Most CNN models are designed for different types of tasks to achieve high accuracy. This approach is adopted in the field of cybersecurity in fraudulent conversations to create a meaningful and robust system to recognize all the emotions in a telephone conversation. The CNN model has three components, namely convolution layers, pooling layers, and fully connected layers. Convolution layers have a large number of filters to calculate the initial feature set, which is then passed to the pooling layer to reduce dimensions for fast processing and calculations. Likewise, the fully connected layers are used to learn global features and recognize hidden clues in the input data, then feed the SoftMax layer to produce the different class probabilities. The simple CNN model is used to extract the features after obtaining the speech spectrograms. This CNN model consists of the first convolution layer containing an argument to specify the shape of each sample in the data that will be used for training then a Maxpooling layer to reduce the size of the images then a dropout layer is used to disable temporarily certain layers of the neural network. The comparisons are made on the predictions and the emotion with the highest prediction is stored in an emotion database created by conversation. However, the CNN model contains a two-step training process like traditional neural networks such as forward propagation and backward propagation. The main objectives of these two steps are to calculate the results of the input data with the current parameters and to update the trainable parameters. Updated parameters recalculate results and show their performance. The model proposes a robust and simple result which is proven in experiment 1. Figure 5 summarizes the proposed CNN architecture as well as the parameters used. the CNN model contains a two-step training process like traditional neural networks such as forward propagation and backward propagation. The main objectives of these two steps are to calculate the results of the input data with the current parameters and to update the trainable parameters. Updated parameters recalculate results and show their performance. The model proposes a robust and simple result which is proven in experiment 1. Figure 5 summarizes the proposed CNN architecture as well as the parameters used. the CNN model contains a two-step training process like traditional neural networks, such as forward propagation and backward propagation. The main objectives of these two steps are to calculate the results of the input data with the current parameters and to update the trainable parameters. Updated parameters recalculate results and show their performance. The model proposes a robust and simple result which is proven in experiment 1. Figure 5 summarizes the proposed CNN architecture as well as the parameters used. The main objectives of these two steps are to calculate the results of the input data with the current parameters and to update the trainable parameters. Updated parameters recalculate results and show their performance. The model proposes a robust and simple result which is proven in experiment 1. Figure 5 summarizes the proposed CNN architecture as well as the parameters used. The main objectives of these two steps are to calculate the results of the input data with the current parameters and to update the trainable parameters. Updated parameters recalculate results and show their performance. The model proposes a robust and simple result which is proven in experiment 1. Figure 5 summarizes the proposed CNN architecture as well as the parameters used.

Figure 5. Summary of architecture CNN

```
Layer (type)                    Output Shape              Param #
=================================================================
conv2d_2 (Conv2D)               (None, 348, 348, 32)      896

conv2d_3 (Conv2D)               (None, 346, 346, 64)      18496

max_pooling2d_1 (MaxPooling     (None, 173, 173, 64)      0
2D)

dropout_2 (Dropout)             (None, 173, 173, 64)      0

flatten_1 (Flatten)             (None, 1915456)           0

dense_2 (Dense)                 (None, 128)               245178496

dropout_3 (Dropout)             (None, 128)               0

dense_3 (Dense)                 (None, 7)                 903

=================================================================
Total params: 245,198,791
Trainable params: 245,198,791
Non-trainable params: 0
```

5. LSTM Architecture

To apply the approach using the LSTM, several treatments were carried out. Spectrograms of the sample were used. The approach consists of a first Lambda layer used to transform the input data to obtain the two-input data only. After this layer, there are four LSTM layers allowing access to both the return sequences and the return state with varying sizes of neurons for each layer; then a dropout layer: Allows randomly deactivating neuron outputs during the learning phase. This amounts to simulating a set of different models and learning them together. For this model, this value is fixed at 0.3. Each neuron is possibly inactive during a learning iteration, this forces each unit to learn well independently of the others and thus avoids co-adaptation. The last two layers are the dense layers or the "fully connected" layer to apply linear combinations, and activation functions and classify the input data. The architecture below summarizes the layers and parameters used for this model.

Researchers label these emotions as follows:

1: for Calm emotion;
2: for the Anger emotion;
3: for Fearful emotion;
4: for the Happy emotion;
5: for the emotion of Disgust;
6: for the Surprise emotion; 6: for the Sad emotion.

Figure 6. LSTM architecture summary

```
Layer (type)              Output Shape              Param #
=================================================================
lambda_2 (Lambda)         (None, 350, 350)          0

lstm_8 (LSTM)             (None, 350, 256)          621568

lstm_9 (LSTM)             (None, 350, 128)          197120

lstm_10 (LSTM)            (None, 350, 64)           49408

lstm_11 (LSTM)            (None, 32)                12416

dropout_2 (Dropout)       (None, 32)                0

flatten_2 (Flatten)       (None, 32)                0

dense_4 (Dense)           (None, 128)               4224

dense_5 (Dense)           (None, 7)                 903

=================================================================
Total params: 885,639
Trainable params: 885,639
Non-trainable params: 0
```

6. Model Validation and Testing

This step consists of applying a set of tests to assess the ability to recognize patterns on unknown statements in the data. The statistical parameters are used to study the effectiveness of the proposed methods. Among the existing metrics, the authors used: The confusion matrix, error rate, precision, recall, and F1 score

1. **Confusion matrix:** It allows us to know on the one hand the different errors made by a prediction algorithm, but more importantly, to know the different types of errors made. For this case, The confusion matrix shows the actual predicted values diagonally and the confusion between them in the corresponding rows. The results of a confusion matrix are classified into four main categories: true positives, true negatives, false positives, and false negatives.
    ◦ The true positives or TP (true positive) indicate the cases where the predictions and the actual values are indeed positive. It is the number of correctly predictable actual positive emotion records,
    ◦ The true negatives or TN (true negative) indicates on the other hand the cases where the predictions and the actual values are both negative.
    ◦ False positives or FP (false positive) indicate a positive prediction contrary to the negative real value. They are also considered type 1 errors.

○ False negatives refer to cases where the predictions are negative while the actual values are positive. They are also considered type 2 errors.

2. **Error rate:** The error rate or ERR is a metric that is calculated by summing all the incorrect predictions over the total number of data (positive and negative). The lower it is, the better. The best possible error rate is 0.

$$ERR= TP+_{NT}PF++FNFP+FN$$

3. **Accuracy: This** parameter sums all the true positives and true negatives and divides it by the total number of instances. It provides an answer to the following question: of all the positive and negative classes, how many of them were predicted correctly? High values of this parameter are often desirable.

4. **The reminder:** Recall is a parameter that measures the number of correct positive predictions out of the total number of positive data. It answers the following question: Of all the positive records, how many were correctly predicted?

5. **The F1 score:** The F1 score (or F-measure) is a harmonic mean of precision and recall. It is equivalent to twice the product of these two parameters over their sum. Its value is maximum when recall and precision are equivalent.

These parameters make it possible to evaluate the reliability, quality, and quantity of learning of the models.

III. EXPERIMENTS AND RESULTS

In this section, it is a question of doing a practical demonstration of the approaches, tested on the sample sets, RAVDESS and TESS. The importance and robustness of the emotion recognition model in conversations are presented in this part.

1. Working Environment

The environment used is ANACONDA and the Jupyter interface. The researchers developed the scripts in Python language. Indeed, Anaconda brings together a set of tools revolving around the Python programming language and notably provides the execution environment. This distribution of Python is data science-oriented machine learning. Anaconda installs on both Windows and Linux. In addition, the choice for the Python language is justified by its ability to offer support for programming filtering, mapping, and reduction functions; list comprehensions, dictionaries, sets, and generator expressions. Python uses typed objects but untyped variable names and type constraints are not checked at compile time. It allows programmers to define their types using classes, which are most often used for object-oriented programming.

New instances of classes are constructed by calling the class, and classes are meta class type instances allowing for meta programming and reflection. Python's standard library is very large, it offers a wide range of tools. The Python libraries used in this work are: it offer a wide range of tools. The Python libraries used in this work are: it offer a wide range of tools. The Python libraries used in this work are:

1. Librosa: is a Python package for music and audio analysis. It provides the basic building blocks needed to create music information retrieval systems. It is installed via the Anaconda GUI or by command prompt.
2. Pydub: is an external module for reading (listening) and manipulating (modifying) sounds (mainly .wav and .mp3 files) this module offers useful options for recreational programming.
3. Tensorflow: is an open-source library offering a different perspective on conceptualizing mathematical actions; With this framework, it is possible to create neural networks and train them. These neural networks are a crucial part of artificial intelligence because they are trained to learn.
4. Numpy: is open-source software for creating and managing multidimensional arrays and matrices. This library includes various functions for handling such complex arrays. This library specializes in providing high-level mathematical functions for managing multidimensional arrays.
5. Sklearn is another free Python library, for creating machine learning models. Closely related to machine learning procedures. It consists of algorithms like support vector machines, gradient boosting, k-means, and random forests.
6. Keras is a Python-based library for developing deep-learning models. It is also compatible with other Python libraries (TensorFlow or Theano as well). The main purpose of this framework is the rapid prototyping of neural networks. Developers can experiment with deep neural networks and train them.
7. Matplotlib is a comprehensive library for creating static, animated, and interactive visualizations in Python.

2. Data Used

a) RAVDESS

The researchers used the Ryerson Audio-Visual of Emotional Speech and Song (RAVDESS) database (Majumder et al., (2019) for this work. It is a database containing 24 professional actors, 12 men, and 12 women, vocalizing two lexically matching statements in a neutral North American accent. Speech includes expressions of calm, joy, sadness, anger, fear, surprise, and disgust. Each expression is produced at two levels of emotional intensity (normal, strong), with an additional neutral expression. Each actor has 60 recordings with different emotions. 2 sentences are used during recordings.

b) TESS

This is a set of 200 target words spoken by two actresses aged 26 and 64. The recordings were made on the set representing each of the seven emotions (anger, disgust, fear, happiness, pleasant surprise, sadness, and neutral). There are 2800 stimuli in total with 400 audio files per emotion (Majumder et al., (2019).

Data partitioning is a method in data analysis that consists of studying a set of unclassified data and grouping them into coherent and homogeneous subsets. Typically, the data used for machine learning is partitioned into training and test data. The percentages of this segmentation may vary; for this work, the authors used 80% of the dataset for training and 20% for model validation.

3. Evaluation and Performance of Models

a) Experiment 1: Learning With CNN

It consists of training and validating the CNN model with the TESS database. This approach uses speech spectrograms as input features and from seven iterations the accuracy is already good. The model increases the level of accuracy and decreases losses during training and testing, which proves the efficiency and robustness of the model. The visual result of the accuracy of the proposed approach is illustrated in Figure 7 which shows the variations in accuracy. As can be seen from the seventh iteration, the curve is constant with an accuracy of 98%.

Unlike accuracy, loss is not a percentage. In FIG. 8 the line converges towards 0 as the number of iterations increases.

According to the confusion matrix, the researchers obtained an accuracy of 85% for the fearful emotion, 83% for the angry emotion, 80% for calm, and 79% for the happy and sad emotions; lower results have an accuracy of 77% for neutral and disgust emotions. The confusion matrix shows the actual predicted values diagonally and the confusion between them in the corresponding rows. The CNN model confusion matrix is shown in Figure 9.

The authors in addition to precision and confusion matrix evaluated the model with other performance metrics and obtained 97% for recall and 98% as f1 score value.

Figure 7. CNN precision curve

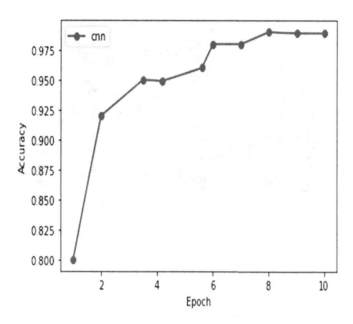

Figure 8. CNN loss curve

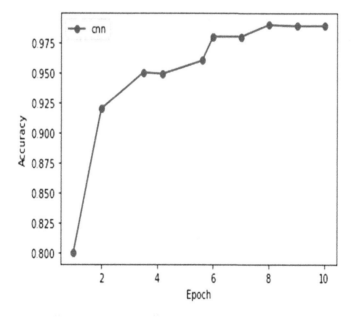

Figure 9. CNN confusion matrix

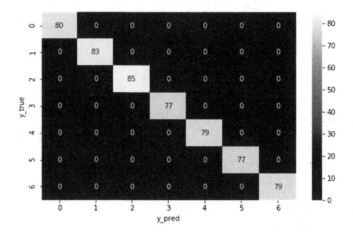

b) Experiment 2: Learning With LSTM

It consists of training the LSTM model with the TESS database. This approach also uses speech spectrograms as input features and the model is trained through 100 iterations. This model is also efficient as can be seen in Figure 10 with an accuracy of 96%.

Unlike accuracy, loss is not a percentage. In figure 11 concerning the loss, it can be seen that the straight line converges towards 0 as the number of iterations increases, this function decreases.

Figure 10. Accuracy curve of LSTM

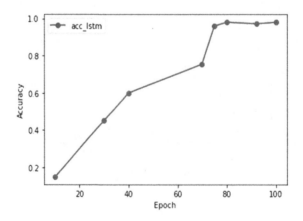

Figure 11. LSTM loss curve

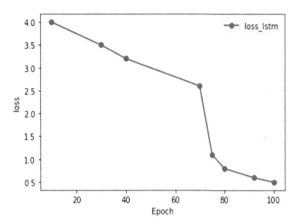

According to the confusion matrix, the authors obtained an accuracy of 88% for the sad emotion, 82% for the angry emotion, 80% for fearful, and 77% for the happy, neutral, and surprised emotions; low accuracy results are 77%. The confusion matrix shows the actual predicted values diagonally and the confusion between them in the corresponding rows. The confusion matrix of the LSTM model is shown in Figure 12

In addition to accuracy and convolution matrix evaluate our model with other performance metrics and researchers got 93% for recall and 95% as f1 score value.

Figure 12. LSTM confusion matrix

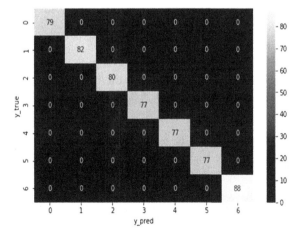

c) Experiment 3: Comparative Analysis

In this section, the researchers compared the two deep learning approaches CNN and LSTM intending to detect the model that displays better learning quality. A model displays better learning quality when it obtains the highest performance value. This comparison will be made according to several criteria: the value of the precision, the loss, and the learning time.

- The value of the precision: The highest precision value indicates a better learning of the model and according to the figure we note that with 10 iterations CNN already obtains a good precision. Unlike LSTM.

Figure 13. CNN and LSTM precision curve

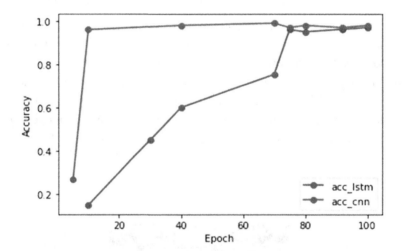

- The loss: the lower this value, the better the model, and as can also be seen, the loss value of the CNN model decreases very quickly. This proves its effectiveness.

Figure 14. CNN and LSTM loss curve

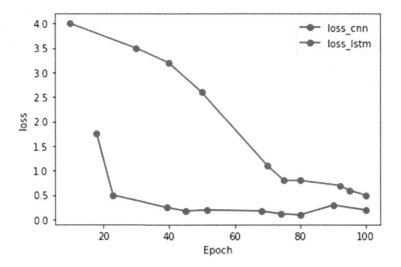

- Time and resource consumption: To analyze the time taken by the model, we take into consideration the number of iterations that the model will be able to perform to learn well and have good precision. The comparison in time consumption of the two models shows that LSTM consumes less time and resources compared to CNN.

The LSTM approach works with large data sets. The performance is good as it gets good accuracy. However, compared to CNN it is less reliable in terms of accuracy. Moreover, the observed results show that compared to CNN, LSTM consumes more training time with more iterations, which shows that this learning method requires much more time than CNN to learn. The proposed CNN approach is reliable, efficient, and robust with good performance in a short time. However, with Deep Learning parameters like size of input data, number of layers, and size of neurons in the layer can affect the quality of learning which makes this method a bit more complex than other methods of deep learning. learning.

The researchers compare the results and performance of the CNN model with existing models using the same dataset or using the deep learning approach to show the importance and robustness of the proposed system. A detailed overview of these comparisons with the authors and the year of publication, the dataset used and the prediction obtained is in Table 1.

The researchers have studied in depth the literature in the field of emotion recognition on audios, Many techniques have been developed but the segmentation is done according to a predefined size and the proposed approaches only detect a single emotion. These questions are addressed and they create a new model for the SER based on an already trained CNN model. The authors applied the code snippets for segmentation and display of multiple emotions. The model has additional modules compared to the existing one and we obtain an accuracy of 98.39% which is not far from the highest accuracy in the literature with 99.52%. With the proposed model, the emotions during a multi-speaker conversation are recognized.

Table 1. Accuracy comparison

Actors and Year	Data Set	Accuracy
Doltka et al (2021)	TESS	99.52%
Meng et al (2019)	IEMOCAP	66,32%
Issa et al. (2020)	IEMOCAP	64,03%
Mustaqeem and Kwon (2020)	EMO-BD	92.02%
Proposed model	TESS	98.39%

4. Model Limitations

Moreover, when training the LSTM model, the authors consider the spectrograms as inputs to the model. Other structures can also be used as inputs and improve the quality of learning. The choice of input data type may have an impact on learning. The segmentation should be made according to the emotions based on some parameters of the voice.

CONCLUSION

In summary, this work focused on the analysis and recognition of emotions in multifaceted conversations. This analysis was done using the CNN and LSTM approaches. It was about presenting a model that allows:

1. Constitute a conversation sample and segment the conversations according to the interventions of the speakers;
2. Design an approach based on deep learning techniques to bring out emotions during multi-speaker conversation;
3. Experiment with the approach on the sample constituted and evaluate the performance of emotion recognition compared to the approaches of the literature.

To achieve this, the researchers explored some existing models and approaches, more specifically the models based on CNNs and LSTMs, they found that the use of these approaches generates better performance with good complexity. To apply the model to the field of cybersecurity, this model is applied to multi-speaker conversations and detects all the emotions felt. A segmentation step by speaker according to the turns of speech based on silence was done, then a representation in the form of a spectrogram and the application of deep learning approaches. The researchers obtained a CNN model that provides results at 98.39% accuracy and the LSTM model with an accuracy of 96% close to reality according to the tests carried out. A comparative study with approaches has been made and it appears that the CNN model is better in terms of its accuracy, training time, and data size compared to LSTM. Comparisons are also made with existing approaches using the same datasets or using a machine learning approach. The model is less efficient in terms of accuracy than one of the literature models with a deviation of 1.2%.

By way of perspectives, it would therefore be a question on the one hand of segmenting conversations according to emotions and on the other hand of applying fraudulent conversations to this model for its use in the fight against vishing techniques.

REFERENCES

Abbaschian, B. J., Sierra-Sosa, D., & Elmaghraby, A. (2021). Deep learning techniques for speech emotion recognition, from databases to models. *Sensors (Basel)*, *21*(4), 1249. doi:10.3390/s21041249 PMID:33578714

Anvarjon, T., Mustaqeem, & Kwon, S. (2020). Deep-net: A lightweight CNN-based speech emotion recognition system using deep frequency features. *Sensors (Basel)*, *20*(18), 5212. doi:10.3390/s20185212 PMID:32932723

Badshah, A. M., Rahim, N., Ullah, N., Ahmad, J., Muhammad, K., Lee, M. Y., Kwon, S., & Baik, S. W. (2019). Deep features-based speech emotion recognition for smart affective services. *Multimedia Tools and Applications*, *78*(5), 5571–5589. doi:10.1007/s11042-017-5292-7

Claudon, P., & Weber, M. (2009). L'émotion: contribution à l'étude psychodynamique du développement de la pensée de l'enfant sans langage en interaction. *Devenir*, *21*(1), 6.

Dasgupta, P. B. (2017). Detection and analysis of human emotions through voice and speech pattern processing. *arXiv preprint arXiv:1710.10198*.

Delacourt, P., & Wellekens, C. J. (2000). DISTBIC: A speaker-based segmentation for audio data indexing. *Speech Communication, 32*(1-2), 111–126. doi:10.1016/S0167-6393(00)00027-3

Ekman, P. (1999). Basic emotions. Handbook of cognition and emotion, 98(45-60), 16.

El Filali, A., El Filali, S., & Jadli, A. (2022, July). Application of Deep Learning in the Supply Chain Management: A comparison of forecasting demand for electrical products using different ANN methods. In *2022 International Conference on Electrical, Computer and Energy Technologies (ICECET)* (pp. 1-7). IEEE. 10.1109/ICECET55527.2022.9872903

Gao, Y., Li, B., Wang, N., & Zhu, T. (2017). Speech emotion recognition using local and global features. In *Brain Informatics: International Conference, BI 2017, Beijing, China, November 16-18, 2017, Proceedings* (pp. 3-13). Springer International Publishing. 10.1007/978-3-319-70772-3_1

Gupta, P., & Rajput, N. (2007). Two-stream emotion recognition for call center monitoring. In *Eighth Annual Conference of the International Speech Communication Association*. 10.21437/Interspeech.2007-609

Hajarolasvadi, N., & Demirel, H. (2019). 3D CNN-based speech emotion recognition using k-means clustering and spectrograms. *Entropy (Basel, Switzerland), 21*(5), 479. doi:10.3390/e21050479 PMID:33267193

Handa, A., Agarwal, R., & Kohli, N. (2021). Audio-visual emotion recognition system using multi-modal features. *International Journal of Cognitive Informatics and Natural Intelligence, 15*(4), 1–14. doi:10.4018/IJCINI.20211001.oa34

Hochreiter, S., & Schmidhuber, J. (1997). Long short-term memory. *Neural Computation, 9*(8), 1735–1780. doi:10.1162/neco.1997.9.8.1735 PMID:9377276

Issa, D., Demirci, M. F., & Yazici, A. (2020). Speech emotion recognition with deep convolutional neural networks. *Biomedical Signal Processing and Control, 59*, 101894. doi:10.1016/j.bspc.2020.101894

Karim, F., Majumdar, S., & Darabi, H. (2019). Insights into LSTM fully convolutional networks for time series classification. *IEEE Access : Practical Innovations, Open Solutions, 7*, 67718–67725. doi:10.1109/ACCESS.2019.2916828

Kerkeni, L. (2020). *Acoustic voice analysis for the detection of speaker emotions*. Diss.

Kwon, S. (2021). MLT-DNet: Speech emotion recognition using 1D dilated CNN based on multi-learning trick approach. *Expert Systems with Applications, 167*, 114177. doi:10.1016/j.eswa.2020.114177

Liu, X., Van De Weijer, J., & Bagdanov, A. D. (2019). Exploiting unlabeled data in cnns by self-supervised learning to rank. *IEEE Transactions on Pattern Analysis and Machine Intelligence*, *41*(8), 1862–1878. doi:10.1109/TPAMI.2019.2899857 PMID:30794168

Luo, J., & Yu, R. (2015). Follow the heart or the head? The interactive influence model of emotion and cognition. *Frontiers in Psychology*, *6*, 573. doi:10.3389/fpsyg.2015.00573 PMID:25999889

Majumder, N., Poria, S., Hazarika, D., Mihalcea, R., Gelbukh, A., & Cambria, E. (2019, July). Dialoguernn: An attentive rnn for emotion detection in conversations. *Proceedings of the AAAI Conference on Artificial Intelligence*, *33*(01), 6818–6825. doi:10.1609/aaai.v33i01.33016818

Mao, Q., Dong, M., Huang, Z., & Zhan, Y. (2014). Learning salient features for speech emotion recognition using convolutional neural networks. *IEEE Transactions on Multimedia*, *16*(8), 2203–2213. doi:10.1109/TMM.2014.2360798

Meng, H., Yan, T., Yuan, F., & Wei, H. (2019). Speech emotion recognition from 3D log-mel spectrograms with deep learning network. *IEEE Access: Practical Innovations, Open Solutions*, *7*, 125868–125881. doi:10.1109/ACCESS.2019.2938007

Mustaqeem, & Kwon, S. (2019). A CNN-assisted enhanced audio signal processing for speech emotion recognition. *Sensors, 20*(1), 183.

Mustaqeem, & Kwon, S. (2020). CLSTM: Deep feature-based speech emotion recognition using the hierarchical ConvLSTM network. *Mathematics, 8*(12), 2133.

Nardelli, M., Valenza, G., Greco, A., Lanata, A., & Scilingo, E. P. (2015). Recognizing emotions induced by affective sounds through heart rate variability. *IEEE Transactions on Affective Computing*, *6*(4), 385–394. doi:10.1109/TAFFC.2015.2432810

Noroozi, F., Sapiński, T., Kamińska, D., & Anbarjafari, G. (2017). Vocal-based emotion recognition using random forests and decision tree. *International Journal of Speech Technology*, *20*(2), 239–246. doi:10.1007/s10772-017-9396-2

Plutchik, R. (1988). The nature of emotions: Clinical implications. In *Emotions and psychopathology* (pp. 1–20). Springer US. doi:10.1007/978-1-4757-1987-1_1

Rana, R., Latif, S., Gururajan, R., Gray, A., Mackenzie, G., Humphris, G., & Dunn, J. (2019). Automated screening for distress: A perspective for the future. *European Journal of Cancer Care*, *28*(4), e13033. doi:10.1111/ecc.13033 PMID:30883964

Ren, Z., Han, J., Cummins, N., & Schuller, B. (2020). *Enhancing transferability of black-box adversarial attacks via lifelong learning for speech emotion recognition models.* Academic Press.

Roberts, L. S. (2012). *A forensic phonetic study of the vocal responses of individuals in distress* (Doctoral dissertation, University of York).

Sajjad, M., & Kwon, S. (2020). Clustering-based speech emotion recognition by incorporating learned features and deep BiLSTM. *IEEE Access : Practical Innovations, Open Solutions, 8*, 79861–79875. doi:10.1109/ACCESS.2020.2990405

Schuller, B., & Batliner, A. (2013). *Computational paralinguistics: emotion, affect and personality in speech and language processing.* John Wiley & Sons. doi:10.1002/9781118706664

Torfi, A., Iranmanesh, S. M., Nasrabadi, N., & Dawson, J. (2017). 3d convolutional neural networks for cross audio-visual matching recognition. *IEEE Access : Practical Innovations, Open Solutions, 5*, 22081–22091. doi:10.1109/ACCESS.2017.2761539

Verkholyak, O., Dvoynikova, A., & Karpov, A. (2021). A Bimodal Approach for Speech Emotion Recognition using Audio and Text. *J. Internet Serv. Inf. Secur., 11*(1), 80–96.

Wang, H., Zhang, Q., Wu, J., Pan, S., & Chen, Y. (2019). Time series feature learning with labeled and unlabeled data. *Pattern Recognition, 89*, 55–66. doi:10.1016/j.patcog.2018.12.026

Wang, K., An, N., Li, B. N., Zhang, Y., & Li, L. (2015). Speech emotion recognition using Fourier parameters. *IEEE Transactions on Affective Computing, 6*(1), 69–75. doi:10.1109/TAFFC.2015.2392101

Why companies want to mine tea secrets in your voice. (n.d.). https://www.theverge.com/2019/3/14/18264458/voice-technology-speech-analysismental-health-riskprivacy

Zhang, S., Zhang, S., Huang, T., & Gao, W. (2017). Speech emotion recognition using deep convolutional neural network and discriminant temporal pyramid matching. *IEEE Transactions on Multimedia, 20*(6), 1576–1590. doi:10.1109/TMM.2017.2766843

Zhu, L., Chen, L., Zhao, D., Zhou, J., & Zhang, W. (2017). Emotion recognition from Chinese speech for smart affective services using a combination of SVM and DBN. *Sensors (Basel), 17*(7), 1694. doi:10.3390/s17071694 PMID:28737705

Chapter 6

Feature Engineering and Computer Vision for Cybersecurity:
A Brief State-of-the-Art

Ismael Abbo
Faculty of Sciences, University of Ngaoundere, Cameroon

Naomi Dassi Tchomte
University Institute of Technology, Cameroon

ABSTRACT

In cybersecurity, the fusion of feature engineering and computer vision presents a promising frontier. This study delves into their symbiotic relationship, highlighting their combined potential in bolstering cybersecurity measures. By examining tailored feature engineering techniques for intrusion detection, malware analysis, access control, and threat intelligence, this work sheds light on the transformative impact of visual data analysis on cybersecurity strategies. Harnessing feature engineering pipelines alongside computer vision algorithms unlocks novel avenues for threat detection, incident response, and risk mitigation. However, challenges such as overfitting, adversarial attacks, and ethical concerns necessitate ongoing research and innovation. This chapter lays the groundwork for future advancements in feature engineering for computer vision in cybersecurity, paving the way for more robust and resilient security solutions.

DOI: 10.4018/978-1-6684-8127-1.ch006

INTRODUCTION

The proliferation of digital assets and interconnected systems, organizations face an ever-growing array of cyber threats ranging from malware, phishing attacks to sophisticated cyber-physical intrusions and data breach each year, which have been forecasted to USD 12 million of cost for 2026 (IBM, 2023). Traditional rule-based approaches often fall short in adequately addressing these dynamic threats, necessitating a paradigm shift towards data-driven methodologies (Jothibasu, 2023)..

Thus, Feature engineering and computer vision are two fundamental concepts in data analysis and image processing, each playing crucial roles in various domains. Firstly, Feature Engineering (F.E.) involves the process of selecting, transforming, and creating meaningful features from raw data to facilitate machine learning algorithms' performance (Sriram, 2020) (Jha, 2023). These features serve as essential descriptors that encapsulate relevant information, enabling algorithms to discern patterns and make accurate predictions. On the other hand, computer vision encompasses the field of artificial intelligence and computer science dedicated to enabling machines to interpret and understand visual information from digital images or videos (Alosaimi, 2023) (Jothibasu, 2023).

Furthermore, the amalgamation of feature engineering and computer vision presents a potent solution to combat evolving threats and vulnerabilities. One compelling application lies in anomaly detection, where the detection of suspicious activities or intrusions within a network is paramount (Gibert, 2022). By harnessing computer vision techniques to analyze network traffic or surveillance footage, coupled with adept feature engineering, cybersecurity professionals can identify aberrant patterns indicative of potential security breaches or malicious activities (Duong, 2023).

In this work, a brief state-of-the-art is realized about feature engineering and computer vision in cybersecurity.

The rest of the document is organized as follows. In section 2, studies that explore FE and CV for cybersecurity issues are discussed followed by problem statement and research methodology respectively in section 2 and 3. In section 4, we detailed the background related to CV and FE. Then, we presented the literature analysis in section 5. Finally, we mentioned open issues in section 6 and conclude with perspectives.

1. RELATED INVESTIGATIONS

Machine Learning (ML) and Deep Learning (DL) techniques have been extensively explored and applied in the domain of cybersecurity to address a wide array of challenges. Notably, (Jha, 2023) surveyed the potential of integrating ML and Natural

Language Processing (NLP) for threat analysis and anomaly detection in Smart Grid Technology. Considering the same use case, (Hasan, 2024) explored ML and DL for threat detection in Smart Grid. (Soman, 2023) reviewed thoroughly deep learning and machine learning architectures with their mathematical background such as Naïve Bayes, Random Forest, Deep Autoencoder (DAE), and Deep Neural Network (DNN). (de Azambuja, 2023) works extensively highlighted the ability of ML/DL algorithms such as convolutional neural networks (CNNs) and recurrent neural networks (RNNs) to enhance the detection and prevention of cybersecurity systems. However, there is a growing need to develop ML/DL techniques capable of handling streaming and real-time data for dynamic threat detection and response in highly dynamic and interconnected environments of Computer Vision. Computer Vision offers novel approaches for threat detection, surveillance, and anomaly identification which (Zhao, 2021) (Ranka, 2023) (Liu, 2023) works overviewed. They informed about the ability to augment traditional cybersecurity measures with visual intelligence capabilities where advanced systems based on CV can analyze visual data from surveillance cameras, satellite imagery, and digital sensors to detect suspicious activities, identify potential threats, and monitor critical infrastructure in real-time. Although CV-based cybersecurity solutions offer a non-intrusive and scalable approach, there is a growing emphasis on the development of multimodal CV systems.

In summary, recent existing works primarily focus on employing machine learning, deep learning, and computer vision techniques to tackle cybersecurity issues broadly, this chapter diverges by critically examining the limitations inherent in leveraging F.E. within C.V. for cybersecurity applications. In essence, the objective shifts from directly addressing cybersecurity concerns to identifying measures aimed at regulating the exploitation of F.E. in C.V. methodologies for cybersecurity.

2. PROBLEM STATEMENT

Cybersecurity mechanisms rely heavily on vast amounts of data, including incoming and outgoing communication flows, access control lists (ACLs), and other authorization and access management data. These datasets encompass various fields, as specified by TCP/IP protocols, such as IP addresses, ports, URLs, among others. Processing this data demands substantial computational resources to extract meaningful information for network or system administrators. In the literature, authors have attempted to address this challenge by transforming the data into formats such as images (Ning, 2021), videos (Duong, 2023), or audio (Odeleye, 2023), aiming to discretize it into easily manipulable structures. Feature engineering (FE) plays a crucial role in this process by enabling the focus on the most relevant fields while ensuring acceptable performance for the given problem. However, throughout this transformation process, information loss or noise often occurs in the data, leading to a lack of robustness and reliability in the proposed approaches. This chapter seeks to conduct a reflective examination to highlight shortcomings that may arise when cybersecurity solutions leveraging computer vision (CV) rely on feature engineering.

The primary concern lies in the potential loss of crucial information during the feature engineering process, which can compromise the effectiveness of cybersecurity measures based on CV. Additionally, the introduction of noise or inaccuracies further exacerbates the challenge, hindering the ability to accurately detect and mitigate cyber threats. Exploiting the wealth of data available within network logs, system metrics, and visual surveillance feeds holds immense potential for bolstering cybersecurity defenses. However, the sheer volume and complexity of this data pose significant challenges in discerning meaningful insights amidst the noise. Thus, there is an imperative to harness the power of feature engineering within computer vision frameworks to distill actionable intelligence from vast datasets and fortify cybersecurity postures proactively.

3. RESEARCH METHODOLOGY

This study outlines several key steps, beginning with planning and establishing a review protocol, followed by formulating research questions and designing the search strategy. Additionally, the current investigation entails defining exclusion and inclusion criteria and selecting relevant data. These steps provide a structured approach to conducting the review and ensure that the methodology is clearly outlined and adhered to throughout the process.

3.1. Research Questions

This work is guided by the following questions:

RQ1: Are there any cybersecurity studies that rely on the CV while exploiting the FE to improve performance?

RQ2: What are the different issues that are raised in these studies?

3.2. Search Strategy

The research conducted an extensive search across various digital libraries including IEEE, ACM Digital Library, Springer, ScienceDirect, and WileyOnline Library, utilizing specific keywords outlined in Table 1 for crawling purposes. Additionally, citation engines such as Google Scholar and Web of Knowledge were employed to ensure comprehensive coverage of relevant literature. Forward research on authors who cited identified papers was also conducted to gather recent works. This thorough approach aimed to minimize the likelihood of overlooking any relevant studies and to provide a comprehensive overview of the existing literature on the topic.

Table 1. Search keywords

Group	Keywords
1	Feature engineering AND|FOR detection of malware
2	Feature engineering AND computer vision AND detection of malware
3`	Feature engineering AND computer vision AND cybersecurity
4	Feature engineering AND cybersecurity
5	Computer vision AND cybersecurity
6	1 OR 2 OR 3 OR 4 OR 5
7	1 AND 2 AND 3 AND 4 AND 5

3.3. Inclusion Criteria

This essay exclusively focuses on studies published from 2019 onwards and restricted to those written in English. Extensive literature searches were conducted to gather relevant literature, including literature reviews and surveys pertaining to feature engineering and computer vision for cybersecurity. These sources are intended for utilization in the "related reviews" section of the research. Papers were selected based on the presence of specific keywords such as "feature engineering for cybersecurity", "computer vision for cybersecurity", and "detection of malware" to ensure alignment with the research objectives.

3.4. Exclusion Criteria

The exclusion criteria for papers encompass those published in predatory journals, papers lacking specificity to feature engineering and computer vision for cybersecurity in their title and abstract, and papers lacking peer review. These criteria ensure the selection of rigorous and relevant literature for the research, excluding sources from questionable publishing outlets and focusing exclusively on papers directly related to the research topic. Abstracts and conclusion sections of all relevant articles were thoroughly examined to ensure their alignment with the study's topic. This scrutiny aimed to verify that the selected articles provide pertinent insights and findings related to feature engineering and computer vision for cybersecurity, confirming their relevance to the research objectives and ensuring the inclusion of high-quality and pertinent literature in the essay.

Data Selection Process

Only studies meeting the inclusion criteria related to feature engineering and computer vision for cybersecurity were considered for further review, with Mendeley utilized for paper organization and duplicate removal. Any works not meeting the exclusion criteria were deemed irrelevant and excluded. While collecting relevant papers ensured inclusion based on criteria, the quality of each paper was ensured through full-text reading. Papers related to feature engineering and computer vision were collected separately and then filtered based on the cybersecurity focuses. These steps finally provided 43 papers.

4. BACKGROUND

To answer the questions that are underlined in previous section, we will delve into concepts behind Computer Vision and Feature Engineering respectively.

4.1. Computer Vision

Computer vision plays a vital role in cybersecurity by providing the capability to analyze and interpret visual data for threat detection and prevention (Alosaimi, 2023). While adversaries are constantly innovating to bypass traditional security measures, computer vision offers a proactive approach to identify and mitigate potential threats (Zhao, 2021). One of the primary applications of computer vision in cybersecurity is in video surveillance systems. These systems leverage computer vision algorithms to analyze live or recorded video feeds for suspicious activities, unauthorized access attempts, or other anomalous behavior (Duong, 2023). By continuously monitoring visual data, video surveillance systems can alert security personnel to potential security breaches in real-time, allowing for prompt intervention. Furthermore, computer vision is instrumental in the development of intrusion detection systems (IDS) and access control mechanisms (Alosaimi, 2023). By analyzing network traffic patterns, system logs, and other data sources, computer vision algorithms can identify anomalous behavior indicative of unauthorized access or malicious activity. This enables organizations to detect and respond to security threats more effectively, minimizing the risk of data breaches or system compromises. In addition to threat detection, computer vision also plays a role in malware detection and analysis (Chen,

2019). By analyzing the visual characteristics of files or code snippets, computer vision algorithms can identify potentially malicious content and flag it for further investigation. This helps security analysts identify and mitigate malware infections before they can cause significant harm to systems or networks.

Overall, computer vision serves as a powerful tool in the cybersecurity arsenal, enabling organizations to detect, analyze, and respond to security threats more effectively. By leveraging feature engineering techniques to extract meaningful visual features, computer vision algorithms can enhance cybersecurity defenses and safeguard sensitive information from malicious actors.

4.2. Feature Engineering in Computer Vision

Feature engineering represents a fundamental aspect of data preprocessing in machine learning and computer vision (Dubey, 2021). It involves the transformation of raw data into a format that is conducive to the performance of machine learning algorithms as shown in Figure 1. In the context of computer vision, feature engineering revolves around extracting meaningful visual attributes or descriptors from images or videos (Ning, 2021). Traditionally, computer vision algorithms relied on handcrafted features, where domain experts manually designed features based on their understanding of the problem domain. However, this approach often lacked scalability and adaptability to diverse datasets and scenarios. With the advent of deep learning and neural networks, feature engineering has undergone a paradigm shift (Elngar, 2021). Instead of relying solely on handcrafted features, deep learning models can automatically learn hierarchical representations directly from raw data, alleviating the need for manual feature engineering to some extent.

Feature engineering remains a critical component in computer vision pipelines, particularly in cybersecurity applications that reduces resource consumption. By carefully selecting, transforming, and creating features from visual data, feature engineering enables machine learning algorithms to discern relevant patterns, anomalies, or threats amidst the complexity of visual information. The detail of each step is as follow:

- Preprocessing: This is the first step in feature engineering, where raw image data undergoes various transformations to remove noise, normalize intensities, and ensure that all images are processed uniformly.
- Feature Selection: After preprocessing, feature selection is the process of identifying relevant features from a large pool of potential descriptors. This step aims to reduce the dimensionality of the data while preserving important information needed for model training. Figure 2 depicts well known feature selection groups.

Figure 1. Feature engineering within computer vision

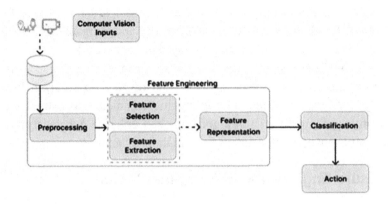

Figure 2. Feature selection methods

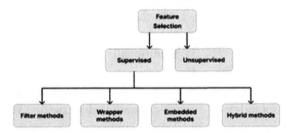

- Feature Extraction: takes place by transforming the raw image data into a more abstract representation that captures important visual information. This step involves applying various algorithms such as edge detection, object detection, and texture analysis to extract meaningful features from images as presented in Figure 3.

Figure 3. Feature extraction process

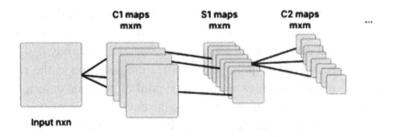

- Feature Representation: Finally, the process of mapping features onto a suitable format that can be fed into machine learning algorithms. Common representations include vectors (e.g., one-hot encoding), matrices (e.g., convolutional neural networks), and tensors (e.g., deep learning models).

4.3. Techniques and Methods of Feature Engineering

Feature engineering encompasses a diverse array of techniques and methods aimed at extracting informative features from raw visual data to enhance the performance of computer vision algorithms (Chandramouli, 2021). In the context of cybersecurity, where accurate threat detection is paramount, the choice of feature engineering techniques can significantly impact the effectiveness of security systems. Let's delve into some common techniques and methods employed in feature engineering for computer vision in cybersecurity.

4.3.1. Principal Component Analysis (PCA)

PCA is a dimensionality reduction technique widely used in feature engineering to reduce the complexity of visual data while preserving its essential characteristics (RM, 2020). By transforming high-dimensional data into a lower-dimensional space, PCA facilitates the identification of principal components or features that capture the most significant variations in the data. In cybersecurity applications, PCA can help alleviate the curse of dimensionality and improve the efficiency of computer vision algorithms for tasks such as anomaly detection and intrusion detection (Bouwmans, 2018). Based on cited works, PCA consists of:

1. **Data Transformation**: with **variables** (features), set of **orthogonal directions** (principal components) that capture the most significant variation in the data,
2. **First Principal Component (PC1)**: which explains the **most variance** in the data. Expressed as:

$$PC1 = w_1 \bullet x_1 + w_2 \bullet x_2 + \ldots + w_p \bullet x_p \qquad (1.1)$$

Where:
  w_i represents the weight (or coefficient) for the (i)-th variable.
  x_i represents the value of the (i)-th variable.
  p is the total number of variables.

3. **Subsequent Principal Components**: explain the most variance after removing the effect of PC1. The process is iterative to find additional principal components until all the variance is explained.
4. **Eigenvalues and Eigenvectors**: The principal components are **eigenvectors** of the data's **covariance matrix**. They represent the **variance** associated with each principal component.

4.3.2. Histogram of Oriented Gradients (HOG)

HOG is a feature descriptor technique that captures local intensity gradients or edge orientations in images (Yerima, 2022), (Bijitha, 2022), (Wang, 2023). By quantifying the distribution of gradient orientations within localized regions of an image, HOG descriptors enable the representation of object shapes and textures effectively. In cybersecurity, HOG features are commonly used in object detection and recognition tasks, such as identifying suspicious objects or individuals in video surveillance footage. Hence, its steps are:

*   The image is divided into small, connected regions called cells,
*   For each pixel within a cell, we compute the gradient direction (orientation),
*   We compile a histogram of gradient directions for each cell,
*   The final HOG descriptor is formed by concatenating these histograms.

4.3.3. Local Binary Patterns (LBP)

LBP is a texture descriptor technique that characterizes the local texture patterns within an image (Yerima, 2022), (Bijitha, 2022), (Wang, 2023). By comparing the intensity values of neighboring pixels in a local neighborhood, LBP descriptors encode information about texture variations and spatial relationships within an image. In cybersecurity applications, LBP features are valuable for detecting texture-based anomalies or identifying specific texture patterns associated with malicious content, such as malware or phishing attacks. For each cell:

*   Compare the pixel to each of its 8 neighbors (left-top, left-middle, left-bottom, right-top, etc.).
*   Follow the pixels along a circle (either clockwise or counterclockwise).
*   If the center pixel's value is greater than the neighbor's value, it is a "0"; otherwise, it is a "1".
*   This gives an 8-digit binary number (which can be converted to decimal for convenience).

- Compute the histogram over the cell, representing the frequency of each binary pattern (256 possible combinations).
- Concatenate (normalized) histograms of all cells to create a feature vector for the entire window.

4.3.4. Scale-Invariant Feature Transform (SIFT)

SIFT is a feature extraction technique designed to identify distinctive key points or interest points within an image invariant to scale, rotation, and illumination changes (Karami, 2017). By detecting and describing local image features based on their scale-space representations, SIFT descriptors enable robust matching and recognition of objects across different viewing conditions. In cybersecurity, SIFT features can be utilized for tasks such as image-based authentication, where invariant feature representations are essential for reliable recognition and verification. The SIFT workflow consists of several calculations where fundamental concept is the Euclidean distance between two feature vectors representing points.

4.3.5. Convolutional Neural Networks (CNNs)

CNNs represent a deep learning approach to feature learning and extraction in computer vision (Elngar, 2021), (Chen, 2019), (Akhtar N. M., 2021), (Sarker, 2021). By employing hierarchical layers of convolutional filters, CNNs can automatically learn hierarchical representations of visual features directly from raw pixel data. In cybersecurity, CNNs have demonstrated remarkable performance in various tasks, including image classification, object detection, and semantic segmentation. By leveraging the expressive power of CNNs, cybersecurity systems can extract discriminative features from visual data and enhance threat detection capabilities.

In summary, feature engineering in computer vision for cybersecurity encompasses a range of techniques and methods tailored to extract meaningful features from visual data. From traditional methods such as PCA and HOG to advanced deep learning approaches like CNNs, feature engineering plays a pivotal role in enhancing the effectiveness and efficiency of cybersecurity systems. By leveraging these techniques, security practitioners can develop robust and adaptive security solutions capable of detecting and mitigating emerging threats effectively.

5. LITERATURE ANALYSIS

In the previous section, we reviewed some commonly used methods of FE in Computer Vision. This section will revolve around related methods within the literature.

5.1. Feature Engineering in Computer Vision

In computer vision, feature engineering plays a central role in enhancing the capabilities of machine learning algorithms for various tasks, including object recognition, image classification, and anomaly detection. Numerous studies and research efforts have explored different techniques and methods of feature engineering to address specific challenges and improve the performance of computer vision systems. Let's explore some notable works and contributions in the field of feature engineering for computer vision.

The studies of (Carta, 2020), (Nakashima, 2021), (Gottwalt, 2019) investigate feature engineering techniques tailored to anomaly detection in network traffic data, addressing a critical aspect of cybersecurity. The authors explore methods for extracting discriminative features from network traffic flows, such as packet size distributions and inter-arrival times. The works highlight the importance of feature engineering in enhancing the accuracy and efficiency of anomaly detection systems in cybersecurity. While the studies provide valuable insights into feature engineering for network anomaly detection, there may be scope for further exploration of advanced feature selection and dimensionality reduction techniques to improve detection accuracy and scalability. Additionally, the studies could benefit from addressing the challenges of robustness to adversarial attacks and the integration of feature engineering with machine learning models for real-time threat detection.

On another hand, some literatures focus on the potential of visual feature engineering techniques in enhancing cybersecurity resilience through computer vision applications. This includes studies such as (Chandramouli, 2021), (Dick, 2019), (Zhang X. I., 2022) which investigate novel methods for extracting informative visual features from surveillance video feeds, addressing the need for robust security measures in critical infrastructure protection. These works demonstrate the potential of feature engineering in improving threat detection and monitoring capabilities in critical infrastructure security. However, there may be opportunities to explore the integration of advanced deep learning techniques for automatic feature extraction and representation learning, as well as addressing the challenges of scalability and real-time processing in large-scale surveillance systems and ethical considerations surrounding the use of visual data in security operations.

Furthermore, (Gibert, 2022), (Akhtar M. S., 2021), (Shaukat, 2023) investigate deep learning-based feature engineering techniques for malware image classification, addressing the growing threat of malware in cybersecurity. These endeavors showcase the potential of deep learning-based feature engineering for enhancing malware detection capabilities in cybersecurity. However, there may be opportunities to investigate the robustness of these techniques to adversarial attacks and generalization performance across diverse malware families. Additionally, addressing challenges of interpretability and transparency in deep learning models for malware analysis and ethical implications of using automated classification systems in cybersecurity operations would further enhance the contributions in the field of study.

5.2. Feature Engineering in Computer Vision for Cybersecurity

In the domain of cybersecurity, the integration of feature engineering techniques with computer vision has garnered significant attention from researchers and practitioners alike. Various studies and research endeavors have explored the application of feature engineering in bolstering cybersecurity defenses through enhanced visual analysis and threat detection capabilities as summarized in Table 2.

Notably, (Yerima, 2022), (Bijitha, 2022), and (Wang, 2023) conducted a comprehensive analysis of feature extraction methods, including Histogram of Oriented Gradients (HOG) and Local Binary Patterns (LBP), showcasing their effectiveness in detecting malware through image-based analysis. These studies demonstrated promising results in terms of accuracy and efficiency, highlighting the potential of feature engineering in bolstering cybersecurity defenses through computer vision. Similarly, (Elngar, 2021), (Chen, 2019), (Akhtar N. M., 2021) and (Sarker, 2021) proposed a novel approach utilizing Convolutional Neural Networks (CNNs) for feature extraction within computer vision field for cybersecurity applications. By leveraging deep learning techniques, their model achieved remarkable performance in identifying and classifying malicious activities in network traffic data. Through extensive experimentation, these works showcased the superior accuracy and scalability of their approach compared to traditional methods, underscoring the transformative impact of feature engineering in computer vision for cybersecurity. Despite the promising advancements, certain limitations persist in the application of feature engineering techniques in computer vision for cybersecurity. One notable challenge is the susceptibility to adversarial attacks, wherein malicious actors can manipulate visual data to evade detection (Rasheed, 2021). This vulnerability underscores the importance of robustness and resilience in feature engineering methodologies. Additionally, the computational complexity associated with some feature extraction algorithms may pose scalability challenges, particularly in real-time threat detection scenarios. Addressing these limitations requires further research and innovation to develop more robust and efficient feature engineering techniques tailored to the unique demands of cybersecurity applications.

These related works highlight the diverse range of approaches and methodologies employed in feature engineering for computer vision, spanning traditional handcrafted features to advanced deep learning techniques. By leveraging these insights and advancements, researchers and practitioners can continue to push the boundaries of feature engineering in computer vision and develop more robust and efficient solutions for cybersecurity and beyond.

Table 2. Literature analysis summary

Ref	FE	CV	Contributions	Limitations
(Carta, 2020), (Nakashima, 2021) and (Gottwalt, 2019)	Yes	No	Anomaly detection with improved accuracy	Not thoroughly overviewed Computer Vision aspect
(Chandramouli, 2021), and (Zhang X. I., 2022)	Yes	Yes	Video feeds for robust security	Advanced DL methods can be used for more robustness
(Gibert, 2022), (Dick, 2019), (Akhtar M. S., 2021) and (Shaukat, 2023)	Yes	Yes	Explored DL methods for secure systems	Can be weak to adversarial attacks
(Yerima, 2022), (Bijitha, 2022), and (Wang, 2023)	Yes	Yes	Image-based threats detection	Real-time threat can be challenging
(Elngar, 2021), (Chen, 2019), (Akhtar N. M., 2021) and (Sarker, 2021)	Yes	Yes	Used CNN in CV to thwart malicious activities	Susceptible to adversarial attacks

6. CHALLENGES AND FUTURE DIRECTIONS

While feature engineering in computer vision has demonstrated significant promise in enhancing cybersecurity capabilities, it also presents several challenges and opportunities for future research and development. Addressing these challenges and exploring new directions in feature engineering is crucial to advancing the effectiveness and applicability of computer vision in cybersecurity. Let's delve into some key challenges and future directions in this field:

- **Overfitting and Dimensionality Reduction:** One of the primary challenges of feature engineering when using in CV to solve cybersecurity issues, is the risk of overfitting, where the model learns to capture noise or irrelevant patterns in the data, leading to decreased generalization performance. Additionally, high-dimensional feature spaces pose challenges in terms of computational complexity and memory requirements. Future research efforts should focus on developing robust feature selection and dimensionality reduction techniques to mitigate overfitting and improve the efficiency of feature engineering pipelines in cybersecurity applications.
- **Robustness to Adversarial Attacks:** Adversarial attacks pose a significant threat to computer vision systems, particularly in cybersecurity applications

where adversaries may attempt to manipulate visual data to evade detection or compromise security measures. Future research should explore methods for enhancing the robustness of feature engineering techniques to adversarial attacks, such as developing adversarial training strategies, incorporating robust feature representations, and designing anomaly detection algorithms capable of detecting adversarial perturbations in visual data.

- **Automated Feature Engineering Techniques**: The manual design and selection of features can be labor-intensive and time-consuming, particularly in complex cybersecurity scenarios with large-scale and high-dimensional data. Future research should explore automated feature engineering techniques, such as genetic algorithms, reinforcement learning, and evolutionary optimization, to automate the process of feature selection, extraction, and transformation. By leveraging automated feature engineering, cybersecurity practitioners can streamline the development and deployment of robust security solutions with minimal human intervention.

- **Ethical and Privacy Considerations**: As feature engineering techniques become more sophisticated and pervasive in cybersecurity applications, it is imperative to address ethical and privacy concerns surrounding the collection, use, and dissemination of visual data. Future research should prioritize the development of privacy-preserving feature engineering techniques, such as differential privacy, federated learning, and secure multiparty computation, to ensure the responsible and ethical use of visual data in cybersecurity operations. Additionally, efforts should be made to promote transparency, accountability, and fairness in the design and implementation of feature engineering pipelines to mitigate potential biases and discrimination in security decision-making processes.

In summary, addressing the challenges and exploring new directions in feature engineering for computer vision is essential for advancing the capabilities of cybersecurity systems. By overcoming obstacles such as overfitting, robustness to adversarial attacks, and ethical considerations, researchers and practitioners can unlock the full potential of feature engineering in enhancing threat detection, incident response, and risk management in cybersecurity.

CONCLUSION AND PERSPECTIVES

In summary, the marriage of feature engineering and computer vision heralds a new era in cybersecurity, where visual data analysis serves as a cornerstone of defense against evolving threats. Through meticulous extraction of relevant features from visual data, cybersecurity practitioners can develop agile and adaptive security frameworks capable of addressing a spectrum of cyber risks. Despite challenges such as overfitting and adversarial attacks, the synergistic integration of feature engineering and computer vision holds immense promise for enhancing cybersecurity resilience. Furthermore, an extension of this essay will be directed into a systematic literature review of related works. As researchers and practitioners continue to innovate and refine feature engineering techniques, the trajectory of cybersecurity stands poised for advancement, ensuring the protection of digital assets and the preservation of trust in an increasingly interconnected world.

REFERENCES

Akhtar, M. S., & Feng, T. (2021). Deep learning-based framework for the detection of cyberattack using feature engineering. *Security and Communication Networks*, *2021*, 1–12. doi:10.1155/2021/6129210

Akhtar, N. M., Mian, A., Kardan, N., & Shah, M. (2021). Advances in adversarial attacks and defenses in computer vision: A survey. *IEEE Access : Practical Innovations, Open Solutions*, *9*, 155161–155196. doi:10.1109/ACCESS.2021.3127960

Alosaimi, S. A., Almutairi, S. M., & Chamato, F. A. (2023). Computer Vision-Based Intrusion Detection System for Internet of Things. *Wireless Communications and Mobile Computing*, *2023*, 2023. doi:10.1155/2023/5881769

Bijitha, C. V., & Nath, H. V. (2022). On the effectiveness of image processing based malware detection techniques. *Cybernetics and Systems*, *53*(7), 615–640. doi:10.1 080/01969722.2021.2020471

Bouwmans, T., Javed, S., Zhang, H., Lin, Z., & Otazo, R. (2018). On the applications of robust PCA in image and video processing. *Proceedings of the IEEE*, *106*(8), 1427–1457. doi:10.1109/JPROC.2018.2853589

Carta, S. P., Podda, A. S., Recupero, D. R., & Saia, R. (2020). A local feature engineering strategy to improve network anomaly detection. *Future Internet*, *12*(10), 177. doi:10.3390/fi12100177

Chandramouli, K. (2021). An Advanced Framework for Critical Infrastructure Protection Using Computer Vision Technologies. In *Cyber-Physical Security for Critical Infrastructures Protection: First International Workshop, CPS4CIP 2020, Guildford, UK, September 18, 2020, Revised Selected Papers 1* (pp. 107-122). Guildford, UK: Springer. 10.1007/978-3-030-69781-5_8

Chen, L. (2019). Understanding the efficacy, reliability and resiliency of computer vision techniques for malware detection and future research directions. *arXiv preprint arXiv:1904.10504*.

de Azambuja, A. J., Plesker, C., Schützer, K., Anderl, R., Schleich, B., & Almeida, V. R. (2023). Artificial Intelligence-Based Cyber Security in the Context of Industry 4.0—A Survey. *Electronics (Basel)*, *12*(8), 1920. doi:10.3390/electronics12081920

Dick, K. R., Russell, L., Souley Dosso, Y., Kwamena, F., & Green, J. R. (2019). Deep learning for critical infrastructure resilience. *Journal of Infrastructure Systems*, *25*(2), 05019003. doi:10.1061/(ASCE)IS.1943-555X.0000477

Dubey, G. P., & Bhujade, D. R. K. (2021). Optimal feature selection for machine learning based intrusion detection system by exploiting attribute dependence. *Materials Today: Proceedings*, *47*, 6325–6331. doi:10.1016/j.matpr.2021.04.643

Duong, H. T. (2023). Deep Learning-Based Anomaly Detection in Video Surveillance: A Survey. Sensors, 23(11), 5024.

Elngar, A. A., Arafa, M., Fathy, A., Moustafa, B., Mahmoud, O., Shaban, M., & Fawzy, N. (2021). Image classification based on CNN: A survey. *Journal of Cybersecurity and Information Management*, *6*(1), 18–50. doi:10.54216/JCIM.060102

Gibert, D. P., Planes, J., Mateu, C., & Le, Q. (2022). Fusing feature engineering and deep learning: A case study for malware classification. *Expert Systems with Applications*, *207*, 117957. doi:10.1016/j.eswa.2022.117957

Gottwalt, F. C. (2019). CorrCorr: A feature selection method for multivariate correlation network anomaly detection techniques. *Computers & Security, 83*, 234-245.

Gu, H. L., Lai, Y., Wang, Y., Liu, J., Sun, M., & Mao, B. (2022). DEIDS: A novel intrusion detection system for industrial control systems. *Neural Computing & Applications*, *34*(12), 9793–9811. doi:10.1007/s00521-022-06965-4

Hasan, M. K., Abdulkadir, R. A., Islam, S., Gadekallu, T. R., & Safie, N. (2024). A review on machine learning techniques for secured cyber-physical systems in smart grid networks. *Energy Reports*, *11*, 1268–1290. doi:10.1016/j.egyr.2023.12.040

IBM. (2023). *Cost of Data Breach 2023*. Retrieved from IBM: https://www.ibm.com/reports/data-breach

Jha, R. K. (2023). Strengthening Smart Grid Cybersecurity: An In-Depth Investigation into the Fusion of Machine Learning and Natural Language Processing. *Journal of Trends in Computer Science and Smart Technology*, *5*(3), 284–301. doi:10.36548/jtcsst.2023.3.005

Jothibasu, M. S. (2023). Improvement of Computer Vision-Based Elephant Intrusion Detection System (EIDS) with Deep Learning Models. *Innovative Engineering with AI Applications*, 131-153.

Karami, E. a. (2017). Image matching using SIFT, SURF, BRIEF and ORB: performance comparison for distorted images. *arXiv preprint arXiv:1710.02726*.

Lim, J. A., Al Jobayer, M. I., Baskaran, V. M., Lim, J. M. Y., See, J., & Wong, K. S. (2021). Deep multi-level feature pyramids: Application for non-canonical firearm detection in video surveillance. *Engineering Applications of Artificial Intelligence*, *97*, 104094. doi:10.1016/j.engappai.2020.104094

Liu, J. &. (2023). A comprehensive survey of robust deep learning in computer vision. *Journal of Automation and Intelligence*.

Nakashima, M. S., Sim, A., Kim, Y., Kim, J., & Kim, J. (2021). Automated feature selection for anomaly detection in network traffic data. *ACM Transactions on Management Information Systems*, *12*(3), 1–28. doi:10.1145/3446636

Naqvi, R. A., Arsalan, M., Qaiser, T., Khan, T. M., & Razzak, I. (2022). Sensor data fusion based on deep learning for computer vision applications and medical applications. *Sensors (Basel)*, *22*(20), 8058. doi:10.3390/s22208058 PMID:36298412

Ning, B., & Na, L. (2021). Deep Spatial/temporal-level feature engineering for Tennis-based action recognition. *Future Generation Computer Systems*, *125*, 188–193. doi:10.1016/j.future.2021.06.022

O'Shaughnessy, S. &. (2022). Image-based malware classification hybrid framework based on space-filling curves. *Computers & Security, 116*, 102660.

Odeleye, B. L., Loukas, G., Heartfield, R., Sakellari, G., Panaousis, E., & Spyridonis, F. (2023). Virtually secure: A taxonomic assessment of cybersecurity challenges in virtual reality environments. *Computers & Security, 124*, 102951. doi:10.1016/j.cose.2022.102951

Ranka, P. S. (2023). Computer Vision-Based Cybersecurity Threat Detection System with GAN-Enhanced Data Augmentation. *International Conference on Soft Computing and its Engineering Applications* (pp. 54-67). Cham: Springer Nature Switzerland.

Rasheed, B. K. (2021). Adversarial attacks on featureless deep learning malicious urls detection. *Computers, Materials & Continua, 68*(1), 921–939. doi:10.32604/cmc.2021.015452

RM, S. P. (. (2020). An effective feature engineering for DNN using hybrid PCA-GWO for intrusion detection in IoMT architecture. *Computer Communications, 160*, 139–149. doi:10.1016/j.comcom.2020.05.048

Sarker, I. H. (2021). Deep cybersecurity: A comprehensive overview from neural network and deep learning perspective. *SN Computer Science, 2*(3), 154. doi:10.1007/s42979-021-00535-6 PMID:33778771

Shaukat, K. L., Luo, S., & Varadharajan, V. (2023). A novel deep learning-based approach for malware detection. *Engineering Applications of Artificial Intelligence, 122*, 106030. doi:10.1016/j.engappai.2023.106030

Singla, R. (2023). Age and gender detection using Deep Learning. *2023 7th International Conference on Computing, Communication, Control and Automation (ICCUBEA)* (pp. 1-6). IEEE.

SomanK. P. (2023). A comprehensive tutorial and survey of applications of deep learning for cyber security. Authorea Preprints.

Sriram, S. S. (2020). DCNN-IDS: deep convolutional neural network based intrusion detection system. *Computational Intelligence, Cyber Security and Computational Models. Models and Techniques for Intelligent Systems and Automation: 4th International Conference, ICC3 2019, December 19-21, 2019, Revised Selected Papers 4.*

Torres, M. Á., Álvarez, R., & Cazorla, M. (2023). A Malware Detection Approach Based on Feature Engineering and Behavior Analysis. *IEEE Access: Practical Innovations, Open Solutions, 11*, 105355–105367. doi:10.1109/ACCESS.2023.3319093

Wang, Z. &. (2023). DAE-IHOG: An Improved Method for Classification Malware. *Proceedings of the 15th International Conference on Digital Image Processing*, (pp. 1-7). 10.1145/3604078.3604144

Yerima, S. Y., & Bashar, A. (2022). A novel Android botnet detection system using image-based and manifest file features. *Electronics (Basel), 11*(3), 486. doi:10.3390/electronics11030486

Zahid, S. M. (2023). A Multi Stage Approach for Object and Face Detection using CNN. *2023 8th International Conference on Communication and Electronics Systems (ICCES)* (pp. 798-803). IEEE.

Zhang, X. I. (2022). Critical Infrastructure Security Using Computer Vision Technologies. *Security Technologies and Social Implications*, 149-180.

Zhang, Z. Q., Qi, P., & Wang, W. (2020). Dynamic malware analysis with feature engineering and feature learning. *Proceedings of the AAAI Conference on Artificial Intelligence*, *34*(1), 1210–1217. doi:10.1609/aaai.v34i01.5474

Zhao, J. M. (2021). A review of computer vision methods in network security. *IEEE Communications Surveys & Tutorials, 23*(3), 1838-1878.

Chapter 7
Object Detection in Cybersecurity:
A Review of Automation of Malware Detection

Stones Dalitso Chindipha
Rhodes University, South Africa

ABSTRACT

With the increase in malware attacks, the need for automated malware detection in cybersecurity has become more important. Traditional methods of malware detection, such as signature-based detection and heuristic analysis, are becoming less effective in detecting advanced and evasive malware. It has the potential to drastically improve the detection of malware, as well as reduce the manual efforts required in scanning and flagging malicious activity. This chapter also examines the advantages and limitations and the challenges associated with deploying object detection in cybersecurity, such as its reliance on labeled data, false positive rates, and its potential for evasion. Finally, the review presents the potential of object detection in cybersecurity, as well as the future research directions needed to make the technique more reliable and useful for cybersecurity professionals. It provides a comparison of the results obtained by these techniques with traditional methods, emphasizing the potential of object detection in detecting advanced and evasive malware.

DOI: 10.4018/978-1-6684-8127-1.ch007

INTRODUCTION

The use of machine learning techniques in cybersecurity has been active for at least two decades and it has produced actionable results that others have built on. For instance, as early as 1998, Machine Learning (ML) techniques were applied to identify the discriminant features of malicious network traffic and classify legitimate network traffic from malicious traffic (Shafiq et al., 2020; Kundu et al., 2022).

It is the same machine-learning technique that emails use to filter out spam. Despite these ML techniques being used, the rapid change in the format of spam emails eludes some of these algorithms, and thus users find these spam emails in their inboxes. Another example of targeted cyber security attacks on machine learning techniques is presented by (Xi, 2020) which involves adversarial attacks against Deep Neural Networks (DNN). DNN has drawn significant attention because of how it is now applied in critical tasks, such as autonomous driving systems and partly automated vehicles. Thus, though the use of ML techniques is good for improving malware detection, some ML models are being targeted by vicious attacks. These too have to be looked at irrespective of the job they do in detecting malware.

While some autonomous malware detection strategies have worked, others have not worked. This chapter reviews and evaluates the peer-reviewed work on autonomous malware detection and looks at the strengths and weaknesses of each technique that has been used thus far and how some of these ML techniques have opened loopholes in systems. For instance, deep neural networks fail to correctly classify adversarial images (Xi, 2020), more work needs to be put into understanding why such is the case by looking at what other researchers have done and reporting those with higher success and what they did differently than the preceding work to achieve greater success. Even ML techniques that work in cyberspace have their attacks designed specifically for them to avoid detection. This includes but is not limited to poisoning attacks and evasion attacks (Xi, 2020).

Poisoning attacks have targeted machine learning techniques for some time. They work by contaminating the training dataset before training which in turn causes a learning model to make costly mistakes (Tian et al., 2022). These poisonous attacks can further be split into targeted attacks or non-target attacks. With targeted attacks, a threat actor works with tailor-made malware that would affect a specific organization while non-targeted attacks aim at reducing the overall accuracy of a learning model thus resulting in a majority of the malware being undetected and damaging systems. A major problem here is that a majority of publicly available datasets are outdated and may not be sufficient in identifying the undocumented behavioural patterns of various cyber-attacks (Xi, 2020). That means due to a lack of freely accessible data, this same dataset can be shared by many people which in turn means that if the data was poisoned at the collection point, then every other finding from such a source will be faulty. Evasion attacks involve the generation of adversarial samples to cause misclassification by a classifier which may also evade detection anomalies or malware by a learning algorithm at the test time (Rey et al., 2022).

Social media sites have also benefited from the use of machine learning techniques in detecting fake friend requests, impersonation, social phishing, hijackings, identity theft, face image retrieval and analysis, and malware detection, among other things (Alsodi et al., 2021). Though this has worked to some extent, it has had its high levels of false positives too because there is a lot of content that is not properly filtered and a lot of misuse of hashtags in their posts to seek likes and attention (Fang et al., 2020). Such incidences escalate to false malware detection, making it very difficult to detect cybersecurity threats and researchers find it very difficult to automatically detect cybersecurity threats from tweets. If a way could be found to remedy the levels of false positives, social media sites could prove a great source of threat intelligence data.

Understanding and processing knowledge of loopholes in the usage of the existing machine learning techniques, the trend and pattern of where the current research on the detection of malware is leading, presenting areas where there are knowledge gaps, and proposing which direction researchers ought to take in this field would help to avoid repeating the same errors in future if we know what is wrong with the current methods. Thus, evaluating the current existing literature on malware detection and identifying the gaps that need more focus is the primary objective of this chapter proposal.

Definition of Malware Detection

Before looking at malware detection, the chapter explains what malware is: It is a short form of malicious software that is designed to take advantage of system vulnerabilities and in the process, disrupt normal system operations, harm the system under attack, or harass users of such applications or systems (Maniriho et al., 2022). Such systems being targeted include but are not limited to servers, and a single computer connected to an entire network. Some of the common malware include viruses, worms, Trojans, spyware, adware, and ransomware among others. If malware remains undetected in the system the damage caused can escalate to a point where it could cause irreparable damage.

Thus systems, tools, and algorithms have been developed to detect, identify, and isolate such malware in order to protect systems and data from the damage that they can cause. The identification of systems works by first establishing a pattern or behaviour in which the malware behaves. Behaviour based malware detection works by using algorithms that capture and analyse any unusual behaviour of the software understudy in order to identify any malicious behaviour. Since the algorithms or software placed on the running system can identify the normal behaviour of the system they are running on. If an unusual behaviour is identified which is consistent with any malware it is trained to identify, it will alert the users who will then have to take action to remedy the situation (Maniriho et al., 2022). In some cases, the malware is identified based on the signature (digital footprint that uniquely identifies the malware). In these detection systems, a database that is populated with well-known malware is used to scan the systems they are on with the objective of identifying any signature that matches with what is in the database (Mahbooba et al., 2021). When identified, an alert is made to the system users who will then have to make a decision to remedy the situation. Anti-viruses work on this logic. However, this chapter will not focus on any of these. Instead, much attention will be sent to detection systems that use machine learning and artificial intelligence which use algorithms and statistical models by training models to analyse large chunks of data in order to identify patterns or behaviour that is identical to malware (Mahbooba et al., 2021; Abu Al-Haija et al., 2022; Botacin et al., 2022). Having trained such models they are deployed in a real environment in which they can successfully detect malware in real-time, including but not limited to new malware that the model has not been trained for. It is this approach that brings about the automation of malware detection as these models will have to make decisions at times without human intervention.

Significance of Automation in Malware Detection

Gone are the days when automation of the detection of cybersecurity threats was seen as an afterthought primarily because people could cope with the use of a few malware signatures and identify them. From the detection of less than 50 million unique malware executables in 2010 to over 900 million in 2019, estimates now show that these 900 million malicious executables will almost quadruple by 2026 (Ahsan et al., 2022). Financially, cybercrimes cost the world economy an estimated USD 400 billion per year and according to Cybercrime magazine[1] these values will go up to over USD 10 trillion per year. These are not values that can easily be ignored hence pushing companies and researchers to find a more efficient way to curb expenditures while keeping their companies safe from malicious software.

Technology-wise, researchers and security experts are now capable of collecting tons of threat intelligence data automatically but until this data is processed, no insights can be extracted from this data. Such large chunks of threat intelligence data need to be processed and analysed quickly so that decisions can be made in time to support the business both in its daily operations as well as defense against the network, application, information, and operational security threats (Ahsan et al., 2022). Machine learning techniques have been used to analyse threat intelligence data in feature reduction, feature selection, regression analysis, unsupervised learning, finding associations, or neural network focused deep learning techniques with the overall objective of extracting insights and/or patterns of security incidents (Dua and Du 2016; Dabney et al., 2018; Buchanan et al., 2020; Xi, 2020). Considering that malware is no longer used as a once-off software (Lakhotia et al., 2018) if malware has been used to attack more than one system and there is data to support this, the automated malware detection systems will improve the accuracy and efficiency with which these reused malwares are detected which could take more time for to be detected without automated systems. The longer the malware remains undetected due to manual analysis, the more damage the malware will cause to computer systems (David and Netanyahu, 2015). Furthermore, automated malware detection systems do not rest like manual applications do, thus being able to detect threats in real-time. Not only do automated malware detection systems bring out fast results but they also improve the accuracy of the results collected particularly because they have gone through large chunks of data in a short space of time. This is significant as any missed malware in this digital age could lead to serious implications for computer systems because they have not been treated in time.

Sometimes there could be minimal adjustments to the original code which can easily be missed by manual analysis but with automated systems, these can easily be identified or a new pattern easily identified due to the large chunks being processed (David and Netanyahu, 2015). This, in turn, reduces the likelihood of false positives and resource wastage as a more thorough analysis would have been made and resources properly allocated. With automated systems, security experts can zero in on specific malware to identify how frequently such malware has been seen in a certain period of time (David and Netanyahu, 2015). This can take a lot of time, with such systems, the experts can focus on other duties and in the process multitask. Though the start-up investment in automated malware detection systems is high, in the long run, the organisations can reduce costs associated with cyber security threats as mitigation steps are taken in time thus reducing the costs of labour and maintenance to damaged property.

It is for these reasons that automation of malware detection is significant as decisions can be made in real-time but also allows security analysts a chance to curb certain threats in time before more damage can be done. Large volumes of threat intelligence data can also be analysed quickly and decisions made. By providing real-time, faster, efficient, more accurate, and more reliable detection of threats, automated malware detection systems can help curb the workload of security professionals and improve the overall security of networks and systems. As such, it is a critical tool in the fight against cyber-attacks.

Purpose and Scope of the Review

The primary objective of this book chapter is to evaluate the current state of affairs in the automation of malware detection using machine learning and artificial intelligence techniques. At the end of the chapter, readers ought to know which machine learning and artificial intelligence techniques offer the best based on their current usage and the kind of malware that they are analysing or trying to automate. It is important to note that machine learning and artificial intelligence techniques are being incorporated into most of the software by companies in order to improve their accuracy and effectiveness in detecting malware and this is what we will be aiming to review.

Due to this, this study will primarily focus on machine learning and artificial intelligence techniques that are currently in use. To be more specific, this chapter will focus on supervised and unsupervised learning techniques, anomaly detection, and deep learning. In each category, the study will look at three examples. For supervised learning, the study will focus on Support Vector Machines (SVM), Random Forest (RF), and Naive Bayes. For unsupervised learning, the study will focus on K-means clustering, Hierarchical Clustering, and Density-Based Clustering (DBSCAN). For anomaly detection, the study will focus on One-Class SVM, Isolation Forest and Gaussian Mixture Model (GMM). This chapter also reviews deep learning techniques as they have proven to be very effective in identifying complex malware. One example, You Only Look Once (YOLO) is reviewed to pinpoint the significance of deep learning techniques as the future of malware detection. The study will also focus on Convolutional Neural Networks (CNN), Recurrent Neural Networks (RNN) and Auto-encoders

OVERVIEW OF EXISTING METHODS OF MALWARE DETECTION

In this section, the study reviewed existing literature on malware detection. The objective of this section is to ensure that the reader has a clear understanding of how the field of malware detection has evolved and also be able to point to where it is heading. It is for this reason that both automated and non-automated methods will be given a quick overview in this section before sorely focusing on the automated methods of malware detection. The four main malware detection methods discussed in this section are signature-based detection, heuristic-based detection, behavioural-based detection, and machine learning-based detection methods.

Signature-Based Detection

Behaviour-based malware detection approaches work by monitoring the behaviour of programs in order to detect malicious activity (Mahbooba et al., 2021; Savenko et al., 2019). To be more precise, it focuses on the behaviour of a binary or executable file, rather than its code or signature, to determine whether it is malicious. Due to this focus, the behaviour-based malware detection approach is effective for detecting unknown or complicated malware, as it does not rely on signatures and can identify suspicious activities even if a program has been changed or packed (Savenko et al., 2019). Because this approach is based on the notion that malware exhibits specific behaviour that make it operate differently from known behaviour, it is very effective at identifying malware that has been previously seen, often referred to as zero-day malware (Savenko et al., 2019). However, this method may face some challenges when dealing with new types of malware binaries which could either be false positives or consistent changes in the behaviour of the malware making it difficult to maintain an up-to-date database or a scenario where some malicious software will not run properly under pro tected environments such as virtual machines or sandbox environments which makes them difficult to monitor accurately using these methods (Mahbooba et al., 2021). Additionally, there are also certain obfuscation techniques that cannot be detected through behavioural analysis alone so other strategies must be employed in order to protect against those threats effectively (Mahbooba et al., 2021). A study conducted by (Savenko et al., (2019) showed that it is possible to attain high levels of accuracy (96.56%) using API call tracing which allows distinguishing malicious programs from benign ones. This is achieved based on the frequency and interaction of critical API calls performed during their execution. Furthermore, using API call tracing, the proposed method for generating signatures can be used to overcome obfuscation techniques employed by malware authors who try to develop software that cannot be detected (Savenko et al., 2019). Worthy of note is that signature-based malware detection is the most common method used by commercial antiviruses (Aslan and Samet, 2020).

Behavioural-Based Detection

Behaviour-based detection approaches on the other hand, observe program behaviour with monitoring tools in order to identify any potential threats from incoming data packets that may contain malicious codes or payloads malware (Mahbooba et al., 2021), Alqurashi and Batarfi (2016). Any suspicious activities that allow the program to behave in a different manner are flagged as a threat. However, as explained in Section 2.1 this method may not always work as some malicious software binaries do not run properly under protected environments such as virtual machines or sandbox environments. (Ferreira et al., 2021) presents work that shows that if behavioural-based detection systems can be modified to operate in real-time, it could be an effective way to combat zero-day threats before they become a problem. This approach involves monitoring the behaviour of a system and its users for any suspicious activity that could indicate malicious software is present or attempting to gain access. However, this leans more toward machine learning as a tool to help enable proactive malware detection in real-time.

Heuristic-Based Detection

According to (Alqurashi and Batarfi (2016), heuristic-based malware detection is an approach that operates by using a set of rules to detect malicious software in order to analyse the code and behaviour of programs for suspicious properties. A study conducted by (Aslan and Samet, 2020; Alsmadi and Alqudah, 2021) showed that heuristic malware detection methods are more effective than signature-based and behavioural-based ones in detecting unknown threats. This is the case because heuristic-based approaches are able to detect malware that might not be caught by behavioural-based detection systems and are better at recognizing previously unknown or polymorphic malware, which can be difficult for traditional signature-based detection methods to identify. For efficiency, heuristic methods have also been used in conjunction with data mining and machine learning techniques to learn the behaviour and characteristics of executable files based on predefined rules, which allows them to detect malicious code that has not been seen before (Pourkhodabakhsh et al., 2022).

Heuristic malware detection methods are also able to detect malware by using algorithms to identify patterns and detect potential malicious code without needing a specific signature. Thus, allowing them (heuristic algorithms) to analyze data for suspicious behaviour or signs of a potential compromise, which traditional signature-based systems are unable to do. Additionally, heuristic systems can detect new and previously unseen forms of malware, whereas signature-based systems are limited to identifying known threats. Finally, heuristic systems are able to detect new variants of existing malware, whereas signature-based systems may not be able to detect new variants. Despite being better than signature-based and behavioural-based detection techniques, heuristics-based detection techniques tend to have higher false positive rates than signature-based techniques (Alsmadi and Alqudah, 2021; Gopinath and Sethuraman, 2023). In another study conducted by (Amini et al., (2016), their results showed that, in some cases, heuristics-based detection techniques showed an average accuracy rate of 95.42%, which was higher than that achieved by machine learning techniques (88.33%). In essence, the study demonstrated that when there are limited training datasets available, a heuristic approach may be more effective at detecting falls accurately compared to using machine learning methods.

Machine Learning-Based Detection

According to a study conducted by (Ahsan et al., 2022), the most effective automatic signature generation mechanism currently available for detecting unknown or complicated malware samples is a combination of data mining and machine learning techniques. Data mining involves analyzing large datasets to identify patterns, while machine learning uses algorithms that can learn from the data in order to make predictions about future events. This combined approach allows signatures generated by these methods to be more accurate than traditional signature-based approaches as they are able to detect both known and unknown threats with greater accuracy (Ahsan et al., 2022). Additionally, this method is also resistant to packing and obfuscation techniques which makes it even more reliable when dealing with complex malicious software samples.

Machine learning-based approaches operate by analyzing the data for meaningful patterns or correlations. Thus, while in the training phase, using any of the identified machine learning techniques, the behaviour of the system is observed in the absence of any attack (Gopinath and Sethuraman, 2023). The primary objective of this training is to create a profile based on this normal behaviour. In the testing phase, the profile that was created during the training phase is compared against current behaviour. Such a comparison enables the training models to identify any differences that may indicate potential attacks.

The results of a study conducted by (Alsmadi and Alqudah, 2021) show that machine-learning algorithms are effective at generating evidence and classifying samples accurately which enables them to detect malicious software faster and with greater accuracy than manual testing. The malware behaviour analysis of this approach, however, ought to be done in a secure sandbox environment to allow researchers to test suspicious code without risking any damage from the code itself (Alsmadi and Alqudah, 2021). The secure sandbox environment also allows faster detection of malicious software than manual testing. The sandbox environment did not seem to have negative effects on the results because when the proposed system was tested with real malware samples, the accuracy scores were very high. The results obtained from testing 500 files showed that it had a reliability score of over 95%, indicating its effectiveness in detecting malicious software accurately and quickly (Alsmadi and Alqudah, 2021).

Machine Learning algorithms can be used to detect malicious applications on mobile phones and other embedded systems by analyzing the behaviour of an application during execution. This analysis is done using a variety of monitored features such as power consumption patterns, code structure, and system calls made by the applications which are then fed into Machine Learning models for classification or anomaly detection. The model will learn from these features in order to classify new (unknown) applications as malicious or benign based on their behaviour.

As with behavioural and signature-based malware detection systems, machine learning algorithms can be used to classify suspicious code retrieved without risk by creating a secure sandbox environment (Alsmadi and Alqudah, 2021). This allows researchers to test the code in an isolated and controlled setting while monitoring its behaviour. The algorithm then uses this information along with other data points such as static analysis techniques or dynamic analysis techniques, which are commonly combined together for extracting major amounts of information from untrusted files (Alsmadi and Alqudah, 2021).

METHODOLOGY

The impact of different feature selection methods on malware detection accuracy depends largely on the number and type of features used. Generally, using more features can lead to higher accuracy but it also increases computational complexity. Feature selection techniques such as Chi-Square, Fisher Score or Info-Gain are commonly used for selecting a subset of relevant features that yield maximum detection accuracy while minimizing computation time. One also needs to consider the False Positive Rate (FPR) and make sure that these are kept to a minimum.

Criteria for Selecting Studies to Review

As explained in Section 1.3, the areas of focus for the existing methods of malware detection will be supervised and unsupervised learning techniques, anomaly detection, and deep learning. The reason for this approach is that based on a survey conducted by (Ahsan et al., 2022; Gopinath and Sethuraman, 2023), their studies explained that though signature-based and heuristic-based techniques are good methods, they can only detect known threats, while behaviour-based, model checking based, cloud-based deep learning techniques have emerged as effective ways to identify both known and unknown malicious software. In addition to this, (Alqurashi and Batarfi, 2016) presented work showing that machine learning-based techniques outperform behavioural-based, signature-based detection, and heuristic based malware detection in terms of accuracy and speed, features that are critical to malware detection. Furthermore, machine learning techniques have a lower false positive rate than the traditional methods of malware detection (signature-based techniques, heuristic-based and behavioural-based). Another factor that was taken into consideration is the IoT device that the identified detection technique is going to be used. For instance, the way desktop computers operate cannot be the same way a mobile device would. IoT devices like routers have very specialized responsibilities and limited operations, which makes their behaviour quite predictable (An et al., 2017). This predictability al lows anomaly detection algorithms to learn the normal patterns of home routers easily so that any deviation from these patterns can be detected as malicious programs or malware (An et al., 2017). Seeing high-performance scores on machine learning algorithms using data from such devices should come as no surprise when one notices that the accuracy scores are low the moment a new dataset from a different device is used. Thus, machine learning algorithms that can be used in these specialized devices had to be considered as well. It is for this reason that the study has included support vector machines, principal component analysis, and a naive anomaly detector based on unseen n-grams as they work well with home routers.

One-class Support Vector Machines (SVMs) is an unsupervised learning algorithm that uses kernel functions to detect anomalies from normal data points by creating hyper-planes around the training dataset. This makes it a powerful tool for malware detection on home routers as it can identify malicious activities even when there are no known examples of such behavior in the training set. Additionally, one-class SVMs have been shown to be more accurate and efficient than other anomaly detectors like principal component analysis or naive anomaly classifiers based on unseen n-grams (An et al., 2017). Principal Component Analysis (PCA) is another unsupervised machine learning technique used for dimensionality reduction which can be applied to identify outliers or anomalous behaviour patterns within datasets. Experimental results show that the one-class SVM using the complete 2-gram space, and the naive anomaly classifier based on unseen n-grams outperform PCA when fragment length is relatively short; while all three anomaly detectors achieve a 100% detection rate and close to zero false alarms when fragment length is sufficiently large (An et al., (2017). Lastly, the naïve anomaly detection approach relies on constructing models of "normal" system call sequences using N-Grams as features and then detecting any deviations from these expected behaviour as potential malicious activities. In the training phase, it learns a normal dictionary which consists of all occurring n-grams from the clean training system call traces; this serves as an indicator for what constitutes normal behaviour so that anything outside this range can be flagged up for further investigation.

Another factor of consideration for the selection of machine learning models included in this study is computational efficiency. For this criteria, Logistic Regression (LR) was chosen because LR has been shown to be more computationally efficient while still providing good accuracy results in many cases compared to other models like Support Vector Machines and Neural Networks (Alsulami et al., 2017). Logistic regression is a machine learning method used in the classification problem when you need to distinguish one class from another. It is a type of supervised learning algorithm that uses a linear equation to predict the probability of a given data point belonging to a certain class (Bui et al., 2017). In the context of malware identification, logistic regression can be used to identify malware by analyzing a set of data and determining whether it contains malicious code or not (Yeboah-Ofori and Boachie, 2019). Logistic regression works by fitting a linear model to the data and then using a sigmoid function to decide whether the data is likely to be malicious or not.

Approach for Conducting the Review

In this study, the paper used bench-marking as a research approach. Unlike in normal setting cases where a system runs a dataset of known malware specimens and measures the accuracy of the system's detection results and compares the results, in this study, bench-marking involved comparing the performance of different automated malware detection systems and identifying strengths and weaknesses of different systems, and provide a basis for evaluating their effectiveness (Samara and El-Alfy 2019; Ravi et al., 2022; Vu et al., 2022). The study selected past research conducted on the automation of malware detection to evaluate the accuracy of different detection methods. The criteria used to select the machine learning technique for bench-marking have been explained in Section 3.1

RESULTS

In this section, the study looked at the different techniques for both machine learning and deep learning by explicitly focusing on the strengths and weaknesses that each method has.

Machine Learning

As explained in Section 1.3 the areas of focus for machine learning are Support Vector Machines (SVM), Random Forest (RF), and Naive Bayes. For unsupervised learning, the study will focus on K-means clustering, Hierarchical Clustering, and Density-Based Clustering (DBSCAN). For anomaly detection, the study will focus on One-Class SVM, Isolation Forest, and Gaussian Mixture Model (GMM) and when looking at deep learning, the study will focus on Convolutional Neural Networks (CNN) and Recurrent Neural Networks (RNN).

Strengths and Weaknesses of Current ML Methods

Decision trees are a popular machine learning technique for malware detection due to their ability to quickly analyze large datasets and identify patterns in the data (Fernando et al., 2020). The main strength of decision trees is their ability to quickly detect anomalies in the data. Additionally, decision trees are able to quickly identify patterns and relationships between different variables, which is useful for malware detection. However, decision trees can suffer from over-fitting, which can lead to inaccurate results (Beaman et al., 2021). Additionally, decision trees can be difficult to interpret and can be prone to bias, as the data used to build the tree can be heavily influenced by the data used to train the model (Fernando et al.,(2020). As such, decision trees should be used with caution when it comes to malware detection.

Support Vector Machines (SVMs) have proven to be one of the most effective techniques for malware detection (Khraisat et al., 2019; Dada et al., 2019), with a high accuracy rate and a low false positive rate. SVMs are particularly good at detecting unknown malware, as they are able to effectively model data that is not linearly separable. However, SVMs can be computationally expensive, which can be a disadvantage when working with large datasets (Khraisat et al., 2019; Dada et al., 2019),. Additionally, SVMs can perform poorly on datasets with high levels of noise or outliers, as they are prone to over-fitting.

The main strength of Random Forest in detecting malware is its ability to process a large number of features from the data and to quickly make accurate predictions (Fernando et al., 2020). Random Forests are also robust to outliers and can handle noisy data well. One of the weaknesses of Random Forest is that it is not particularly good at detecting rare events or small changes in data, and can sometimes produce overly simplified models that are not suitable for complex data (Fernando et al., 2020). Additionally, Random Forests can be computationally expensive, as they require a large number of trees to be trained.

The strengths of using Naive Bayes in detecting malware are that it is fast to train and can handle large datasets (Khraisat et al., 2019). It is also relatively simple to understand and implement. Its weaknesses include that it is not very accurate in predicting rare events, and it assumes that all features are independent of each other, which is not always the case (Khraisat et al., 2019). Additionally, Naive Bayes does not provide good estimates of class probabilities, which can be an issue when dealing with malware detection.

The strengths of K-Means Clustering in detecting malware include its scalability, speed, and accuracy in detecting malicious code (Bohara et al., 2020). Additionally, K-Means Clustering is capable of detecting complex data structures and is easy to implement. The weaknesses of K-Means Clustering include its sensitivity to outliers, as well as its inability to handle noise and overlapping clusters (Bohara et al., 2020). Additionally, K-Means Clustering can be computationally expensive, which can limit its use in real-time applications. Finally, K-Means Clustering relies on predetermined parameters, which can limit its accuracy in some situations.

The main strength of hierarchical clustering in detecting malware is its ability to identify patterns in large datasets and classify them into clusters (Bohara et al., 2020; Fernando et al., 2020). This can help detect anomalies or malicious activities in a network. Additionally, hierarchical clustering can be used to identify clusters within a network and identify potential threats. The main weaknesses of hierarchical clustering in detecting malware are its reliance on prior knowledge and its inability to accurately detect new or unknown malware (Bohara et al., 2020; Fernando et al., 2020). Additionally, hierarchical clustering can be computationally expensive, making it less suitable for large datasets. Additionally, hierarchical clustering may not be able to detect more complex malicious activities.

The current strengths of Density-Based Clustering (DBSCAN) in detecting malware are that it is able to detect complex patterns in data and is able to distinguish between normal and abnormal data. It is also able to identify outliers in data, which can be useful for detecting new or unknown malicious activity (Sarker (2021). One of the weaknesses of DBSCAN is that it is sensitive to noise and outliers, which may lead to false positives (Bohara et al., (2020), Sarker (2021). Additionally, DBSCAN is not suitable for large datasets due to its computational complexity

Literature also reports that the current strengths of using the Gaussian Mixture Model (GMM) in detecting malware are its ability to detect unknown and new types of malicious behavior as well as its ability to approximate the distributions of known malicious behaviour. GMM is also capable of clustering threat classes, allowing it to detect different kinds of malicious behaviour. The current weaknesses of using GMM in detecting malware are its potential for false positives, as well as its inability to detect behaviour that is not part of the clusters it is trained on. Additionally, GMM requires a significant amount of data in order to accurately detect malicious behavior and may not be suitable for environments with limited data (Aryal, 2018; Park et al., 2019).

Based on the criteria explained in Section 3.1 will have to identify which ML best meets their need and what features the user will prioritize in order to get the intended results.

Deep Learning

Deep learning algorithms can be used for feature engineering in malware detection by using a variety of techniques to identify patterns and features in the data which can help identify malicious behaviour. For example, deep learning algorithms can use techniques such as convolutional neural networks (CNNs) to extract features from data such as images or text, which can then be used to help detect more sophisticated malware. Additionally, deep learning algorithms can also use techniques such as recurrent neural networks (RNNs) to analyze sequences of data such as log files, which can help detect malware that is more difficult to identify. In general, deep learning algorithms provide more accurate feature engineering for malware detection than more traditional machine learning approaches. In this section, the study focused on the strengths and weaknesses of deep learning techniques.

Strengths and Weaknesses of Current DL Methods

Convolutional Neural Networks (CNN) have their strengths and weaknesses. The current strengths of Convolutional Neural Networks (CNN) for malware detection include the ability to detect complex patterns in malicious code, the ability to identify and classify malware even when it has been slightly modified, and the ability to adapt to new types of malicious code. The main weaknesses of CNNs for malware detection are the potential for false positives due to the fact that CNNs are prone to over-fitting, their potential for under-fitting due to the complex nature of malware, and their limited ability to detect unknown malware (Naway and Li, 2018; Catalano et al., 2022).

Lastly, the study looked at Recurrent Neural Networks (RNNs). The current strengths of RNNs in detecting malware include their ability to process and understand large amounts of data, their ability to detect complex patterns in data, and their ability to identify subtle changes in data. The weaknesses of RNNs in malware detection include the difficulty of training them properly, the large amount of data required for accurate results, and the lack of interpretability of their results. Additionally, RNNs can be prone to over-fitting and require careful tuning to optimize their performance (Islam et al., 2020).

You Only Look Once (YOLO) is a deep learning technique that has been successfully used for object detection, and it has also been used for malware detection (Yuan et al., 2019; Zhu et al., 2023). Compared to other deep learning techniques, YOLO is generally faster and more efficient at detecting objects in an image. In terms of malware detection, YOLO has been shown to be relatively effective, especially in detecting malicious objects in dynamic environments such as in malware samples (Zhu et al., 2023). However, YOLO is not as effective as other deep learning techniques, such as Convolutional Neural Networks (CNNs) or Recurrent Neural Networks (RNNs), in detecting malicious objects in static environments (Yuan et al., 2019; Ahmad et al., 2020). This is because YOLO is designed to be used in real-time applications, where it is expected that the objects being detected may be moving around or changing in size or shape (Yuan et al., 2019; Zhu et al., 2023). In contrast, CNNs and RNNs are better suited to static environments, as they can be trained on a dataset of static images and used to detect objects in those images. Additionally, CNNs and RNNs are better at object recognition, since they are able to recognize objects even when they are partially obscured, which is not something that YOLO is designed to do (Yuan et al., 2019; Ahmad et al., 2020).

CONCLUSION

In this section, the chapter concludes by splitting the section into two parts: the first part explains the key findings of the evaluation, and the second part makes recommendations for future work and areas where future studies need to focus more.

Summary of Key Findings

Machine learning algorithms have successfully been used to detect unknown malware that is not detected by traditional methods like signature-based and behaviour-based techniques. Furthermore, ML has been shown to detect unknown malware more accurately with less false positive rate than signature-based and behaviour-based techniques. In addition to this, ML also helps reduce the time taken for manual analysis of thousands of incoming malwares on a daily basis thus making it easier to protect computer systems from advanced threats quickly and efficiently.

The best-performing machine-learning techniques for malware detection include decision trees, random forests, k-nearest neighbours, naive Bayes, support vector machines, and deep learning algorithms. Decision trees are useful for quickly classifying data and can be used to detect malware quickly and accurately. Random forests are also effective for malware detection and can provide more accurate results than decision trees. K-nearest neighbours is a computationally efficient algorithm that is often used for malware detection, as it can quickly generate accurate results. Naive Bayes is another algorithm commonly used for malware detection, as it can easily handle large datasets and is relatively fast to train. Support vector machines are powerful algorithms capable of detecting nonlinear relationships and can be used for malware detection. Finally, deep learning algorithms are useful for feature engineering and can help detect more sophisticated malware. It is important to note that there can never be a one-size-fits-all algorithm because the performance of different algorithms depends on a variety of factors such as the size of the dataset, the complexity of the neural network architecture, the device that was affected by the malware and the hardware used for training and testing.

RECOMMENDATIONS FOR FUTURE RESEARCH

Future studies will do best to lean more towards deep learning than traditional machine learning techniques. This is the case because deep learning techniques are more efficient than traditional machine learning techniques in detecting sophisticated malware. This is the case because deep learning models are also able to analyze large datasets more quickly and accurately than traditional machine learning models, and can more effectively identify patterns and anomalies within the data. Additionally, deep learning models are better able to identify trends and patterns in malware behaviour, allowing them to more accurately detect sophisticated malware threats.

A good case study would be to use You Only Look Once (YOLO). YOLO is a powerful tool for feature engineering and can help detect more sophisticated malware. YOLO is a deep-learning object detection system that can identify objects in an image within seconds. It works by using a convolutional neural network (CNN) to detect objects within an image and then draw a bounding box around each object. YOLO is able to detect multiple objects in an image, and it can detect objects in different sizes and shapes. Furthermore, YOLO can be used to identify and classify objects in an image and can be used to identify and classify malware. YOLO can also be used to detect and classify more sophisticated malware, as it is able to identify patterns and features that are unique to specific types of malwares.

REFERENCES

Abu Al-Haija, Q., Odeh, A., & Qattous, H. (2022). PDF malware detection based on optimizable decision trees. *Electronics (Basel)*, *11*(19), 3142. doi:10.3390/electronics11193142

Ahmad, T., Ma, Y., Yahya, M., Ahmad, B., Nazir, S., & Haq, A. U. (2020). Object detection through modified YOLO neural network. *Scientific Programming*, *2020*, 1–10. doi:10.1155/2020/8403262

Ahsan, M., Nygard, K. E., Gomes, R., Chowdhury, M. M., Rifat, N., & Connolly, J. F. (2022). Cybersecurity threats and their mitigation approaches using Machine Learning—A Review. *Journal of Cybersecurity and Privacy*, *2*(3), 527–555. doi:10.3390/jcp2030027

Alqurashi, S., & Batarfi, O. (2016). A comparison of malware detection techniques based on hidden Markov model. *Journal of Information Security*, *7*(3), 215–223. doi:10.4236/jis.2016.73017

Alsmadi, T., & Alqudah, N. (2021, July). A survey on malware detection techniques. In 2021 international conference on information technology (ICIT) (pp. 371-376). IEEE. doi:10.1109/ICIT52682.2021.9491765

Alsodi, O., Zhou, X., Gururajan, R., & Shrestha, A. (2021, October). A Survey on Detection of cybersecurity threats on Twitter using deep learning. In *2021 8th International Conference on Behavioral and Social Computing (BESC)* (pp. 1-5). IEEE. 10.1109/BESC53957.2021.9635406

Alsulami, B., Srinivasan, A., Dong, H., & Mancoridis, S. (2017, October). Lightweight behavioral malware detection for windows platforms. In *2017 12th International Conference on Malicious and Unwanted Software (MALWARE)* (pp. 75-81). IEEE. 10.1109/MALWARE.2017.8323959

Amini, A., Banitsas, K., & Cosmas, J. (2016, May). A comparison between heuristic and machine learning techniques in fall detection using Kinect v2. In *2016 IEEE International Symposium on Medical Measurements and Applications (MeMeA)* (pp. 1-6). IEEE. 10.1109/MeMeA.2016.7533763

An, N., Duff, A., Naik, G., Faloutsos, M., Weber, S., & Mancoridis, S. (2017, October). Behavioral anomaly detection of malware on home routers. In *2017 12th International Conference on Malicious and Unwanted Software (MALWARE)* (pp. 47-54). IEEE. 10.1109/MALWARE.2017.8323956

Aryal, S. (2018). Anomaly detection technique robust to units and scales of measurement. *Advances in Knowledge Discovery and Data Mining: 22nd Pacific-Asia Conference, PAKDD 2018, Melbourne, VIC, Australia, June 3-6, 2018 Proceedings*, 22(Part I), 589–601.

Aslan, Ö. A., & Samet, R. (2020). A comprehensive review on malware detection approaches. *IEEE Access : Practical Innovations, Open Solutions*, 8, 6249–6271. doi:10.1109/ACCESS.2019.2963724

Beaman, C., Barkworth, A., Akande, T. D., Hakak, S., & Khan, M. K. (2021). Ransomware: Recent advances, analysis, challenges and future research directions. *Computers & Security*, 111, 102490. doi:10.1016/j.cose.2021.102490 PMID:34602684

Bohara, B., Bhuyan, J., Wu, F., & Ding, J. (2020). A survey on the use of data clustering for intrusion detection system in cybersecurity. *International Journal of Network Security & its Applications*, 12(1), 1–18. doi:10.5121/ijnsa.2020.12101 PMID:34290487

Botacin, M., Alves, M. Z., Oliveira, D., & Grégio, A. (2022). HEAVEN: A Hardware-Enhanced AntiVirus ENgine to accelerate real-time, signature-based malware detection. *Expert Systems with Applications*, *201*, 117083. doi:10.1016/j.eswa.2022.117083

Buchanan, B., Bansemer, J., Cary, D., Lucas, J., & Musser, M. (2020). Automating cyber attacks. Center for Security and Emerging Technology, 13-32.

Bui, N., Cesana, M., Hosseini, S. A., Liao, Q., Malanchini, I., & Widmer, J. (2017). A survey of anticipatory mobile networking: Context-based classification, prediction methodologies, and optimization techniques. *IEEE Communications Surveys and Tutorials*, *19*(3), 1790–1821. doi:10.1109/COMST.2017.2694140

Catalano, C., Chezzi, A., Angelelli, M., & Tommasi, F. (2022). Deceiving AI-based malware detection through polymorphic attacks. *Computers in Industry, 143*, 103751.

Dada, E. G., Bassi, J. S., Chiroma, H., Adetunmbi, A. O., & Ajibuwa, O. E. (2019). Machine learning for email spam filtering: Review, approaches and open research problems. *Heliyon*, *5*(6), e01802. doi:10.1016/j.heliyon.2019.e01802 PMID:31211254

David, O. E., & Netanyahu, N. S. (2015, July). Deepsign: Deep learning for automatic malware signature generation and classification. In *2015 International Joint Conference on Neural Networks (IJCNN)* (pp. 1-8). IEEE. 10.1109/IJCNN.2015.7280815

Dua, S., & Du, X. (2016). *Data mining and machine learning in cybersecurity*. CRC press. doi:10.1201/b10867

Fang, Y., Gao, J., Liu, Z., & Huang, C. (2020). Detecting cyber threat event from twitter using IDCNN and BiLSTM. *Applied Sciences (Basel, Switzerland)*, *10*(17), 5922. doi:10.3390/app10175922

Fernando, D. W., Komninos, N., & Chen, T. (2020). A study on the evolution of ransomware detection using machine learning and deep learning techniques. *IoT*, *1*(2), 551–604. doi:10.3390/iot1020030

Ferreira, A. P., Gupta, C., Inácio, P. R., & Freire, M. M. (2021). Behaviour-based Malware Detection in Mobile AndroidPlatforms Using Machine Learning Algorithms. *J. Wirel. Mob. Networks Ubiquitous Comput. Dependable Appl., 12*(4), 62-88.

Gopinath, M., & Sethuraman, S. C. (2023). A comprehensive survey on deep learning based malware detection techniques. *Computer Science Review, 47*, 100529. doi:10.1016/j.cosrev.2022.100529

Islam, M. R., Liu, S., Wang, X., & Xu, G. (2020). Deep learning for misinformation detection on online social networks: A survey and new perspectives. *Social Network Analysis and Mining*, *10*(1), 82. doi:10.1007/s13278-020-00696-x PMID:33014173

Khraisat, A., Gondal, I., Vamplew, P., & Kamruzzaman, J. (2019). Survey of intrusion detection systems: Techniques, datasets and challenges. *Cybersecurity*, *2*(1), 1–22. doi:10.1186/s42400-019-0038-7

Kundu, P. P., Truong-Huu, T., Chen, L., Zhou, L., & Teo, S. G. (2022). Detection and classification of botnet traffic using deep learning with model explanation. *IEEE Transactions on Dependable and Secure Computing*.

Lakhotia, A., Notani, V., & LeDoux, C. (2018, June). Malware economics and its implication to anti-malware situational awareness. In *2018 International Conference On Cyber Situational Awareness, Data Analytics And Assessment* (Cyber SA) (pp. 1-8). IEEE. 10.1109/CyberSA.2018.8551388

Mahbooba, B., Timilsina, M., Sahal, R., & Serrano, M. (2021). Explainable artificial intelligence (XAI) to enhance trust management in intrusion detection systems using decision tree model. *Complexity*, *2021*, 1–11. doi:10.1155/2021/6634811

Maniriho, P., Mahmood, A. N., & Chowdhury, M. J. M. (2022). A study on malicious software behaviour analysis and detection techniques: Taxonomy, current trends and challenges. *Future Generation Computer Systems*, *130*, 1–18. doi:10.1016/j.future.2021.11.030

Naway, A., & Li, Y. (2018). A review on the use of deep learning in android malware detection. *arXiv preprint arXiv:1812.10360*.

Park, M., Han, J., Oh, H., & Lee, K. (2019). Threat assessment for android environment with connectivity to IoT devices from the perspective of situational awareness. *Wireless Communications and Mobile Computing*, *2019*, 1–14. doi:10.1155/2019/5121054

Pourkhodabakhsh, N., Mamoudan, M. M., & Bozorgi-Amiri, A. (2023). Effective machine learning, Meta-heuristic algorithms and multi-criteria decision making to minimizing human resource turnover. *Applied Intelligence*, *53*(12), 16309–16331. doi:10.1007/s10489-022-04294-6 PMID:36531972

Ravi, V., Alazab, M., Selvaganapathy, S., & Chaganti, R. (2022). A Multi-View attention-based deep learning framework for malware detection in smart healthcare systems. *Computer Communications*, *195*, 73–81. doi:10.1016/j.comcom.2022.08.015

Rey, V., Sánchez, P. M. S., Celdrán, A. H., & Bovet, G. (2022). Federated learning for malware detection in IoT devices. *Computer Networks*, *204*, 108693. doi:10.1016/j. comnet.2021.108693

Samara, M., & El-Alfy, E. S. M. (2019, November). Benchmarking open-source android malware detection tools. In *2019 2nd IEEE Middle East and North Africa COMMunications Conference (MENACOMM)* (pp. 1-6). IEEE. 10.1109/ MENACOMM46666.2019.8988532

Sarker, I. H. (2021). Machine learning: Algorithms, real-world applications and research directions. *SN Computer Science*, *2*(3), 160. doi:10.1007/s42979-021-00592-x PMID:33778771

Savenko, O., Nicheporuk, A., Hurman, I., & Lysenko, S. (2019, June). Dynamic Signature-based Malware Detection Technique Based on API Call Tracing. In ICTERI workshops (pp. 633-643). Academic Press.

Shafiq, M., Tian, Z., Bashir, A. K., Du, X., & Guizani, M. (2020). CorrAUC: A malicious bot-IoT traffic detection method in IoT network using machine-learning techniques. *IEEE Internet of Things Journal*, *8*(5), 3242–3254. doi:10.1109/ JIOT.2020.3002255

Tian, Z., Cui, L., Liang, J., & Yu, S. (2022). A comprehensive survey on poisoning attacks and countermeasures in machine learning. *ACM Computing Surveys*, *55*(8), 1–35. doi:10.1145/3551636

Vu, D. L., Newman, Z., & Meyers, J. S. (2022). A benchmark comparison of python malware detection approaches. *arXiv preprint arXiv:2209.13288*.

Xi, B. (2020). Adversarial machine learning for cybersecurity and computer vision: Current developments and challenges. *Wiley Interdisciplinary Reviews: Computational Statistics*, *12*(5), e1511. doi:10.1002/wics.1511

Yeboah-Ofori, A., & Boachie, C. (2019, May). Malware attack predictive analytics in a cyber supply chain context using machine learning. In *2019 International conference on cyber security and Internet of Things (ICSIoT)* (pp. 66-73). IEEE. 10.1109/ICSIoT47925.2019.00019

Yuan, X., He, P., Zhu, Q., & Li, X. (2019). Adversarial examples: Attacks and defenses for deep learning. *IEEE Transactions on Neural Networks and Learning Systems*, *30*(9), 2805–2824. doi:10.1109/TNNLS.2018.2886017 PMID:30640631

Zhu, Y., Wang, M., Yin, X., Zhang, J., Meijering, E., & Hu, J. (2022). Deep learning in diverse intelligent sensor based systems. *Sensors (Basel)*, *23*(1), 62. doi:10.3390/ s23010062 PMID:36616657

ENDNOTE

[1]   https://cybersecurityventures.com/hackerpocalypse-cybercrime-report-2016/

Chapter 8

Role of Blockchain in Digital Forensics:
A Systematic Study

Amit Kumar Tyagi

https://orcid.org/0000-0003-2657-8700
National Institute of Fashion Technology, New Delhi, India

Bukola Fatimah Balogun
Kwara State University Malete, Nigeria

Shrikant Tiwari

https://orcid.org/0000-0001-6947-2362
Galgotias University, Greater Noida, India

ABSTRACT

Digital forensics plays an important role in investigating cybercrimes, data breaches, and other digital misdeeds in an increasingly connected world. With the proliferation of blockchain technology, a new dimension has emerged in the world of digital forensics. This work presents a comprehensive review of the intersection between blockchain and digital forensics, exploring the various ways blockchain technology influences and challenges the traditional practices of digital forensic investigations. This work begins by elucidating the fundamental concepts of blockchain technology, emphasizing its decentralized and immutable nature, cryptographic underpinnings, and its uses in cryptocurrency transactions. Subsequently, it delves into the potential benefits of blockchain for digital forensics, such as providing transparent and tamper-proof logs of digital activities and transactions. However, this chapter also discusses the unique challenges posed by blockchain in digital forensic investigations.

DOI: 10.4018/978-1-6684-8127-1.ch008

INTRODUCTION TO BLOCKCHAIN AND DIGITAL FORENSICS

A. Blockchain Fundamentals: Definition, Concepts, Types, Key Components of Blockchain Technology

Blockchain is a distributed and decentralized digital ledger technology that records transactions across multiple computers in a way that ensures the security, transparency, and immutability of the data (Al-Khateeb, Epiphaniou, & Daly 2019; Kumari, Tyagi, & Rekha, 2021). It consists of a chain of blocks, each containing a batch of transactions, which are linked together and secured through cryptographic hashes. Now here few of the key concepts of Blockchain are:

- Decentralization: Blockchain operates on a decentralized network of computers (nodes) rather than relying on a central authority. Each node has a copy of the entire blockchain ledger, ensuring redundancy and resilience.
- Distributed Ledger: The ledger, containing transaction data, is distributed across multiple nodes. This distribution prevents a single point of failure and enhances transparency.
- Blocks: Transactions are grouped into blocks, and each block contains a set of transactions. Blocks are linked together chronologically to form a chain.
- Transactions: Transactions represent actions or data changes recorded on the blockchain. These can include cryptocurrency transfers, smart contract executions, or any data update relevant to the blockchain's purpose.
- Consensus Mechanisms: Blockchain networks use consensus algorithms to validate and agree on the state of the ledger. Common consensus mechanisms include Proof of Work (PoW), Proof of Stake (PoS), and Delegated Proof of Stake (DPoS).
- Cryptography: Cryptographic techniques, such as hashing and digital signatures, secure data on the blockchain. Hashes uniquely identify blocks and their contents, while digital signatures ensure transaction authenticity.
- Immutability: Once data is added to the blockchain, it becomes extremely difficult to alter. This immutability ensures the historical integrity of transactions.
- Public vs. Private Blockchains: Public blockchains, like Bitcoin and Ethereum, are open to anyone, while private blockchains restrict access to authorized participants. Consortium blockchains are semi-private, allowing a group of organizations to participate.
- Smart Contracts: Smart contracts are self-executing contracts with predefined rules and conditions. They automatically execute actions when the specified conditions are met, providing automation and trust in various applications.

Further, types of Blockchains are;

- Public Blockchain: Open to anyone and maintained by a decentralized network of nodes. Examples include Bitcoin and Ethereum.
- Private Blockchain: Restricted access and controlled by a single organization or consortium of organizations. Used for internal purposes, such as supply chain management.
- Consortium Blockchain: A semi-private blockchain controlled by a group of organizations. It provides more control than public blockchains while maintaining some level of decentralization.

Key Components of Blockchain Technology are;

- Cryptographic Hash: Blocks are linked using cryptographic hashes, which are unique identifiers generated from block data. Changing any data in a block would require recalculating the hash for that block and all subsequent blocks.
- Decentralized Network: A network of nodes (computers) maintains the blockchain, ensuring that no single entity has control. This decentralization enhances security and reliability.
- Consensus Mechanism: Consensus algorithms determine how nodes agree on the validity of transactions and the addition of new blocks to the chain. Examples include PoW, PoS, and DPoS (Tibrewal, Srivastava, & Tyagi, 2022).
- Transactions: Transactions represent data changes recorded on the blockchain. They include inputs, outputs, and digital signatures for verification.
- Smart Contracts: Code that automatically executes predefined actions when specific conditions are met. Smart contracts are a key feature of blockchain platforms like Ethereum.

Digital Signatures: Digital signatures verify the authenticity of transactions and ensure that only authorized parties can make changes to the blockchain.

- Public/Private Key Pairs: Users on the blockchain have public and private key pairs. Public keys serve as addresses for receiving funds or data, while private keys are kept secret and used for signing transactions.

Note that, Blockchain technology has several applications beyond cryptocurrencies, including supply chain management, voting systems, healthcare, finance, and more. Its fundamental concepts of decentralization, distributed ledgers, and cryptographic security makes it a powerful tool for enhancing trust and transparency in various industries.

B. Security and Consensus Mechanisms of Blockchain Technology

Blockchain technology depends on security mechanisms and consensus algorithms to ensure the integrity, trustworthiness, and immutability of data (Mishra, & Tyagi, 2019). Here, we explain the security features and consensus mechanisms commonly used in blockchain technology:

Security Mechanisms

Cryptography

- Hash Functions: Blockchain uses cryptographic hash functions to create unique, fixed-length representations (hashes) of data. Hashes are used to link blocks in the chain and ensure data integrity.
- Digital Signatures: Digital signatures are used to verify the authenticity of transactions and ensure that only authorized parties can modify the blockchain. They provide non-repudiation, meaning a party cannot deny their involvement in a transaction.
- Immutable Ledger: Once data is added to a blockchain, it becomes extremely difficult to alter or delete. This immutability ensures the historical integrity of the ledger.
- Decentralization: Blockchain operates on a decentralized network of nodes (computers). This distribution prevents a single point of failure and enhances security, as there is no central authority that can be compromised.
- Consensus Mechanisms: Consensus mechanisms are important for validating and agreeing on the state of the blockchain. They prevent double-spending, ensure the order of transactions, and maintain network security.

Common Consensus Mechanisms

- Proof of Work (PoW): In PoW, miners compete to solve complex mathematical puzzles. The first miner to solve the puzzle gets the right to add a new block to the chain and is rewarded with cryptocurrency. PoW is used in Bitcoin and Ethereum.
- Proof of Stake (PoS): PoS replaces miners with validators who are chosen to create new blocks based on the amount of cryptocurrency they hold and are

willing to "stake" as collateral. PoS is considered more energy-efficient than PoW and is used in networks like Ethereum 2.0.

- Delegated Proof of Stake (DPoS): DPoS is a variation of PoS in which token holders vote for a select group of delegates who validate transactions and create blocks. DPoS aims to improve scalability and speed, and it is used in networks like EOS and TRON.

- Proof of Authority (PoA): In PoA, block validators are known and trusted entities or organizations. They take turns creating blocks. PoA is used in private and consortium blockchains where trust among participants is established.

- Proof of Space (PoSpace) and Proof of Time (PoTime): PoSpace and PoTime consensus mechanisms use storage space and time as the basis for validating transactions. Chia, for example, uses PoSpace to secure its blockchain.

- Hybrid Consensus: Some blockchain networks combine multiple consensus mechanisms to balance security, scalability, and energy efficiency. For example, Algorand uses both PoS and PoA in its hybrid consensus.

Security Challenges (Krishna, & Tyagi, 2020)

- 51% Attacks: In PoW blockchains, a malicious entity with over 50% of the network's computational power can potentially control the blockchain, leading to double-spending and other security issues.

- Sybil Attacks: In PoS and DPoS, attackers can create several pseudonymous nodes or stake large amounts of cryptocurrency to gain undue influence in the network.

- Smart Contract Vulnerabilities: Vulnerabilities in smart contract code can lead to security breaches and exploits. Regular audits and code reviews are essential to identify and mitigate these risks.

- Quantum Threat: Quantum computers, once sufficiently advanced, could potentially break existing blockchain encryption methods, necessitating the adoption of quantum-resistant cryptographic solutions.

- Regulatory and Compliance Issues: Blockchain must related to legal and regulatory requirements in various jurisdictions, which can be challenging due to the global and decentralized nature of the technology.

- Privacy Issues: Balancing transparency with privacy is an ongoing challenge in blockchain. Some networks, like Monero and Zcash, prioritize privacy, making it challenging for investigators to trace transactions.

Hence, blockchain technology continues to evolve, and security mechanisms and consensus algorithms are frequently refined to address these challenges and enhance the security and trustworthiness of blockchain networks.

C. Forensics Fundamentals, Definition, Types, and Role of Digital Forensics in Cybersecurity

Forensics, in a broad sense, refers to the application of scientific methods and techniques to investigate and solve crimes, legal disputes, or incidents. Digital forensics specifically focuses on the investigation of digital devices, data, and systems to collect, preserve, analyze, and present evidence for legal purposes. As defined, Digital forensics, also known as computer forensics or cyber forensics, is the process of collecting, preserving, analyzing, and presenting digital evidence from digital devices and electronic systems. This evidence is often used in legal proceedings to investigate cybercrimes, security breaches, fraud, and other digital incidents. There are different types of Digital Forensics, as mentioned in table 1.

Table 1. Types of digital forensics

Type	Description
Computer Forensics	This involves the examination of computers, laptops, servers, and storage devices to recover and analyze digital evidence. It includes data recovery, file analysis, and the identification of malware or unauthorized activities.
Mobile Device Forensics	Mobile forensics focuses on smartphones, tablets, and other mobile devices. Investigators extract data such as call logs, text messages, emails, and app usage to uncover relevant evidence.
Network Forensics	Network forensics analyzes network traffic to detect and investigate security incidents. It helps identify intrusions, unauthorized access, and the flow of data between devices.
Malware Analysis:	Malware forensics involves the examination of malicious software, such as viruses, Trojans, and ransomware. Analysts dissect malware to understand its functionality and origin.
Incident Response	Incident response forensics is the process of quickly identifying and mitigating security incidents. It involves real-time analysis of systems and networks to contain threats.
Forensic Data Analysis:	This type of analysis involves examining large datasets to identify patterns, anomalies, and trends. It's used in financial investigations, fraud detection, and cybersecurity analysis.
Cloud Forensics:	With the growing use of cloud services, cloud forensics deals with collecting and analyzing data stored in the cloud, such as emails, documents, and server logs.
IoT (Internet of Things) Forensics	IoT forensics focuses on connected devices, such as smart appliances, wearable technology, and IoT sensors. Investigators analyze data generated by these devices (refer figure 1).

Figure 1. IoT forensics or Internet of forensics

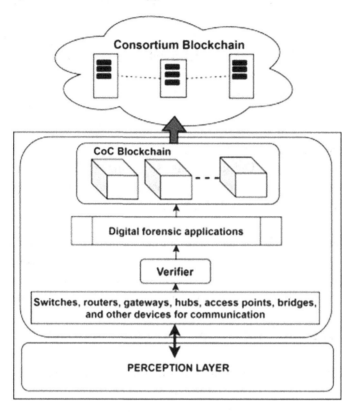

Role of Digital Forensics in Cybersecurity: It can be discussed as:

- Incident Investigation: Digital forensics plays an important role in investigating cybersecurity incidents. It helps determine the scope of a breach, the tactics used by attackers, and the extent of the damage.
- Evidence Collection: Digital forensics collects and preserves digital evidence that can be used to identify cybercriminals, understand the attack vectors, and support legal actions.
- Attribution: Forensic analysis can help attribute cyberattacks to specific individuals, groups, or nation-states. This is essential for holding perpetrators accountable and taking appropriate actions.
- Cybercrime Prevention: By analyzing past cyber incidents and vulnerabilities, digital forensics can inform proactive cybersecurity measures to prevent future attacks.

- Compliance and Legal Support: Digital forensics assists organizations in complying with legal and regulatory requirements related to data breaches and cyber incidents. It provides evidence for use in legal proceedings.
- Recovery and Remediation: After a cyber incident, digital forensics helps organizations recover compromised systems, remove malware, and implement security improvements to prevent future attacks.
- Threat Intelligence: Information extracted from forensic investigations contributes to threat intelligence, allowing organizations to stay informed about emerging threats and vulnerabilities.
- Employee Training: Digital forensics findings can be used to educate employees about cybersecurity best practices, social engineering techniques, and the consequences of negligent behavior.

Hence, Digital forensics is an important component of modern cybersecurity, helping organizations respond to and recover from cyber incidents while also aiding law enforcement in prosecuting cybercriminals. It contributes to the overall security posture of organizations and assists in reducing the impact of cyber threats.

D. Limitations and Challenges in Digital Forensics

Digital forensics, while an emerging/ important field for investigating cybercrimes and incidents, faces several limitations and challenges that impact its effectiveness and scope. Here are some key limitations and challenges in digital forensics:

- Rapid Technological Advancements: The pace of technological advancement is relentless, and new devices, software, and storage technologies constantly emerge. Digital forensics tools and techniques must continually evolve to keep up with these changes.
- Encryption and Privacy Issues: The widespread use of encryption technologies, especially end-to-end encryption, can make it difficult to access and analyze digital data, even for legitimate investigative purposes. Balancing privacy rights with the need for digital evidence is an ongoing challenge.
- Data Volume and Storage: The sheer volume of digital data generated daily can overwhelm forensic investigators. Collecting, processing, and analyzing large datasets require essential resources and time.
- Data Fragmentation: Digital data is often fragmented and dispersed across various devices, cloud services, and storage media. Reconstructing a complete picture from fragmented data can be challenging.

- Anti-Forensic Techniques: Malicious actors use anti-forensic techniques to hide their tracks and make investigations more difficult. These techniques include file wiping, data encryption, and data obfuscation.
- Jurisdictional and Legal Challenges: Digital evidence often crosses international borders, making jurisdictional issues and differences in legal standards major challenge. Harmonizing legal frameworks is essential for effective cross-border investigations.
- Lack of Standardization: Digital forensics lacks global standardization in terms of tools, procedures, and methodologies. This can lead to inconsistencies in evidence handling and reporting.
- Chain of Custody Issues: Maintaining the chain of custody for digital evidence is important for its admissibility in court. Mishandling evidence or failing to establish a proper chain of custody can jeopardize cases.
- Forensic Tool Limitations: Digital forensics tools may have limitations in terms of compatibility with various devices and file formats. They may not always support the latest technologies or obscure file types.
- Insider Threats: Insider threats, where individuals within an organization abuse their access to digital systems, can be challenging to detect and investigate, as the perpetrators may know forensic techniques.
- Evolving Cyber Threats: Cyber threats continually evolve, with attackers using sophisticated techniques to cover their tracks. Digital forensics must adapt to keep pace with evolving attack methods.
- Digital Evidence Preservation: Preserving digital evidence in a forensically sound manner is essential. The failure to do so can lead to the contamination or loss of important evidence.
- Resource and Budget Constraints: Many organizations, especially smaller ones, may lack the resources and budget required to establish and maintain a comprehensive digital forensics capability.
- Data Deletion and Overwriting: The overwriting of data, whether accidental or intentional, can result in the loss of potential evidence. Recovery from overwritten data can be challenging or impossible.
- Zero-Day Vulnerabilities: Attacks that exploit zero-day vulnerabilities can leave little or no trace, making it difficult to detect and investigate the breach.

Hence, these limitations and challenges in digital forensics require ongoing research, collaboration among practitioners and law enforcement agencies, and the development of innovative tools and methodologies (Jayaprakash, & Tyagi, 2022). It also necessitates a strong emphasis on training and education to ensure that digital forensic experts have the skills and knowledge to navigate these complex and dynamic landscapes.

E. Organization of the Work

This work is summarized into 7 sections.

BLOCKCHAIN APPLICATIONS IN DIGITAL FORENSICS

Blockchain technology has several applications in the field of digital forensics, providing solutions to various challenges and enhancing the integrity and security of digital evidence (Deshmukh, Sreenath, et al., (2022). Here are some key applications of blockchain in digital forensics:

- Immutable Evidence Storage: Blockchain's immutability ensures that once digital evidence is recorded on the blockchain, it cannot be altered or deleted. This property helps preserve the integrity of evidence, making it tamper-proof and admissible in legal proceedings.
- Chain of Custody Management: Maintaining a secure and transparent chain of custody is important in digital forensics. Blockchain can be used to record and track the custody of digital evidence, providing an auditable and unforgeable history of who accessed or modified the evidence and when.
- Timestamping: Blockchain provides reliable and verifiable timestamps for digital files and records. This is important for establishing the sequence of events in investigations, especially when determining the timeline of cyber incidents.
- Digital Identity Verification: Blockchain-based digital identities can enhance the verification of individuals and entities involved in online transactions. This helps in verifying the authenticity of parties and preventing identity theft in digital investigations.
- Cross-Chain Forensic Analysis: Many blockchain networks operate independently. Cross-chain forensic analysis involves tracking digital assets as they move between different blockchains, aiding in the investigation of cryptocurrency-related crimes that span multiple networks.
- Anti-Money Laundering (AML): Blockchain analysis tools can assist in AML efforts by tracking the movement of funds through cryptocurrency networks. This helps financial institutions and law enforcement agencies identify money laundering activities and comply with regulatory requirements.
- Fraud Detection: Blockchain analytics tools can identify patterns and anomalies in transaction data, flagging potentially fraudulent or suspicious activities. This is particularly useful for uncovering Ponzi schemes, scams, and fraudulent investments.

- Smart Contract Audits: Smart contracts, which execute automatically when conditions are met, can contain vulnerabilities or exploits that malicious actors may exploit. Blockchain forensics experts can audit smart contracts to identify and analyze such issues.

- Evidence Transparency: Blockchain provides transparency in the handling and presentation of digital evidence. Parties involved in legal proceedings can verify the integrity and authenticity of evidence stored on the blockchain.

- Digital Asset Tracking: In cases involving stolen cryptocurrencies or digital assets, blockchain analysis can help trace the movement of funds across the blockchain, providing information about the flow of illicit assets.

- Regulatory Compliance: Blockchain can assist organizations and law enforcement agencies in maintaining compliance with data protection and evidence-handling regulations, simplifying the audit process.

- Chain of Evidence Preservation: Storing forensic evidence on the blockchain ensures that it cannot be tampered with or altered, safeguarding its admissibility in court (refer figure 2).

Figure 2. Blockchain for chain of evidence management in IoT

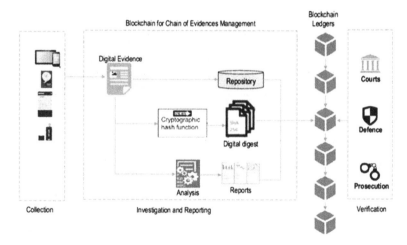

- Cross-Border Investigations: Blockchain enables international collaboration in digital forensics by providing a secure and transparent platform for sharing evidence and information across borders.

- Digital Investigations Training: Blockchain-based educational platforms can provide training and certification in digital forensics, enhancing the skills of investigators and forensic experts.

Blockchain technology continues to evolve, and its applications in digital forensics are expanding. As digital crimes become more sophisticated, the integration of blockchain into forensic investigations provides new tools and methods for addressing emerging challenges. A few other applications are: Immutable Data Storage, Chain of Custody and Evidence Integrity, Timestamping and Audit Trails, Fraud Detection and Investigation and Case Management and Chain of Custody

BENEFITS, LIMITATIONS, ISSUES, AND CHALLENGES OF BLOCKCHAIN IN DIGITAL FORENSICS

Blockchain technology provides several benefits and advantages in the context of digital forensics (Tyagi, Chandrasekaran, & Sreenath, 2022). However, it also comes with limitations, issues, and challenges that need to be considered. Here's an overview of the benefits, limitations, issues, and challenges of using blockchain in digital forensics, as mentioned in table 2.

Table 2. Benefits, limitations, issues, and challenges of using blockchain in digital forensics

Types	Uses	Explanation
Benefits of Blockchain in Digital Forensics	Immutability	Blockchain's immutability ensures that once data is recorded, it cannot be altered or deleted. This feature is important for preserving the integrity of digital evidence.
	Tamper-Proof Evidence	Blockchain can be used to create a tamper-proof chain of custody for digital evidence, preventing unauthorized access or tampering during an investigation.
	Transparency	Transactions on the blockchain are transparent and can be audited by authorized parties. This transparency aids in tracking and verifying digital evidence
	Timestamping	Blockchain provides reliable and verifiable timestamps for digital files, helping establish the timeline of digital events during investigations.
	Cross-Chain Analysis	Blockchain can facilitate cross-chain analysis, allowing investigators to track digital assets and transactions across different blockchain networks
	Smart Contract Audits:	Forensic experts can audit smart contracts to identify vulnerabilities or exploits that may have been used in malicious activities.
	Data Integrity	Blockchain ensures data integrity by providing cryptographic proof of the information recorded, making it suitable for preserving forensic evidence.

Table 2 continued

Types	Uses	Explanation
Limitations of Blockchain in Digital Forensics	Pseudonymity	Blockchain addresses are often pseudonymous, making it challenging to identify the real-world individuals or entities behind transactions.
	Privacy Coins	Privacy-focused cryptocurrencies like Monero and Zcash obscure transaction details, hindering forensic analysis.
	Smart Contract Complexity	Analyzing complex smart contracts can be challenging, as they may involve intricate logic and interactions.
	Regulatory Variability	Different countries have varying regulations related to blockchain and cryptocurrencies, creating legal and jurisdictional challenges for digital forensics.
	Data Size	Blockchain data can be substantial, leading to storage and processing challenges for investigators.
Issues and Challenges of Blockchain in Digital Forensics	Privacy and Anonymity	The inherent privacy and pseudonymity of blockchain can impede investigations into illicit activities, particularly when privacy coins are involved.
	Cryptocurrency Theft	Investigating cryptocurrency thefts, such as hacks or scams, requires specialized knowledge of blockchain technology and cryptocurrency markets.
	Cross-Chain Complexity	Tracking assets across multiple blockchain networks presents technical and logistical challenges for investigators
	Quantum Threat	The potential future threat of quantum computers breaking existing blockchain encryption methods requires preparation for quantum-resistant cryptographic solutions.
	Legal Compliance	Ensuring that investigations and evidence collection comply with evolving legal and regulatory frameworks is a persistent challenge.
	Resource Intensiveness	Blockchain forensic investigations can be resource-intensive, requiring access to specialized tools and expertise.
	Scalability	As blockchain networks grow, scalability challenges may affect the speed and efficiency of investigations.
	Lack of Standardization	The lack of standardized practices and certification in blockchain forensics can lead to inconsistencies in investigations.
	Privacy Issues	Balancing the need for transparency in investigations with privacy issues related to blockchain data is an ongoing challenge.
	Education and Training	There is a need for specialized education and training programs to develop expertise in blockchain forensics.

In summary, while blockchain technology provides major advantages for digital forensics, it also presents challenges related to privacy, scalability, complexity, and legal compliance. Digital forensics professionals and investigators must navigate these issues to effectively use blockchain in their investigations and maintain the integrity of digital evidence.

USE CASES OF BLOCKCHAIN IN DIGITAL FORENSICS

Blockchain technology has several compelling use cases in the field of digital forensics (Tyagi et al., 2023; Deekshetha, & Tyagi, 2023). It can enhance the transparency, security, and integrity of digital evidence while providing new avenues for tracking and analyzing illicit activities. Here are some notable use cases of blockchain in digital forensics:

- Immutable Evidence Storage: Blockchain's immutability ensures that digital evidence, once stored on the blockchain, cannot be altered or deleted. This feature is valuable for preserving the integrity of important evidence.
- Chain of Custody Tracking: Blockchain can be used to create a tamper-proof chain of custody for digital evidence. Smart contracts can automate the tracking of evidence throughout the investigation process, providing transparency and accountability.
- Timestamping: Blockchain can be used to timestamp digital files, ensuring their authenticity and proving that they existed at a specific point in time. This is important for verifying the timeline of digital events.
- Digital Asset Tracking: In cases involving stolen cryptocurrencies or digital assets, blockchain analysis can help trace the movement of funds across the blockchain, providing information about the flow of illicit assets.
- Fraud Detection: Blockchain analytics tools can identify patterns and anomalies in transaction data, flagging potentially fraudulent or suspicious activities. This is particularly useful for uncovering Ponzi schemes, scams, and fraudulent investments.
- Anti-Money Laundering (AML): Blockchain analysis can assist in AML efforts by tracking the movement of funds through cryptocurrency networks. It helps financial institutions and law enforcement agencies identify money laundering activities.
- Digital Identity Verification: Blockchain-based digital identities can be used to verify the authenticity of individuals or entities involved in online transactions. This is relevant for fraud prevention and identity theft investigations.

- Smart Contract Audits: Digital forensics experts can audit smart contracts to identify vulnerabilities or exploits that may have been used in malicious activities. This is essential for investigating incidents involving decentralized applications (DApps) and DeFi platforms.

- Cross-Chain Investigations: Cross-chain forensic analysis involves tracking digital assets as they move between different blockchain networks. This is important for cases involving assets that have been transferred across multiple blockchains.

- Evidence Transparency: Blockchain provides transparency in the handling and presentation of digital evidence. Parties involved in legal proceedings can verify the integrity of evidence stored on the blockchain.

- Anti-Counterfeiting Measures: Blockchain can be used to track the provenance of physical and digital goods, such as luxury items, pharmaceuticals, and art. It helps in detecting counterfeit products and supply chain fraud.

- Evidence Tampering Prevention: Storing forensic evidence on the blockchain ensures that it cannot be tampered with or altered, safeguarding its admissibility in court.

- Cross-Border Investigations: Blockchain enables international collaboration in digital forensics by providing a secure and transparent platform for sharing evidence and information across borders.

- Digital Investigations Training: Blockchain-based educational platforms can provide training and certification in digital forensics, enhancing the skills of investigators and forensic experts.

Hence, Blockchain technology continues to evolve, and its applications in digital forensics are expanding. As digital crimes become more sophisticated, the integration of blockchain into forensic investigations provides new tools and methods for addressing emerging challenges Few other use cases are: Digital Evidence Preservation, Authentication of Digital Evidence, Incident Response and Investigation, Chain of Custody in Legal Proceedings

A. Digital Forensics as a Service (DFaaS)

Digital Forensics as a Service (DFaaS) is a model that provides digital forensic investigation and analysis capabilities to individuals, organizations, or law enforcement agencies on a subscription or on-demand basis. DFaaS uses cloud computing, specialized tools, and expertise to provide scalable and cost-effective solutions for digital investigations. Here are the key aspects of DFaaS:

- Cloud-Based Infrastructure: DFaaS depends on cloud infrastructure, enabling users to access forensic services and tools remotely. This eliminates the need for extensive on-premises hardware and reduces the upfront costs associated with setting up a forensic lab.
- Scalability: DFaaS platforms can scale resources up or down based on demand. This flexibility is valuable for handling varying workloads and addressing large-scale investigations or incidents.
- Specialized Tools and Software: DFaaS providers provide access to a range of specialized digital forensic tools and software. These tools facilitate data collection, analysis, and reporting for various digital devices and platforms.
- Remote Access: Users can access DFaaS platforms from anywhere with an internet connection. This feature is particularly advantageous for remote or distributed teams conducting investigations.
- Expertise On-Demand: DFaaS services may include access to experienced digital forensic experts who can assist with complex investigations, provide guidance, and provide support when needed.
- Cost-Efficiency: By eliminating the need for essential upfront investments in hardware and software, DFaaS can be a cost-effective solution for organizations that require digital forensic capabilities only periodically.
- Reduced Maintenance: Maintenance, updates, and upgrades of forensic tools and infrastructure are typically managed by the DFaaS provider, relieving users of these responsibilities.
- Customization: DFaaS can be tailored to meet specific investigative needs or compliance requirements, providing flexibility in terms of the services and tools included in the subscription.
- Data Security and Compliance: DFaaS providers often implement robust security measures and compliance standards to protect sensitive data and ensure that investigations related to legal and regulatory requirements.
- Rapid Response: DFaaS is well-suited for rapid response to incidents, enabling organizations to initiate investigations promptly without the need to procure and set up forensic infrastructure.
- Evidence Preservation: DFaaS providers have procedures in place to preserve digital evidence in a forensically sound manner, ensuring its admissibility in legal proceedings.
- Chain of Custody Management: Maintaining the chain of custody is an important aspect of digital forensics. DFaaS platforms incorporate features to track and document the handling and transfer of digital evidence.

Hence, DFaaS can benefit huge range of users, including law enforcement agencies, cybersecurity teams, legal professionals, corporate investigators, and incident response teams. It provides accessibility, cost savings, and expertise on-demand, making it a valuable option for organizations and individuals requiring digital forensic capabilities without the overhead of maintaining an in-house forensic lab.

SECURITY AND PRIVACY ISSUES TOWARDS BLOCKCHAIN FOR DIGITAL FORENSICS

Blockchain technology presents unique security and privacy challenges for digital forensics, complicating the investigation and analysis of digital crimes. Some of the key security and privacy issues associated with blockchain for digital forensics are mentioned in Table 3.

Table 3. Key security and privacy issues associated with blockchain for digital forensics

Sr. No	Encryption Mechanisms	Issues	Implications
1	Pseudonymity and Anonymity	Blockchain transactions often use pseudonyms or wallet addresses, making it challenging to identify real-world individuals or entities behind transactions.	Investigators may struggle to link blockchain addresses to specific individuals or entities involved in criminal activities.
2	Privacy Coins	Privacy-focused cryptocurrencies like Monero and Zcash are designed to obscure transaction details, including sender, receiver, and transaction amounts.	Tracking illicit activities involving privacy coins is extremely difficult, as the inherent privacy features hinder forensic analysis.
3	Decentralization	Blockchain's decentralized nature means that there is no central authority controlling transactions, making it challenging to impose regulations.	Criminal activities can be conducted on decentralized platforms with little oversight, complicating investigations and regulatory efforts.
4	Immutable Transactions	Once recorded on the blockchain, transactions are immutable and cannot be altered or deleted.	Even if illegal activities are identified, it is impossible to erase or modify the evidence, requiring forensic experts to work within the constraints of immutability.
5	Smart Contracts Vulnerabilities	Smart contracts are not immune to vulnerabilities or exploits, leading to thefts or fraudulent	Digital forensics experts must investigate and analyze the code of smart contracts to identify vulnerabilities that may have been exploited.

Table 3 continued

Sr. No	Encryption Mechanisms	Issues	Implications
6	Insider Threats	Insider threats from blockchain developers or administrators can compromise the integrity of blockchain networks.	Digital forensics professionals must consider the possibility of insider attacks when investigating security breaches or fraud on blockchain platforms.
7	Quantum Computing Threat	Quantum computers, once sufficiently advanced, could potentially break existing blockchain encryption methods.	The security of blockchain networks may be compromised by quantum computing, requiring a shift to quantum-resistant cryptographic algorithms.
8	Lack of Global Standards	There are no standardized procedures or protocols for blockchain forensics investigations.	Investigations may lack consistency and face legal challenges due to the absence of established standards.
9	Cross-Chain Transactions	Tracking digital assets and transactions across different blockchains can be complex.	Investigators may need to develop methods and tools to trace assets across multiple blockchain networks.
10	Data Privacy and Consent	Privacy regulations like GDPR can conflict with the transparency of blockchain data.	Investigators must navigate the legal and ethical issues surrounding data privacy and consent when collecting blockchain-related evidence.
11	Scalability Challenges	Scalability issues in blockchain networks can lead to delayed transactions and congestion.	Delays in transaction processing may hinder timely forensic investigations, especially in cases where quick action is required.

Hence, these security and privacy challenges in the context of blockchain for digital forensics require the development of new investigative techniques, tools, and methodologies. Moreover, collaboration between blockchain developers, law enforcement agencies, and regulatory bodies is important which strikes a balance between privacy, security, and law enforcement needs in the evolving blockchain landscape.

FUTURE TRENDS AND EMERGING TECHNOLOGIES TOWARDS BLOCKCHAIN FOR DIGITAL FORENSICS

Future trends and emerging technologies in the field of blockchain for digital forensics are poised to shape the way cybercrimes are investigated and digital evidence is analyzed. As blockchain technology continues to evolve, some of the key trends and emerging technologies to watch for are discussed in Table 4.

Table 4. Trends and description of Blockchain for digital forensics

Sr. No.	Types	Trend	Description
1	Advanced Blockchain Analytics Tools	The development of more sophisticated blockchain analytics tools.	As blockchain networks become more complex, analytics tools are evolving to provide deeper information about into transaction histories, token movements, and wallet addresses. These tools will be important for forensic investigators to trace and analyze digital transactions effectively.
2	Privacy-Preserving Blockchain Solutions	Increased focus on privacy-preserving blockchain technologies	Privacy coins and blockchain platforms that emphasize user anonymity, such as Monero and Zcash, pose challenges for digital forensics. Researchers are working on new techniques to analyze transactions on these privacy-focused blockchains without violating user privacy.
3	Smart Contract Forensics	The growing importance of smart contract forensics.	With the proliferation of decentralized applications (DApps) and smart contracts on blockchain platforms like Ethereum, forensic experts will need to specialize in analyzing these self-executing contracts for vulnerabilities, fraudulent activities, and legal compliance.
4	AI and Machine Learning Integration	Increased use of AI and machine learning in blockchain forensics.	Machine learning algorithms can assist in identifying suspicious patterns and anomalies within blockchain data. AI-powered tools can automate the process of tracing and flagging potentially illicit transactions.
5	Interoperability Solutions	Development of interoperability protocols for cross-chain investigations.	As blockchain ecosystems diversify, interoperability protocols will become essential for tracking digital assets and transactions across multiple blockchains. Investigative tools that can work seamlessly with various blockchains will gain prominence.
6	Decentralized Identity and Attestation	Adoption of decentralized identity solutions	Decentralized identity platforms like SelfKey and uPort provide users control over their personal information. Forensic experts will need to adapt to these new identity paradigms and develop techniques for verifying decentralized identities.
7	Quantum-Safe Blockchain	Research and development of quantum-safe blockchain protocols.	With the potential threat of quantum computers breaking existing cryptographic algorithms, blockchain developers are exploring quantum-resistant cryptographic solutions. Forensic experts will need to adapt to these new security measures.
8	Regulatory Compliance and Reporting Tools	Enhanced regulatory compliance tools for blockchain forensics.	As governments and regulatory bodies implement stricter cryptocurrency regulations, forensic investigators will require advanced reporting and compliance tools to ensure related to legal requirements.
9	Blockchain Governance and Consensus Mechanism Analysis	Deeper analysis of blockchain governance and consensus mechanisms.	Understanding the governance structures and consensus algorithms of various blockchains is important for forensic experts. Changes in these mechanisms can impact how investigations are conducted.

Hence, the intersection of blockchain and digital forensics is evolving rapidly, and staying up-to-date with these emerging technologies and trends will be essential for forensic experts, law enforcement agencies, and cybersecurity professionals. As blockchain technology continues to mature, the tools and techniques used to investigate and analyze digital crimes on blockchain networks will also evolve.

A. Blockchain Integration With AI in Digital Forensics

The integration of blockchain technology with artificial intelligence (AI) in digital forensics has the potential to revolutionize the way cybercrimes are investigated, evidence is collected, and security breaches are analyzed (Deshmukh, Patil, et al., 2023), (Ryu, Sharma, et al., 2019), (Borse, Patole, et al., 2021), (Kaushik, Dahiya, & Sharma, 2022). Here's how blockchain and AI can be integrated in the field of digital forensics:

- Immutable Evidence Storage: Blockchain's immutability ensures that digital evidence, once stored on the blockchain, cannot be altered or deleted. AI can be used to automate the process of timestamping and securely storing digital evidence on the blockchain, ensuring its integrity and reliability for forensic investigations.
- Chain of Custody Tracking: Blockchain can be used to create a tamper-proof chain of custody for digital evidence. AI-driven smart contracts can automate the tracking of evidence throughout the investigation process, providing transparency and accountability.
- Enhanced Data Analysis: AI algorithms can be applied to analyze large amounts of data on the blockchain, identifying patterns, anomalies, and potential cyber threats. This can aid investigators in proactively detecting and preventing cybercrimes.
- Transaction Monitoring: AI-powered monitoring systems can continuously track blockchain transactions in real-time. Suspicious or fraudulent activities can trigger alerts for investigators, allowing them to take early action.
- Natural Language Processing (NLP): NLP algorithms can be used to analyze text-based blockchain data, such as chat logs, emails, and social media messages. This can help in identifying cyber threats and evidence of malicious intent.
- Behavioral Analytics: AI-driven behavioral analytics can profile users and entities on the blockchain. Deviations from established behavioral patterns can raise red flags for potential cybercrimes, enabling early intervention.

- Cryptocurrency Tracing: AI can assist in tracing cryptocurrency transactions across the blockchain. This is important for investigating ransomware attacks, money laundering, and other financial cybercrimes.
- Image and Video Analysis: AI-based image and video analysis tools can be used to extract and analyze multimedia content from the blockchain. This can help in identifying illegal content, such as child exploitation materials.
- Predictive Analysis: AI can predict potential security breaches or cyberattacks based on historical data and emerging trends in blockchain networks. This proactive approach can help organizations preemptively strengthen their cybersecurity measures.
- Cross-Chain Investigations: AI can facilitate cross-chain investigations by analyzing data from multiple blockchain networks. This is essential for tracking assets and evidence that may move across different blockchains.
- Fraud Detection and Prevention: AI-powered fraud detection models can identify fraudulent transactions and activities on the blockchain. These models can continuously learn and adapt to evolving fraud tactics.
- Automated Reporting: AI-driven reporting tools can generate detailed forensic reports based on blockchain data analysis. These reports can be used as evidence in legal proceedings.
- Scalable Analysis: AI can handle the scalability challenges posed by the increasing volume of blockchain data. Machine learning models can process and analyze data efficiently, even in large-scale blockchain networks.

Hence, the integration of blockchain and AI in digital forensics provides the potential for more efficient, accurate, and proactive investigations. It enables investigators to harness the transparency and security of blockchain while using AI's analytical and predictive capabilities to combat cybercrimes effectively. As the synergy between blockchain and AI technologies continues to evolve, digital forensics is poised to become more sophisticated and adaptive in addressing modern cybersecurity challenges.

B. Cross-Chain Forensic Analysis

Cross-chain forensic analysis is the process of investigating and analyzing digital transactions, assets, and activities that span multiple blockchain networks. This emerging field is important for digital forensics experts, investigators, and law enforcement agencies as cryptocurrencies and decentralized applications (DApps) become more interconnected across different blockchain platforms. Here are key aspects of cross-chain forensic analysis:

- Interconnected Blockchain Networks: Cross-chain forensic analysis is necessary because cryptocurrencies and digital assets can move between various blockchain networks. This movement might be intentional, as users seek to diversify their holdings or access specific features, or it could be due to illicit activities, such as money laundering or token theft.

- Tracking Digital Assets: One of the primary goals of cross-chain forensic analysis is to track digital assets as they move from one blockchain to another. This involves tracing transactions and wallet addresses across different blockchains to establish a comprehensive transaction history.

- Decentralized Exchanges (DEXs): DEXs allow users to trade cryptocurrencies across different blockchain networks without relying on centralized intermediaries. Cross-chain forensic analysis often focuses on investigating transactions conducted through DEXs to identify illicit activities or money flows.

- Smart Contract Interaction: Some blockchain platforms, like Ethereum, enable smart contracts to interact with each other and with assets on different blockchains. Investigating these cross-chain smart contract interactions is essential for understanding how assets are transferred and used.

- Data Aggregation and Correlation: Investigators use specialized tools and techniques to aggregate and correlate data from multiple blockchains. This involves collecting data from public blockchain explorers, blockchain APIs, and other sources to create a unified view of cross-chain activities.

- Anonymity and Privacy Challenges: Cross-chain forensic analysis faces the challenge of pseudonymous blockchain addresses and privacy coins. It can be difficult to identify the real-world entities or individuals involved in cross-chain transactions, especially when privacy-enhancing technologies are used.

- Legal and Jurisdictional Issues: Investigating cross-chain activities may involve legal and jurisdictional challenges. Different countries have varying regulations related to cryptocurrencies and blockchain. Digital forensics experts must navigate these complexities while ensuring compliance with applicable laws.

- Blockchain Analytics Tools: Specialized blockchain analytics tools and platforms are important for cross-chain forensic analysis. These tools provide features for tracking assets, identifying patterns, and flagging suspicious activities across multiple blockchains.

- Collaboration and Knowledge Sharing: As cross-chain forensic analysis is a relatively new field, collaboration and knowledge sharing among investigators and forensic experts are essential. Sharing best practices, tools, and research findings can help advance the capabilities of cross-chain investigations.

- Training and Education: Digital forensics professionals require specialized training and education to become proficient in cross-chain forensic analysis. This includes understanding the technical aspects of various blockchain networks and their interoperability.
- Future Developments: As blockchain technology and cross-chain capabilities continue to evolve, cross-chain forensic analysis will become more complex. New techniques, standards, and tools will emerge to address the challenges of investigating increasingly interconnected blockchain ecosystems.

Hence, cross-chain forensic analysis is an important component of modern digital forensics, enabling investigators to trace and understand the flow of digital assets across multiple blockchain networks. As cryptocurrencies and blockchain applications become more integrated into everyday financial activities, the need for cross-chain forensic expertise will continue to grow.

C. Standardization and Certification in Blockchain Forensics

Standardization and certification in blockchain forensics are essential to ensure the quality, consistency, and credibility of investigations and analyses in the field. These efforts help establish recognized practices, methodologies, and qualifications for digital forensics experts working with blockchain technology. Now we will discuss a few key issues related to standardization and certification in blockchain forensics, as mentioned in table 5.

Table 5. Standardization and certification in blockchain forensics (with overcoming issues)

Types	Use	Explanation
Standardization	Development of Best Practices	Standardization involves the development of best practices for conducting blockchain forensic investigations. These practices cover data collection, analysis, reporting, and compliance with legal and ethical guidelines.
	Documentation and Reporting Standards	Standardized documentation and reporting templates ensure that forensic reports are comprehensive, transparent, and consistent. These standards help investigators communicate their findings effectively.
	Interoperability Standards	With the emergence of cross-chain and multi-chain investigations, interoperability standards ensure that investigators can work safely with data from different blockchain networks.
	Data Collection and Preservation	Standardized procedures for collecting and preserving blockchain-related data, including transaction records, wallet addresses, and smart contract codes, are important to maintain the integrity of evidence.

Table 5 continued

Types	Use	Explanation
Certification	Professional Certification	Professional certification programs for blockchain forensics experts validate their expertise and knowledge in the field. Certification bodies can provide examinations and assessments to verify an individual's skills.
	Education and Training	Certified training programs provide comprehensive education on blockchain forensics, covering both theoretical and practical aspects. These programs equip professionals with the necessary skills and knowledge.
	Continuing Education	Certification programs often require individuals to engage in continuous learning and professional development to stay up-to-date with evolving blockchain technologies and investigative techniques.
	Recognition of Expertise	Certification serves as a recognition of an individual's expertise in blockchain forensics. It enhances their credibility and can lead to career advancement opportunities.
	Global Recognition	Certification programs should aim for global recognition, allowing blockchain forensic experts to work across borders and jurisdictions with a standardized skill set.
	Collaboration with Industry	Certification bodies should collaborate with industry stakeholders, law enforcement agencies, and regulatory authorities to ensure that certification programs align with real-world requirements.
Challenges and Issues	Evolving Technology	Blockchain technology is continually evolving. Standardization and certification efforts must adapt to keep pace with new developments and challenges.
	Legal and Jurisdictional Variations	Different countries have varying regulations related to blockchain and cryptocurrencies. Certification programs should consider these legal differences.
	Privacy and Data Protection	Ethical issues regarding data privacy and protection are paramount in blockchain forensic investigations. Certification programs should address these ethical issues.
	Multidisciplinary Skills	Blockchain forensics often requires multidisciplinary skills, including cryptography, computer science, and legal knowledge. Certification programs should encompass a broad range of expertise.
	Resource Constraints	Developing standardized practices and certification programs can be resource-intensive. Funding and support from industry, academia, and government bodies are important.

Hence, standardization and certification play an important role in ensuring the credibility and effectiveness of blockchain forensics investigations. They assure stakeholders that digital forensic experts possess the necessary skills and related to established best practices, ultimately enhancing trust in the field.

CONCLUSION

This chapter explains the importance of blockchain technology as a double-edged sword in the field of digital forensics. While it presents opportunities for transparency and accountability, it simultaneously introduces unprecedented complexities and anonymity. As blockchain continues to permeate various sectors, the digital forensics community faces the formidable task of adapting and innovating to stay ahead in the pursuit of truth and justice in the digital world. Finally, this chapter explains this topic as a basic resource for researchers, etc., striving to understand the multifaceted relationship between blockchain and digital forensics.

REFERENCES

Al-Khateeb, H., Epiphaniou, G., & Daly, H. (2019). Blockchain for modern digital forensics: The chain-of-custody as a distributed ledger. *Blockchain and Clinical Trial: Securing Patient Data*, 149-168. doi:10.1186/s13635-023-00142-3

Borse, Y., Patole, D., Chawhan, G., Kukreja, G., Parekh, H., & Jain, R. (2021, May). Advantages of Blockchain in Digital Forensic Evidence Management. *Proceedings of the 4th International Conference on Advances in Science & Technology (ICAST2021)*.

Deekshetha, H. R., & Tyagi, A. K. (2023). Automated and intelligent systems for next-generation-based smart applications. In *Data Science for Genomics* (pp. 265–276). Academic Press. doi:10.1016/B978-0-323-98352-5.00019-7

Deshmukh, A., Patil, D. S., Soni, G., & Tyagi, A. K. (2023). Cyber Security: New Realities for Industry 4.0 and Society 5.0. In A. Tyagi (Ed.), *Handbook of Research on Quantum Computing for Smart Environments* (pp. 299–325). IGI Global. doi:10.4018/978-1-6684-6697-1.ch017

Deshmukh, A., Sreenath, N., Tyagi, A. K., & Abhichandan, U. V. E. (2022, January). Blockchain enabled cyber security: A comprehensive survey. In *2022 International Conference on Computer Communication and Informatics (ICCCI)* (pp. 1-6). IEEE. 10.1109/ICCCI54379.2022.9740843

Jayaprakash, V., & Tyagi, A. K. (2022). Security Optimization of Resource-Constrained Internet of Healthcare Things (IoHT) Devices Using Lightweight Cryptography. In Information Security Practices for the Internet of Things, 5G, and Next-Generation Wireless Networks (pp. 179-209). IGI Global.

Kaushik, K., Dahiya, S., & Sharma, R. (2022). Role of blockchain technology in digital forensics. In *Blockchain Technology* (pp. 235–246). CRC Press. doi:10.1201/9781003138082-14

Krishna, A. M., & Tyagi, A. K. (2020, February). Intrusion detection in intelligent transportation system and its applications using blockchain technology. In 2020 international conference on emerging trends in information technology and engineering (IC-ETITE) (pp. 1-8). IEEE. doi:10.1109/ic-ETITE47903.2020.332

Kumari, S., Tyagi, A. K., & Rekha, G. (2021). Applications of Blockchain Technologies in Digital Forensics and Threat Hunting. In *Recent Trends in Blockchain for Information Systems Security and Privacy* (pp. 159–173). CRC Press. doi:10.1201/9781003139737-12

Mishra, S., & Tyagi, A. K. (2019, December). Intrusion detection in Internet of Things (IoTs) based applications using blockchain technolgy. In *2019 third international conference on I-SMAC (IoT in social, mobile, analytics and cloud)(I-SMAC)* (pp. 123-128). IEEE.

Ryu, J. H., Sharma, P. K., Jo, J. H., & Park, J. H. (2019). A blockchain-based decentralized efficient investigation framework for IoT digital forensics. *The Journal of Supercomputing*, 75(8), 4372–4387. doi:10.1007/s11227-019-02779-9

Tibrewal, I., Srivastava, M., & Tyagi, A. K. (2022). Blockchain technology for securing cyber-infrastructure and internet of things networks. *Intelligent Interactive Multimedia Systems for e-Healthcare Applications*, 337-350.

Tyagi, A. K., Chandrasekaran, S., & Sreenath, N. (2022, May). Blockchain technology:–a new technology for creating distributed and trusted computing environment. In *2022 International Conference on Applied Artificial Intelligence and Computing (ICAAIC)* (pp. 1348-1354). IEEE. 10.1109/ICAAIC53929.2022.9792702

Tyagi, A. K., Dananjayan, S., Agarwal, D., & Thariq Ahmed, H. F. (2023). Blockchain—Internet of Things Applications: Opportunities and Challenges for Industry 4.0 and Society 5.0. *Sensors (Basel)*, 23(2), 947. doi:10.3390/s23020947 PMID:36679743

Chapter 9

Securing Digital Photography Images by Encryption– Watermarking CFA (Color Filter Array) Images

Hervé Abena Ndongo
University of Ngaoundere, Cameroon

Tieudjo Daniel
University of Ngaoundere, Cameroon

Bitjoka Laurent
University of Ngaoundere, Cameroon

ABSTRACT

Research in image processing of digital color photography is in full expansion, especially on CFA (color filter array) images. These raw CFA images are very important for image analysis because they have not undergone any processing (interpolation, demosaicking, etc.) that would alter their reliability. The chapter presents three robust hybrid algorithms combining chaotic encryption and blind watermarking techniques of CFA images based on the quaternionic wavelet transform (QWT) to propose solutions related to the problems of confidentiality, security, authenticity of these images transmitted over digital networks, the size of some CFA images, and the large amount of data to be transferred in a non-secure environment where resources in terms of throughput and bandwidth are quite limited. The three hybrid algorithms were implemented simultaneously and successively.

DOI: 10.4018/978-1-6684-8127-1.ch009

INTRODUCTION

Today's digital networks are so highly developed that they have become an essential communication medium. They enable the transmission of all kinds of information: text, sound and above all, images. The increased use of the latter is reinforced by the emergence of cameras, digital cameras, cell phones, scanners and IRM.

The rapid development of communication technologies and image-processing tools raises a number of important issues: illegal distribution, duplication, falsification, confidentiality and so on. Authors and providers of multimedia data are reluctant to allow their data to be distributed in a networked environment because they fear unrestricted duplication and dissemination of copyrighted material.

These problems have prompted a number of researchers to take an interest in securing digital data through various protection techniques such as steganography, encryption, watermarking and even encryption-watermarking. The hybrid method of encryption-watermarking is the one we'll be studying in our work with a view to *i)* ensuring the secure transfer of digital photographic images *ii)* achieving a better compromise between invulnerability (robustness and security) and the amount of information to be embedded (capacity and imperceptibility).

To meet these needs, a new line of research is rapidly developing: hybrid encryption-watermarking algorithms. In this work, our contribution is to propose three robust hybrid algorithms combining chaotic encryption and blind watermarking of CFA images based on the quaternionic wavelet transform (QWT) to solve the various problems posed in our approach.

Although the hybrid encryption-watermarking algorithm is a new line of research, it has gained a lot of attention and evolved very rapidly. In the literature, several efficient encryption-watermarking methods have been developed, satisfying certain conditions depending on the problem at hand. However, earlier work includes that of Puech et al. (2001), who proposed a hybrid encryption-watermarking technique for secure image transfer. After generating a key to encrypt the image, they watermark this encrypted image with two components: the encryption key and the text data associated with the image. Puech et al. (2001) present a combination of image encryption and watermarking techniques. They proposed a system for securely transferring medical images by generating a key to encrypt the image, then watermarking the image with the encryption key and patient data. Autrusseau et al. (2003) present an algorithm for Mojette encryption-watermarking of medical images. This algorithm is a combination of watermarking based on the Mojette transform (MT), the Fourier transform (FT) of an image, and Mojette encryption so as to memorize the list of unambiguous matches during direct MT, then keep a unique path in this list, then scramble (encrypt) unused bins and finally drown in encrypted data, the plaintext data kept. Puech and Rodrigues (2005) present a new method combining encryption and image watermarking for secure data transfer. The method is based on a combination of public-private key encryption, secret key encryption and watermarking algorithms. The image encryption algorithm uses a secret key. They then encrypt this secret key with an asymmetric algorithm. This encrypted secret key is then watermarked into the encrypted image. J. Shuhong and G. Robert (2007) propose a method combining stenography and cryptography, by embedding a hidden message into a 2D black-and-white medical image of any modality, including all the information needed to identify the patient, his or her history, the conditions of the examination (nature, place, date), as well as the radiologist's observations, diagnosis and comments. Benlcouiri et al. (2012) present an algorithm for symmetric encryption-watermarking of still digital images, using symmetric noise injection on the architecture of multilayer neural networks executed at compressed images. Rakotondraina et al. (2013) present a new approach for secure image transfer. It comprises three treatments, namely: compression based on the Discrete Fourier Transform (DFT), a symmetrical encryption operation and a Hidden Data Insertion or HDI (image watermarking) technique for transporting sensitive information. Ralaivao et al. (2016) present a new technique for secure digital image transfer based on the combination of Verman stream encryption and watermarking based on Discrete Cosine Transform (DCT) and Singular Value Decomposition (SVD). Noura et al. (2017) present a robust image encryption-watermarking algorithm for the secure transfer of medical images. This hybrid algorithm is based on watermarking using the Discrete Wavelet Transform (DWT) and Discrete Cosine Transform (DCT) of an audio signal and chaos-based encryption by generating (chaotic generator) a key to encrypt the watermarked image. Bhnassy et al. (2019) present a new technique for secure transfer of grayscale images based on the combination of CHP (Chaotic Hopping Pattern) based watermarking and DPRE (Double Random Phase Encoding) based encryption using DDCHP (Dynamic Delay Chaotic Hopping Pattern).

We note that in the literature, the majority of contributions have been made to grayscale images, and even more so to medical images. The analysis of these images is very delicate due to the appearance of certain artefacts caused by prior processing of the raw images.

Our work presents three robust hybrid algorithms combining chaotic encryption and blind watermarking of CFA images based on the Quaternionic Wavelet Transform (QWT). The three hybrid algorithms were implemented simultaneously and successively. The first method is the hybrid algorithm implemented simultaneously (known as the EncrypWatermarking algorithm), the second and third methods are based on the implementation of this hybrid algorithm in succession, respectively encryption then watermarking (already known as the encryption-watermarking algorithm) and watermarking then encryption (also known as the watermarking-encryption algorithm).

In this chapter, we will propose the three robust hybrid algorithm methods that have been developed to cope with the various problems described above. We also present examples and experimental results obtained after simulations of these proposed hybrid algorithms on real CFA images. A comparative study of the three proposed methods has been carried out with the aim of determining the most robust method.

1. DEFINITION AND INTEREST OF CFA IMAGES

Generally speaking, the CFA image is a black-and-white image showing the signal received by each pixel of the sensor. These pixels are alternately covered with a mosaic of red (R), green (G) and blue (B) filters. For example, if the scene observed is uniformly red, only pixels covered with a red filter will be illuminated, while green and blue pixels will appear very dark in the CFA image (Lukac and Plataniotis, 2005; Y. Yang et al., 2007; Gwet et al., 2018). In short, then, the CFA image is one in which a single-color component level (R or G or B) is present in each pixel. It depends on the CFA filters and their arrangement.

In the literature, several efficient image encryption-watermarking methods have been developed, satisfying certain conditions depending on the problem addressed. Most contributions have been made to grayscale images and even more so to medical images. However, to our knowledge, CFA (Color Filter Array) images generated by digital photography (Lukac and Plataniotis, 2010) have not yet been subject to encryption-watermarking. These images are very important for image analysis because they have not undergone any processing (interpolation, demosaicking, etc.) altering their reliability, and raw CFA images are no longer regularly manipulated within our Laboratory (LESIA) as shown by the work of (Laurent et al., 2010; Boukara et al., 2013), (Ndongo et al., 2013, 2021, 2022; Gwet et al., 2018), and by other foreign laboratories. For a good collaboration with these different foreign laboratories, it is important to ensure the fast, simple and secure transfer of these images exposed to piracy.

2. DEFINITION AND INTEREST OF QUATERNIONIC WAVELET TRANSFORM (QWT)

Quaternions are an extension of the complex numbers (Lord William Hamilton in the 19th century) with a real part and three imaginary parts as follows:

$q=a+ib+jc+kd$, with $\boldsymbol{a,b,c,d} \in \mathcal{R}$, and $i^2=j^2=k^2=ijk= -1$ (1)

The multiplication of two of these imaginary numbers i, j, k behaves like the vector product of orthogonal unit vectors:

$$\begin{cases} i*j = -j*i = k \\ j*k = -k*j = i \\ k*i = -i*k = j \end{cases} \tag{2}$$

The polar writing of a quaternion is, analogous to the exponential complex: $q = |q|e^{i\alpha}e^{j\theta}e^{k\beta}$, giving access to the module/argument representation that allows us to separately represent the presence of local components in the image (amplitude), and their structures (phase). The conjugate and the standard of a quaternion are calculated in a similar way to complex numbers. The multiplication of quaternions is associative but not commutative. Quaternions can be represented as a linear combination, a vector of four coefficients, a scalar for the coefficient of the actual part and as a vector for the coefficients of the imaginary part (Bülow, 1999; Le Bihan, 2003).

The ongoing search for improvements and the design of new encryption-watermarking algorithms are driving researchers to work continuously in this field. These performances, which do not reach theoretical limits, justify intensified research into the improvement of existing algorithms and the development of new ones. The good properties of quaternionic wavelets demonstrated in the literature (finer decomposition, more thorough image analysis, translation invariance of amplitude and finesse of sub-band orientation enable classical wavelets to be outperformed thanks to richer, more stable descriptors) justify their use in developing new algorithms. The aim is to develop a robust algorithm combining encryption and watermarking of CFA digital photography images in order to improve the accuracy of algorithms for the secure transfer of CFA images while guaranteeing good extracted watermark quality.

Our contribution will therefore be to propose hybrid, robust algorithms for encryption-watermarking CFA images.

The originality of this work lies in the analysis of CFA images using quaternions. The scientific contribution (interest) of our work concerns the development of robust hybrid algorithms for encryption-watermarking based on the quaternionic wavelet transform, which enables us to obtain a quaternionic representation (one real part and 3 imaginary parts) of the raw CFA image with no artifacts and reduced execution time compared with color images, and to generate the encryption keys k and insertion keys q from its sub-bands of detail (imaginary parts).

3. THE DIFFERENT PROPOSED ALGORITHMS

The digital revolution, the explosion of communication networks and the public ever-growing enthusiasm for new information technologies mean that digital data (images, videos, texts, sounds, etc.) are increasingly circulating (disseminating, duplicating, transforming, etc.). The scale of these phenomena is such that fundamental questions now arise concerning the control and protection of exchanged data. For reasons of confidentiality and security, it is very important to protect this digital data in an unsecured environment. We have therefore proposed hybrid encryption-watermarking algorithms that combine chaotic encryption and blind watermarking algorithms to ensure the secure transfer of CFA images.

3.1. Chaotic Encryption Algorithm

The cryptographic method used here is the symmetrical chaotic encryption. The encryption key will still be used for decryption at the receiver level. The approach to the chaotic encryption technique applied here is simple and straightforward. It consists of mixing information with a chaotic sequence from a sender, usually described by a state representation with a state vector. Only the sender's output is transmitted to the receiver. The role of the receiver is to extract the original information from the signal received. The recovery of information is usually based on the synchronization of the states of the sender and the states of the receiver (Nkapkop et al., 2016). We define our discrete-time chaotic system as follows:

$$
\begin{cases}
\dot{x}_1 = x_3 \\
\dot{x}_2 = \mu_1\left(x_3 - v\right) \\
\dot{x}_3 = \sigma\left(x_3 - x_2 - x_1\right) \\
\dot{v} = \mu_2\left(x_2 - \gamma \sinh(v)\right)
\end{cases}
\tag{3}
$$

Using chaotic sequences of system (4.3) the image is then encrypted in the following steps and the schematic diagram depicted in Figure 1.

- Select the initial values $(x_{10}, x_{20}, x_{30}, v_0, \varepsilon_1, \varepsilon_2, \sigma, \gamma)$ of system (4.3) to achieve chaotic state. This yields to four real sequences $\{X1\}$, $\{X2\}$, $\{X3\}$ and $\{V\}$;
- Convert the real sequence X1, X2 and V to integer as $X1 = fix(X1_i \times 10^{16} \bmod 256)$, $X1 = fix(X1_i \times 10^{16} \bmod 256)$ and $V = fix(V_i \times 10^{16} \bmod 256)$;

- Read the original image as $m \times n \times k$ image. Perform the confusion (permutation) of rows and column of the image respectively using the key sequences X1 and X2 to achieve the permuted image P.
- Apply Bit-XORed based diffusion process on the permuted image P using the sequence X3 and V of the proposed chaotic system. The encrypted image is then achieved.

Decryption process is the reverse of this encryption scheme.

Figure 1. Block diagram of the encryption scheme

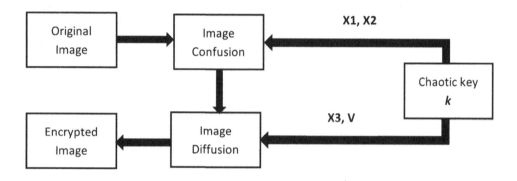

3.2. Blind Watermarking Algorithm

The watermarking algorithm used here is blind watermarking using the substitution method. The coefficients (pixels) of the watermark (patient data, encryption key k, etc.) have been embedded by replacing the coefficients of the host image with those of the watermark, using a secret key q. This key determines where the elements of the watermark should be embedded and controls the visibility of the watermarking. As the extraction mode used is blind, we only need the secret key *q* to extract the watermark hidden in the watermarked image. The block diagram of the embedding process is shown in Figure 2 (Ndongo et al., 2021), and is summarized by the following steps:

- Break down the original image I_0 using the quaternionic wavelets transform in ℓ levels of resolution. We then obtain $(3\ell+1)$ quaternionic sub-bands (**LL, LH, HL, HH**) and $(3\ell+1)*4$ elements that make up the matrix w of the QWT. We calculate the module of each sub-band from the elements of the

QWT in order to obtain the matrix w_r Representing the standard format of the wavelets transforms;

- Select a sub-band among the sub-bands of details of the last level of resolution ℓ, i.e., a sub-band among the sub-bands: $\{HH_\ell, HL_\ell, LH_\ell\}$;
- Calculate the new matrix G that represents the subtraction of the matrix of the selected sub-band and that of the watermark;
- Set the secret key q from the matrix G in order to control the visibility of the watermark. This key is defined here as an interval of thresholds;
- Replace the coefficients of the host image (selected sub-band) with those of the watermark using the secret key q. We obtain a new matrix T representing the modified selected sub-band;
- Calculate the reverse quaternionic wavelets transform (IQWT) of the elements of the new matrix w' from the matrix w_r' made up of the modified selected sub-band and the remaining sub-bands. We then obtain our watermarked image I_t.

Figure 2. Block diagram of the watermark embedding process

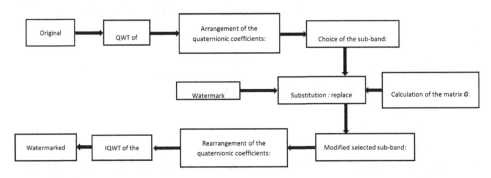

The watermark extraction process is the inverse of the embedding process.

3.3. Hybrid Encryption-Watermarking Algorithms

In this section, we present hybrid CFA image watermarking algorithms combining chaotic encryption and blind watermarking techniques based on the quaternionic wavelet transform. These proposed techniques can be implemented both simultaneously and successively.

3.3.1. Simultaneous Encryption-Watermarking Algorithm: EncrypWatermarking

The hybrid algorithm proposed here is a simultaneous combination of chaotic encryption and blind watermarking techniques. Consider the original image I_0, a CFA image of $m*n$ pixels and the watermark image M, a grayscale image of $k*l$ pixels. The block diagram of the emission process is shown in Figure 3 (Ndongo et al., 2021), and is summarized by the following steps:

- Break down the original image I_0 through the quaternionic wavelets transform *(QWT)* in ℓ resolution levels. This results in a $(3\ell+1)$ quaternionic sub-bands *(LL, LH, HL, HH)* and $(3\ell+1)*4$ elements that make up the matrix w of the QWT. We calculate the module of each sub-band from the elements of the QWT in order to obtain the matrix w_r representing the standard format of the wavelets;
- Select a sub-band among the sub-bands of details from the last resolution level ℓ, i.e., a sub-band among the sub-bands: $\{HH_\ell, HL_\ell, LH_\ell\}$;
- Randomly generate from a chaotic generator, the encryption key k of the selected sub-band;
- Encrypt with the encryption key k, the approximate component *(LL)* corresponding to the coefficients representing the information;
- Generate from a pseudo-random generator, the secret key q of one of the two remaining sub-bands;
- Embedded with the secret key q, the watermark in the other remaining sub-band;
- Calculate the inverse quaternionic wavelets transform *(IQWT)* of the elements of the new matrix w' from the matrix w_r' modified selected sub-bands and other remaining sub-bands. We then get our encrypted-watermarked image I_{ct}.

The reception process is the reverse of this emission process scheme to obtain reconstructed image I_r.

3.3.2. Successive Encryption-Watermarking Algorithm

The hybrid algorithm proposed here is a successive combination of chaotic encryption and blind watermarking techniques. In this case, we have two ways of successively combining these two protection techniques: chaotic encryption followed by blind watermarking, and blind watermarking followed by chaotic encryption.

Figure 3. Block diagram of the emission process of the hybrid simultaneous encryption and watermarking algorithm

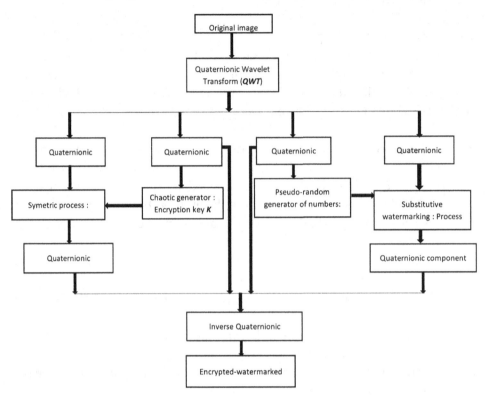

3.3.2.1. Hybrid Encryption and Watermarking Algorithm: Encryption-Watermarking

The hybrid algorithm proposed here is a successive combination of chaotic encryption and blind watermarking. Consider the original image I_0, a CFA image of $m*n$ pixels and the watermark image M, a grayscale image of $k*l$ pixels. The block diagram of the emission process is shown in Figure 4 (Ndongo et al., 2022), and is summarized by the following steps:

- Define a chaotic system and the encryption key k;
- Encrypt (confuse and broadcast) the original image using the key k: encrypted image I_c;
- Break down the encrypted image I_c through the quaternionic wavelets transform *(QWT)* in ℓ resolution levels. This results in a $(3\ell+1)$ quaternionic sub-bands *(LL, LH, HL, HH)* and $(3\ell+1)*4$ elements that make up the matrix w of the QWT. We calculate the module of each sub-band from the elements

of the QWT in order to obtain the matrix w_r representing the standard format of the wavelets transforms;

- Embedded using the key q, the watermark M into one of the quaternionic sub-bands of details of the last level of resolution ℓ (LH_ℓ, HL_ℓ, HH_ℓ);
- Calculate the inverse quaternionic wavelet transform ($IQWT$) of the elements of the new matrix w' from the matrix w_r' modified selected sub-bands and other remaining sub-bands. We then obtain our encrypted-watermarked image I_{ct}.

Figure 4. Block diagram of the emission process of the hybrid encryption and watermarking algorithm

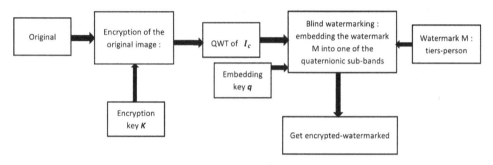

The reception process is the reverse of this emission process scheme to obtain reconstructed image I_r.

3.3.2.2. Hybrid Watermarking and Encryption Algorithm: Watermarking-Encryption

The hybrid algorithm proposed here is a combination of blind watermarking and chaotic encryption. Consider the original image I_0, a CFA image of $m*n$ pixels and the watermark image M, a grayscale image of $k*l$ pixels. The block diagram of the emission process is shown in Figure 5, and is summarized by the following steps:

- Break down the original image I_0 through the quaternionic wavelets transform (QWT) in ℓ resolution levels. This results in a $(3\ell+1)$ quaternionic sub-bands (LL, LH, HL, HH) and $(3\ell+1)*4$ elements that make up the matrix w of the QWT. We calculate the module of each sub-band from the elements of the QWT in order to obtain the matrix w_r representing the standard format of the wavelets transforms;

- Select a sub-band from the detail sub-bands of the last resolution level ℓ, i.e., a sub-band from the sub-bands: $\{HH_\ell, HL_\ell, LH_\ell\}$;
- Calculate the new matrix G which represents the subtraction of the matrix of the selected sub-band and that of the watermark;
- Define the secret key q from the matrix G to control the visibility of the watermarking. This key is defined here as a threshold interval;
- Replace the coefficients of the host image (selected sub-band) by those of the watermark using the secret key q. We get a new matrix T representing the modified selected sub-band;
- Calculate the inverse quaternionic wavelet transform ($IQWT$) of the elements of the new matrix w' from the matrix w_r' modified selected sub-bands and other remaining sub-bands. We get our watermarked image I_t;
- Encrypt (confusion and diffusion) the watermarked image I_t with the key k: we get the watermarked-encrypted image I_{tc}.

Figure 5. Block diagram of the emission process of the hybrid watermarking and encryption algorithm

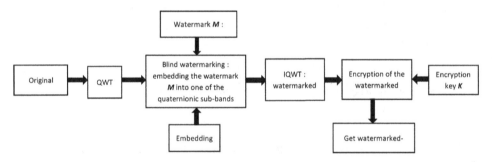

The reception process is the reverse of this emission process scheme to obtain reconstructed image I_r.

4. RESULTS, SIMULATION, AND DISCUSSION

The aim of our work was therefore to develop hybrid and robust algorithms that simultaneously and successively combine chaotic encryption techniques and blind watermarking of digital photographic images using quaternions to enable secure transfer of CFA images. The calculations of the various evaluation parameters (the Peak Signal to Noise Ratio (PSNR) and the Correlation Coefficient (CC)) were carried out with the aim of determining the robustness of our algorithm against some attacks. The expressions of these different parameters are:

$$PSNR = 10 \log_{10} \left(\frac{\max \left(\max \left(I_o \right)^2 \right)}{MSE} \right) \qquad (4)$$

Where MSE is mean squared error between original and reconstructed images, which is defined as follow:

$$MSE = \sum_{i=1}^{m} \sum_{j=1}^{n} \frac{\left(I_o \left(i,j \right) - I_r \left(i,j \right) \right)^2}{m * n} \qquad (5)$$

$$CC = \frac{\sum_{i=1}^{m} \sum_{j=1}^{n} \left(I_o \left(i,j \right) * I_r \left(i,j \right) \right)}{\sqrt{\left(\sum_{i=1}^{m} \sum_{j=1}^{n} I_o^2 \left(i,j \right) * \sum_{i=1}^{m} \sum_{j=1}^{n} I_r^2 \left(i,j \right) \right)}} \qquad (6)$$

Generally, the CC value obtained between 0.7 and 1 is acceptable. It is important to mention that bigger the PSNR values more than obtains a high quality of reconstructed image. For PSNR=30dB, the quality of image is acceptable (Manoury, 2001; Autrusseau et al., 2003; Gunjal and Mali, 2011; Rey, 2003).

In the next, we will present an example of the application of these hybrids algorithms on image 2 illustrated above (Figure 6).

The raw CFA images of a size of $512 * 512$ and $1024 * 1024$ pixels used (Figure 6) in this work come from color images obtained by 3CCD cameras (Li et al., 2008; Zhang et al., 2011). The watermark image used of a size of $323 * 124$ pixels (Figure 6) represent the tiers-person data. The algorithms were implemented using MATLAB software (version 8.3) installed on an 8GB RAM microcomputer, 1TB of hard drive and 2.4GHz frequency with a Windows 10 Professional Edition environment.

4.1. Hybrid EncrypWatermarking Algorithm

The results obtained after simulation of this hybrid encrypwatermarking algorithm are presented as follows:

Figure 6. Raw CFA images (image 1, ..., image 6) and watermark image

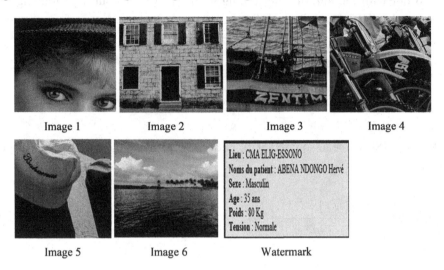

Image 1   Image 2   Image 3   Image 4

Image 5   Image 6   Watermark

Figure 7. Original image (a), watermark image (b), encrypted-watermarked image (c), and their histograms

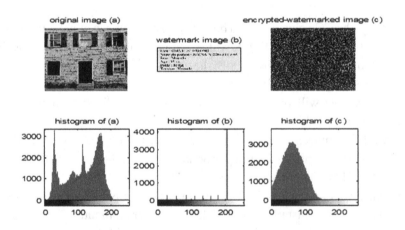

According to the human visual system, we find that from this figure (Figure 7, 8, 9 and 10), it is difficult to differentiate the original image from the reconstructed image after simultaneous encryption-watermarking. Based on the calculated evaluation parameters, we find that the operation results in a loss of information equivalent to the correlation coefficient CC=0.9928 and a peak signal-to-noise ratio PSNR=34.4040dB. So, we can say that our encryption-watermarking of CFA images was successful.

Figure 8. Original image (a), encrypted-watermarked image (b), reconstructed image (c), and their histograms

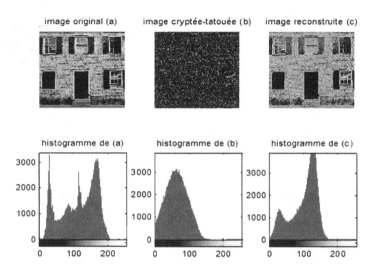

Figure 9. Original image (a), reconstructed image (b), difference between the original image and the reconstructed image (c), and their histograms

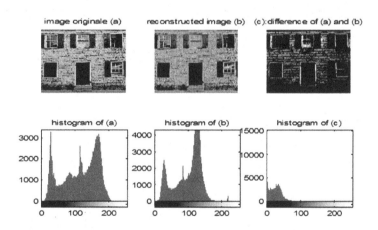

In order to assess the robustness of our technique of encryption-watermarking of CFA images, several types of attacks classified in two classes, have been implemented. The first class consists of geometric attacks (Figure 11) which aims to sufficiently distort the encrypted-watermarked image. While, the second class consists of erasure attacks (Figure 12) aimed extracted watermark in the encrypted-watermarked image.

Figure 10. Watermark image (a), extracted watermark (b), difference between the watermark and the extracted watermark (c), and their histograms

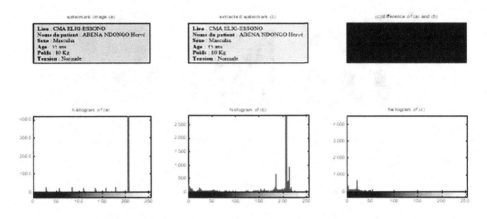

Figure 11. Performance against geometric attacks: watermarks extracted from encrypted-watermarked images and attacked

Figure 12. Performance against erasure attacks: watermarks extracted from encrypted-watermarked images and attacked

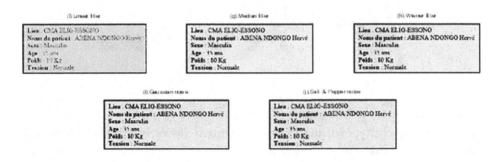

We find that from Figure 11 and 12, our simultaneous hybrid method for encryption-watermarking of CFA images resists geometric and erasure operations because the reconstructed images and the extracted watermark after these operations are easily recognized by the human visual system. Experimental results (Table 1) show that our simultaneous hybrid method encryption-watermarking CFA image maintains a good quality of reconstructed images and extracted watermark, and a good robustness against some conventional attacks.

The results obtained for the hybrid method simultaneous encryption-watermarking of CFA images on our various host images (Figure 6) are presented in Table 1.

From the results presented in Table 1, we find that we have good correlation coefficient (CC) values, which attests to the good quality of the reconstructed images despite the various attacks made on our encrypted-watermarked images.

In order to compare our results obtained with those obtained by Rakotondraina et al. (2013) we have also implemented our proposed algorithm on grayscale images (Lena image). The results are shown in Table 2 below.

The obtained results (Table 2) show that, our hybrid algorithm is better suited and more robust than that proposed by Rakotondraina et al. (2013) (MSE=6,3947<47,4619, PSNR=40,0719>31,3674, and CC=0,9993>0,9933). We obtained the better results with CFA images than grayscale images.

4.2. Successive Hybrid Encryption Then Watermarking Algorithm

The results obtained after simulation of this successive hybrid algorithm of chaotic encryption and blind watermarking are presented as follows:

According to the human visual system, we note that from this figure (Figure 13, 14, 15 and 16), that it is difficult to differentiate the original image from the reconstructed image and the same to the watermark from the extracted watermark after encryption and then watermarking. According to the calculated evaluation parameters, we find that the operation generates an information loss equivalent to the correlation coefficient CC=0.9996 (with CC $\approx$ 1) and a peak signal-to-noise ratio PSNR=42.4562dB (already > 30dB). So, we can say that our algorithm for successive encryption-watermarking of CFA images was successful depending on the standards described in the literature.

In order to evaluate the robustness of our hybrid algorithm of successive CFA image encryption, several types of attacks existing in two classes, have been implemented. The first class consists of geometric attacks (Figure 17) which aims to sufficiently distort the encrypted-watermarked image. While, the second class consists of erasure attacks (Figure 18) aimed extracted watermark in the encrypted-watermarked image.

Table 1. Evaluation parameters for the hybrid method simultaneous encryption-watermarking of CFA images.

DESIGNATIONS		IMAGE 1		IMAGE 2		IMAGE 3		IMAGE 4		IMAGE 5		IMAGE 6	
		PSNR (db)	CC	PSNR (db)	CC	PSNR (db)	CC	PSNR (db)	CC	PSNR (db)	CC	PSNR (db)	CC
NO ATTACK	No attack	42.0515	0.9987	34.4040	0.9928	36.8989	0.9957	35.2372	0.9873	35.6311	0.9913	34.5683	0.9890
GEOMETRIC ATTACKS	Rotation 10°	39.2265	0.9979	34.3610	0.9926	36.7867	0.9955	35.1348	0.9865	35.2894	0.9896	34.5422	0.9889
	Contrast	39.2462	0.9980	34.3644	0.9926	36.7928	0.9955	35.1405	0.9866	35.3065	0.9897	34.5445	0.9889
	Horizontal Flipping	38.8056	0.9975	34.3575	0.9926	36.7574	0.9954	35.1088	0.9863	35.1911	0.9890	34.5408	0.9889
	Vertical Flipping	39.5676	0.9983	34.3558	0.9926	36.7703	0.9955	35.1053	0.9863	35.2477	0.9894	34.5403	0.9889
	Total Flipping	38.8005	0.9975	34.3566	0.9926	36.7536	0.9954	35.0972	0.9862	35.2163	0.9892	34.5402	0.9889
ERASURE ATTACKS	Linear filter	37.0868	0.9942	34.1126	0.9912	35.7141	0.9918	34.5541	0.9807	34.4259	0.9834	34.4022	0.9881
	Median filter	39.2422	0.9979	34.3624	0.9926	36.7896	0.9955	35.1379	0.9865	35.3042	0.9897	34.5428	0.9889
	Wiener filter	39.3153	0.9980	34.3634	0.9926	36.7952	0.9955	35.1422	0.9866	35.2622	0.9894	34.5440	0.9889
	De-debugging salt and peppers	39.2461	0.9980	34.3634	0.9926	36.7928	0.9955	35.1404	0.9866	35.3064	0.9897	34.5445	0.9889
	Gaussian de-delusing	39.2461	0.9983	34.3634	0.9926	36.7952	0.9955	35.1404	0.9866	35.3063	0.9897	34.5445	0.9889

Table 2. Comparison of hybrid algorithm method and evaluation parameters with other approaches.

DESIGNATIONS		Rakotondraina et al. (2013)	PROPOSED METHOD	
HYBRID ALGORITHM	Encryption-watermarking	simultaneous	simultaneous	
	Used transform	Discrete Fourier Transform (DFT)	Quaternionic Wavelets Transform (QWT)	
	Applied to embeded	A part of image	All image	
	Images type	**Grayscale image**	**Grayscale image**	**CFA image**
EVALUATION PARAMETERS	MSE	47,4619	6,3947	4,0544
	PSNR (dB)	31,3674	40,0719	42.0515
	CC	0,9933	0,9993	0.9987

Figure 13. Original image (a), watermark image (b), encrypted-watermarked image (c), and their histograms

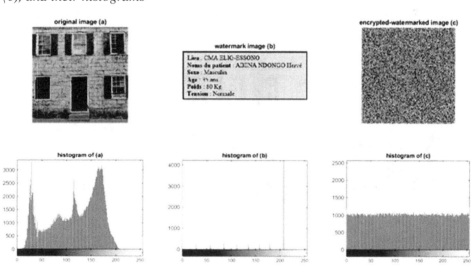

We find that from Figure 17 and 18, our successively implemented hybrid CFA image encryption-watermarking algorithm is well resilient to geometric and erasure operations, as the watermarks extracted after these operations are easily recognized by the human visual system. The values of different evaluation parameters for the hybrid successive encryption- watermarking algorithm are presented in Table 3.

Figure 14. Encrypted-watermarked image (a), extracted watermark (b), reconstructed image (c), and their histograms

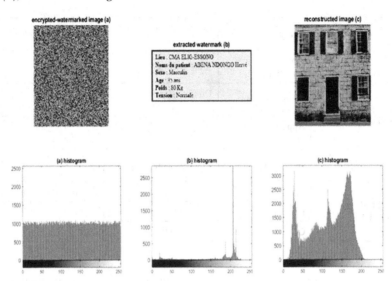

Figure 15. Original image (a), reconstructed image (b), difference between the original image and the reconstructed image (c), and their histograms

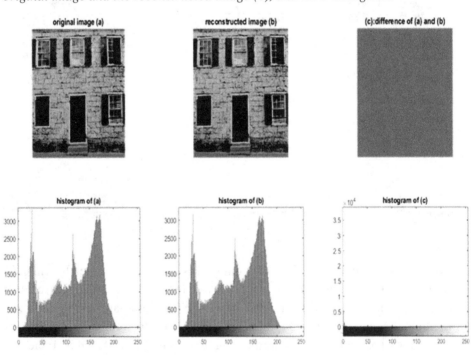

Figure 16. Watermark image (a), extracted watermark (b), difference between the watermark and the extracted watermark (c), and their histograms

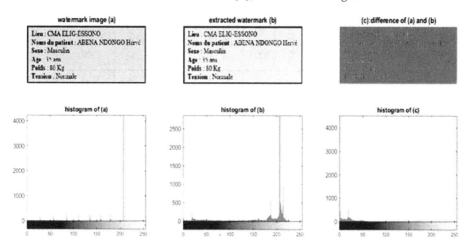

Figure 17. Performance against geometric attacks: watermarks extracted from encrypted then watermarked images and attacked

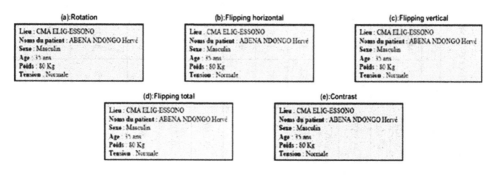

Figure 18. Performance against erasure attacks: watermarks extracted from encrypted then watermarked images and attacked

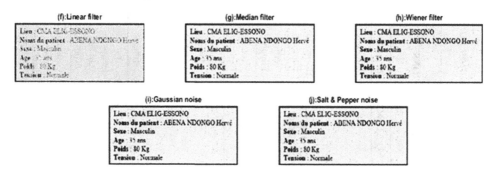

Table 3. Evaluation parameters for the hybrid method successive encryption-watermarking of CFA images

DESIGNATIONS		IMAGE 1		IMAGE 2		IMAGE 3		IMAGE 4		IMAGE 5		IMAGE 6	
		PSNR (dB)	CC	PSNR (dB)	CC	PSNR (dB)	CC	PSNR (dB)	CC	PSNR (dB)	CC	PSNR (dB)	CC
NO ATTACK	No attack	41,8956	0,9993	42,4562	0,9996	41,9432	0,9994	42,1124	0,9992	41,8772	0,9996	42,7459	0,9996
GEOMETRIC ATTACKS	Rotation 10⁰	37,0250	0,9983	35,9579	0,9963	35,5676	0,9963	37,5729	0,9983	37,5633	0,9983	35,9805	0,9964
	Contrast	36,7605	0,9981	35,6735	0,9958	35,2846	0,9958	37,3469	0,9981	37,3233	0,9981	35,7079	0,9959
	Horizontal Flipping	36,8662	0,9981	35,9289	0,9963	35,4782	0,9961	37,4171	0,9981	37,3962	0,9981	35,8939	0,9962
	Vertical Flipping	36,8777	0,9981	35,9019	0,9962	35,5003	0,9962	37,4025	0,9981	37,4221	0,9981	35,8953	0,9962
	Total Flipping	36,8624	0,9981	35,9002	0,9962	35,4704	0,9961	37,4207	0,9981	37,4200	0,9981	35,8877	0,9962
ERASURE ATTACKS	Linear filter	33,8101	0,9923	33,2677	0,9875	32,8930	0,9875	34,3502	0,9924	34,3466	0,9924	33,2945	0,9876
	Median filter	37,1101	0,9984	36,0053	0,9964	35,6075	0,9964	37,6702	0,9984	37,6596	0,9984	36,0271	0,9965
	Wiener filter	36,9526	0,9982	35,8476	0,9962	35,4661	0,9962	37,5276	0,9983	37,5081	0,9983	35,8730	0,9962
	De-debugging salt and peppers	36,7606	0,9981	35,6737	0,9958	35,2848	0,9958	37,3470	0,9981	37,3235	0,9981	35,7079	0,9959
	Gaussian de-debugging	36,7606	0,9981	35,6736	0,9958	35,2848	0,9958	37,3471	0,9981	37,3234	0,9981	35,7079	0,9959

The results obtained after simulation (presented in Table 3) show that our successive CFA image encryption-watermarking algorithm maintains a good quality of the extracted watermarks and a good robustness against some conventional attacks which is acceptable.

We compare our results obtained by our hybrid successive encryption then watermarking algorithm with those of the works of Khalfallah et al. (2006), Puech et al. (2008) and Bhnassy et al. (2019). The results obtained are presented in Table 4:

Table 4. Comparison of the quality of the reconstructed image without attacks of the encrypted-watermarked image

Authors	Khalfallah et al. (2006)	Puech et al. (2008)	Bhnassy et al. (2019)	Proposed method
Calculed parameters	PSNR (dB)	PSNR (dB)	PSNR (dB)	PSNR (dB)
No attack	34,2500	38,7500	33,0119	**42,4562**

We can see from Table 4 that our results are better on the quality of the reconstructed image since our value (in bold) of PSNR is largely above theirs.

4.3. Successive Hybrid Watermarking Then Encryption Algorithm

The results obtained after simulation of this successive hybrid algorithm of blind watermarking and chaotic encryption are presented as follows:

According to the human visual system, we note that from these figure (Figure 19, 20, 21 and 22), that it is difficult to differentiate the original image from the reconstructed image and the same to the watermark from the extracted watermark after watermarking then encryption. According to the calculated evaluation parameters, we find that the operation generates an information loss equivalent to the correlation coefficient CC=1,0000 and a peak signal-to-noise ratio PSNR=51,5303dB (already > 30dB). So, we can say that our algorithm for successive watermarking-encryption of CFA images was successful depending on the standards described in the literature.

In order to evaluate the robustness of our hybrid algorithm of successive CFA image encryption, several types of attacks existing in two classes, have been implemented. The first class consists of geometric attacks (Figure 23) which aims to sufficiently distort the watermarked-encrypted image. While, the second class consists of erasure attacks (figure 24) aimed extracted watermark in the watermarked-encrypted image.

Figure 19. Original image (a), watermark image (b), watermarked-encrypted image (c), and their histograms

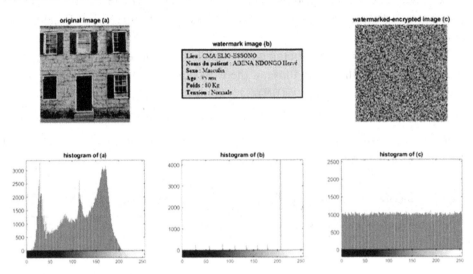

Figure 20. Watermarked-encrypted image (a), extracted watermark (b), reconstructed image (c), and their histograms

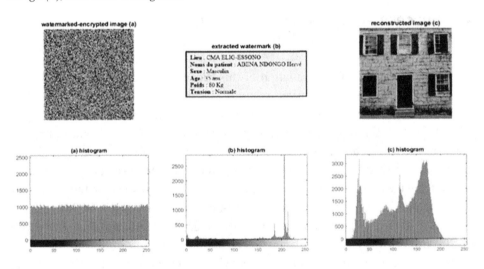

Figure 21. Original image (a), reconstructed image (b), difference between the original image and the reconstructed image (c), and their histograms

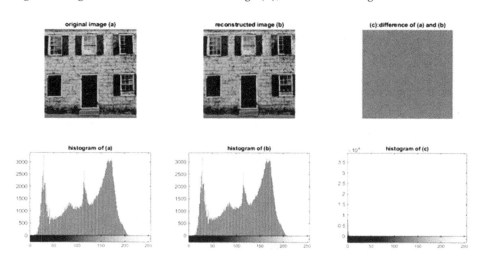

Figure 22. Watermark image (a), extracted watermark (b), difference between the watermark and the extracted watermark (c), and their histograms

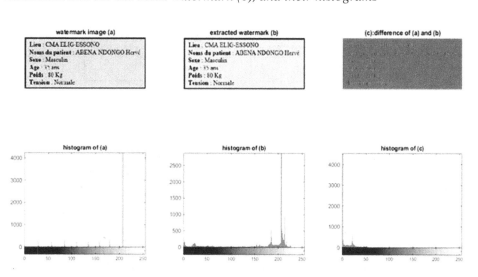

Figure 23. Performance against geometric attacks: watermarks extracted from watermarked then encrypted images and attacked

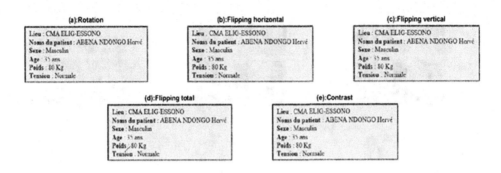

Figure 24. Performance against erasure attacks: watermarks extracted from watermarked then encrypted images and attacked

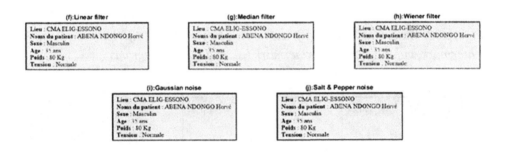

We find that from Figure 23 and 24, our successively implemented hybrid CFA image watermarking-encryption algorithm is well resilient to geometric and erasure operations, as the watermarks extracted after these operations are easily recognized by the human visual system. The values of different evaluation parameters for the hybrid successive watermarking-encryption algorithm are presented in Table 5 below:

The results obtained after simulation (shown in Table 5) show that our successive watermarking then encryption algorithm of CFA images maintains good quality of extracted marks and good robustness against some conventional attacks.

We compare our results obtained by our successive hybrid watermarking then encryption algorithm with those of the work of Sunjay et al., and Noura et al. (2017). The results obtained are presented in Table 6.

Table5. Evaluation parameters for the hybrid method successive watermarking-encryption of CFA images

DESIGNATIONS		IMAGE 1		IMAGE 2		IMAGE 3		IMAGE 4		IMAGE 5		IMAGE 6	
		PSNR (dB)	CC	PSNR (dB)	CC	PSNR (dB)	CC	PSNR (dB)	CC	PSNR (dB)	CC	PSNR (dB)	CC
NO ATTACK	No attack	51,3385	1,0000	51,5303	1,0000	51,9601	1,0000	52,5758	1,0000	51,6907	1,0000	51,4948	1,0000
GEOMETRIC ATTACKS	Rotation 10^0	35,3765	0,9962	34,1946	0,9916	34,0371	0,9925	34,7963	0,9937	36,3676	0,9969	34,0927	0,9912
	Contrast	35,3768	0,9962	34,1921	0,9916	33,9936	0,9923	34,7950	0,9937	36,4383	0,9985	34,0968	0,9913
	Horizontal Flipping	35,3598	0,9962	34,2240	0,9918	34,0406	0,9925	34,7866	0,9936	36,4261	0,9970	34,1338	0,9914
	Vertical Flipping	35,3841	0,9962	34,2176	0,9917	34,0209	0,9924	34,8070	0,9937	36,3973	0,9970	34,1365	0,9914
	Total Flipping	35,3604	0,9962	34,2144	0,9917	33,9985	0,9923	34,7993	0,9937	36,3913	0,9970	34,1120	0,9913
	Linear filter	36,1317	0,9973	35,0288	0,9943	34,7723	0,9946	35,8312	0,9961	37,1497	0,9979	34,9779	0,9942
	Median filter	35,4664	0,9964	34,3401	0,9922	34,1724	0,9929	34,8893	0,9939	36,5005	0,9971	34,2349	0,9918
	Wiener filter	35,4959	0,9964	34,3472	0,9922	34,1528	0,9929	34,9453	0,9941	36,5058	0,9971	34,2581	0,9919
ERASURE ATTACKS	De-debugging salt and peppers	37,4090	0,9985	36,3795	0,9970	36,0147	0,9970	37,8448	0,9985	37,9613	0,9985	36,3937	0,9970
	Gaussian de-debugging	36,9915	0,9982	35,8977	0,9962	35,6067	0,9964	36,9743	0,9977	37,7111	0,9984	35,8198	0,9961

Table 6. Comparison of robustness after attacks on the successively watermarked-encrypted image

Authors	Sunjay et al., in 2011		Noura et al., 2017		Proposed method	
Calculed parameters	PSNR (dB)	CC	PSNR (dB)	CC	PSNR (dB)	CC
Median filter	34,9500	0,9200	36,2400	0,9400	**35,4664**	**0,9964**
Rotation	10,8600	0,9200	12,0100	0,9300	**35,3765**	**0,9962**
De-debugging salt and peppers	25,2300	0,9900	27,1500	0,8900	**37,4090**	**0,9985**

We see from Table 6 that our results are better on the quality of the watermarked and then encrypted image and the extracted watermarks respectively after these attacks seen that our values (in bold) of PSNR and CC in general, are largely above theirs. So, our algorithm is more robust than theirs.

4.5. Comparison of Proposed Hybrid Algorithms

In order to determine the most robust of the various hybrid algorithms proposed, we compare the results obtained (after simulation of these algorithms) of PSNR values after attacks of these algorithms according to the human visual system and statistical analysis (by doing an ANOVA: *analysis of variance*).

4.5.1. The Human Visual System

The results are presented in Table 7 for the different CFA images (image 1, ..., image 3) in Figure 6:

The results of PSNR values presented in Table 7 show that our simultaneous hybrid algorithm (brown values) is more robust than the successive hybrid algorithms (red values) on CFA images 1 and 3, but not completely (the simultaneous hybrid algorithm is only more robust than the successive hybrid algorithm of watermarking then encryption, but not at all on the successive hybrid algorithm of encryption then watermarking) on CFA image 2. These results also show that the successive hybrid encryption-then-encryption algorithm is more robust than the watermarking-then-encryption algorithm on all 3 CFA images.

Table 7. Comparison of the values of the evaluation parameters of the different proposed hybrid algorithms

CFA IMAGES	PROPOSED HYBRID ALGORITHMS	DIFFERENT TYPES OF ATTACKS	PSNR (DB)
IMAGE 1	Hybrid simultaneous encryption and watermarking algorithm	Geometric attacks (rotation 10⁰, contrast, vertical flipping, horizontal flipping, total flipping)	39,2265
			39,2462
			38,8056
			39,5676
			38,8005
		Erasure attacks (linear filter, median filter, wiener filter, salt & peppers noise, gaussian noise)	37,0868
			39,2422
			39,3153
			39,2461
			39,2461
	Successive hybrid algorithm of encryption and watermarking	Geometric attacks (rotation 10⁰, contrast, vertical flipping, horizontal flipping, total flipping)	37,0250
			36,7605
			36,8662
			36,8777
			36,8624
		Erasure attacks (linear filter, median filter, wiener filter, salt & peppers noise, gaussian noise)	33,8101
			37,1101
			36,9526
			36,7606
			36,7606
	Successive hybrid algorithm of watermarking and encryption	Geometric attacks (rotation 10⁰, contrast, vertical flipping, horizontal flipping, total flipping)	35,3765
			35,3768
			35,3598
			35,3841
			35,3604
		Erasure attacks (linear filter, median filter, wiener filter, salt & peppers noise, gaussian noise)	36,1317
			35,4664
			35,4959
			37,4090
			36,9915

Table 7 continued

CFA IMAGES	PROPOSED HYBRID ALGORITHMS	DIFFERENT TYPES OF ATTACKS	PSNR (DB)
IMAGE 2	Hybrid simultaneous encryption and watermarking algorithm	Geometric attacks (rotation 10⁰, contrast, vertical flipping, horizontal flipping, total flipping)	34,3610
			34,3644
			34,3575
			34,3558
			34,3566
		Erasure attacks (linear filter, median filter, wiener filter, salt & peppers noise, gaussian noise)	34,1126
			34,3624
			34,3634
			34,3634
			34,3634
	Successive hybrid algorithm of encryption and watermarking	Geometric attacks (rotation 10⁰, contrast, vertical flipping, horizontal flipping, total flipping)	**35,9579**
			35,6735
			35,9289
			35,9019
			35,9002
		Erasure attacks (linear filter, median filter, wiener filter, salt & peppers noise, gaussian noise)	33,2677
			36,0053
			35,8476
			35,6737
			35,6736
	Successive hybrid algorithm of watermarking and encryption	Geometric attacks (rotation 10⁰, contrast, vertical flipping, horizontal flipping, total flipping)	36,7867
			36,7928
			36,7574
			36,7703
			36,7536
		Erasure attacks (linear filter, median filter, wiener filter, salt & peppers noise, gaussian noise)	35,7141
			36,7896
			36,7952
			36,7928
			36,7952

Table 7 continued

CFA IMAGES	PROPOSED HYBRID ALGORITHMS	DIFFERENT TYPES OF ATTACKS	PSNR (DB)
IMAGE 3	Hybrid simultaneous encryption and watermarking algorithm	Geometric attacks (rotation 10^0, contrast, vertical flipping, horizontal flipping, total flipping)	**36,7867**
			36,7928
			36,7574
			36,7703
			36,7536
		Erasure attacks (linear filter, median filter, wiener filter, salt & peppers noise, gaussian noise)	**35,7141**
			36,7896
			36,7952
			36,7928
			36,7952
	Successive hybrid algorithm of encryption and watermarking	Geometric attacks (rotation 10^0, contrast, vertical flipping, horizontal flipping, total flipping)	**35,5676**
			35,2846
			35,4782
			35,5003
			35,4704
		Erasure attacks (linear filter, median filter, wiener filter, salt & peppers noise, gaussian noise)	32,8930
			35,6075
			35,4661
			35,2848
			35,2848
	Successive hybrid algorithm of watermarking and encryption	Geometric attacks (rotation 10^0, contrast, vertical flipping, horizontal flipping, total flipping)	34,0371
			33,9936
			34,0406
			34,0209
			33,9985
		Erasure attacks (linear filter, median filter, wiener filter, salt & peppers noise, gaussian noise)	**34,7723**
			34,1724
			34,1528
			36,0147
			35,6067

4.5.2. Statistical Analysis

In statistics, ANOVA (analysis of variance) is a set of statistical models used to check whether group means come from the same population. The groups correspond to the modalities of a qualitative variable, and the means are calculated from a continuous variable. This test is applied when one or more categorical explanatory variables (then called variability factors, their different modalities sometimes referred to as "levels") have an influence on the law of a continuous variable to be explained. Analysis is referred to as one-factor analysis when the model is described by a single variability factor, and as two-factor analysis or multifactor analysis otherwise.

Analysis of variance is used to study the behavior of a quantitative variable to be explained as a function of one or more categorical variables. When we wish to study the explanatory power of several categorical variables at once, we use a multiple analysis of variance (MANOVA). If a model contains categorical and continuous explanatory variables, and we wish to study the laws linking the continuous explanatory variables with the quantitative variable to be explained as a function of each modality of the categorical variables, then we use an analysis of covariance (ANCOVA).

In this work, the quantitative variable will be represented by the PSNR values and the categorical or qualitative variables will be characterized by: the proposed hybrid algorithms, the CFA images used in the simulations and the different types of attacks. The objective will therefore be to see how the dependent (quantitative) variable changes according to the levels of the independent (categorical) variables. So, the null hypothesis of the ANOVA is that there is no statistically significant difference between the means, and the alternative hypothesis is that the means are different from each other.

In the one-way ANOVA, we will first model the PSNR values as a function of the "different types of attacks" used.

Table 8. Modeling of PSNR values according to "different types of attacks"

Designations	Df	Sum Sq	Mean Sq	F value	P value (Pr>F)
Different types of attacks	1	0.09	0.0899	0.037	0.847
Residuals	88	212.00	2.4091	-	-

The P value of the variable "different types of attacks" (Table 8) is high (0.847 > 0.001), so it seems that this variable used has no impact on the final result of the obtained PSNR values.

Then, we model the PSNR values according to the "proposed hybrid algorithms".

Table 9. Modeling of PSNR values according to the "proposed hybrid algorithms"

Designations	Df	Sum Sq	Mean Sq	F value	P value (Pr>F)
proposed hybrid algorithms	2	41.21	20.607	10.49	8.28e-05
Residuals	87	170.87	1.964	-	-

The P-value of the variable "proposed hybrid algorithms" (Table 9) is low ($P=8.28*10^{-5} < 0.001$), so it appears that this variable used has a real impact on the final result of the obtained PSNR values.

Finally, we model the PSNR values according to the "CFA images" presented in Figure 6.

Table 10. Modeling of PSNR values according to the "CFA images".

Designations	Df	Sum Sq	Mean Sq	F value	P value (Pr>F)
CFA Images	2	82.56	41.28	27.73	4.84e-10
Residuals	87	129.53	1.49	-	-

The P-value of the variable "CFA images" (Table 10) is low ($P=4.84*10^{-10} < 0.001$), so it seems that the CFA images used have a real impact on the final result of the obtained PSNR values.

In order to obtain a correct model, we will take into account the two categorical variables ("proposed hybrid algorithms" and "CFA images") that have a real impact on the final result of the obtained PSNR values. We obtain the table below:

Table 11. Modeling of PSNR values according to the variables "proposed hybrid algorithms" and "CFA images"

Designations	Df	Sum Sq	Mean Sq	F value	P value (Pr>F)
proposed hybrid algorithms	2	41.21	20.61	19.83	8.53e-08
CFA Images	2	82.56	41.28	39.73	6.58e-13
Residuals	85	88.32	1.04	-	-

We see (Table 11) that including these two variables appears to have improved the model: it reduced the residual variance (the sum of the residual squares went from 170.87 to 88.32), and they are both statistically significant (P values < 0.001).

So far, the ANOVA has told us whether there are differences between the means of the groups, but not what those differences are. To find out which groups are statistically different from each other, we can perform a Tukey's Honestly Significant Difference (HSD) post-hoc test for pairwise comparisons: so, we get the table below:

With for the categorical variable "proposed hybrid algorithms": 1=simultaneous hybrid algorithm, 2=successive hybrid algorithm of encryption and then watermarking and 3=successive hybrid algorithm of watermarking and then encryption; and for the categorical variable "CFA images used": 1=CFA image 1, 2=CFA image 2 and 3=CFA image 3.

Table 12. Pairwise comparison of the variables "proposed hybrid algorithms" and "CFA images": post-hoc TukeyHSD test

Designations	proposed hybrid algorithms			CFA images used		
	2-1	3-1	3-2	2-1	3-1	3-2
diff	-0.8812567	-1.6564467	-0.7751900	-2.256467	-1.684207	0.572260
lwr	-1.509081	-2.284271	-1.403015	-2.88429118	-2.31203118	-0.05556451
upr	-0.2534322	-1.0286222	-0.1473655	-1.628642	-1.056382	1.200085
P adj	0.0034424	0.0000000	0.0114777	0.0000000	0.0000000	0.0814757

From the results of the post-hoc test (Table 12), we see that there are statistically significant differences (P adj < 0.05) between the proposed hybrid algorithms 3 and 1 groups, between the proposed hybrid algorithms 3 and 2 groups, between the proposed hybrid algorithms 2 and 1 groups, and there is also a significant difference between the CFA Images 2 and 1 group, between the CFA Images 3 and 1 group. However, the difference between the CFA Images 3 and 2 groups is not statistically significant.

In order to show which combinations of proposed hybrid algorithms + CFA Images are statistically different from each other, we will perform another ANOVA + TukeyHSD test, using the interaction between proposed hybrid algorithms and CFA Images. We do this not to find out if the interaction term is significant, but rather to find out which group means are statistically different from each other. We obtain the figure below:

Figure 25. Level difference of means for proposed hybrid algorithms: CFA images

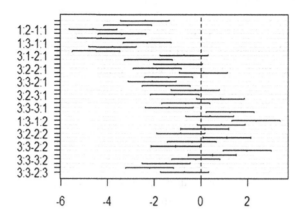

Significant pairwise differences are those for which the 95% confidence interval does not include zero. This is another way of saying that the P-value for these pairwise differences is < 0.05. From this graph (Figure 4.25), we can see that the proposed hybrid algorithms + CFA images combinations that are significantly different from each other are 2:1-1:1, 3:1-1:1, 1:2-1:1, 2:2-1:1, and 3:2-2:1... etc.

Figure 26. Difference in the means of PSNR values according to the variables "proposed hybrid algorithms" and "CFA images"

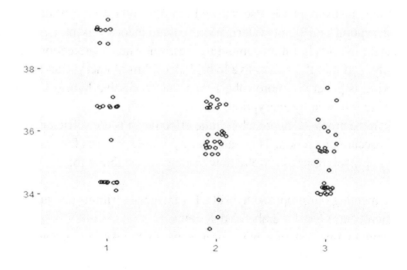

Figure 26 allowed us to find a statistically significant difference in the Mean PSNR value both by type of proposed hybrid algorithms and by CFA images. The comparison by group showed the largest PSNR gains for CFA image 1 and the proposed hybrid algorithm 1 (simultaneous), suggesting that this proposed hybrid algorithm mix is the most advantageous for the "PSNR value" under our experimental conditions.

CONCLUSION

At the end of our work, we were able to achieve our goal of developing a robust hybrid algorithm for encryption-watermarking CFA images using quaternions. In the course of this research work, we studied the problem of simple, fast and secure image transfer. The problem concerns the confidentiality, security and authenticity of images transmitted over digital networks in an insecure environment. After studying a wide range of image protection techniques, we developed three hybrid algorithms that simultaneously and successively combine chaotic encryption and blind watermarking techniques to address the various issues raised. These proposed algorithms have been implemented on a Windows PC platform, taking into account the trade-off between visual quality of modified images (encrypted-watermarked) and robustness against the different types of attacks used. The hypotheses put forward during this research work have been verified, and analysis of the results obtained after simulation has shown that these proposed hybrid methods offer better values for the evaluation criteria proposed in the literature. These methods are effective for the confidentiality, integrity and authentication of digital documents.

The results analysis phase also showed that the hybrid algorithm combining chaotic encryption and blind watermarking simultaneously is particularly more robust than the hybrid algorithm combining these same image protection techniques successively; and that the successive hybrid algorithm of encryption followed by watermarking is generally more robust than the successive hybrid algorithm of watermarking followed by encryption.

Although the proposed approach is quite effective, it is not sufficient to achieve completely secure protection. There are many possible avenues for improving and developing new solutions. So, we're now turning our attention to:

- Implementing our proposed hybrid CFA image algorithms on hardware such as microcontrollers for embedded systems.
- Automating our system using neural networks to take into account all types of images for real-time applications.

REFERENCES

Autrusseau, F., Guédon, J. P., & Bizais, Y. (2003). Watermarking and cryptographic schemes for medical imaging. In SPIE Medical Imaging (pp. 958-965). Academic Press.

Benlcouiri, Y., Ismaili, M., Azizi, A., & Benabdellah, M. (2012). Securing images by secret key steganography. *Applied Mathematical Sciences*, *6*(111), 5513–5523.

Bhnassy, M. A., Hagras, E. A., El-Badawy, E. S. A., Mokhtar, M. A., & Aly, M. H. (2019). Image encryption and watermarking combined dynamic chaotic hopping pattern with double random phase encoding DRPE. *Optical and Quantum Electronics*, *51*(7), 246. doi:10.1007/s11082-019-1961-2

Boukara, O., Bitjokaa, L., & Djaowéa, G. (2013). Nondestructive determination of beans water absorption capacity using CFA images analysis for Hard-To-Cook evaluation. *Iranian Journal of Electrical and Computer Engineering*, *3*(3), 317–328.

Bülow, T. (1999). *Hypercomplex spectral signal representations for the processing and analysis of images* (Doctoral dissertation).

Gwet, D. L. L., Otesteanu, M., Libouga, I. O., Bitjoka, L., & Popa, G. D. (2018). A review on image segmentation techniques and performance measures. *International Journal of Computer and Information Engineering*, *12*(12), 1107–1117.

Khalfallah, A., Kammoun, F., Bouhlel, M. S., & Olivier, C. (2006, April). A new scheme of watermarking in multi-resolution filed by 5/3 wavelet: Family signature combined with the adapted embedding strength. *2006 2nd International Conference on Information & Tongxin Jishu*, *1*, 1145–1152.

Laurent, B., Ousman, B., Dzudie, T., Carl, M. M., & Emmanuel, T. (2010). Digital camera images processing of hard-to-cook beans. *Journal of Engineering and Technology Research*, *2*(9), 177–188.

Le Bihan, N. (2003). *Quaternionic processing of color images*. Conferences on Signal and Image Processing.

Li, X., Gunturk, B., & Zhang, L. (2008, January). Image demosaicing: A systematic survey. In *Visual Communications and Image Processing 2008* (Vol. 6822, pp. 489–503). SPIE. doi:10.1117/12.766768

Lukac, R., & Plataniotis, K. N. (2005). Color filter arrays: Design and performance analysis. *IEEE Transactions on Consumer Electronics*, *51*(4), 1260–1267. doi:10.1109/TCE.2005.1561853

Lukac, R., & Plataniotis, K. N. (Eds.). (2018). *Color image processing: methods and applications.* CRC press. doi:10.1201/9781315221526

Manoury, A. (2001). *Tatouage d'images numériques par paquets d'ondelettes* (Doctoral dissertation, Ecole Centrale de Nantes (ECN); Université de Nantes).

Ndongo, H. A., Barzina, R., Ousman, B., & Bitjoka, L. (2013). *Comparison of CFA and color image tattoos.* Dans le 2ème Atelier annuel sur la Cryptographie, Algèbre et Géométrie (CRAG 2), Pages: 113-120 du 03-07/12/2012 à l'Université de Ngaoundéré.

Ndongo, H. A., Ledoux, E. E. B., Paul, A. M., & Alexendre, N. (2021). Hybrid compression-encryption-watermarking image algorithm based on the quaternionic wavelets transform (QWT). *IACSIT International Journal of Engineering and Technology*, *10*(2), 208–214.

Ndongo, H. A., Vournone, M., Pouyap, M., Ngakawa, T., & Malobe, P. A. (2022). Hybrid Successive CFA Image Encryption-Watermarking Algorithm Based on the Quaternionic Wavelet Transform (QWT). *Journal of Information Security*, *13*(4), 244–256. doi:10.4236/jis.2022.134013

Nkapkop, J. D., Effa, J. Y., Borda, M., Ciprian, A., Bitjoka, L., & Mohamadou, A. (2016). Efficient Chaos-Based Cryptosystem for Real Time Applications. *Acta Technica Napocensis*, *57*(4), 5.

NouraA.NtsamaP.BitjokaL. (2017). A robust biomedical images watermarking scheme based on chaos. *International Journal of Computer Science and Security,* *11*(1).

Puech, W., Charre, J. J., & Dumas, M. (2001). Secure image transfer using Vigenère encryption. NimesTic 2001, The Human-System relationship: Complex, Nîmes, France, 167-171.

Puech, W., Chaumont, M., & Strauss, O. (2008, March). A reversible data hiding method for encrypted images. In *Security, forensics, steganography, and watermarking of multimedia contents X* (Vol. 6819, pp. 534–542). SPIE. doi:10.1117/12.766754

Puech, W., & Rodrigues, J. M. (2005, September). Crypto-compression of medical images by selective encryption of DCT. In *2005 13th European signal processing conference* (pp. 1-4). IEEE.

Rakotondraina, T.E., Ramafiarisona, H.M., & Randriamitantsoa, A.A. (2013). Secure transfer of images in the domain of TFD. *MADA-ETI.*

Ralaivao, HH, Randriamitantsoa, PA, & Raminoson, T. (2016). Security of images by combination of tattooing and encryption. *MADA-ETI.*

Rey, C. (2003, January). *Image watermarking: gain in robustness and integrity of images.* Avignon.

Yang, Y., Losson, O., & Duvieubourg, L. (2007, December). Quality evaluation of color demosaicing according to image resolution. In *2007 Third International IEEE Conference on Signal-Image Technologies and Internet-Based System* (pp. 689-695). IEEE. 10.1109/SITIS.2007.33

Zhang, L., Wu, X., Buades, A., & Li, X. (2011). Color demosaicking by local directional interpolation and nonlocal adaptive thresholding. *Journal of Electronic Imaging, 20*(2), 023016–023016. doi:10.1117/1.3600632

ADDITIONAL READING

Adams, M. D., & Ward, R. (2001, August). Wavelet transforms in the JPEG-2000 standard. In *2001 IEEE Pacific Rim Conference on Communications, Computers and Signal Processing (IEEE Cat. No. 01CH37233)* (Vol. 1, pp. 160-163). IEEE. 10.1109/PACRIM.2001.953547

Anstett, F. (2006). *Chaotic dynamic systems for encryption: synthesis and cryptanalysis* (Doctoral dissertation, Université Henri Poincaré-Nancy I).

Bayer, B. (1976). Color imaging array. *United States Patent, no. 3971065.*

Bayram, S., Sencar, H. T., & Memon, N. (2008). Classification of digital camera models based on demosaicing artifacts. *Digital Investigation, 5*(1-2), 49-59.

Bender, W., Gruhl, D., Morimoto, N., & Lu, A. (1996). Techniques for data hiding. *IBM systems journal, 35*(3.4), 313-336.

Bhattacharjee, S., & Kutter, M. (1998, October). Compression tolerant image authentication. In *Proceedings 1998 International Conference on Image Processing. ICIP98 (Cat. No. 98CB36269)* (Vol. 1, pp. 435-439). IEEE. 10.1109/ICIP.1998.723518

Boccaletti, S., Kurths, J., Osipov, G., Valladares, D. L., & Zhou, C. S. (2002). The synchronization of chaotic systems. *Physics Reports, 366*(1-2), 1–101. doi:10.1016/S0370-1573(02)00137-0 PMID:12443117

Campisi, P., Carli, M., Giunta, G., & Neri, A. (2003). Blind quality assessment system for multimedia communications using tracing watermarking. *IEEE Transactions on Signal Processing, 51*(4), 996–1002. doi:10.1109/TSP.2003.809381

Celik, T., & Tjahjadi, T. (2009). Multiscale texture classification using dual-tree complex wavelet transform. *Pattern Recognition Letters, 30*(3), 331–339. doi:10.1016/j.patrec.2008.10.006

Celik, T., & Tjahjadi, T. (2011). Bayesian texture classification and retrieval based on multiscale feature vector. *Pattern Recognition Letters, 32*(2), 159–167. doi:10.1016/j.patrec.2010.10.003

Chan, W. L., Choi, H., & Baraniuk, R. (2004, October). Quaternion wavelets for image analysis and processing. In *2004 International Conference on Image Processing, 2004. ICIP'04.* (Vol. 5, pp. 3057-3060). IEEE. 10.1109/ICIP.2004.1421758

Chan, W. L., Choi, H., & Baraniuk, R. G. (2008). Coherent multiscale image processing using dual-tree quaternion wavelets. *IEEE Transactions on Image Processing, 17*(7), 1069–1082. doi:10.1109/TIP.2008.924282 PMID:18586616

Chandra, D. S. (2002, August). Digital image watermarking using singular value decomposition. In *The 2002 45th Midwest Symposium on Circuits and Systems, 2002. MWSCAS-2002.* (Vol. 3, pp. III-III). IEEE. 10.1109/MWSCAS.2002.1187023

Chang, C. C., Hu, Y. S., & Lin, C. C. (2007). A digital watermarking scheme based on singular value decomposition. In *Combinatorics, Algorithms, Probabilistic and Experimental Methodologies: First International Symposium, ESCAPE 2007, Hangzhou, China, April 7-9, 2007, Revised Selected Papers* (pp. 82-93). Springer Berlin Heidelberg. 10.1007/978-3-540-74450-4_8

De Rivaz, P., & Kingsbury, N. (1999, October). Complex wavelet features for fast texture image retrieval. In *Proceedings 1999 International Conference on Image Processing (Cat. 99CH36348)* (Vol. 1, pp. 109-113). IEEE. 10.1109/ICIP.1999.821576

Demba, M., & Zaid, O. M. A. (2013). A proposed confusion algorithm based on Chen's chaotic system for securing colored images. *System, 10*(13), 296-301.

Diffle, W., & Hellman, M. E. (1976). New directions in cryptography. *IEEE Transactions on Information Theory, 22*(6), 644–654. doi:10.1109/TIT.1976.1055638

Dugelay, J. L., & Roche, S. (1999). Introduction au tatouage d'images. *Annales des Télécommunications, 54*(9-10), 427–437. doi:10.1007/BF02996385

Effa, J. Y., Nkapkop, J. D. D., Cislariu, M., & Borda, M. (2016). Comparative Analysis of Different Structures of Chaos-Based Cryptosystems: A Survey. *Acta Technica Napocensis, 57*(2), 36.

Eggers, J. J., Bauml, R., Tzschoppe, R., & Girod, B. (2003). Scalar costa scheme for information embedding. *IEEE Transactions on Signal Processing, 51*(4), 1003–1019. doi:10.1109/TSP.2003.809366

El-Taweel, G. S., Onsi, H. M., Samy, M., & Darwish, M. G. (2005). Secure and non-blind watermarking scheme for color images based on DWT. *ICGST International Journal on Graphics. Vision and Image Processing, 5*, 1–5.

Elbasi, E., & Eskicioglu, A. M. (2006, March). A Semi-Blind Watermarking Scheme for Images using a Tree Structure. In *2006 IEEE Sarnoff Symposium* (pp. 1-4). IEEE. 10.1109/SARNOF.2006.4534757

ElGamal, T. (1985). A public key cryptosystem and a signature scheme based on discrete logarithms. *IEEE Transactions on Information Theory, 31*(4), 469–472. doi:10.1109/TIT.1985.1057074

Eloundou, B. L. E., Oyobe, A. J., Abena, H., & Ele, P. (2021). Compression of medical images by quaternionic wavelet transform. *IACSIT International Journal of Engineering and Technology, 10*(2), 89–94.

Eloundou, P. N., Ele, P., & Tonye, E. (2004). Robust compression of the ElectroMyoGraphique (EMG) signal using the B-spline transform. *Proc. 7th CARI*, 22-25.

Jiansheng, M., Sukang, L., & Xiaomei, T. (2009). A digital watermarking algorithm based on DCT and DWT. In *Proceedings. The 2009 International Symposium on Web Information Systems and Applications (WISA 2009)* (p. 104). Academy Publisher.

Kingsbury, N. (2001). Complex wavelets for shift invariant analysis and filtering of signals. *Applied and Computational Harmonic Analysis, 10*(3), 234–253. doi:10.1006/acha.2000.0343

Koblitz, N. (1987). Elliptic curve cryptosystems. *Mathematics of Computation, 48*(177), 203–209. doi:10.1090/S0025-5718-1987-0866109-5

Kundur, D., & Hatzinakos, D. (1997, October). A robust digital image watermarking method using wavelet-based fusion. *Proceedings - International Conference on Image Processing, 1*, 544–547. doi:10.1109/ICIP.1997.647970

Kundur, D., & Hatzinakos, D. (1998, May). Digital watermarking using multiresolution wavelet decomposition. In *Proceedings of the 1998 IEEE International Conference on Acoustics, Speech and Signal Processing, ICASSP'98 (Cat. No. 98CH36181)* (Vol. 5, pp. 2969-2972). IEEE. 10.1109/ICASSP.1998.678149

Kuno, T., & Sugiura, H. (2006). *U.S. Patent No. 7,019,774*. Washington, DC: U.S. Patent and Trademark Office.

Langelaar, G. C., van der Lubbe, J. C., & Lagendijk, R. L. (1997, January). Robust labeling methods for copy protection of images. In *Storage and retrieval for Image and Video databases V* (Vol. 3022, pp. 298–309). SPIE. doi:10.1117/12.263418

Le Guelvouit, G. (2003). *Robust tattooing by spread spectrum taking into account adjacent information* (Doctoral dissertation, INSA Rennes).

Liu, X. L., Lin, C. C., & Yuan, S. M. (2016). Blind dual watermarking for color images' authentication and copyright protection. *IEEE Transactions on Circuits and Systems for Video Technology, 28*(5), 1047–1055. doi:10.1109/TCSVT.2016.2633878

Madhu, C., & Shankar, E. A. (2018). Image compression using Quaternion wavelet transform. *HELIX, 8*(1), 2691–2695. doi:10.29042/2018-2691-2695

Maranhão, D. M., & Prado, C. P. (2005). Evolution of chaos in the Matsumoto-Chua circuit: A symbolic dynamics approach. *Brazilian Journal of Physics, 35*(1), 162–169. doi:10.1590/S0103-97332005000100013

Masuda, N., & Aihara, K. (2002). Cryptosystems with discretized chaotic maps. *Ieee transactions on circuits and systems i: fundamental theory and applications, 49*(1), 28-40.

Monno, Y., Kiku, D., Tanaka, M., & Okutomi, M. (2015, September). Adaptive residual interpolation for color image demosaicking. In *2015 IEEE International Conference on Image Processing (ICIP)* (pp. 3861-3865). IEEE. 10.1109/ICIP.2015.7351528

Nkapkop, J. D. D., Effa, J. Y., Borda, M., Bitjoka, L., & Mohamadou, A. (2017). Chaotic encryption scheme based on a fast permutation and diffusion structure. *The International Arab Journal of Information Technology, 14*(6), 812–819.

Parulski, K. A. (1985). Color filters and processing alternatives for one-chip cameras. *IEEE Transactions on Electron Devices, 32*(8), 1381–1389. doi:10.1109/T-ED.1985.22133

Planitz, B., & Maeder, A. (2005, February). Medical image watermarking: a study on image degradation. *Proc. Australian Pattern Recognition Society Workshop on Digital Image Computing, WDIC.*

Rodrigues, J. M. (2006). *Transfert sécurisé d'Images par combinaison de techniques de compression, cryptage et de marquage* (Doctoral dissertation, Université Montpellier II-Sciences et Techniques du Languedoc).

Sangwine, S. J. (1996). Fourier transforms of colour images using quaternion or hypercomplex, numbers. *Electronics Letters*, *32*(21), 1979–1980. doi:10.1049/el:19961331

Sangwine, S. J. (2002, January). Mathematical approaches to linear vector filtering of color images. In *Conference on Colour in Graphics, Imaging, and Vision* (Vol. 1, pp. 348-351). Society of Imaging Science and Technology. 10.2352/CGIV.2002.1.1.art00073

Schneier, B. (2000). A self-study course in block-cipher cryptanalysis. *Cryptologia*, *24*(1), 18–33. doi:10.1080/0161-110091888754

Selesnick, I. W., Baraniuk, R. G., & Kingsbury, N. C. (2005). The dual-tree complex wavelet transform. *IEEE Signal Processing Magazine*, *22*(6), 123–151. doi:10.1109/MSP.2005.1550194

Shannon, C. E. (1949). Communication theory of secrecy systems. *The Bell System Technical Journal*, *28*(4), 656–715. doi:10.1002/j.1538-7305.1949.tb00928.x

Soulard, R., & Carré, P. (2011). Quaternionic wavelets for texture classification. *Pattern Recognition Letters*, *32*(13), 1669–1678. doi:10.1016/j.patrec.2011.06.028

Starck, J. L., Murtagh, F., & Fadili, J. M. (2010). *Sparse image and signal processing: wavelets, curvelets, morphological diversity*. Cambridge university press. doi:10.1017/CBO9780511730344

Tareef, A., Song, Y., Cai, W., Wang, Y., Feng, D. D., & Chen, M. (2016, April). Automatic nuclei and cytoplasm segmentation of leukocytes with color and texture-based image enhancement. In *2016 IEEE 13th International symposium on Biomedical imaging (ISBI)* (pp. 935-938). IEEE. 10.1109/ISBI.2016.7493418

Trémeau, A., Fernandez-Maloigne, C., Bonton, P., & Chassery, J. M. (2004). *Image numérique couleur: de l'acquisition au traitement: cours*. Dunod.

Tsafack, N., Kengne, J., Abd-El-Atty, B., Iliyasu, A. M., Hirota, K., & Abd EL-Latif, A. A. (2020). Design and implementation of a simple dynamical 4-D chaotic circuit with applications in image encryption. *Information Sciences*, *515*, 191–217. doi:10.1016/j.ins.2019.10.070

Tsafack, N., Sankar, S., Abd-El-Atty, B., Kengne, J., Jithin, K. C., Belazi, A., ... Abd El-Latif, A. A. (2020). A new chaotic map with dynamic analysis and encryption application in internet of health things. *IEEE Access : Practical Innovations, Open Solutions, 8*, 137731–137744. doi:10.1109/ACCESS.2020.3010794

Ventura, R. F., Vandergheynst, P., & Frossard, P. (2006). Low-rate and flexible image coding with redundant representations. *IEEE Transactions on Image Processing, 15*(3), 726–739. doi:10.1109/TIP.2005.860596 PMID:16519358

Villalobos-Castaldi, F. M., Felipe-Riverón, E. M., & Sánchez-Fernández, L. P. (2010). A fast, efficient and automated method to extract vessels from fundus images. *Journal of Visualization / the Visualization Society of Japan, 13*(3), 263–270. doi:10.1007/s12650-010-0037-y

Wang, Z., Bovik, A. C., Sheikh, H. R., & Simoncelli, E. P. (2004). Image quality assessment: From error visibility to structural similarity. *IEEE Transactions on Image Processing, 13*(4), 600–612. doi:10.1109/TIP.2003.819861 PMID:15376593

Weszka, J. S., & Rosenfeld, A. (1978). Threshold evaluation techniques. *IEEE Transactions on Systems, Man, and Cybernetics, 8*(8), 622–629. doi:10.1109/TSMC.1978.4310038

Yadav, S., & Rawat, T. K. (2013). Transform Based Hybrid Image Compression Tech-niques in Conjunction with Fractal Image Compression Scheme. *International Journal of Advancements in Research & Technology, 1*(4).

Yang, C. C. (2006). Image enhancement by modified contrast-stretching manipulation. *Optics & Laser Technology, 38*(3), 196–201. doi:10.1016/j.optlastec.2004.11.009

Yang, T., & Chua, L. O. (1996). Secure communication via chaotic parameter modulation. *IEEE Transactions on Circuits and Systems. I, Fundamental Theory and Applications, 43*(9), 817–819. doi:10.1109/81.536758

Compilation of References

Abbaschian, B. J., Sierra-Sosa, D., & Elmaghraby, A. (2021). Deep learning techniques for speech emotion recognition, from databases to models. *Sensors (Basel)*, *21*(4), 1249. doi:10.3390/s21041249 PMID:33578714

AbdAlmageed, W., Wu, Y., Rawls, S., Harel, S., Hassner, T., Masi, I., Choi, J., Lekust, J., Kim, J., & Natarajan, P. (2016). Face recognition using deep multi-pose representations. 2016 IEEE winter conference on applications of computer vision (WACV), 1–9.

Abijah Roseline, S., Hari, G., Geetha, S., & Krishnamurthy, R. (2020). Vision-based malware detection and classification using lightweight deep learning paradigm. In *Computer Vision and Image Processing: 4th International Conference, CVIP 2019, Jaipur, India, September 27–29, 2019, Revised Selected Papers, Part II 4* (pp. 62-73). Springer Singapore. 10.1007/978-981-15-4018-9_6

Abioye, S. O., Oyedele, L. O., Akanbi, L., Ajayi, A., Davila Delgado, J. M., Bilal, M., Akinade, O. O., & Ahmed, A. (2021). Artificial intelligence in the construction industry: A review of present status, opportunities and future challenges. *Journal of Building Engineering*, *44*, 103299. doi:10.1016/j.jobe.2021.103299

Abu Al-Haija, Q., Odeh, A., & Qattous, H. (2022). PDF malware detection based on optimizable decision trees. *Electronics (Basel)*, *11*(19), 3142. doi:10.3390/electronics11193142

Adali, S., & Golbeck, J. (2012). Predicting personality with social behavior. *2012 IEEE/ACM International Conference on Advances in Social Networks Analysis and Mining*, 302–309. 10.1109/ASONAM.2012.58

Adam, H. (2023, August 25). *10 Important Cryptocurrencies Other Than Bitcoin*. Retrieved February 09, 2024, from https://www.investopedia.com/tech/most-important-cryptocurrencies-other-than-bitcoin/

Adedoyin, A., Kapetanakis, S., Petridis, M., & Panaousis, E. (2016). Evaluating Case-Based Reasoning Knowledge Discovery in Fraud Detection. In ICCBR Workshops (pp. 182-191). Academic Press.

Adeto, Y. (2019). Transformative Pedagogy for Building Peace. In *Reconciliation, Peace and Global Citizenship Education: Pedagogy and Practice*. Author.

Agarwal, S., Farid, H., El-Gaaly, T., & Lim, S. (2020). Detecting Deep-Fake Videos from Appearance and Behavior. *WIFS, 2020*(December), 6–11. doi:10.1109/WIFS49906.2020.9360904

Agrawal, A., & Cleland-Huang, J. (2021). Explaining autonomous decisions in swarms of human-on-the-loop small unmanned aerial systems. *Proceedings of the AAAI Conference on Human Computation and Crowdsourcing, 9*, 15–26. 10.1609/hcomp.v9i1.18936

Ahmad, T., Ma, Y., Yahya, M., Ahmad, B., Nazir, S., & Haq, A. U. (2020). Object detection through modified YOLO neural network. *Scientific Programming, 2020*, 1–10. doi:10.1155/2020/8403262

Ahmed, M., Afreen, N., Ahmed, M., Sameer, M., & Ahamed, J. (2023). An inception V3 approach for malware classification using machine learning and transfer learning. *International Journal of Intelligent Networks, 4*, 11–18. doi:10.1016/j.ijin.2022.11.005

Ahsan, M., Nygard, K. E., Gomes, R., Chowdhury, M. M., Rifat, N., & Connolly, J. F. (2022). Cybersecurity threats and their mitigation approaches using Machine Learning—A Review. *Journal of Cybersecurity and Privacy, 2*(3), 527–555. doi:10.3390/jcp2030027

Akhtar, M. a. (2021). An overview of the applications of Artificial Intelligence in Cybersecurity. *EAI Endorsed Transactions on Creative Technologies, 8*(29).

Akhtar, M. S., & Feng, T. (2021). Deep learning-based framework for the detection of cyberattack using feature engineering. *Security and Communication Networks, 2021*, 1–12. doi:10.1155/2021/6129210

Akhtar, N. M., Mian, A., Kardan, N., & Shah, M. (2021). Advances in adversarial attacks and defenses in computer vision: A survey. *IEEE Access : Practical Innovations, Open Solutions, 9*, 155161–155196. doi:10.1109/ACCESS.2021.3127960

Al-Abri, A. A., & Salih, N. K. (2023, September). Mobile Application Malware Self-Diagnosis. In *2023 10th International Conference on Electrical Engineering, Computer Science and Informatics (EECSI)* (pp. 338-342). IEEE. 10.1109/EECSI59885.2023.10295583

Alam, M. A. U. (2020). AI-fairness towards activity recognition of older adults. *MobiQuitous 2020-17th EAI International Conference on Mobile and Ubiquitous Systems: Computing, Networking and Services*, 108–117.

Albahar, M. (2017). Cyber Attacks and Terrorism: A Twenty-First Century Conundrum. *Sci Eng Ethics*. DOI doi:10.1007/s11948-016-9864

Al-Khateeb, H., Epiphaniou, G., & Daly, H. (2019). Blockchain for modern digital forensics: The chain-of-custody as a distributed ledger. *Blockchain and Clinical Trial: Securing Patient Data*, 149-168. doi:10.1186/s13635-023-00142-3

Almomani, I., Alkhayer, A., & El-Shafai, W. (2022). An automated vision-based deep learning model for efficient detection of android malware attacks. *IEEE Access : Practical Innovations, Open Solutions, 10*, 2700–2720. doi:10.1109/ACCESS.2022.3140341

Al-Mousa, M. R. (2021). Analyzing cyber-attack intention for digital forensics using case-based reasoning. *arXiv preprint arXiv:2101.01395.*

Alosaimi, S. A., Almutairi, S. M., & Chamato, F. A. (2023). Computer Vision-Based Intrusion Detection System for Internet of Things. *Wireless Communications and Mobile Computing, 2023*, 2023. doi:10.1155/2023/5881769

Alqurashi, S., & Batarfi, O. (2016). A comparison of malware detection techniques based on hidden Markov model. *Journal of Information Security, 7*(3), 215–223. doi:10.4236/jis.2016.73017

Alshareef, N., Yuan, X., Roy, K., & Atay, M. (2021). A study of gender bias in face presentation attack and its mitigation. *Future Internet, 13*(9), 234. doi:10.3390/fi13090234

Alsmadi, T., & Alqudah, N. (2021, July). A survey on malware detection techniques. In 2021 international conference on information technology (ICIT) (pp. 371-376). IEEE. doi:10.1109/ICIT52682.2021.9491765

Alsodi, O., Zhou, X., Gururajan, R., & Shrestha, A. (2021, October). A Survey on Detection of cybersecurity threats on Twitter using deep learning. In *2021 8th International Conference on Behavioral and Social Computing (BESC)* (pp. 1-5). IEEE. 10.1109/BESC53957.2021.9635406

Alsulami, B., Srinivasan, A., Dong, H., & Mancoridis, S. (2017, October). Lightweight behavioral malware detection for windows platforms. In *2017 12th International Conference on Malicious and Unwanted Software (MALWARE)* (pp. 75-81). IEEE. 10.1109/MALWARE.2017.8323959

Amini, A., Banitsas, K., & Cosmas, J. (2016, May). A comparison between heuristic and machine learning techniques in fall detection using Kinect v2. In *2016 IEEE International Symposium on Medical Measurements and Applications (MeMeA)* (pp. 1-6). IEEE. 10.1109/MeMeA.2016.7533763

An, N., Duff, A., Naik, G., Faloutsos, M., Weber, S., & Mancoridis, S. (2017, October). Behavioral anomaly detection of malware on home routers. In *2017 12th International Conference on Malicious and Unwanted Software (MALWARE)* (pp. 47-54). IEEE. 10.1109/MALWARE.2017.8323956

Analyzing and reducing the damage of dataset bias to face recognition with synthetic data. (2019). *IEEE/CVF Conference on Computer Vision and Pattern Recognition Workshops (CVPRW)*, 2261–2268. doi:10.1109/CVPRW.2019.00279

Anandita Iyer, A., & Umadevi, K. S. (2023). Role of AI and its impact on the development of cyber security applications. In *Artificial Intelligence and Cyber Security in Industry 4.0* (pp. 23–46). Springer Nature Singapore. doi:10.1007/978-981-99-2115-7_2

Antonios, G., Christos, K. G., & Georgios, D. (2023, Decembre 23). A Comparative Analysis of Ethereum Solidity and Sui Move Smart Contract Languages: Advantages and Trade-Offs. *2023 6th World Symposium on Communication Engineering (WSCE)*. 10.1109/WSCE59557.2023.10365887

Anvarjon, T., Mustaqeem, & Kwon, S. (2020). Deep-net: A lightweight CNN-based speech emotion recognition system using deep frequency features. *Sensors (Basel), 20*(18), 5212. doi:10.3390/s20185212 PMID:32932723

Anzum, F., Asha, A. Z., & Gavrilova, M. L. (2022). Biases, fairness, and implications of using AI in social media data mining. *2022 International Conference on Cyberworlds (CW)*, 251–254. 10.1109/CW55638.2022.00056

Anzum, F., & Gavrilova, M. L. (2023). Emotion detection from micro-blogs using novel input representation. *IEEE Access : Practical Innovations, Open Solutions*, *11*, 19512–19522. doi:10.1109/ACCESS.2023.3248506

Aramanda, A., Abdul, S. M., & Vedala, R. (2021). Refining user ratings using user emotions for recommender systems. *The 23rd International Conference on Information Integration and Web Intelligence. Linz, Austria*, 3–10.

Aryal, S. (2018). Anomaly detection technique robust to units and scales of measurement. *Advances in Knowledge Discovery and Data Mining: 22nd Pacific-Asia Conference, PAKDD 2018, Melbourne, VIC, Australia, June 3-6, 2018 Proceedings*, *22*(Part I), 589–601.

Asha, A. Z., & Sharlin, E. (2023). Designing inclusive interaction with autonomous vehicles for older passengers. *Proceedings of the 2023 ACM Designing Interactive Systems Conference*, 2138–2154. 10.1145/3563657.3596045

Aslan, Ö. A., & Samet, R. (2020). A comprehensive review on malware detection approaches. *IEEE Access : Practical Innovations, Open Solutions*, *8*, 6249–6271. doi:10.1109/ACCESS.2019.2963724

Atzei, N., Bartoletti, M., & Cimoli, T. (2017). A survey of attacks on ethereum smart contracts (sok). *Principles of Security and Trust: 6th International Conference, POST 2017, Held as Part of the European Joint Conferences on Theory and Practice of Software, ETAPS 2017, Uppsala, Sweden, April 22-29, 2017 Proceedings*, *6*, 164–186.

Autrusseau, F., Guédon, J. P., & Bizais, Y. (2003). Watermarking and cryptographic schemes for medical imaging. In SPIE Medical Imaging (pp. 958-965). Academic Press.

Azoulay, A. (2018). Towards an Ethics of Artificial Intelligence. New Technologies: Where To?

Babaei, M., Kulshrestha, J., Chakraborty, A., Redmiles, E. M., Cha, M., & Gummadi, K. P. (2021). Analyzing biases in perception of truth in news stories and their implications for fact checking. *IEEE Transactions on Computational Social Systems*, *9*(3), 839–850. doi:10.1109/TCSS.2021.3096038

Bachir, N. a. (2024). Benchmarking YOLOv5 models for improved human detection in search and rescue missions. *Journal of Electronic Science and Technology*, 100243.

Badshah, A. M., Rahim, N., Ullah, N., Ahmad, J., Muhammad, K., Lee, M. Y., Kwon, S., & Baik, S. W. (2019). Deep features-based speech emotion recognition for smart affective services. *Multimedia Tools and Applications*, *78*(5), 5571–5589. doi:10.1007/s11042-017-5292-7

Badurdeen, F. (2018). Online Radicalisation and Recruitment: Al-Shabaab Luring Strategies with New Technology. In M. Ruteere & P. Mutahi (Eds.), *Confronting Violent Extremism in Kenya: Debates, Ideas and Challenges*. Centre for Human Rights and Policy Studies.

Compilation of References

Balmau, O., Guerraoui, R., Kermarrec, A.-M., Maurer, A., Pavlovic, M., & Zwaenepoel, W. (2018). Limiting the spread of fake news on social media platforms by evaluating users' trustworthiness. *arXiv preprint arXiv:1808.09922*.

Bari, A. H., Sieu, B., & Gavrilova, M. L. (2020). Aestheticnet: Deep convolutional neural network for person identification from visual aesthetic. *The Visual Computer*, *36*(10-12), 2395–2405. doi:10.1007/s00371-020-01893-7

Barnett, A. J. (2021). Interpretable mammographic image classification using case-based reasoning and deep learning. arXiv preprint arXiv:2107.05605.

Basheer Ahmed, M. I., Zaghdoud, R., Ahmed, M. S., Sendi, R., Alsharif, S., Alabdulkarim, J., Albin Saad, B. A., Alsabt, R., Rahman, A., & Krishnasamy, G. (2023). A real-time computer vision based approach to detection and classification of traffic incidents. *Big Data and Cognitive Computing, 7*(1), 22.

Bastiaan, M. (2015, January). *Preventing the 51%-attack: a stochastic analysis of two phase proof of work in bitcoin*. Available at http://referaat. cs. utwente. nl/conference/22/paper/7473/ preventingthe-51-attack-a-stochasticanalysis-oftwo-phase-proof-of-work-in-bitcoin. pdf

Beaman, C., Barkworth, A., Akande, T. D., Hakak, S., & Khan, M. K. (2021). Ransomware: Recent advances, analysis, challenges and future research directions. *Computers & Security, 111*, 102490. doi:10.1016/j.cose.2021.102490 PMID:34602684

Belghith, H. Y. (2017). A Multi-Agent Case-Based Reasoning Architecture for Phishing Detection. *Procedia Computer Science, 110*, 492–497. doi:10.1016/j.procs.2017.06.131

Belghith, H. Y. (2017). Using Case-Based Reasoning for Phishing Detection. *Procedia Computer Science, 109*, 281288. doi:10.1016/j.procs.2017.05.352

Beliz, N., Rangel, J. C., & Hong, C. S. (2012). Detecting DoS attack in Web services by using an adaptive multiagent solution. *ADCAIJ: Advances in Distributed Computing and Artificial Intelligence Journal, 1*(2), 57–63. doi:10.14201/ADCAIJ2012125763

Ben Abdel Ouahab, I., Elaachak, L., & Bouhorma, M. (2023). Enhancing Malware Classification with Vision Transformers: A Comparative Study with Traditional CNN Models. In *Proceedings of the 6th International Conference on Networking, Intelligent Systems & Security* (pp. 1-5). Academic Press.

Benlcouiri, Y., Ismaili, M., Azizi, A., & Benabdellah, M. (2012). Securing images by secret key steganography. *Applied Mathematical Sciences, 6*(111), 5513–5523.

Besenyö, J., & Sinkó, G. (2021). The Social Media Use of African Terrorist Organizations: A Comparative Study of Al-Qaeda in the Islamic Maghreb, Al-Shabaab and Boko Haram. *Insights into Regional Development, 3*(3), 66–78. doi:10.9770/IRD.2021.3.3(4)

Bhatt, D., Patel, C., Talsania, H., Patel, J., Vaghela, R., Pandya, S., Modi, K., & Ghayvat, H. (2021). CNN variants for computer vision: History, architecture, application, challenges and future scope. *Electronics (Basel), 10*(20), 2470. doi:10.3390/electronics10202470

271

Bhnassy, M. A., Hagras, E. A., El-Badawy, E. S. A., Mokhtar, M. A., & Aly, M. H. (2019). Image encryption and watermarking combined dynamic chaotic hopping pattern with double random phase encoding DRPE. *Optical and Quantum Electronics*, *51*(7), 246. doi:10.1007/s11082-019-1961-2

Bijitha, C. V., & Nath, H. V. (2022). On the effectiveness of image processing based malware detection techniques. *Cybernetics and Systems*, *53*(7), 615–640. doi:10.1080/01969722.2021.2020471

Bird, S., Dudík, M., Edgar, R., Horn, B., Lutz, R., Milan, V., Sameki, M., Wallach, H., & Walker, K. (2020). Fairlearn: A toolkit for assessing and improving fairness in ai. *Microsoft, Tech. Rep. MSR-TR-2020-32*.

Boehmer, W. (2010). Analyzing human behavior using case-based reasoning with the help of forensic questions. In *2010 24th IEEE International Conference on Advanced Information Networking and Applications* (pp. 1189-1194). IEEE. 10.1109/AINA.2010.73

Bohara, B., Bhuyan, J., Wu, F., & Ding, J. (2020). A survey on the use of data clustering for intrusion detection system in cybersecurity. *International Journal of Network Security & its Applications*, *12*(1), 1–18. doi:10.5121/ijnsa.2020.12101 PMID:34290487

Borse, Y., Patole, D., Chawhan, G., Kukreja, G., Parekh, H., & Jain, R. (2021, May). Advantages of Blockchain in Digital Forensic Evidence Management. *Proceedings of the 4th International Conference on Advances in Science & Technology (ICAST2021)*.

Botacin, M., Alves, M. Z., Oliveira, D., & Grégio, A. (2022). HEAVEN: A Hardware-Enhanced AntiVirus ENgine to accelerate real-time, signature-based malware detection. *Expert Systems with Applications*, *201*, 117083. doi:10.1016/j.eswa.2022.117083

Botchkarev, A. (2018). Performance metrics (error measures) in machine learning regression, forecasting and prognostics: Properties and typology. *arXiv preprint arXiv:1809.03006*.

Boukara, O., Bitjokaa, L., & Djaowéa, G. (2013). Nondestructive determination of beans water absorption capacity using CFA images analysis for Hard-To-Cook evaluation. *Iranian Journal of Electrical and Computer Engineering*, *3*(3), 317–328.

Bouwmans, T., Javed, S., Zhang, H., Lin, Z., & Otazo, R. (2018). On the applications of robust PCA in image and video processing. *Proceedings of the IEEE*, *106*(8), 1427–1457. doi:10.1109/JPROC.2018.2853589

Bozkir, A. S., Tahillioglu, E., Aydos, M., & Kara, I. (2021). Catch them alive: A malware detection approach through memory forensics, manifold learning and computer vision. *Computers & Security*, *103*, 102166. doi:10.1016/j.cose.2020.102166

Buchanan, B., Bansemer, J., Cary, D., Lucas, J., & Musser, M. (2020). Automating cyber attacks. Center for Security and Emerging Technology, 13-32.

Bui, N., Cesana, M., Hosseini, S. A., Liao, Q., Malanchini, I., & Widmer, J. (2017). A survey of anticipatory mobile networking: Context-based classification, prediction methodologies, and optimization techniques. *IEEE Communications Surveys and Tutorials*, *19*(3), 1790–1821. doi:10.1109/COMST.2017.2694140

Bülow, T. (1999). *Hypercomplex spectral signal representations for the processing and analysis of images* (Doctoral dissertation).

Buolamwini, J., & Gebru, T. (2018). Gender shades: Intersectional accuracy disparities in commercial gender classification. *Conference on fairness, accountability and transparency. New York, USA*, 77–91.

Burton, J. (2020). *Christchurch's Legacy of Fighting Violent Extremism Online Must go Further Deep into the Dark Web.* Retrieved August 23, 2023 from https://theconversation.com/christchurchs-legacy-of-fighting-violent-extremism-online-must-go-further-deep-into-the-dark-web-133159

Buttarelli, G. (2018). *What Do we Learn from Machine Learning?* European Data Protection Supervisor. Retrieved January 3, 2023 from https://edps.europa.eu/press-publications/press-news/blog/what-do-we-learn-machine-learning_en

Byrne et al. (2018) *The Evolution of the Salafi-Jihadist Threat: Current and Future Challenges from the Islamic State, Al-Qaeda, and Other Groups.* A Report of Center for Strategic and International Studies Transnational Threat Project.

Cai, C., He, R., & McAuley, J. (2017). SPMC: Socially-aware personalized markov chains for sparse sequential recommendation. *arXiv preprint arXiv:1708.04497.* doi:10.24963/ijcai.2017/204

Carlos, G., Carlis, R., & Julio, L. (2022, September 29). eSi-BTC: an energy efficient Bitcoin mining core. *2022 35th SBC/SBMicro/IEEE/ACM Symposium on Integrated Circuits and Systems Design (SBCCI).* 10.1109/SBCCI55532.2022.9893218

Carta, S. P., Podda, A. S., Recupero, D. R., & Saia, R. (2020). A local feature engineering strategy to improve network anomaly detection. *Future Internet*, *12*(10), 177. doi:10.3390/fi12100177

Catalano, C., Chezzi, A., Angelelli, M., & Tommasi, F. (2022). Deceiving AI-based malware detection through polymorphic attacks. *Computers in Industry, 143*, 103751.

Cavazos, J. G., Phillips, P. J., Castillo, C. D., & O'Toole, A. J. (2020). Accuracy comparison across face recognition algorithms: Where are we on measuring race bias? *IEEE Transactions on Biometrics, Behavior, and Identity Science*, *3*(1), 101–111. doi:10.1109/TBIOM.2020.3027269 PMID:33585821

Caverlee, J. (2008). A large-scale study of myspace: Observations and implications for online social networks. *Proceedings of the International AAAI Conference on Web and Social Media, 2* (1), 36–44.

Chandramouli, K. (2021). An Advanced Framework for Critical Infrastructure Protection Using Computer Vision Technologies. In *Cyber-Physical Security for Critical Infrastructures Protection: First International Workshop, CPS4CIP 2020, Guildford, UK, September 18, 2020, Revised Selected Papers 1* (pp. 107-122). Guildford, UK: Springer. 10.1007/978-3-030-69781-5_8

Chen, L. (2019). Understanding the efficacy, reliability and resiliency of computer vision techniques for malware detection and future research directions. *arXiv preprint arXiv:1904.10504.*

Chen, M.-Y. a. (2023). Guest editorial: Machine learning-based decision support systems in IoT systems. *Computer Science and Information Systems, 20*(2).

Chen, H., Pendleton, M., Njilla, L., & Xu, S. (2020). A survey on ethereum systems security: Vulnerabilities, attacks, and defenses. *ACM Computing Surveys, 53*(3), 1–43. doi:10.1145/3391195

Chernobrov, D. (2022). Diasporas as Cyberwarriors: Infopolitics, Participatory Warfare and the 2020 Karabakh War. *International Affairs, 98*(2), 631–651. doi:10.1093/ia/iiac015

Chien, S.-Y., Yang, C.-J., & Yu, F. (2022). Xflag: Explainable fake news detection model on social media. *International Journal of Human-Computer Interaction, 38*(18-20), 1808–1827. doi:10.1080/10447318.2022.2062113

Christian, H., Suhartono, D., Chowanda, A., & Zamli, K. Z. (2021). Text based personality prediction from multiple social media data sources using pre-trained language model and model averaging. *Journal of Big Data, 8*(1), 1–20. doi:10.1186/s40537-021-00459-1 PMID:33425651

Claudon, P., & Weber, M. (2009). L'émotion: contribution à l'étude psychodynamique du développement de la pensée de l'enfant sans langage en interaction. *Devenir, 21*(1), 6.

Collmann, J., & Matei, S. A. (2016). *Ethical reasoning in big data: An exploratory analysis.* Springer. doi:10.1007/978-3-319-28422-4

Colome, M., Nunes, R. C., & de Lima Silva, L. A. (2019). Case-Based Cybersecurity Incident Resolution. In SEKE (pp. 253-330). doi:10.18293/SEKE2019-204

Comito, C., Caroprese, L., & Zumpano, E. (2023). Multimodal fake news detection on social media: A survey of deep learning techniques. *Social Network Analysis and Mining, 13*(1), 101. doi:10.1007/s13278-023-01104-w

Confalonieri, R., Coba, L., Wagner, B., & Besold, T. R. (2021). A historical perspective of explainable artificial intelligence. *Wiley Interdisciplinary Reviews. Data Mining and Knowledge Discovery, 11*(1), e1391. doi:10.1002/widm.1391

Conti, M., Kumar, E. S., Lal, C., & Ruj, S. (2018). A survey on security and privacy issues of bitcoin. *IEEE Communications Surveys and Tutorials, 20*(4), 3416–3452. doi:10.1109/COMST.2018.2842460

Crawford, B., Keen, F., & Suarez de-Tangil, G. (2020). *Memetic Irony and the Promotion of Violence within Chan Cultures.* CREST Centre for Research and Evidence on Security Threats.

Dada, E. G., Bassi, J. S., Chiroma, H., Adetunmbi, A. O., & Ajibuwa, O. E. (2019). Machine learning for email spam filtering: Review, approaches and open research problems. *Heliyon*, *5*(6), e01802. doi:10.1016/j.heliyon.2019.e01802 PMID:31211254

Dangi, A. K., Pant, K., Alanya-Beltran, J., Chakraborty, N., Akram, S. V., & Balakrishna, K. (2023). A Review of use of Artificial Intelligence on Cyber Security and the Fifth-Generation Cyber-attacks and its analysis. In *2023 International Conference on Artificial Intelligence and Smart Communication (AISC)* (pp. 553-557). IEEE. 10.1109/AISC56616.2023.10085175

Dasgupta, P. B. (2017). Detection and analysis of human emotions through voice and speech pattern processing. *arXiv preprint arXiv:1710.10198.*

David, O. E., & Netanyahu, N. S. (2015, July). Deepsign: Deep learning for automatic malware signature generation and classification. In *2015 International Joint Conference on Neural Networks (IJCNN)* (pp. 1-8). IEEE. 10.1109/IJCNN.2015.7280815

De Azambuja, A. J. G., Plesker, C., Schützer, K., Anderl, R., Schleich, B., & Almeida, V. R. (2023). Artificial intelligence-based cyber security in the context of industry 4.0—A survey. *Electronics (Basel)*, *12*(8), 1920. doi:10.3390/electronics12081920

Decker, C., & Wattenhofer, R. (2013, September). Information propagation in the bitcoin network. In IEEE P2P 2013 Proceedings (pp. 1-10). IEEE. doi:10.1109/P2P.2013.6688704

Deekshetha, H. R., & Tyagi, A. K. (2023). Automated and intelligent systems for next-generation-based smart applications. In *Data Science for Genomics* (pp. 265–276). Academic Press. doi:10.1016/B978-0-323-98352-5.00019-7

Delacourt, P., & Wellekens, C. J. (2000). DISTBIC: A speaker-based segmentation for audio data indexing. *Speech Communication*, *32*(1-2), 111–126. doi:10.1016/S0167-6393(00)00027-3

Deshmukh, A., Patil, D. S., Soni, G., & Tyagi, A. K. (2023). Cyber Security: New Realities for Industry 4.0 and Society 5.0. In A. Tyagi (Ed.), *Handbook of Research on Quantum Computing for Smart Environments* (pp. 299–325). IGI Global. doi:10.4018/978-1-6684-6697-1.ch017

Deshmukh, A., Sreenath, N., Tyagi, A. K., & Abhichandan, U. V. E. (2022, January). Blockchain enabled cyber security: A comprehensive survey. In *2022 International Conference on Computer Communication and Informatics (ICCCI)* (pp. 1-6). IEEE. 10.1109/ICCCI54379.2022.9740843

Dhelim, S., Aung, N., Bouras, M. A., Ning, H., & Cambria, E. (2022). A survey on personality-aware recommendation systems. *Artificial Intelligence Review*, 1–46.

Dick, K. R., Russell, L., Souley Dosso, Y., Kwamena, F., & Green, J. R. (2019). Deep learning for critical infrastructure resilience. *Journal of Infrastructure Systems*, *25*(2), 05019003. doi:10.1061/(ASCE)IS.1943-555X.0000477

Directive on automated decision-making. (2019). Government of Canada.

Dolph, C. V., Tran, L., & Allen, B. D. (2018). *Towards explainability of uav-based convolutional neural networks for object classification. 2018 Aviation Technology.* Integration, and Operations Conference.

Doshi-Velez, F., & Kim, B. (2017). Towards a rigorous science of interpretable machine learning. *arXiv preprint arXiv:1702.08608.*

Doumit, S., & Minai, A. (2011). Online news media bias analysis using an lda-nlp approach. *International Conference on Complex Systems.*

Dua, S., & Du, X. (2016). *Data mining and machine learning in cybersecurity.* CRC press. doi:10.1201/b10867

Dubey, G. P., & Bhujade, D. R. K. (2021). Optimal feature selection for machine learning based intrusion detection system by exploiting attribute dependence. *Materials Today: Proceedings, 47,* 6325–6331. doi:10.1016/j.matpr.2021.04.643

Duenser, A., & Douglas, D. M. (2023). Whom to trust, how and why: Untangling artificial intelligence ethics principles, trustworthiness, and trust. *IEEE Intelligent Systems, 38*(6), 19–26. doi:10.1109/MIS.2023.3322586

Du, N., Robert, L., & Yang, X. J. (2023). Cross-cultural investigation of the effects of explanations on drivers' trust, preference, and anxiety in highly automated vehicles. *Transportation Research Record: Journal of the Transportation Research Board, 2677*(1), 554–561. doi:10.1177/03611981221100528

Duong, H. T. (2023). Deep Learning-Based Anomaly Detection in Video Surveillance: A Survey. Sensors, 23(11), 5024.

Ekman, P. (1999). Basic emotions. Handbook of cognition and emotion, 98(45-60), 16.

El Ajjouri, M., Benhadou, S., & Medromi, H. (2016). LnaCBR: Case Based Reasoning Architecture for Intrusion Detection to Learning New Attacks. *Revue Méditerranéenne des Télécommunications, 6*(1).

El Filali, A., El Filali, S., & Jadli, A. (2022, July). Application of Deep Learning in the Supply Chain Management: A comparison of forecasting demand for electrical products using different ANN methods. In *2022 International Conference on Electrical, Computer and Energy Technologies (ICECET)* (pp. 1-7). IEEE. 10.1109/ICECET55527.2022.9872903

El-Ghamry, A., Gaber, T., Mohammed, K. K., & Hassanien, A. E. (2023). Optimized and efficient image-based IoT malware detection method. *Electronics (Basel), 12*(3), 708. doi:10.3390/electronics12030708

Elngar, A. A., Arafa, M., Fathy, A., Moustafa, B., Mahmoud, O., Shaban, M., & Fawzy, N. (2021). Image classification based on CNN: A survey. *Journal of Cybersecurity and Information Management, 6*(1), 18–50. doi:10.54216/JCIM.060102

Elphinston, R. A., Vaezipour, A., Fowler, J. A., Russell, T. G., & Sterling, M. (2023). Psychological therapy using virtual reality for treatment of driving phobia: A systematic review. *Disability and Rehabilitation*, *45*(10), 1582–1594. doi:10.1080/09638288.2022.2069293 PMID:35532316

Erbacher, R. F., & Hutchinson, S. E. (2013). *Extending Case-Based Reasoning (CBR) Approaches to Semi-automated Network Alert Reporting*. Academic Press.

Eyal, I., & Sirer, E. G. (2014). *How to disincentivize large bitcoin mining pools*. http://hackingdistributed. com/2014/06/18/how-to-disincentivize-large-bitcoin-mining-pools

Faia, R., Pinto, T., Abrishambaf, O., Fernandes, F., Vale, Z., & Corchado, J. M. (2017). Case based reasoning with expert system and swarm intelligence to determine energy reduction in buildings energy management. *Energy and Building*, *155*, 269281. doi:10.1016/j.enbuild.2017.09.020

Fang, Y., Gao, J., Liu, Z., & Huang, C. (2020). Detecting cyber threat event from twitter using IDCNN and BiLSTM. *Applied Sciences (Basel, Switzerland)*, *10*(17), 5922. doi:10.3390/app10175922

Fernando, D. W., Komninos, N., & Chen, T. (2020). A study on the evolution of ransomware detection using machine learning and deep learning techniques. *IoT*, *1*(2), 551–604. doi:10.3390/iot1020030

Ferreira, A. P., Gupta, C., Inácio, P. R., & Freire, M. M. (2021). Behaviour-based Malware Detection in Mobile AndroidPlatforms Using Machine Learning Algorithms. *J. Wirel. Mob. Networks Ubiquitous Comput. Dependable Appl.*, *12*(4), 62-88.

Firdaus, A., AlDharhani, G. S., Ismail, Z., & Razak, M. F. (2023, January 23). The Summer Heat of Cryptojacking Season: Detecting Cryptojacking using Heatmap and Fuzzy. *2022 International Conference on Cyber Resilience (ICCR)*. 10.1109/ICCR56254.2022.9995891

Flaxman, S., Goel, S., & Rao, J. M. (2016). Filter bubbles, echo chambers, and online news consumption. *Public Opinion Quarterly*, *80*(S1), 298–320. doi:10.1093/poq/nfw006

Franco, D., Oneto, L., Navarin, N., & Anguita, D. (2021). Toward learning trustworthily from data combining privacy, fairness, and explainability: An application to face recognition. *Entropy (Basel, Switzerland)*, *23*(8), 1047. doi:10.3390/e23081047 PMID:34441187

Gao, Y., Li, B., Wang, N., & Zhu, T. (2017). Speech emotion recognition using local and global features. In *Brain Informatics: International Conference, BI 2017, Beijing, China, November 16-18, 2017, Proceedings* (pp. 3-13). Springer International Publishing. 10.1007/978-3-319-70772-3_1

Gavrilova, M. L. (2023). Responsible artificial intelligence and bias mitigation in deep learning systems. *2023 27th International Conference Information Visualisation (IV)*, 329–333.

Gavrilova, M., Ahmed, F., Azam, S., Paul, P. P., Rahman, W., Sultana, M., & Zohra, F. T. (2017). Emerging trends in security system design using the concept of social behavioural biometrics. *Information Fusion for Cyber-Security Analytics*, 229–251.

Gavrilova, M. L., Ahmed, F., Bari, A. H., Liu, R., Liu, T., Maret, Y., Sieu, B. K., & Sudhakar, T. (2021). Multi-modal motion-capture-based biometric systems for emergency response and patient rehabilitation. In *Research anthology on rehabilitation practices and therapy* (pp. 653–678). IGI global.

Gavrilova, M. L., Anzum, F., Hossain Bari, A., Bhatia, Y., Iffath, F., Ohi, Q., Shopon, M., & Wahid, Z. (2022). A multifaceted role of biometrics in online security, privacy, and trustworthy decision making. In *Breakthroughs in digital biometrics and forensics* (pp. 303–324). Springer. doi:10.1007/978-3-031-10706-1_14

Gibert, D. P., Planes, J., Mateu, C., & Le, Q. (2022). Fusing feature engineering and deep learning: A case study for malware classification. *Expert Systems with Applications*, *207*, 117957. doi:10.1016/j.eswa.2022.117957

Gilson, A., Safranek, C. W., Huang, T., Socrates, V., Chi, L., Taylor, R. A., & Chartash, D. (2023). How does chatgpt perform on the united states medical licensing examination? the implications of large language models for medical education and knowledge assessment. *JMIR Medical Education*, *9*(1), e45312. doi:10.2196/45312 PMID:36753318

Gopinath, M., & Sethuraman, S. C. (2023). A comprehensive survey on deep learning based malware detection techniques. *Computer Science Review*, *47*, 100529. doi:10.1016/j.cosrev.2022.100529

Gosse, C., & Hodson, J. (2021). *Not two Different Worlds: QAnon and the Offline Dangers of Online Speech*. Retrieved August 23, 2023 from https://theconversation.com/not-two-different-worlds-qanon-and-the-offline-dangers-of-online-speech-159668

Gottwalt, F. C. (2019). CorrCorr: A feature selection method for multivariate correlation network anomaly detection techniques. *Computers & Security, 83*, 234-245.

Govindan, K., & Mohapatra, P. (2011). Trust computations and trust dynamics in mobile adhoc networks: A survey. *IEEE Communications Surveys and Tutorials*, *14*(2), 279–298. doi:10.1109/SURV.2011.042711.00083

Granatyr, J., Barddal, J. P., Weihmayer Almeida, A., Enembreck, F., & dos Santos Granatyr, A. P. (2016). Towards emotion-based reputation guessing learning agents. *2016 International Joint Conference on Neural Networks (IJCNN)*, 3801–3808. 10.1109/IJCNN.2016.7727690

Granatyr, J., Botelho, V., Lessing, O. R., Scalabrin, E. E., Barthès, J.-P., & Enembreck, F. (2015). Trust and reputation models for multiagent systems. *ACM Computing Surveys*, *48*(2), 1–42. doi:10.1145/2816826

Granatyr, J., Gomes, H. M., Dias, J. M., Paiva, A. M., Nunes, M. A. S. N., Scalabrin, E. E., & Spak, F. (2019). Inferring trust using personality aspects extracted from texts. *2019 IEEE International Conference on Systems, Man and Cybernetics (SMC)*, 3840–3846. 10.1109/SMC.2019.8914641

Granatyr, J., Osman, N., Dias, J., Nunes, M. A. S. N., Masthoff, J., Enembreck, F., Lessing, O. R., Sierra, C., Paiva, A. M., & Scalabrin, E. E. (2017). The need for affective trust applied to trust and reputation models. *ACM Computing Surveys*, *50*(4), 1–36. doi:10.1145/3078833

Gravel, J., D'Amours-Gravel, M., & Osmanlliu, E. (2023). Learning to fake it: Limited responses and fabricated references provided by chatgpt for medical questions. *Mayo Clinic Proceedings. Digital Health*, *1*(3), 226–234. doi:10.1016/j.mcpdig.2023.05.004

Grosse, K., Papernot, N., Manoharan, P., Backes, M., & McDaniel, P. (2017). Adversarial examples for malware detection. *Computer Security–ESORICS 2017: 22nd European Symposium on Research in Computer Security, Oslo, Norway, September 11-15, 2017 Proceedings*, *22*(Part II), 62–79.

Guerra, P. A. C., Barcelos, F. A., Nunes, R. C., De Freitas, E. P., & Silva, L. A. D. L. (2023). An Artificial Intelligence Framework for the Representation and Reuse of Cybersecurity Incident Resolution Knowledge. In *Proceedings of the 12th Latin-American Symposium on Dependable and Secure Computing* (pp. 136-145). 10.1145/3615366.3615369

Guffond, J. (2020). *The Web Never Forgets*. Retrieved January 10, 2023 from http://jasmineguffond.com/?path=art/The+Web+Never+Forgets

Gu, H. L., Lai, Y., Wang, Y., Liu, J., Sun, M., & Mao, B. (2022). DEIDS: A novel intrusion detection system for industrial control systems. *Neural Computing & Applications*, *34*(12), 9793–9811. doi:10.1007/s00521-022-06965-4

Gupta, D., & Krishnan, T. (2020). Algorithmic bias: Why bother. *California Management Review*, *63*(3).

Gupta, P., & Rajput, N. (2007). Two-stream emotion recognition for call center monitoring. In *Eighth Annual Conference of the International Speech Communication Association*. 10.21437/Interspeech.2007-609

Gwet, D. L. L., Otesteanu, M., Libouga, I. O., Bitjoka, L., & Popa, G. D. (2018). A review on image segmentation techniques and performance measures. *International Journal of Computer and Information Engineering*, *12*(12), 1107–1117.

Hajarolasvadi, N., & Demirel, H. (2019). 3D CNN-based speech emotion recognition using k-means clustering and spectrograms. *Entropy (Basel, Switzerland)*, *21*(5), 479. doi:10.3390/e21050479 PMID:33267193

Hamedani, R. M., Ali, I., Hong, J., & Kim, S.-W. (2021). TrustRec: An effective approach to exploit implicit trust and distrust relationships along with explicitones for accurate recommendations. *Computer Science and Information Systems*, *18*(1), 93–114. doi:10.2298/CSIS200608039H

Handa, A., Agarwal, R., & Kohli, N. (2021). Audio-visual emotion recognition system using multi-modal features. *International Journal of Cognitive Informatics and Natural Intelligence*, *15*(4), 1–14. doi:10.4018/IJCINI.20211001.oa34

Han, M. L., Han, H. C., Kang, A. R., Kwak, B. I., Mohaisen, A., & Kim, H. K. (2016, October). WHAP: Web-hacking profiling using case-based reasoning. In *2016 IEEE Conference on Communications and Network Security (CNS)* (pp. 344-345). IEEE. 10.1109/CNS.2016.7860503

Hasan, M. K., Abdulkadir, R. A., Islam, S., Gadekallu, T. R., & Safie, N. (2024). A review on machine learning techniques for secured cyber-physical systems in smart grid networks. *Energy Reports*, *11*, 1268–1290. doi:10.1016/j.egyr.2023.12.040

Hashemi, H., & Hamzeh, A. (2019). Visual malware detection using local malicious pattern. *Journal of Computer Virology and Hacking Techniques*, *15*(1), 1–14. doi:10.1007/s11416-018-0314-1

Hassanalian, M., & Abdelkefi, A. (2017). Classifications, applications, and design challenges of drones: A review. *Progress in Aerospace Sciences*, *91*, 99–131. doi:10.1016/j.paerosci.2017.04.003

Heidelberg Institute for International Conflict Research (HIIK). (2022). *Conflict Barometer*. Author.

Heilman, E. K. (2016, October). Eclipse attacks on bitcoin's peer-to-peer network. *Proceedings of the 2016 ACM SIGSAC conference on computer and communications security*.

He, L., Aouf, N., & Song, B. (2021). Explainable deep reinforcement learning for uav autonomous path planning. *Aerospace Science and Technology*, *118*, 107052. doi:10.1016/j.ast.2021.107052

Hemalatha, J., Roseline, S. A., Geetha, S., Kadry, S., & Damaševičius, R. (2021). An efficient densenet-based deep learning model for malware detection. *Entropy (Basel, Switzerland)*, *23*(3), 344. doi:10.3390/e23030344 PMID:33804035

Hochreiter, S., & Schmidhuber, J. (1997). Long short-term memory. *Neural Computation*, *9*(8), 1735–1780. doi:10.1162/neco.1997.9.8.1735 PMID:9377276

Hogan, M., Aouf, N., Spencer, P., & Almond, J. (2022). Explainable object detection for uncrewed aerial vehicles using kernelshap. *2022 IEEE International Conference on Autonomous Robot Systems and Competitions (ICARSC)*, 136–141. 10.1109/ICARSC55462.2022.9784772

Horsman, G., Laing, C., & Vickers, P. (2011). *A case-based reasoning system for automated forensic examinations*. Academic Press.

Hossain, M. Z., Sohel, F., Shiratuddin, M. F., & Laga, H. (2019). A comprehensive survey of deep learning for image captioning. *ACM Computing Surveys*, *51*(6), 1–36. doi:10.1145/3295748

Huang, T. H. D. (2018). Hunting the ethereum smart contract: Color-inspired inspection of potential attacks. *arXiv preprint arXiv:1807.01868*.

IBM. (2023). *Cost of Data Breach 2023*. Retrieved from IBM: https://www.ibm.com/reports/data-breach

Iffath, F., & Gavrilova, M. (2023). Raif: A deep learning-based architecture for multi-modal aesthetic biometric system. *Computer Animation and Virtual Worlds*, *34*(3-4), 2163. doi:10.1002/cav.2163

Iffath, F., & Gavrilova, M. L. (2022). A novel three stage framework for person identification from audio aesthetic. *IEEE Access : Practical Innovations, Open Solutions*, *10*, 90229–90243. doi:10.1109/ACCESS.2022.3200166

Compilation of References

Indrawan, P., Budiyatno, S., Ridho, N. M., & Sari, R. F. (2013). Face recognition for social media with mobile cloud computing. *International Journal on Cloud Computing: Services and Architecture*, *3*(1), 23–35. doi:10.5121/ijccsa.2013.3102

Islam, M. R., Liu, S., Wang, X., & Xu, G. (2020). Deep learning for misinformation detection on online social networks: A survey and new perspectives. *Social Network Analysis and Mining*, *10*(1), 82. doi:10.1007/s13278-020-00696-x PMID:33014173

Issa, D., Demirci, M. F., & Yazici, A. (2020). Speech emotion recognition with deep convolutional neural networks. *Biomedical Signal Processing and Control*, *59*, 101894. doi:10.1016/j.bspc.2020.101894

Jaafar, R. a. (2023). CBHIR-based approach for histological image analysis on large scale datasets. *2023 International Conference on Cyberworlds (CW)* (pp. 502-503). IEEE. 10.1109/CW58918.2023.00088

Jain, A. K., Deb, D., & Engelsma, J. J. (2021). Biometrics: Trust, but verify. *IEEE Transactions on Biometrics, Behavior, and Identity Science*, *4*(3), 303–323. doi:10.1109/TBIOM.2021.3115465

Jain, A. K., & Nandakumar, K. (2012). Biometric authentication: System security and user privacy. *Computer*, *45*(11), 87–92. doi:10.1109/MC.2012.364

Jamie Kay Graham. (2022). *The Dark Web and Human Trafficking*. PhD Dissertation Liberty University.

Jayaprakash, V., & Tyagi, A. K. (2022). Security Optimization of Resource-Constrained Internet of Healthcare Things (IoHT) Devices Using Lightweight Cryptography. In Information Security Practices for the Internet of Things, 5G, and Next-Generation Wireless Networks (pp. 179-209). IGI Global.

Jega, A. D. (2014, September 18). Bitcoin mining acceleration and performance quantification. *2014 IEEE 27th Canadian Conference on Electrical and Computer Engineering (CCECE)*.

Jens, D. (2022, June). *Satoshi Nakamoto and the Origins of Bitcoin — Narratio in Nomine, Datis et Numeris*. doi:/arXiv.2206.10257 doi:10.48550

Jha, R. K. (2023). Strengthening Smart Grid Cybersecurity: An In-Depth Investigation into the Fusion of Machine Learning and Natural Language Processing. *Journal of Trends in Computer Science and Smart Technology*, *5*(3), 284–301. doi:10.36548/jtcsst.2023.3.005

Jiang, Q., & Sun, M. (2011, June). Semi-supervised simhash for efficient document similarity search. In *Proceedings of the 49th annual meeting of the association for computational linguistics: Human language technologies* (pp. 93-101). Academic Press.

Jiang, F., Gu, T., Chang, L., & Xu, Z. (2014). Case retrieval for network security emergency response based on description logic. *Intelligent Information Processing VII: 8th IFIP TC 12 International Conference, IIP 2014, Hangzhou, China, October 17-20, 2014 Proceedings*, *8*, 284–293.

Jiang, Y., Wu, S., Yang, H., Luo, H., Chen, Z., Yin, S., & Kaynak, O. (2022). Secure data transmission and trustworthiness judgement approaches against cyber-physical attacks in an integrated data-driven framework. *IEEE Transactions on Systems, Man, and Cybernetics. Systems, 52*(12), 7799–7809. doi:10.1109/TSMC.2022.3164024

Jian, Y., Kuang, H., Ren, C., Ma, Z., & Wang, H. (2021). A novel framework for image-based malware detection with a deep neural network. *Computers & Security, 109,* 102400. doi:10.1016/j.cose.2021.102400

Jing, T., Xia, H., Tian, R., Ding, H., Luo, X., Domeyer, J., Sherony, R., & Ding, Z. (2022). Inaction: Interpretable action decision making for autonomous driving. *European Conference on Computer Vision,* 370–387. 10.1007/978-3-031-19839-7_22

Jirotka, M. (2021). Explanations in autonomous driving: A survey. *IEEE Transactions on Intelligent Transportation Systems,* 23.

Joonseok, P., Sumin, J., & Keunhyuk, Y. (2023, July). Smart Contract Broker: Improving Smart Contract Reusability in a Blockchain Environment. *Sensors (Basel), 13*(13), 6149. Advance online publication. doi:10.3390/s23136149

Jothibasu, M. S. (2023). Improvement of Computer Vision-Based Elephant Intrusion Detection System (EIDS) with Deep Learning Models. *Innovative Engineering with AI Applications,* 131-153.

Kapetanakis, S., Filippoupolitis, A., Loukas, G., & Al Murayziq, T. S. (2014). *Profiling cyber attackers using case-based reasoning.* Academic Press.

Kapoor, N., Sulke, P., Pardeshi, P., Kakad, R., & Badiye, A. (2023). Introduction to Forensic Science. In *Textbook of Forensic Science* (pp. 41–66). Springer Nature Singapore. doi:10.1007/978-981-99-1377-0_2

Karami, E. a. (2017). Image matching using SIFT, SURF, BRIEF and ORB: performance comparison for distorted images. *arXiv preprint arXiv:1710.02726.*

Karduni, A., Wesslen, R., Markant, D., & Dou, W. (2023). Images, emotions, and credibility: Effect of emotional facial expressions on perceptions of news content bias and source credibility in social media. *Proceedings of the International AAAI Conference on Web and Social Media, 17,* 470–481. 10.1609/icwsm.v17i1.22161

Karim, F., Majumdar, S., & Darabi, H. (2019). Insights into LSTM fully convolutional networks for time series classification. *IEEE Access : Practical Innovations, Open Solutions, 7,* 67718–67725. doi:10.1109/ACCESS.2019.2916828

Karmakar, G., Chowdhury, A., Das, R., Kamruzzaman, J., & Islam, S. (2021). Assessing trust level of a driverless car using deep learning. *IEEE Transactions on Intelligent Transportation Systems, 22*(7), 4457–4466. doi:10.1109/TITS.2021.3059261

Kaur, N., Rani, S., & Kaur, S. (2024). Real-time video surveillance based human fall detection system using hybrid haar cascade classifier. *Multimedia Tools and Applications,* 1–19. doi:10.1007/s11042-024-18305-w

Kaur, R., Gabrijelčič, D., & Klobučar, T. (2023). Artificial intelligence for cybersecurity: Literature review and future research directions. *Information Fusion*, *97*, 101804. doi:10.1016/j. inffus.2023.101804

Kaushik, K., Dahiya, S., & Sharma, R. (2022). Role of blockchain technology in digital forensics. In *Blockchain Technology* (pp. 235–246). CRC Press. doi:10.1201/9781003138082-14

Kerkeni, L. (2020). *Acoustic voice analysis for the detection of speaker emotions*. Diss.

Kessler, G. (2018). Technology and the future of language teaching. *Foreign Language Annals*, *51*(1), 205–218. doi:10.1111/flan.12318

Khalfallah, A., Kammoun, F., Bouhlel, M. S., & Olivier, C. (2006, April). A new scheme of watermarking in multi-resolution filed by 5/3 wavelet: Family signature combined with the adapted embedding strength. *2006 2nd International Conference on Information & Tongxin Jishu*, *1*, 1145–1152.

Khraisat, A., Gondal, I., Vamplew, P., & Kamruzzaman, J. (2019). Survey of intrusion detection systems: Techniques, datasets and challenges. *Cybersecurity*, *2*(1), 1–22. doi:10.1186/s42400-019-0038-7

Kiffer, L., Levin, D., & Mislove, A. (2017, November). Stick a fork in it: Analyzing the ethereum network partition. In *Proceedings of the 16th ACM Workshop on Hot Topics in Networks* (pp. 94-100). 10.1145/3152434.3152449

Kim, A., Moravec, P. L., & Dennis, A. R. (2019). Combating fake news on social media with source ratings: The effects of user and expert reputation ratings. *Journal of Management Information Systems*, *36*(3), 931–968. doi:10.1080/07421222.2019.1628921

Kim, J., Rohrbach, A., Darrell, T., Canny, J., & Akata, Z. (2018). Textual explanations for self-driving vehicles. *Proceedings of the European conference on computer vision (ECCV)*, 563–578.

KN, P. K., & Gavrilova, M. L. (2021). Latent personality traits assessment from social network activity using contextual language embedding. *IEEE Transactions on Computational Social Systems*, *9*(2), 638–649.

Knapič, S., Malhi, A., Saluja, R., & Främling, K. (2021). Explainable artificial intelligence for human decision support system in the medical domain. *Machine Learning and Knowledge Extraction*, *3*(3), 740–770. doi:10.3390/make3030037

Koehler, D. (2017). *Understanding Deradicalization Methods, tools and programs for countering violent extremism*. Routledge.

Kolodner, J. L. (1994). Understanding creativity: A case-based approach. Lecture Notes in Computer Science (including subseries Lecture Notes in Artificial Intelligence and Lecture Notes in Bioinformatics), 837, 3-20. doi:10.1007/3-540-58330-0_73

Kolodner, J. L. (1992). An introduction to case-based reasoning. *Artificial Intelligence Review*, *6*(1), 3–34. doi:10.1007/BF00155578

Krishna, A. M., & Tyagi, A. K. (2020, February). Intrusion detection in intelligent transportation system and its applications using blockchain technology. In 2020 international conference on emerging trends in information technology and engineering (IC-ETITE) (pp. 1-8). IEEE. doi:10.1109/ic-ETITE47903.2020.332

Krüger, M. (2022). An Approach to Profiler Detection of Cyber Attacks using Case-based Reasoning. In LWDA (pp. 234-245). Academic Press.

Ku, L.-W., & Chen, H.-H. (2007). Mining opinions from the web: Beyond relevance retrieval. *Journal of the American Society for Information Science and Technology, 58*(12), 1838–1850. doi:10.1002/asi.20630

Kumari, S., Tyagi, A. K., & Rekha, G. (2021). Applications of Blockchain Technologies in Digital Forensics and Threat Hunting. In *Recent Trends in Blockchain for Information Systems Security and Privacy* (pp. 159–173). CRC Press. doi:10.1201/9781003139737-12

Kundu, P. P., Truong-Huu, T., Chen, L., Zhou, L., & Teo, S. G. (2022). Detection and classification of botnet traffic using deep learning with model explanation. *IEEE Transactions on Dependable and Secure Computing.*

Kurt Knutsson. (2023). *Turn this Gmail Security Feature on ASAP*. Retrieved January 2, 2023 from https://www.foxnews.com/tech/turn-gmail-security-feature-asap

Kwon, N., Cho, J., Lee, H.-S., Yoon, I., & Park, M. (2019). Compensation Cost Estimation Model for Construction Noise Claims Using Case-Based Reasoning. *Journal of Construction Engineering and Management, 145*(8), 04019047. Advance online publication. doi:10.1061/(ASCE)CO.1943-7862.0001675

Kwon, S. (2021). MLT-DNet: Speech emotion recognition using 1D dilated CNN based on multi-learning trick approach. *Expert Systems with Applications, 167*, 114177. doi:10.1016/j.eswa.2020.114177

Lago, F., Phan, Q.-T., & Boato, G. (2019). Visual and textual analysis for image trustworthiness assessment within online news. *Security and Communication Networks, 2019*, 2019. doi:10.1155/2019/9236910

Lakhotia, A., Notani, V., & LeDoux, C. (2018, June). Malware economics and its implication to anti-malware situational awareness. In *2018 International Conference On Cyber Situational Awareness, Data Analytics And Assessment* (Cyber SA) (pp. 1-8). IEEE. 10.1109/CyberSA.2018.8551388

Lamy, J.-B., Sekar, B., Guezennec, G., Bouaud, J., & Séroussi, B. (2019). Explainable artificial intelligence for breast cancer: A visual case-based reasoning approach. *Artificial Intelligence in Medicine, 94*, 42–53. doi:10.1016/j.artmed.2019.01.001 PMID:30871682

Langguth, J., Pogorelov, K., Brenner, S., Filkuková, P., & Schroeder, D. T. (2021). Don't trust your eyes: Image manipulation in the age of deepfakes. *Frontiers in Communication, 6*, 632317. doi:10.3389/fcomm.2021.632317

Lansley, M., Polatidis, N., Kapetanakis, S., Amin, K., Samakovitis, G., & Petridis, M. (2019). Seen the villains: detecting social engineering attacks using case-based reasoning and deep learning. *Proceedings of the ICCBR Workshops*, 39–48.

Laurent, B., Ousman, B., Dzudie, T., Carl, M. M., & Emmanuel, T. (2010). Digital camera images processing of hard-to-cook beans. *Journal of Engineering and Technology Research, 2*(9), 177–188.

Le Bihan, N. (2003). *Quaternionic processing of color images.* Conferences on Signal and Image Processing.

Lee, S. H., Purnima, M. M., Jonathan, P., & Peter, L. (n.d.). *An Integrated Smart Contract Vulnerability Detection Tool Using Multi-layer Perceptron on Real-time Solidity Smart Contracts.* IEEE. doi:10.1109/ACCESS.2024.3364351

Leite, A., & Girardi, R. (2017). A hybrid and learning agent architecture for network intrusion detection. *Journal of Systems and Software, 130*, 59–80. doi:10.1016/j.jss.2017.01.028

Lex, E., Kowald, D., Seitlinger, P., Tran, T. N. T., Felfernig, A., & Schedl, M. (2021). Psychology-informed recommender systems. *Foundations and Trends® in Information Retrieval, 15*(2), 134–242.

Liao, M., Sundar, S. S., & Walther, B., J. (2022). User trust in recommendation systems: A comparison of content-based, collaborative and demographic filtering. *Proceedings of the 2022 CHI Conference on Human Factors in Computing Systems*, 1–14. 10.1145/3491102.3501936

Li, B., Qi, P., Liu, B., Di, S., Liu, J., Pei, J., Yi, J., & Zhou, B. (2023). Trustworthy ai: From principles to practices. *ACM Computing Surveys, 55*(9), 1–46. doi:10.1145/3555803

Lieber, J. (2008). *Contributions à la conception de systèmes de raisonnement à partir de cas.* Academic Press.

Lim, J. A., Al Jobayer, M. I., Baskaran, V. M., Lim, J. M. Y., See, J., & Wong, K. S. (2021). Deep multi-level feature pyramids: Application for non-canonical firearm detection in video surveillance. *Engineering Applications of Artificial Intelligence, 97*, 104094. doi:10.1016/j.engappai.2020.104094

Linardatos, P., Papastefanopoulos, V., & Kotsiantis, S. (2020). Explainable ai: A review of machine learning interpretability methods. *Entropy (Basel, Switzerland), 23*(1), 18. doi:10.3390/e23010018 PMID:33375658

Liu, J. &. (2023). A comprehensive survey of robust deep learning in computer vision. *Journal of Automation and Intelligence.*

Liu, X., Van De Weijer, J., & Bagdanov, A. D. (2019). Exploiting unlabeled data in cnns by self-supervised learning to rank. *IEEE Transactions on Pattern Analysis and Machine Intelligence, 41*(8), 1862–1878. doi:10.1109/TPAMI.2019.2899857 PMID:30794168

Li, X., Gunturk, B., & Zhang, L. (2008, January). Image demosaicing: A systematic survey. In *Visual Communications and Image Processing 2008* (Vol. 6822, pp. 489–503). SPIE. doi:10.1117/12.766768

Li, X., Yang, J., & Ma, J. (2021). Recent developments of content-based image retrieval (CBIR). *Neurocomputing*, *452*, 675–689. doi:10.1016/j.neucom.2020.07.139

López, B. (2022). *Case-based reasoning: a concise introduction.* Springer Nature.

Lopez-Sanchez, D., Herrero, J. R., Arrieta, A. G., & Corchado, J. M. (2018). Hybridizing metric learning and case-based reasoning for adaptable clickbait detection. *Applied Intelligence*, *48*(9), 29672982. doi:10.1007/s10489-017-1109-7

Lovato, P., Perina, A., Sebe, N., Zandonà, O., Montagnini, A., Bicego, M., & Cristani, M. (2012). Tell me what you like and i'll tell you what you are: Discriminating visual preferences on flickr data. *Proceedings of the 11th Asian conference on Computer Vision*, 45–56.

Luc, L. G. (2014). *Raisonnement à base de cas textuels-état de l'art et perspectives.* Academic Press.

Lukac, R., & Plataniotis, K. N. (2005). Color filter arrays: Design and performance analysis. *IEEE Transactions on Consumer Electronics*, *51*(4), 1260–1267. doi:10.1109/TCE.2005.1561853

Lukac, R., & Plataniotis, K. N. (Eds.). (2018). *Color image processing: methods and applications.* CRC press. doi:10.1201/9781315221526

Luo, J., & Yu, R. (2015). Follow the heart or the head? The interactive influence model of emotion and cognition. *Frontiers in Psychology*, *6*, 573. doi:10.3389/fpsyg.2015.00573 PMID:25999889

Luu, L., Chu, D. H., Olickel, H., Saxena, P., & Hobor, A. (2016, October). Making smart contracts smarter. In *Proceedings of the 2016 ACM SIGSAC conference on computer and communications security* (pp. 254-269). 10.1145/2976749.2978309

Lyu, D., Yang, F., Kwon, H., Dong, W., Yilmaz, L., & Liu, B. (2021). Tdm: Trustworthy decision-making via interpretability enhancement. *IEEE Transactions on Emerging Topics in Computational Intelligence*, *6*(3), 450–461. doi:10.1109/TETCI.2021.3084290

Mahbooba, B., Timilsina, M., Sahal, R., & Serrano, M. (2021). Explainable artificial intelligence (XAI) to enhance trust management in intrusion detection systems using decision tree model. *Complexity*, *2021*, 1–11. doi:10.1155/2021/6634811

Mahony, C., Brumby, J., & Thi Lan Tran, H. (2021). *AI can help trace language to violence.* Retrieved August 24, 2023 from https://blogs.worldbank.org/governance/ai-can-help-trace-language-violence

Mair, D. (2016). Westgate: a Case Study-How al-Shabaab Used Twitter During an Ongoing Attack. In A. Aly, S. Macdonald, L. Jarvis, & T. Chen (Eds.), *Violent Extremism Online: New Perspectives on Terrorism and the Internet.* Routledge Publishers.

Majd, S. (2023, October). Dissecting Smart Contract Languages. *Survey (London, England)*, 6. arXiv2310.02799v2 [cs.CR]

Majumder, N., Poria, S., Hazarika, D., Mihalcea, R., Gelbukh, A., & Cambria, E. (2019, July). Dialoguernn: An attentive rnn for emotion detection in conversations. *Proceedings of the AAAI Conference on Artificial Intelligence, 33*(01), 6818–6825. doi:10.1609/aaai.v33i01.33016818

Makhortykh, M., Urman, A., & Ulloa, R. (2021). Detecting race and gender bias in visual representation of ai on web search engines. *International Workshop on Algorithmic Bias in Search and Recommendation*, 36–50. 10.1007/978-3-030-78818-6_5

Maniriho, P., Mahmood, A. N., & Chowdhury, M. J. M. (2022). A study on malicious software behaviour analysis and detection techniques: Taxonomy, current trends and challenges. *Future Generation Computer Systems, 130*, 1–18. doi:10.1016/j.future.2021.11.030

Manku, G. S., Jain, A., & Das Sarma, A. (2007, May). Detecting near-duplicates for web crawling. In *Proceedings of the 16th international conference on World Wide Web* (pp. 141-150). 10.1145/1242572.1242592

Manoury, A. (2001). *Tatouage d'images numériques par paquets d'ondelettes* (Doctoral dissertation, Ecole Centrale de Nantes (ECN); Université de Nantes).

Mao, Q., Dong, M., Huang, Z., & Zhan, Y. (2014). Learning salient features for speech emotion recognition using convolutional neural networks. *IEEE Transactions on Multimedia, 16*(8), 2203–2213. doi:10.1109/TMM.2014.2360798

Maras, M. (2017). Social Media Platforms: Targeting the "Found Space" of Terrorists. *Journal of International Law.*

Meguehout, T. B.-T. (2013). *Un Raisonnement à Partir de Cas pour la Traduction Automatique Arabe-Francais Basée sur la Sémantique*. Academic Press.

Mehrabi, N., Morstatter, F., Saxena, N., Lerman, K., & Galstyan, A. (2021). A survey on bias and fairness in machine learning. *ACM Computing Surveys, 54*(6), 1–35. doi:10.1145/3457607

Meng, H., Yan, T., Yuan, F., & Wei, H. (2019). Speech emotion recognition from 3D log-mel spectrograms with deep learning network. *IEEE Access : Practical Innovations, Open Solutions, 7*, 125868–125881. doi:10.1109/ACCESS.2019.2938007

Minaee, S., Abdolrashidi, A., Su, H., Bennamoun, M., & Zhang, D. (2023). Biometrics recognition using deep learning: A survey. *Artificial Intelligence Review, 56*(8), 8647–8695. doi:10.1007/s10462-022-10237-x

Mishra, S., & Tyagi, A. K. (2019, December). Intrusion detection in Internet of Things (IoTs) based applications using blockchain technolgy. In *2019 third international conference on I-SMAC (IoT in social, mobile, analytics and cloud)(I-SMAC)* (pp. 123-128). IEEE.

Mohammed Benamina, B. A. (2018). Diabetes Diagnosis by Case-Based Reasoning and Fuzzy Logic. *Int. J. Interact. Multimed. Artif. Intell., 4*(7), 7280. doi:10.9781/jimai.2017.03.003

Monika, A., & Gernot, S. (2019, July 16). Collateral Use of Deployment Code for Smart Contracts in Ethereum. *2019 10th IFIP International Conference on New Technologies, Mobility and Security (NTMS)*. 10.1109/NTMS.2019.8763828

Mubashar, I., & Raimundas, M. (2021, May 19). *Exploring Sybil and Double-Spending Risks in Blockchain Systems*. doi:10.1109/ACCESS.2021.3081998

Müller, J. M. (2019). Comparing technology acceptance for autonomous vehicles, battery electric vehicles, and car sharing—A study across europe, china, and north america. *Sustainability (Basel)*, *11*(16), 4333. doi:10.3390/su11164333

Muro, D. (2017). Engineers of Jihad: The Curious Connection between Violent Extremism and Education. *Terrorism and Political Violence*, *29*(6), 1154–1156. doi:10.1080/09546553.2017.1377559

Mustaqeem, & Kwon, S. (2019). A CNN-assisted enhanced audio signal processing for speech emotion recognition. *Sensors, 20*(1), 183.

Mustaqeem, & Kwon, S. (2020). CLSTM: Deep feature-based speech emotion recognition using the hierarchical ConvLSTM network. *Mathematics, 8*(12), 2133.

Nabila, N. a. (2013). *Une approche d'optimisation par essaim de particules pour la recherche en mémoire de cas* [PhD thesis]. University of Montreal, Canada.

Nakashima, M. S., Sim, A., Kim, Y., Kim, J., & Kim, J. (2021). Automated feature selection for anomaly detection in network traffic data. *ACM Transactions on Management Information Systems*, *12*(3), 1–28. doi:10.1145/3446636

Nakid, S. S. (2021). *Evaluation and detection of cybercriminal attack type using machine learning* (Doctoral dissertation, Dublin, National College of Ireland).

Naqvi, R. A., Arsalan, M., Qaiser, T., Khan, T. M., & Razzak, I. (2022). Sensor data fusion based on deep learning for computer vision applications and medical applications. *Sensors (Basel)*, *22*(20), 8058. doi:10.3390/s22208058 PMID:36298412

Nardelli, M., Valenza, G., Greco, A., Lanata, A., & Scilingo, E. P. (2015). Recognizing emotions induced by affective sounds through heart rate variability. *IEEE Transactions on Affective Computing*, *6*(4), 385–394. doi:10.1109/TAFFC.2015.2432810

Naway, A., & Li, Y. (2018). A review on the use of deep learning in android malware detection. *arXiv preprint arXiv:1812.10360*.

Ndongo, H. A., Barzina, R., Ousman, B., & Bitjoka, L. (2013). *Comparison of CFA and color image tattoos*. Dans le 2ème Atelier annuel sur la Cryptographie, Algèbre et Géométrie (CRAG 2), Pages: 113-120 du 03-07/12/2012 à l'Université de Ngaoundéré.

Ndongo, H. A., Ledoux, E. E. B., Paul, A. M., & Alexendre, N. (2021). Hybrid compression-encryption-watermarking image algorithm based on the quaternionic wavelets transform (QWT). *IACSIT International Journal of Engineering and Technology*, *10*(2), 208–214.

Ndongo, H. A., Vournone, M., Pouyap, M., Ngakawa, T., & Malobe, P. A. (2022). Hybrid Successive CFA Image Encryption-Watermarking Algorithm Based on the Quaternionic Wavelet Transform (QWT). *Journal of Information Security, 13*(4), 244–256. doi:10.4236/jis.2022.134013

Ni, J., Li, J., & McAuley, J. (2019). Justifying recommendations using distantly-labeled reviews and fine-grained aspects. *Proceedings of the 2019 conference on empirical methods in natural language processing and the 9th international joint conference on natural language processing (EMNLP-IJCNLP)*, 188–197. 10.18653/v1/D19-1018

Ning, B., & Na, L. (2021). Deep Spatial/temporal-level feature engineering for Tennis-based action recognition. *Future Generation Computer Systems, 125*, 188–193. doi:10.1016/j.future.2021.06.022

Nkapkop, J. D., Effa, J. Y., Borda, M., Ciprian, A., Bitjoka, L., & Mohamadou, A. (2016). Efficient Chaos-Based Cryptosystem for Real Time Applications. *Acta Technica Napocensis, 57*(4), 5.

Nnam, M., & Ajah, B. (2019). The War Must be Sustained: An Integrated Theoretical Perspective of the Cyberspace-Boko Haram Terrorism Nexus in Nigeria. *International Journal of Cyber Criminology, 13*(2).

Noroozi, F., Sapiński, T., Kamińska, D., & Anbarjafari, G. (2017). Vocal-based emotion recognition using random forests and decision tree. *International Journal of Speech Technology, 20*(2), 239–246. doi:10.1007/s10772-017-9396-2

Noura A. Ntsama P. Bitjoka L. (2017). A robust biomedical images watermarking scheme based on chaos. *International Journal of Computer Science and Security, 11*(1).

Nunes, R. C., Colomé, M., Barcelos, F. A., Garbin, M., Paulus, G. B., & Silva, L. A. D. L. (2019). A case-based reasoning approach for the cybersecurity incident recording and resolution. *International Journal of Software Engineering and Knowledge Engineering, 29*(11-12), 1607-1627.

O'Shaughnessy, S. &. (2022). Image-based malware classification hybrid framework based on space-filling curves. *Computers & Security, 116*, 102660.

Odeleye, B. L., Loukas, G., Heartfield, R., Sakellari, G., Panaousis, E., & Spyridonis, F. (2023). Virtually secure: A taxonomic assessment of cybersecurity challenges in virtual reality environments. *Computers & Security, 124*, 102951. doi:10.1016/j.cose.2022.102951

OECD. (2022). *Recommendation of the Council on Artificial Intelligence*, OECD/LEGAL/0449. http://www.jasmineguffond.com/?path=art/Listening+Back

Oggero. (2018). Content-based Multimedia Analytics: US and NATO Research. *Proc. SPIE.* doi:10.1117/12.2307756

Ogunlana, S. (2019). Halting Boko Haram / Islamic State's West Africa Province Propaganda in Cyberspace with Cybersecurity Technologies. *Journal of Strategic Security, 12*(1), 72–106. doi:10.5038/1944-0472.12.1.1707

OSCE & ODIHR. (2018). *Challenging Conspiracy Theories*. Authors.

Ozkan-Ozay, M., Akin, E., Aslan, Ö., Kosunalp, S., Iliev, T., Stoyanov, I., & Beloev, I. (2024). A Comprehensive Survey: Evaluating the Efficiency of Artificial Intelligence and Machine Learning Techniques on Cyber Security Solutions. *IEEE Access : Practical Innovations, Open Solutions, 12*, 12229–12256. doi:10.1109/ACCESS.2024.3355547

Palmieri, F. A., Baldi, M., Buonanno, A., Di Gennaro, G., & Ospedale, F. (2020). Probing a deep neural network. *Neural Approaches to Dynamics of Signal Exchanges*, 201–211.

Panimalar, P., & Rameshkumar, K. (2019). A novel traffic analysis model for botnet discovery in dynamic network. *Arabian Journal for Science and Engineering, 44*(4), 3033–3042. doi:10.1007/s13369-018-3319-7

Papathanasaki, M., & Maglaras, L. (2020). *The Current Posture of Cyber Warfare and Cyber Terrorism*. Global Foundation for Cyber Studies and Research.

Paradesi, S., Doshi, P., & Swaika, S. (2009). Integrating behavioral trust in web service compositions. *2009 IEEE International Conference on Web Services*, 453–460. 10.1109/ICWS.2009.106

Park, M., Han, J., Oh, H., & Lee, K. (2019). Threat assessment for android environment with connectivity to IoT devices from the perspective of situational awareness. *Wireless Communications and Mobile Computing, 2019*, 1–14. doi:10.1155/2019/5121054

Park, Y.-J., Kim, B.-C., & Chun, S.-H. (2006). New knowledge extraction technique using probability for case-based reasoning: Application to medical diagnosis. *Expert Systems: International Journal of Knowledge Engineering and Neural Networks, 23*(1), 2–20. doi:10.1111/j.1468-0394.2006.00321.x

Paul, K. (2023, November 3). *Satoshi Nakamoto created Bitcoin in 2009. He mysteriously vanished in 2011, with billions to his name*. Retrieved February 09, 2024, from https://www.cbc.ca/documentaries/the-passionate-eye/satoshi-nakamoto-created-bitcoin-in-2009-he-mysteriously-vanished-in-2011-with-billions-to-his-name-1.7014958

Paul, P. P., Gavrilova, M., & Klimenko, S. (2014). Situation awareness of cancelable biometric system. *The Visual Computer, 30*(9), 1059–1067. doi:10.1007/s00371-013-0907-0

Pauwels, E. (2020). *Artificial Intelligence and Data Capture Technologies in Violence and Conflict Prevention: Opportunities and Challenges for the International Community*. Global Center on Cooperative Security.

Peng, Y. (2018). Same candidates, different faces: Uncovering media bias in visual portrayals of presidential candidates with computer vision. *Journal of Communication, 68*(5), 920–941. doi:10.1093/joc/jqy041

Peter, G. K. (2023, December 21). Blockchain Ethics. Philosophies, 9(2). https://doi.org/doi:10.3390

Pienta, D., Tams, S., & Thatcher, J. (2020). Can trust be trusted in cybersecurity? Roshchina, A., Cardiff, J., & Rosso, P. (2015). TWIN: Personality-based intelligent recommender system. *Journal of Intelligent & Fuzzy Systems, 28*(5), 2059–2071.

Pinzón Trejos, C., De Paz, J., Bajo, J., & Corchado, J. (2015). *An Adaptive Mechanism to Protect Databases against SQL Injection.* Academic Press.

Plutchik, R. (1988). The nature of emotions: Clinical implications. In *Emotions and psychopathology* (pp. 1–20). Springer US. doi:10.1007/978-1-4757-1987-1_1

Pourkhodabakhsh, N., Mamoudan, M. M., & Bozorgi-Amiri, A. (2023). Effective machine learning, Meta-heuristic algorithms and multi-criteria decision making to minimizing human resource turnover. *Applied Intelligence, 53*(12), 16309–16331. doi:10.1007/s10489-022-04294-6 PMID:36531972

Puech, W., & Rodrigues, J. M. (2005, September). Crypto-compression of medical images by selective encryption of DCT. In *2005 13th European signal processing conference* (pp. 1-4). IEEE.

Puech, W., Charre, J. J., & Dumas, M. (2001). Secure image transfer using Vigenère encryption. NimesTic 2001, The Human-System relationship: Complex, Nîmes, France, 167-171.

Puech, W., Chaumont, M., & Strauss, O. (2008, March). A reversible data hiding method for encrypted images. In *Security, forensics, steganography, and watermarking of multimedia contents X* (Vol. 6819, pp. 534–542). SPIE. doi:10.1117/12.766754

Qaisar, Z. H., & Li, R. (2022). Multimodal information fusion for android malware detection using lazy learning. *Multimedia Tools and Applications, 81*(9), 1–15. doi:10.1007/s11042-021-10749-8

Rakotondraina, T.E., Ramafiarisona, H.M., & Randriamitantsoa, A.A. (2013). Secure transfer of images in the domain of TFD. *MADA-ETI.*

Ralaivao, HH, Randriamitantsoa, PA, & Raminoson, T. (2016). Security of images by combination of tattooing and encryption. *MADA-ETI.*

RAN. (2021). *Digital Challenges: Terrorists' Use of the Internet and the Challenges Coming out of Covid.* Author.

Rana, R., Latif, S., Gururajan, R., Gray, A., Mackenzie, G., Humphris, G., & Dunn, J. (2019). Automated screening for distress: A perspective for the future. *European Journal of Cancer Care, 28*(4), e13033. doi:10.1111/ecc.13033 PMID:30883964

Ranka, P. S. (2023). Computer Vision-Based Cybersecurity Threat Detection System with GAN-Enhanced Data Augmentation. *International Conference on Soft Computing and its Engineering Applications* (pp. 54-67). Cham: Springer Nature Switzerland.

Rasheed, B. K. (2021). Adversarial attacks on featureless deep learning malicious urls detection. *Computers, Materials & Continua, 68*(1), 921–939. doi:10.32604/cmc.2021.015452

Ravi, A., Chaturvedi, V., & Shafique, M. (2023). ViT4Mal: Lightweight Vision Transformer for Malware Detection on Edge Devices. *ACM Transactions on Embedded Computing Systems, 22*(5s), 1–26. doi:10.1145/3609112

Ravi, V., & Alazab, M. (2023). Attention-based convolutional neural network deep learning approach for robust malware classification. *Computational Intelligence, 39*(1), 145–168. doi:10.1111/coin.12551

Ravi, V., Alazab, M., Selvaganapathy, S., & Chaganti, R. (2022). A Multi-View attention-based deep learning framework for malware detection in smart healthcare systems. *Computer Communications, 195*, 73–81. doi:10.1016/j.comcom.2022.08.015

Recio-Garcia, J. A., Orozco-del Castillo, M. G., & Soladrero, J. A. (2023). Case-based Explanation of Classification Models for the Detection of SQL Injection Attacks. *Proceedings of the: XCBR, 23*.

Ren, Z., Han, J., Cummins, N., & Schuller, B. (2020). *Enhancing transferability of black-box adversarial attacks via lifelong learning for speech emotion recognition models*. Academic Press.

Rey, C. (2003, January). *Image watermarking: gain in robustness and integrity of images*. Avignon.

Rey, V., Sánchez, P. M. S., Celdrán, A. H., & Bovet, G. (2022). Federated learning for malware detection in IoT devices. *Computer Networks, 204*, 108693. doi:10.1016/j.comnet.2021.108693

RM, S. P. (. (2020). An effective feature engineering for DNN using hybrid PCA-GWO for intrusion detection in IoMT architecture. *Computer Communications, 160*, 139–149. doi:10.1016/j.comcom.2020.05.048

Roberto, I. (2019). *Building Ethereum Dapps: Decentralized applications on the Ethereum blockchain*. Academic Press.

Roberts, L. S. (2012). *A forensic phonetic study of the vocal responses of individuals in distress* (Doctoral dissertation, University of York).

Rocco. (2021). Toward a Critique of Algorithmic Violence. *International Political Sociology, 15*(1), 121–150. Advance online publication. doi:10.1093/ips/olab003

Rohatgi, S. a. (2023). Introduction to Artificial Intelligence and Cybersecurity for Industry. *Artificial Intelligence and Cyber Security in Industry 4.0*, 1-22.

Roy Chowdhury, A., Banerjee, S., & Chatterjee, T. (2020). A cybernetic systems approach to abnormality detection in retina images using case based reasoning. *SN Applied Sciences, 2*(8), 1–15. doi:10.1007/s42452-020-3187-0

Roy, C., Shanbhag, M., Nourani, M., Rahman, T., Kabir, S., Gogate, V., Ruozzi, N., & Ragan, E. D. (2019). Explainable activity recognition in videos. *IUI Workshops, 2*(4).

Rudin, C. (2019). Stop explaining black box machine learning models for high stakes decisions and use interpretable models instead. *Nat Mach Intell, 1*, 206–215.. doi:10.1038/s42256-019-0048-x

Rudner, M. (2013). Cyber-Threats to Critical National Infrastructure: An Intelligence Challenge. *International Journal of Intelligence and CounterIntelligence, 26*(3), 453–481. doi:10.1080/08850607.2013.780552

Ryu, J. H., Sharma, P. K., Jo, J. H., & Park, J. H. (2019). A blockchain-based decentralized efficient investigation framework for IoT digital forensics. *The Journal of Supercomputing*, *75*(8), 4372–4387. doi:10.1007/s11227-019-02779-9

Saad, M., Njilla, L., Kamhoua, C., Kim, J., Nyang, D., & Mohaisen, A. (2019, May). Mempool optimization for defending against DDoS attacks in PoW-based blockchain systems. In *2019 IEEE international conference on blockchain and cryptocurrency (ICBC)* (pp. 285-292). IEEE.

Sachin, S., & Kaushal, S. (2022, July 18). Exploring Security Threats on Blockchain Technology along with possible Remedies. *2022 IEEE 7th International conference for Convergence in Technology (I2CT)*. 10.1109/I2CT54291.2022.9825123

Sajjad, M., & Kwon, S. (2020). Clustering-based speech emotion recognition by incorporating learned features and deep BiLSTM. *IEEE Access : Practical Innovations, Open Solutions*, *8*, 79861–79875. doi:10.1109/ACCESS.2020.2990405

Saleh, K., Hossny, M., & Nahavandi, S. (2017). Towards trusted autonomous vehicles from vulnerable road users perspective. *2017 Annual IEEE International Systems Conference (SysCon)*, 1–7. 10.1109/SYSCON.2017.7934782

Samara, M., & El-Alfy, E. S. M. (2019, November). Benchmarking open-source android malware detection tools. In *2019 2nd IEEE Middle East and North Africa COMMunications Conference (MENACOMM)* (pp. 1-6). IEEE. 10.1109/MENACOMM46666.2019.8988532

Sanclemente, G. L. (2022). Reliability: Understanding cognitive human bias in artificial intelligence for national security and intelligence analysis. *Security Journal*, *35*(4), 1328–1348. doi:10.1057/s41284-021-00321-2

Sarker, I. H. (2021). Deep cybersecurity: A comprehensive overview from neural network and deep learning perspective. *SN Computer Science*, *2*(3), 154. doi:10.1007/s42979-021-00535-6 PMID:33778771

Sarker, I. H. (2021). Machine learning: Algorithms, real-world applications and research directions. *SN Computer Science*, *2*(3), 160. doi:10.1007/s42979-021-00592-x PMID:33778771

Sarker, I. H. (2022). Ai-based modeling: Techniques, applications and research issues towards automation, intelligent and smart systems. *SN Computer Science*, *3*(2), 158. doi:10.1007/s42979-022-01043-x PMID:35194580

Sarker, I. H. (2023). Multi-aspects AI-based modeling and adversarial learning for cybersecurity intelligence and robustness: A comprehensive overview. *Security and Privacy*, *6*(5), 295. doi:10.1002/spy2.295

Sarvajcz, K., Ari, L., & Menyhart, J. (2024). AI on the Road: NVIDIA Jetson Nano-Powered Computer Vision-Based System for Real-Time Pedestrian and Priority Sign Detection. *Applied Sciences (Basel, Switzerland)*, *14*(4), 1440. doi:10.3390/app14041440

Savenko, O., Nicheporuk, A., Hurman, I., & Lysenko, S. (2019, June). Dynamic Signature-based Malware Detection Technique Based on API Call Tracing. In ICTERI workshops (pp. 633-643). Academic Press.

Saxena, A., Gutiérrez Bierbooms, C., & Pechenizkiy, M. (2023). Fairness-aware fake news mitigation using counter information propagation. *Applied Intelligence*, *53*(22), 27483–27504. doi:10.1007/s10489-023-04928-3

Scavarelli, A., Arya, A., & Teather, R. J. (2021). Virtual reality and augmented reality in social learning spaces: A literature review. *Virtual Reality (Waltham Cross)*, *25*(1), 257–277. doi:10.1007/s10055-020-00444-8

Schoenborn, J. M., & Althoff, K. D. (2021). Detecting SQL-Injection and Cross-Site Scripting Attacks Using Case-Based Reasoning and SEASALT. In LWDA (pp. 66-77). Academic Press.

Schoenborn, J. M., & Althoff, K. D. (2022). Multi-Agent Case-Based Reasoning: a Network Intrusion Detection System. In LWDA (pp. 258-269). Academic Press.

Schuller, B., & Batliner, A. (2013). *Computational paralinguistics: emotion, affect and personality in speech and language processing*. John Wiley & Sons. doi:10.1002/9781118706664

Seneviratne, S., Shariffdeen, R., Rasnayaka, S., & Kasthuriarachchi, N. (2022). Self-supervised vision transformers for malware detection. *IEEE Access : Practical Innovations, Open Solutions*, *10*, 103121–103135. doi:10.1109/ACCESS.2022.3206445

Shafiq, M., Tian, Z., Bashir, A. K., Du, X., & Guizani, M. (2020). CorrAUC: A malicious bot-IoT traffic detection method in IoT network using machine-learning techniques. *IEEE Internet of Things Journal*, *8*(5), 3242–3254. doi:10.1109/JIOT.2020.3002255

Shah, S. S. H., Ahmad, A. R., Jamil, N., & Khan, A. U. R. (2022). Memory forensics-based malware detection using computer vision and machine learning. *Electronics (Basel)*, *11*(16), 2579. doi:10.3390/electronics11162579

Shaukat, K. L., Luo, S., & Varadharajan, V. (2023). A novel deep learning-based approach for malware detection. *Engineering Applications of Artificial Intelligence*, *122*, 106030. doi:10.1016/j.engappai.2023.106030

Shin, Y., Choi, Y., Won, J., Hong, T., & Koo, C. (2024). A new benchmark model for the automated detection and classification of a wide range of heavy construction equipment. *Journal of Management Engineering*, *40*(2), 04023069. doi:10.1061/JMENEA.MEENG-5630

Sieu, B., & Gavrilova, M. (2021). Multi-modal aesthetic system for person identification. *2021 International Conference on Cyberworlds (CW)*. doi:10.1109/ACCESS.2021.3096776

Singla, R. (2023). Age and gender detection using Deep Learning. *2023 7th International Conference on Computing, Communication, Control and Automation (ICCUBEA)* (pp. 1-6). IEEE.

Solat, S., & Potop-Butucaru, M. (2017). Brief announcement: Zeroblock: Timestamp-free prevention of block-withholding attack in bitcoin. *Stabilization, Safety, and Security of Distributed Systems: 19th International Symposium, SSS 2017, Boston, MA, USA, November 5–8, 2017 Proceedings, 19,* 356–360.

SomanK. P. (2023). A comprehensive tutorial and survey of applications of deep learning for cyber security. Authorea Preprints.

Sousa, A. J. (2018). *Application of knowledge acquisition methods in a casebased reasoning tool.* Master thesis, FEUP.

Sriram, S. S. (2020). DCNN-IDS: deep convolutional neural network based intrusion detection system. *Computational Intelligence, Cyber Security and Computational Models. Models and Techniques for Intelligent Systems and Automation: 4th International Conference, ICC3 2019, December 19-21, 2019, Revised Selected Papers 4.*

Sudhani, V., Divakar, Y., & Girish, C. (2022, January). Introduction of Formal Methods in Blockchain Consensus Mechanism and Its Associated Protocols. *IEEE Access : Practical Innovations, Open Solutions, 10,* 66611–66624. doi:10.1109/ACCESS.2022.3184799

Sujeetha, R., & Preetha, C. S. D. (2021, October). A literature survey on smart contract testing and analysis for smart contract based blockchain application development. In *2021 2nd International Conference on Smart Electronics and Communication (ICOSEC)* (pp. 378-385). IEEE.

Sun, K. H., Huh, H., Tama, B. A., Lee, S. Y., Jung, J. H., & Lee, S. (2020). Vision-based fault diagnostics using explainable deep learning with class activation maps. *IEEE Access : Practical Innovations, Open Solutions, 8,* 129169–129179. doi:10.1109/ACCESS.2020.3009852

Tann, W. J. W., Han, X. J., Gupta, S. S., & Ong, Y. S. (2018). Towards safer smart contracts: A sequence learning approach to detecting security threats. *arXiv preprint arXiv:1811.06632.*

Tchomté, S. A. (2019). A Case Based Reasoning Coupling Multi-Criteria Decision Making with Learning and Optimization Intelligences: Application to Energy Consumption. *EAI Endorsed Trans. Smart Cities, 4*(9), 162-292. doi:10.4108/eai.26-6-2018.162292

Tech Against Terrorism. (2020-2021). *Transparency Report: Terrorist Content Analytics Platform.* Author.

Tech Against Terrorism. (2023). *The Disruption Report.* Retrieved August 24, 2023 from https://www.techagainstterrorism.org/2023/07/31/the-disruption-report/

Teicher, F. (2019). The role of Media and Information Literacy. In *Reconciliation, Peace and Global Citizenship Education: Pedagogy and Practice.* Author.

Thiebes, S., Lins, S., & Sunyaev, A. (2021). Trustworthy artificial intelligence. *Electronic Markets, 31*(2), 447–464. doi:10.1007/s12525-020-00441-4

Tian, Z., Cui, L., Liang, J., & Yu, S. (2022). A comprehensive survey on poisoning attacks and countermeasures in machine learning. *ACM Computing Surveys, 55*(8), 1–35. doi:10.1145/3551636

Tibrewal, I., Srivastava, M., & Tyagi, A. K. (2022). Blockchain technology for securing cyber-infrastructure and internet of things networks. *Intelligent Interactive Multimedia Systems for e-Healthcare Applications*, 337-350.

Torfi, A., Iranmanesh, S. M., Nasrabadi, N., & Dawson, J. (2017). 3d convolutional neural networks for cross audio-visual matching recognition. *IEEE Access : Practical Innovations, Open Solutions*, 5, 22081–22091. doi:10.1109/ACCESS.2017.2761539

Torres, M. Á., Álvarez, R., & Cazorla, M. (2023). A Malware Detection Approach Based on Feature Engineering and Behavior Analysis. *IEEE Access : Practical Innovations, Open Solutions*, 11, 105355–105367. doi:10.1109/ACCESS.2023.3319093

Tripathi, V. a. (2022). Enhanced CNN Is Used For Mal Image Anomaly Detection And Classification. *Scandinavian Journal of Information Systems*, 34(2), 37–44.

Tyagi, A. K., Chandrasekaran, S., & Sreenath, N. (2022, May). Blockchain technology:–a new technology for creating distributed and trusted computing environment. In *2022 International Conference on Applied Artificial Intelligence and Computing (ICAAIC)* (pp. 1348-1354). IEEE. 10.1109/ICAAIC53929.2022.9792702

Tyagi, A. K., Dananjayan, S., Agarwal, D., & Thariq Ahmed, H. F. (2023). Blockchain—Internet of Things Applications: Opportunities and Challenges for Industry 4.0 and Society 5.0. *Sensors (Basel)*, 23(2), 947. doi:10.3390/s23020947 PMID:36679743

Uncovska, M., Freitag, B., Meister, S., & Fehring, L. (2023). Patient acceptance of prescribed and fully reimbursed mhealth apps in germany: An utaut2-based online survey study. *Journal of Medical Systems*, 47(1), 14. doi:10.1007/s10916-023-01910-x PMID:36705853

UNESCO. (2018). *Journalism, 'Fake News' and Disinformation*. UNESCO.

UNESCO-IICBA. (2019). *Youth Empowerment for Peace and Resilience Building and Prevention of Violent Extremism in Sahel and Surrounding Countries: A Guide for Teachers*. UNESCO-IICBA.

United Nations Office on Drugs and Crime (UNODC). (2012). *The Use of the Internet for Terrorist Purposes*. Author.

USA Department of Homeland Security. (2019). *Strategic Framework for Countering Terrorism and Targeted Violence*. Author.

van der Stigchel, B., van den Bosch, K., van Diggelen, J., & Haselager, P. (2023). Intelligent decision support in medical triage: Are people robust to biased advice? *Journal of Public Health (Oxford, England)*, 45(3), fdad005. doi:10.1093/pubmed/fdad005 PMID:36947701

Venmaa Devi, P., & Karpagam, G. R (2018). R4 Model for Malware Detection And Prevention Using Case Based Reasoning. *IJCRT, 6*(2).

Verkholyak, O., Dvoynikova, A., & Karpov, A. (2021). A Bimodal Approach for Speech Emotion Recognition using Audio and Text. *J. Internet Serv. Inf. Secur.*, 11(1), 80–96.

Victor, P., De Cock, M., & Cornelis, C. (2011). Trust and recommendations. *Recommender systems handbook*, 645–675.

Vinayakumar, R., Alazab, M., Soman, K. P., Poornachandran, P., & Venkatraman, S. (2019). Robust intelligent malware detection using deep learning. *IEEE Access : Practical Innovations, Open Solutions, 7*, 46717–46738. doi:10.1109/ACCESS.2019.2906934

Vu, D. L., Newman, Z., & Meyers, J. S. (2022). A benchmark comparison of python malware detection approaches. *arXiv preprint arXiv:2209.13288.*

Vultureanu-Albişi, A., & Bădică, C. (2021). Recommender systems: An explainable ai perspective. *2021 International Conference on INnovations in Intelligent SysTems and Applications (INISTA)*, 1–6. 10.1109/INISTA52262.2021.9548125

Vyas, C. A. (2014). M. Security concerns and issues for bitcoin. *International Journal of Computer Applications*. Retrieved from https://goo.gl/cNACCq

Wade, L., & Robinson, R. (2012). *The psychology of trust and its relation to sustainability*. Global Sustainability Institute (Briefing Note 2).

Waelen, R. A. (2023). The ethics of computer vision: An overview in terms of power. *AI and Ethics*, 1–10.

Waisberg, E., Ong, J., Masalkhi, M., Zaman, N., Sarker, P., Lee, A. G., & Tavakkoli, A. (2023). Meta smart glasses—Large language models and the future for assistive glasses for individuals with vision impairments. *Eye (London, England)*, 1–3. PMID:38049627

Wang, Y. (2023). *Vision-assisted behavior-based construction safety: Integrating computer vision and natural language processing*. Academic Press.

Wang, H., Zhang, Q., Wu, J., Pan, S., & Chen, Y. (2019). Time series feature learning with labeled and unlabeled data. *Pattern Recognition, 89*, 55–66. doi:10.1016/j.patcog.2018.12.026

Wang, K., An, N., Li, B. N., Zhang, Y., & Li, L. (2015). Speech emotion recognition using Fourier parameters. *IEEE Transactions on Affective Computing, 6*(1), 69–75. doi:10.1109/TAFFC.2015.2392101

Wang, M., & Deng, W. (2020). Mitigating bias in face recognition using skewness-aware reinforcement learning. *Proceedings of the IEEE/CVF conference on computer vision and pattern recognition. Seattle, USA*, 9322–9331. 10.1109/CVPR42600.2020.00934

Wang, S., Zou, P., Gong, X., Song, M., Peng, J., & Jiao, J. R. (2024). Visual analytics and intelligent reasoning for smart manufacturing defect detection and judgement: A meta-learning approach with knowledge graph embedding case-based reasoning. *Journal of Industrial Information Integration, 37*, 100536. doi:10.1016/j.jii.2023.100536

Wang, X. (2013). Intelligent multi-camera video surveillance: A review. *Pattern Recognition Letters, 34*(1), 3–19. doi:10.1016/j.patrec.2012.07.005

Wang, Y., Howard, N., Kacprzyk, J., Frieder, O., Sheu, P., Fiorini, R. A., Gavrilova, M. L., Patel, S., Peng, J., & Widrow, B. (2018). Cognitive informatics: Towards cognitive machine learning and autonomous knowledge manipulation. *International Journal of Cognitive Informatics and Natural Intelligence*, *12*(1), 1–13. doi:10.4018/IJCINI.2018010101

Wang, Z. &. (2023). DAE-IHOG: An Improved Method for Classification Malware. *Proceedings of the 15th International Conference on Digital Image Processing*, (pp. 1-7). 10.1145/3604078.3604144

Why companies want to mine tea secrets in your voice. (n.d.). https://www.theverge.com/2019/3/14/18264458/voice-technology-speech-analysismental-health-riskprivacy

Wilms, M., Bannister, J. J., Mouches, P., MacDonald, M. E., Rajashekar, D., Langner, S., & Forkert, N. D. (2022). Invertible modeling of bidirectional relationships in neuroimaging with normalizing flows: Application to brain aging. *IEEE Transactions on Medical Imaging*, *41*(9), 2331–2347. doi:10.1109/TMI.2022.3161947 PMID:35324436

Wu, H., Albiero, V., Krishnapriya, K., King, M. C., & Bowyer, K. W. (2023). Face recognition accuracy across demographics: Shining a light into the problem. *Proceedings of the IEEE/CVF Conference on Computer Vision and Pattern Recognition*, 1041–1050. 10.1109/CVPRW59228.2023.00111

Wu, J., Cai, R., & Wang, H. (2020). Déjà vu: A contextualized temporal attention mechanism for sequential recommendation. *Proceedings of The Web Conference 2020*, 2199–2209. 10.1145/3366423.3380285

Xi, B. (2020). Adversarial machine learning for cybersecurity and computer vision: Current developments and challenges. *Wiley Interdisciplinary Reviews: Computational Statistics*, *12*(5), e1511. doi:10.1002/wics.1511

Yan, J. a. (2024). Exploring better image captioning with grid features. *Complex & Intelligent Systems*, 1-16.

Yang, D., Ding, Y., Zhang, H., & Li, Y. (2024). PVitNet: An Effective Approach for Android Malware Detection Using Pyramid Feature Processing and Vision Transformer. In *ICASSP 2024-2024 IEEE International Conference on Acoustics, Speech and Signal Processing (ICASSP)* (pp. 2440-2444). IEEE.

Yang, Y., Gupta, A., Feng, J., Singhal, P., Yadav, V., Wu, Y., Natarajan, P., Hedau, V., & Joo, J. (2022). Enhancing fairness in face detection in computer vision systems by demographic bias mitigation. *Proceedings of the 2022 AAAI/ACM Conference on AI, Ethics, and Society. Oxford, United Kingdom*, 813–822. 10.1145/3514094.3534153

Yang, Y., Losson, O., & Duvieubourg, L. (2007, December). Quality evaluation of color demosaicing according to image resolution. In *2007 Third International IEEE Conference on Signal-Image Technologies and Internet-Based System* (pp. 689-695). IEEE. 10.1109/SITIS.2007.33

Yazid, A. C. (2023). Blockchain Technology in Financial Transactions under Sharia Banking Practice. *Jurnal Ekonomi dan Bisnis, 7*, 65-75. Retrieved from doi:10.14421/EkBis.2023.7.2.2049

Yeboah-Ofori, A., & Boachie, C. (2019, May). Malware attack predictive analytics in a cyber supply chain context using machine learning. In *2019 International conference on cyber security and Internet of Things (ICSIoT)* (pp. 66-73). IEEE. 10.1109/ICSIoT47925.2019.00019

Yerima, S. Y., & Bashar, A. (2022). A novel Android botnet detection system using image-based and manifest file features. *Electronics (Basel), 11*(3), 486. doi:10.3390/electronics11030486

Yuan, X., He, P., Zhu, Q., & Li, X. (2019). Adversarial examples: Attacks and defenses for deep learning. *IEEE Transactions on Neural Networks and Learning Systems, 30*(9), 2805–2824. doi:10.1109/TNNLS.2018.2886017 PMID:30640631

Zablocki, É., Ben-Younes, H., Pérez, P., & Cord, M. (2022). Explainability of deep vision-based autonomous driving systems: Review and challenges. *International Journal of Computer Vision, 130*(10), 2425–2452. doi:10.1007/s11263-022-01657-x

Zahid, S. M. (2023). A Multi Stage Approach for Object and Face Detection using CNN. *2023 8th International Conference on Communication and Electronics Systems (ICCES)* (pp. 798-803). IEEE.

Zakaria, W. Z. A. (2015). Application of case based reasoning in it security incident response. In *Int. Conf. Recent Trends in Engineering and Technology* (pp. 106-109). Academic Press.

Zakaria, W. Z. A., & Kiah, M. L. M. (2012). A review on artificial intelligence techniques for developing intelligent honeypot. In *2012 8th International Conference on Computing Technology and Information Management (NCM and ICNIT)* (Vol. 2, pp. 696-701). IEEE.

Zhang, X. I. (2022). Critical Infrastructure Security Using Computer Vision Technologies. *Security Technologies and Social Implications*, 149-180.

Zhang, L., Wu, X., Buades, A., & Li, X. (2011). Color demosaicking by local directional interpolation and nonlocal adaptive thresholding. *Journal of Electronic Imaging, 20*(2), 023016–023016. doi:10.1117/1.3600632

Zhang, S., Zhang, S., Huang, T., & Gao, W. (2017). Speech emotion recognition using deep convolutional neural network and discriminant temporal pyramid matching. *IEEE Transactions on Multimedia, 20*(6), 1576–1590. doi:10.1109/TMM.2017.2766843

Zhang, Z. Q., Qi, P., & Wang, W. (2020). Dynamic malware analysis with feature engineering and feature learning. *Proceedings of the AAAI Conference on Artificial Intelligence, 34*(1), 1210–1217. doi:10.1609/aaai.v34i01.5474

Zhao, J. M. (2021). A review of computer vision methods in network security. *IEEE Communications Surveys & Tutorials, 23*(3), 1838-1878.

Zhao, D., Wang, A., & Russakovsky, O. (2021). Understanding and evaluating racial biases in image captioning. *Proceedings of the IEEE/CVF International Conference on Computer Vision*, 14830–14840. 10.1109/ICCV48922.2021.01456

Zhu, S., Yu, T., Xu, T., Chen, H., Dustdar, S., Gigan, S., Gunduz, D., Hossain, E., Jin, Y., & Lin, F. (2023). Intelligent computing: The latest advances, challenges, and future. *Intelligent Computing, 2*, 6.

Zhuang, Y., Liu, Z., Qian, P., Liu, Q., Wang, X., & He, Q. (2021, January). Smart contract vulnerability detection using graph neural networks. In *Proceedings of the Twenty-Ninth International Conference on International Joint Conferences on Artificial Intelligence* (pp. 3283-3290). Academic Press.

Zhu, H., Wei, H., Wang, L., Xu, Z., & Sheng, V. S. (2023). An effective end-to-end android malware detection method. *Expert Systems with Applications, 218*, 119593. doi:10.1016/j.eswa.2023.119593

Zhu, L., Chen, L., Zhao, D., Zhou, J., & Zhang, W. (2017). Emotion recognition from Chinese speech for smart affective services using a combination of SVM and DBN. *Sensors (Basel), 17*(7), 1694. doi:10.3390/s17071694 PMID:28737705

Zhu, Y., Wang, M., Yin, X., Zhang, J., Meijering, E., & Hu, J. (2022). Deep learning in diverse intelligent sensor based systems. *Sensors (Basel), 23*(1), 62. doi:10.3390/s23010062 PMID:36616657

About the Contributors

Franklin Tchakounte is an Associate Professor and researcher in computer science with more than 10 years of experience in cybersecurity and data intelligence. He received his M.Sc. in Computer engineering from the University of Ngaoundere (Cameroon, 2010) and his Ph.D. in Mobile Security from the University of Bremen (Germany, 2015). Franklin owns several IT certifications. He authored books, book chapters, and several research papers in cyber security. He is the founder of the Cybersecurity with Computational and Artificial Intelligence (CyComAI,) company. He has been involved in international projects. He is a fellow of DAAD Staff Exchange in Sub-Saharan Africa, Research Mobility grants in Cameroon, and the WebWeWant F.A.S.T project. He is a member of numerous societies: EAI, ISOC SIG Cybersecurity, ISOC SIG Cybersecurity Training and Education, Research Data Alliance (RDA), AuthorAID, and Africa Association of Entrepreneurs (AAE). He is currently the Cameroonian representative of Responsibility in AI in Africa (RAIN) and his interests include cyber security and artificial/digital intelligence.

* * *

Ismael Abbo graduated with a M.Sc. degree at University of Ngaoundere in 2023 and interests revolved around contributing to the field of IoT security.

Fahim Anzum is a Computer Science Ph.D. candidate at the University of Calgary (uCalgary), Calgary, AB, Canada and an Alberta Innovates and Eyes High Doctoral scholar. He is conducting research under the supervision of Dr. Marina L. Gavrilova in the Biometric Technologies Laboratory (BT Lab). Fahim's research investigates novel and effective strategies to enhance the explainability of large language models (LLMs) for responsible and trustworthy decision-making in online social media (OSM) applications. His research interests extend to the application of deep learning models in areas such as emotion detection and user-behavior analysis in online social media by leveraging natural language processing techniques. In 2021, Fahim received his M.Sc. in Computer Science from uCalgary, where he conducted research under the supervision of Dr. Mario Costa Sousa and Dr. Usman Alim. During his master's study, he achieved the Mitacs-Accelerate Graduate Research Scholarship and worked with Suncor Energy Inc. as a research intern. Before joining uCalgary, he served at the United International University (UIU), Bangladesh as a Lecturer (currently on study leave) in the Computer Science and Engineering (CSE) department. Fahim completed his B.Sc. in CSE from the Military Institute of Science and Technology (MIST), Dhaka, Bangladesh.

Ashratuz Zavin Asha is a third-year Ph.D. student in the Department of Computer Science (CPSC) at the University of Calgary (UofC), Alberta, Canada. She works in the Interactions Lab (iLab) under the supervision of Dr. Ehud Sharlin. Her research interest broadly sits in the domains of Human-Computer Interaction (HCI) and Interaction Design. During her Ph.D. study, she explores in-vehicle interfaces for marginalized and vulnerable populations (older adults and women) to promote inclusivity, trust, and acceptability toward autonomous vehicles (AVs). She completed her master's from CPSC at UofC in Aug 2021. Her master's research explored the emerging new domain of interaction between pedestrians and AVs, with a strong focus on designing inclusive interfaces for vulnerable road users: pedestrians using wheelchairs, hearing aids, etc. Her works have been published in top HCI and computer science conferences, including CHI and DIS. She has earned prestigious awards for her research contributions, including the Alberta Innovates and Eyes High Doctoral Scholarships.

Lily Dey's research delves into cutting-edge areas such as Social Media Analysis, employing Machine Learning (ML) and Natural Language Processing (NLP) techniques to extract and comprehend emotions from vast datasets. This multidisciplinary approach not only enhances the depth of my investigations but also aligns with the evolving landscape of emotion recognition technologies. Eager to broaden my horizons, I actively stay abreast of emerging trends within the field, fostering collaborations with peers across disciplines. Participating in conferences and workshops has not only allowed me to present my work but has also enabled networking with fellow researchers, inspiring novel research avenues.

Artemy Gavrilov is a Computer Science student at the University of Calgary, a Chancellor Scholarship award recipient and an Information Security Club executive. His research interests are in the domains of Artificial Intelligence, Cybersecurity, and Behavioural Science.

Marina L. Gavrilova is a Full Professor at the University of Calgary and Research Excellence Chair in Trustworthy an Explainable AI. She directs the Biometric Technologies Laboratory and has published over 300 books, conference proceedings, and peer-reviewed articles in the domains of biometric security, machine learning, pattern recognition, and information fusion. Her professional excellence was recognized by the Canada Foundation for Innovation, the Killam Foundation, and the Order of the University of Calgary. She is the Founding Editor-in-Chief of Transactions on Computational Sciences (Springer), and serves on the editorial boards for the IEEE Transactions on Computational Sciences, IEEE Access, The Visual Computer, Sensors, IJPRAI and the International Journal of Biometrics.

Fariha Iffath received B.Sc. in computer science and engineering from the Chittagong University of Engineering and Technology, Bangladesh in 2019. She is currently pursuing her M.Sc. degree in computer science at the University of Calgary, Canada, under the supervision of Professor Marina L. Gavrilova. She published research in the MDPI Computers Journal, International Conference on Intelligent Computing Optimization 2021, Proceedings of the International Conference on Big Data, IoT, and Machine Learning 2022, New Approaches for Multidimensional Signal Processing 2022, IEEE Access Journal, Computer Animation and Virtual Worlds (CAVW) Journal. Her research interests include computer vision, deep learning, biometrics, and audio/visual aesthetics.

Abu Quwsar Ohi is a master's student at the University of Calgary. His research focuses on deep learning algorithms, pattern recognition, computer vision, and reinforcement learning.

Md Shopon earned a B.Sc. in Computer Science and Engineering from the University of Asia Pacific in 2018 and an M.Sc. in Computer Science from the University of Calgary in 2022. Currently pursuing a Ph.D. in Computer Science at the University of Calgary, Canada, supervised by Prof. Marina L. Gavrilova. Formerly a Lecturer at the University of Asia Pacific (Sep 2018 - Sep 2020), he has authored 15+ international conference papers and journals, focusing on computer vision, deep learning, and behavioral biometrics.

Amit Kumar Tyagi is working as Assistant Professor, at National Institute of Fashion Technology, 110016, New Delhi, India. Previously he has worked as Assistant Professor (Senior Grade 2), and Senior Researcher at Vellore Institute of Technology (VIT), Chennai Campus, 600127, Chennai, Tamilandu, India for the period of 2019-2022. He received his Ph.D. Degree (Full-Time) in 2018 from Pondicherry Central University, 605014, Puducherry, India. About his academic experience, he joined the Lord Krishna College of Engineering, Ghaziabad (LKCE) for the periods of 2009-2010, and 2012-2013. He was an Assistant Professor and Head- Research, Lingaya's Vidyapeeth (formerly known as Lingaya's University), Faridabad, Haryana, India for the period of 2018-2019. His supervision experience includes more than 10 Masters' dissertations and one PhD thesis. He has contributed to several projects such as "AARIN" and "P3- Block" to address some of the open issues related to the privacy breaches in Vehicular Applications (such as Parking) and Medical Cyber Physical Systems (MCPS). He has published over 150 papers in refereed high impact journals, conferences and books.

Index

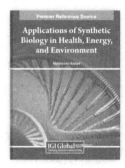

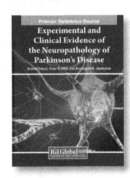

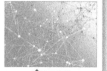

Printed in the United States
by Baker & Taylor Publisher Services